Understanding Rabbinic Judaism

From Talmudic to Modern Times

Edited by

Jacob Neusner

KTAV PUBLISHING HOUSE, INC.

NEW YORK

ANTI-DEFAMATION LEAGUE OF B'NAI B'RITH

NEW YORK

Library of Congress Cataloging in Publication Data

Neusner, Jacob, 1932—   comp.
   Understanding rabbinic Judaism, from Talmudic to modern times.

   "Bibliography of rabbinic Judaism from Talmudic to modern times, by David Goodblatt": p.
   1. Judaism—History—Addresses, essays, lectures. 2. Rabbis. 3. Rabbinical literature—History and criticism. I. Title.
BM155.2.N48   296   73-22167
ISBM 0-87068-238-5

MANUFACTURED IN THE UNITED STATES OF AMERICA

TABLE OF CONTENTS

PART I

THE TALMUDIC HERITAGE

PART II

THE FOUNDATIONS OF RABBINIC JUDAISM

PART III
MASTERS OF THE LAW

PART IV
RABBINIC JUDAISM IN THE THEOLOGICAL IDIOM

PART V
RABBINIC JUDAISM IN THE MYSTICAL IDIOM

PART VI
RABBINIC JUDAISM AT THE THRESHHOLD
OF MODERNITY

ACKNOWLEDGEMENTS

The editor gratefully acknowledges permission to reprint excerpts from various books and papers granted by the following:

Dr. Ira Eisenstein and The Jewish Reconstructionist Foundation for Mordecai M. Kaplan, *The Greater Judaism in the Making.* © 1960 by Jewish Reconstructionist Foundation Inc., sponsor of The Reconstructionist Press.

Holt, Rinehart, and Winston for *Philosophies of Judaism* by Julius Guttmann. Translated by David W. Silverman. © 1964 by Holt Rinehart and Winston, Inc. Reprinted by permission of Holt, Rinehart, and Winston, Inc.

American Jewish Congress for Eliezer Berkovits, *Authentic Judaism and Halakhah,* in *Judaism,* Winter, 1970, pp. 66-76. © 1970 by American Jewish Congress.

Yeshiva University Press for Mendell Lewittes, *The Nature and History of Jewish Law,* in *Studies in Torah Judaism,* edited by Leon D. Stitskin. © 1969 by Yeshiva University Press.

The Jewish Publication Society of America for Israel Abrahams, *Jewish Life in the Middle Ages;* Louis Ginzberg, *Students, Scholars, and Saints;* and Alexander Marx, *Essays in Jewish Biography.* Copyright: © 1948 for Marx. © 1928, 1956 for Ginzberg. © 1958 for Abrahams. By The Jewish Publication Society of America.

Mrs. Minnie Slonimsky for H. Slonimsky, *Judah Halevi. The Kuzari.* © 1964 by Schocken Books.

Mr. Neal Kozodoy, Editor, *Library of Jewish Studies,* and Behrman House, for Isadore Twersky, *A Maimonides Reader.* © 1972 by Isadore Twersky. Reprinted by permission of Behrman House.

The Jewish Publication Society of America for Solomon Schechter, *Studies in Judaism.* © 1958 by The Jewish Publication Society of America.

Harper & Row, Publishers, Inc., for *The Mystical Element in Judaism* by Abraham J. Heschel, in *The Jews: Their History, Culture, and Religion,* 2nd edition, Volume I (Hardbound edition), edited by Louis Finkelstein © 1949, 1955 by Louis Finkelstein, and reprinted by permission of Harper & Row, Publishers, Inc.

Whitehall Co. for *Medieval Jewish Mysticism. Book of the Pious,* by Sholom Alchanan Singer. © 1971 by Whitehall Co.

Rabbi Leo Jung for Charles B. Chavel, *Shneyur Zalman of Liady* and S. Ehrman, *Moses Sofer,* in *Jewish Leaders* (1750-1940) edited by Leo Jung. © 1953 by Leo Jung.

Schocken Books for Gershom G. Scholem, *Major Trends in Jewish Mysticism.* © 1946, 1954 by Schocken Books Inc.

Dickenson Publishing Co. for pp. 35-37 of *The Way of Torah, An Introduction to Judaism,* by Jacob Neusner. © 1970 by Dickenson Publishing Co., Inc., Belmont, California. Reprinted by permission of the publisher.

For

John Giles and Anne Lally Milhaven

PREFACE

Rabbinic Judaism—that mode of Judaic religion created by the rabbis of the early centuries of the Common Era and eventually embodied in the laws and doctrines of the Talmud—is a single, seamless, all-encompassing religious structure, continuing essentially in its classic form from its very beginnings to the present day. The legal component of the tradition exhibits the most striking evidence of continuity, of a harmonious and continuous development for nearly twenty centuries. For each master of the law draws upon all that has gone before and remains in close and constant contact with the heritage of the ages. The commentaries on the Talmud, codes of law based upon the Talmud, and responses to and decisions on specific legal questions, produced from the end of Talmudic literary activity, in the sixth century C.E., to the present simply develop lines of thought laid down long ago. Each stage in the development and articulation of Talmudic and later rabbinic law—that is, of all we know as "Jewish" law—is closely related to the foregoing and just as tightly joined to what would follow.

But the same is true of the lives and doctrines of important figures in the philosophical and mystical traditions within rabbinic Judaism, many of whom were themselves also major legal authorities. These distinctive modes of thought and religious expression, to be sure, make use of particular, idiomatic ways of creativity. Yet a single, underlying perspective, the viewpoint of rabbinic Judaism, is at the base of both mystical and philosophical trends within rabbinic Judaism. Until now works on "Jewish" mysticism and "Jewish" philosophy have tended to neglect, or to take for granted, the mystics' and philosophers' fundamentally rabbinic context, the recourse to the specific symbols, ideas, and religious experiences created by Talmudic and later rabbinic Judaism. Or, to put it differently, the philosopher and the mystic as deeply reflected the values of rabbinic Judaism as did the commentator on the Talmud or the legislator and codifier of its law. All shared a single, unitary, and harmonious heritage of symbols and religious perspectives, and the work of each was to spell out, in his particular idiom, implications of that heritage. The purpose of this reader is to illustrate that fundamental theory of the history of Judaism.

1

We must furthermore recognize that the classic rabbinic tradition continues in modern times. This is in two ways.

First, everyone knows that Reform, Conservative, and Modern Orthodox Judaism draw heavily, in various ways and for various purposes, upon the legal, philosophical, and mystical heritage created by rabbinic Judaism. More significantly, all three contemporary movements lay serious claim to represent, for this day and age, what the creators of classical rabbinic Judaism would have said and done had they lived in our times. To be sure, when Conservative and Reform Jews claim to carry on the rabbinic tradition, they have also to take account of ways in which they depart from its literal requirements. But those Modern Orthodox Jews, and they are many, who believe one should both remain perfectly faithful to the tradition and its law and enter into the life of Western civilization have also to establish the legitimacy of their conviction in terms of a tradition which endures in a second, important form.

And that second form is classical rabbinism continued in its traditional ways, without a break, either intellectual and religious, as with Reform and Conservative Judaism, or cultural and social, as with Modern Orthodoxy.

Most of the essays collected here deal with men and ideas regarded as "medieval." People suppose that the classic, rabbinic tradition goes down to "the modern period," at which point it is superseded by Orthodoxy, Reform, Conservative, and other expressions of "modern Judaism." Yet three of the masters before us, Elijah, the Gaon of Vilna, Moses Sofer, and Israel Salanter, lived at the threshold of modern times and in their setting they faced the same intellectual, social, and cultural issues confronting Western Jewry as well. They were in their setting as radical reformers as the Reform rabbis of Germany. These three, among many traditionalists in modern times, certainly did take seriously the challenges of modernity as these were beginning to unfold, and did respond to them. It is therefore difficult to know why they should be regarded as "medieval" or "pre-modern," while their contemporaries in Germany, France, or, somewhat later, America and Canada, should be understood as "modern" or at least "post-medieval."

The problem, I think, is in the gross categorization of the history of Judaism into four rigid periods, biblical, Talmudic, medieval, and modern. That is, when people come to divide and study the various data—the facts—about Judaism as a religious tradition, they tend to treat it as essentially in four distinct units. The "biblical" period goes from the beginnings down to the time of the Maccabees, when it is conventionally supposed that the Talmudic period begins. This, as is clear, extends to the seventh century C.E., the time of the Moslem conquest of the Middle East, at which point "medieval" Judaism begins. "Medieval" is everything from the seventh to the nineteenth century—a very long time.

Not solely the extraordinary length of the "medieval period" poses problems, but also the obscuring, through that periodization, of the authentic continuities of what is called "medieval" into the nineteenth and twentieth centuries leads to serious misinterpretation. For the rabbinic tradition not only produced revisions and generated modifications in modern times, but it also continued without significant break as well. Therefore we may locate in the last third of the twentieth century numerous Jews, including nearly the whole of Israeli Judaism, who stand in an unbroken connection to that Judaism known to us in the "medieval" sources. The *yeshiva*-movement in America and Western Europe, the Israeli *yeshivot* and rabbinate as a whole, and many ordinary Jews who live their lives entirely in conformity to traditional Judaism, its laws and doctrines—these constitute continuations of the rabbinic tradition. The claim, moreover, of Reform, Conservative, and Modern, or Westernized Orthodoxy to link up with that rabbinic tradition cannot be ignored. We surely cannot regard the former, traditionalist group as merely a fossil or a relic, given its vitality and capacity to transmit its mode of living and way of interpreting Jewish existence, and not only to transmit these things but also to enhance and enrich them. Nor can we ignore the claim of the latter, modernist and modernizing groups to perpetuate in the present age the fundamental values and ideals of rabbinic Judaism.

I have selected two sorts of materials and deliberately omitted a third. First, I have sought general introductions to types of expression within rabbinic Judaism, so that each major unit, on law, philosophy, and mysticism, begins with an overview of primary ideas and expressions. Second, I have then provided accounts of specific important individuals, particularly some of those authorities who continue to this day to have an impact upon the mind of contemporary Judaism. What seemed to me important in the biographies is the demonstration of the essential unity of rabbinic Judaism, however disparate the ways in which it was expressed. The philosophers, theologians and mystics turn out also to have been lawyers and political figures. The great legal authorities also mastered mystical lore. Ascetics produced ethics, and ethical thinkers and mystics founded schools for the study of Talmud. One therefore best gains a sense of the essential unity of rabbinic Judaism, its constant reference to a single, integrated mythic structure, by attending to the ways in which important and representative figures in their own lives and works united the discrete, but not disparate, elements of rabbinism into a single harmonious, individual expression.

I did not choose translations of the original writings except as these are given in the essays before us, because I do not believe that much is gained, especially at the beginning of study, from the direct encounter with primary sources. To be sure, I might have given selections of Talmudic and post-Talmudic rabbinic writings, of philosophical essays, or of mystical sayings. But without an extensive introduction as to the importance of these particular items and how they illustrate the much larger system of which they form a small part, and without an elaborate account of the context and larger meaning of snippets of an exceedingly complex literature such as is given by the essays before us, I do not think much is gained. I am a historian, and therefore have some experience of how difficult it is to make sense out of primary sources. Merely reading the sources, without significant and extended guidance, seems to me inevitably to produce either drastic misinterpretation, on the one side, or the illusion of meaningful knowledge where there is none, on the other.

I have selected materials which have not been anthologized before. In the bibliographical afterword I have explained the relationship between this reader and others I have edited.

J.N.

INTRODUCTION

What do we mean by "rabbinic civilization"? Why do we claim that the widely separated and culturally diverse Jewish communities of the past eighteen centuries together constitute an essentially harmonious expression of a single set of values and ideals, so as to be accurately characterized as a distinctive 'civilization' among mankind?

The answer is that nearly the whole of world Jewry from Talmudic times to the nineteenth century in the West, and to the Holocaust in the East, and a large part of world Jewry today—nearly the whole of the Orthodox sector—share a single, far-ranging and inclusive view of life and way of living. That view is built upon a single symbol, "Torah," articulated in a disciplined way, and interprets everyday affairs and historical events alike in terms of a single symbol, "Torah." The pervasive and universal presence of "Torah," the proximate uniformity of the institutions—the rabbi, the synagogue, the law—which expressed and embodied that symbol the widespread acceptance of the authority of those institutions and the meaningfulness of that symbol—these together justify our characterizing the Jews as living a single mode of life, constituting a unique civilization. And since the rabbi and the Torah were at the center of that civilization, we call it "rabbinic."

Before we expand our definition of these terms and suggest the main outlines of their origin, let us first exclude from consideration two other, perhaps equally helpful categories of analysis.

The first and most important exclusion is "nation." Why is it difficult to regard the Jews as a nation? One useful definition of nation, which in theory is fruitful, is that of Joseph Stalin, who in 1913 stated, "A nation is a historically constituted, stable community of people, formed on the basis of a common language, territory, economic life, and psychological make-up manifested in common culture . . . It must be emphasized that none of these characteristics taken separately is sufficient to define a nation. More than that, it is sufficient for a single one of these characteristics to be lacking and the nation ceases to be a nation." Stalin's definition, deriving, as it does, from nineteenth-century romantic nationalistic thought, clearly will regard the Jews as a nation at some points in their

5

history, and not as a nation at others. When the majority of the Jews lived outside of the land of Israel, as has been the case since the second century C.E., then that important component of nation-hood is absent. But it also is the fact that the Jews lack a common language, do not make up a single economic entity, and, given the diversities of cultures in which they participated, cannot have exhibited a uniform psychological make-up.

Having excluded "nation" as a viable mode of definition, we must also remove from consideration the category of "culture," for people who do not have a common language or territory or psychological make-up also cannot be thought to form a common "culture."

Yet without "culture" and "nation," we are left with the anomaly that the Jews exhibited much in common, wherever they lived. In the centuries under consideration, they did have access to a common language, Hebrew, and they did live under a single law, the Talmud's. They did say the same prayers, those in the Jewish prayerbook, the *Siddur*. They did observe the same holy days and follow the same organization of time in a single, common calendar. They did see themselves as a single holy community, Israel, and the unity of their fate, their interdependence, and their profound concern for one another—these things do prove that the Jews constituted an uncommonly united group. And the unities were more than confessional, it goes without saying. The things they had in common are united by a single, fundamental, and universally shared perspective on the meaning of reality, a consistent formative and interpretive view of all of life, in this world and in eternity, a view of reality transcending the everyday and the secular.

For without a shared imagination of the meaning and structure of being, the common language and law would not have meant the one and the same thing, as they certainly did, to Jews wherever they lived. The common prayers would have obscured the vast differences in what was meant in the saying of them. The common calendar would have brought merely a series of temporal coincidences. The sense of community and mutual concern would have yielded little more than pragmatic and expedient wisdom that it is better to insure one another's welfare than to languish alone. It is the Torah—symbol of rabbinic Judaism —which transformed merely secular facts and common traits into transcendent modes of being, which made the secular and contingent into the sacred and eternal, and which rendered 'being Jewish' into a distinctive mode of being and of living.

Let us now define the central myth of rabbinic civilization and explain the primary rituals which express and realize that symbol.

The Symbol of Torah

The central conception of rabbinic Judaism is the belief that the ancient Scriptures constituted divine revelation, but only a part of it. At Sinai, God had handed down a dual revelation: the written part known to one and all, but also the oral part preserved by the great scriptural heroes, passed on by prophets to various ancestors in the obscure past, finally and most openly handed down to the rabbis who created the Palestinian and Babylonian Talmuds. The "whole Torah" thus consisted of both written and oral parts. The rabbis taught that that "whole Torah" was studied by David, augmented by Ezekiel, legislated by Ezra, and embodied in the schools and by the sages of every period in Israelite history from Moses to the present. It is a singular, linear conception of a revelation, preserved only by the few, pertaining to the many, and in time capable of bringing salvation to all.

The rabbinic conception of Torah further regards Moses as "our rabbi," the first and prototypical figure of the ideal Jew. It holds that whoever embodies the teachings of Moses "our rabbi" thereby conforms to the will of God—and not to God's will alone, but also to his *way*. In heaven God and the angels study Torah just as rabbis do on earth. God dons phylacteries like a Jew. He prays in the rabbinic mode. He carries out the acts of compassion called for by Judaic ethics. He guides the affairs of the world according to the rules of Torah, just as does the rabbi in his court. One exegesis of the creation legend taught that God had looked into the Torah and therefrom had created the world.

The symbol of Torah is multidimensional. It includes the striking detail that whatever the most recent rabbi is destined to discover through proper exegesis of the tradition is as much a part of the Torah revealed to Moses as is a sentence of Scripture itself. It therefore is possible to participate even in the giving of the law by appropriate, logical inquiry into the law. God himself, studying and living by Torah, is believed to subject himself to these same rules of logical inquiry. If an earthly court overrules the testimony, delivered through miracles, of the heavenly one, God would rejoice, crying out, "My sons have conquered me! My sons have conquered me!"

In a word, before us is a mythicoreligious system in which earth and heaven correspond to one another, with Torah as the nexus and model of both. The heavenly paradigm is embodied upon earth. Moses "our rabbi" is the pattern for the ordinary sage of the streets of Jerusalem, Pumbedita, Mainz, London, Lvov, Bombay, Dallas, or New York. And God himself participates in the system, for it is his image which, in the end, forms that cosmic paradigm. The faithful Jew constitutes the pro-

jection of the divine on earth. Honor is due to the learned rabbi more
than to the scroll of the Torah, for through his learning and logic he may
alter the very content of Mosaic revelation. He *is* Torah, not merely because he lives by it, but because at his best he forms as compelling an
embodiment of the heavenly model as did a Torah scroll itself.

The final element in the rabbinic conception of Torah concerns
salvation. It takes many forms. One salvific teaching holds that had Israel
not sinned—that is, disobeyed the Torah—the Scriptures would have
closed with the story of the conquest of Palestine. From that eschatological time forward, the sacred community would have lived in eternal peace
under the divine law. Keeping the Torah was therefore the veritable
guarantee of salvation. The opposite is said in many forms as well. Israel
had sinned, therefore God had called the Assyrians, Babylonians, and
Romans to destroy the Temple of Jerusalem; but in his mercy he would
be equally faithful to restore the fortunes of the people when they,
through their suffering and repentance, had expiated the result and the
cause of their sin.

So in both negative and positive forms, the rabbinic idea of Torah
tells of a necessary connection between the salvation of the people and
of the world and the state of Torah among them. For example, if all
Israel would properly keep a single Sabbath, the Messiah would come.
Of special interest here is the rabbinic saying that the rule of the pagans
depends upon the sin of Israel. If Israel would constitute a full and complete replication of "Torah," that is, of heaven, then pagan rule would
come to an end. It would end because all Israel then, like some few
rabbis even now, would attain to the creative, theurgical powers inherent
in Torah. Just as God had created the world through Torah, so saintly
rabbis could now create a sacred community. When Israel makes itself
worthy through its embodiment of Torah, that is, through its perfect
replication of heaven, then the end will come.

Learning thus finds a central place in the rabbinic tradition because
of the belief that God had revealed his will to mankind through the
medium of a written revelation, given to Moses at Mount Sinai, accompanied by oral traditions taught in the rabbinical schools and preserved
in the Talmuds and related literature. The text without the oral traditions
might have led elsewhere than into the academy, for the biblicism of
other groups yielded something quite different from Jewish religious
intellectualism. But belief in the text was coupled with the belief that
oral traditions were also revealed. In the books composed in the rabbinical academies, as much as in the Hebrew Bible itself, was contained
God's will for man.

The act of study, memorization, and commentary upon the sacred books is holy. The study of sacred texts therefore assumes a *central* position in Judaism. Other traditions had their religious virtuosi whose virtuosity consisted in knowledge of a literary tradition; but few held, as does Judaism, that everyone must become such a virtuoso.

Traditional processes of learning are discrete and exegetical. Creativity is expressed not through abstract dissertation, but rather through commentary upon the sacred writings, or, more likely in later times, commentary upon earlier commentaries. One might also prepare a code of the law, but such a code represented little more than an assemblage of authoritative opinions of earlier times, with a decision being offered upon those few questions the centuries had left unanswered.

The chief glory of the commentator is his *hiddush,* "novelty." The *hiddush* constitutes a scholastic disquisition upon a supposed contradiction between two earlier authorities, chosen from any period, with no concern for how they might in fact relate historically, and upon a supposed harmonization of their "contradiction." Or a new distinction might be read into an ancient law, upon which basis ever more questions might be raised and solved. The focus of interest quite naturally lies upon law, rather than theology, history, philosophy, or other sacred sciences. But within the law it rests upon legal theory, and interest in the practical consequences of the law is decidedly subordinated.

The devotion of the Jews to study of the Torah, as here defined, is held by them to be their chief glory. This sentiment is repeated in song and prayer, and shapes the values of the common society. The important Jew is the learned man. The child many times is blessed, starting at birth, "May he grow in Torah, commandments, good deeds."

The central *ritual* of the rabbinic tradition, therefore, is study. Study as a natural action entails learning of traditions and executing them—in this context, in school or in court. Study becomes a *ritual action* when it is endowed with values *extrinsic* to its ordinary character, when set into a mythic context. When a disciple memorizes his master's traditions and actions, he participates in the rabbinic view of Torah as the organizing principle of reality. His study is thereby endowed with the sanctity that ordinarily pertains to prayer or other cultic matters. Study loses its referent in intellectual attainment. The *act* of study itself becomes holy, so that its original purpose, which was mastery of particular information, ceases to matter much. What matters is piety, piety expressed through the rites of studying. Repeating the words of the oral revelation, even without comprehending them, might produce reward, just as imitating the master matters, even without really being able to explain the reasons for his actions.

The separation of the value, or sanctity, of the act of study from the natural, cognitive result of learning therefore transforms studying from a natural to a ritual action. That separation is accomplished in part by the rabbis' conception of Torah, and in part by the powerful impact of the academic environment itself.

A striking illustration of the distinction between mere learning and learning as part of ritual life derives from the comment of Mar Zutra, a fifth-century A.D. Babylonian rabbi, on Isaiah 14:5, "The Lord has broken the staff of the wicked, the scepter of rulers." He said, "These are disciples of the sages who teach public laws to boorish judges." The fact that the uncultivated judge would know the law did not matter, for he still was what he had been, a boor, not a disciple of the sages. Mere knowledge of the laws does not transform an ordinary person, however powerful, into a sage. Learning carried with it more than naturalistic valence, as further seen in the saying of Amemar, a contemporary of Mar Zutra: "A sage is superior to a prophet, as Scripture says, 'And a prophet has a heart of wisdom'" (Psalm 90:12). What characterized the prophet was, Amemar said, sagacity. Since the prophet was supposed to reveal the divine will, it was not inconsequential that his revelation depended *not* upon gifts of the spirit but upon *learning*.

The rabbi functioned in the Jewish community as judge and administrator. But he lived in a society in some ways quite separate from that of Jewry as a whole. The rabbinical academy was, first, a law school. Some of its graduates served as judges and administrators of the law. The rabbinical school was by no means a center for merely legal study. It was, like the Christian monastery, the locus for a peculiar kind of religious living. Only one of its functions concerned those parts of the Torah to be applied in everyday life through the judiciary.

The school, or *Yeshiva* (literally, "session") was a council of Judaism, a holy community. In it men learned to live a holy life, to become saints. When they left, sages continued to live by the discipline of the school. They invested great efforts in teaching that discipline by example and precept to ordinary folk. Through the school classical Judaism transformed the Jewish people into its vision of the true replica of Mosaic revelation.

The schools, like other holy communities, imposed their own particular rituals, intended, in the first instance, for the disciples and masters. Later, it was hoped, all Jews would conform to those rituals and so join the circle of master and disciples.

As with study, the schools' discipline transformed other ordinary, natural actions, gestures, and functions into rituals—the rituals of "being a rabbi." Everyone ate. Rabbis did so in a "rabbinic" manner. That is to say, what others regarded as matters of mere etiquette, formalities and conventions intended to render eating aesthetically agreeable, rabbis regarded as matters of "Torah," something to be *learned*. It was "Torah" to do things one way, and it was equally "ignorance" to do them another (though not heresy, for theology was no issue).

The master of Torah, whether disciple or teacher, would demonstrate his mastery not merely through what he said in the discussion of legal traditions or what he did in court. He would do so by how he sat at the table, by what ritual formulas he recited before eating one or another kind of fruit or vegetable, by how he washed his hands. Everyone had to relieve himself. The sage would do so according to "Torah." The personality traits of men might vary. Those expected of, and inculcated into, a sage were of a single fabric.

We must keep in mind the fundamental difference between the way of Torah and ways to salvation explored by other holy men and sacred communities. The rabbi at no point would admit that his particular rites were imposed upon him alone, apart from all Israel. He ardently "spread Torah" among the Jews at large. He believed he had to, because Torah was revealed to all Israel at Sinai and required of all Israel afterward. If he was right that Moses was "our rabbi" and even God kept the commandments as he did, then he had to ask of everyone what he demanded of himself: conformity to the *halakhah,* the way of Torah. His task was facilitated by the widespread belief that Moses had indeed revealed the Torah and that some sort of interpretation quite naturally was required to apply it to everyday affairs. The written part of Torah generally shaped the life of ordinary pious folk. What the rabbi had to accomplish was to persuade the outsider that the written part of the Torah was partial and incomplete, requiring further elaboration through the oral traditions he alone possessed and embodied.

The Origins of Rabbinic Judaism

While the rabbinic conception of Torah naturally is believed, by people within rabbinic Judaism, to originate with Moses at Sinai and to constitute nothing other than a statement of historical facts, the beginnings of the rabbinic structure are to be located in the aftermath of the destruction of the Second Temple in 70 C.E. At that time, remnants of various groups in the Judaism of the period before 70 gathered at Yavneh, and, under the leadership of Yohanan ben Zakkai, began to construct the ruins of the old age into a new synthesis.

Before the destruction, there was a common "Judaism" in the Land of Israel, and it was by no means identical to what we now understand as rabbinic Judaism. The common religion of the country consisted of three main elements, first, the Hebrew Scriptures, second, the Temple, and third, the common and accepted practices of the ordinary folk—their calendar, their mode of living, their everyday practices and rites, based on these first two. In addition we know of a number of peculiar groups, or sects, which took a distinctive position on one or another aspect of the inherited religious culture. Among these sects, the best known are the Pharisees, the Sadducees, and the Essenes; this third group, described chiefly in the writings of Josephus, a historian who wrote at the end of the first century, exhibits traits in common with the group known to us from the so-called Dead Sea Scrolls, but cannot have been identical to it in every respect.

When the Temple was destroyed, it is clear, the foundations of the country's religious-cultural life were destroyed. The reason is that the Temple had constituted one of the primary, unifying elements in that common life. The structure not only of political life and of society, but also of the imaginative life of the country, depended upon the Temple and its worship and cult. It was there that people believed they served God. On the Temple the lines of structure—both cosmic and social—converged. The Temple, moreover, served as the basis for those many elements of autonomous self-government and political life left in the Jews' hands by the Romans. Consequently, the destruction of the Temple meant not merely a significant alteration in the cultic or ritual life of the Jewish people, but also a profound and far-reaching crisis in their inner and spiritual existence.

The reconstruction of a viable cultural-religious existence is the outcome of the next half-century, for between ca. 70 and ca. 120, we know in retrospect, a number of elements of the religious-cultural structure of the period before 70 were put together into a new synthesis, the synthesis we now call rabbinic Judaism. It was in response to the disaster of the destruction that rabbinic Judaism took shape, and its success was in its capacity to claim things had not changed at all—hence the assertion that even at the start, Moses was "our rabbi"—while making the very destruction of the Temple itself into the verification and vindication of the new structure. Rabbinic Judaism claimed that it was possible to serve God not only through sacrifice, but also through study of Torah. There is a priest in charge of the life of the community—but a new priest, the rabbi. The old sin-offerings still may be carried out, through deeds of loving kindness. Not only so, but when the whole Jewish people will fully carry out the teachings of the Torah, then the Temple itself will be rebuilt. To be sure, the Temple will be reconstructed along lines laid out in the Torah—that is, in the whole Torah of Moses, the Torah taught by the rabbis. And, like the prophets and historians in the time of the First Destruction, the rabbis further claimed that it was because the people had sinned, that is, had not kept the Torah, that the Temple had been destroyed. So the disaster itself was made to vindicate the rabbinic teaching and to verify its truth.

Now let us stand back from this synthesis and ask, How was it put together? What are its primary elements? What trends or movements before 70 are represented by these elements?

Two primary components in the Yavneh synthesis are to be discerned, first, the emphases of Pharisaism before 70, second, the values of the scribal profession before that time. The former lay stress upon universal keeping of the law, so that every Jew is obligated to do what only the elite—the priests—are normally expected to accomplish. Pre-70 Pharisaism thus contributed the stress on the universal keeping of the law. The second component derives from the scribes, whose professional ideal stressed the study of Torah and the centrality of the learned man in the religious system.

The unpredictable, final element in the synthesis of Pharisaic stress on widespread law—including ritual-law, observance and scribal emphasis on learning—is what makes rabbinic Judaism distinctive, and that is the conviction that the community now stands in the place of the Temple. The ruins of the cult, after all, did not mark the end of the collective life of Israel. What survived was the *people*. It was the genius of rabbinic Judaism to recognize that the people might reconstitute the Temple in its own collective life. Therefore the people had to be made holy, as the Temple had been holy, and the people's social life had to be sanctified as the surrogate for what had been lost. The rabbinic ideal further maintained that the rabbi served as the new priest, the study of Torah substituted for the Temple sacrifice, and deeds of loving kindness were the social surrogate for the sin-offering, that is, personal sacrifice instead of animal sacrifice.

Pre-70 Pharisaism is clearly defined by the Gospels' Pharisaic stories and the rabbinic traditions about the Pharisees. Both stress the same concerns: first, eating secular food in a state of ritual purity; second, careful tithing and giving of agricultural offerings to the priests, and obedience to the biblical rules and taboos concerning raising crops; third, to a lesser degree, some special laws on keeping the Sabbaths and festivals; and finally, still less commonly, rules on family affairs. Therefore, late Pharisaism—that which flourished in the last decades of the Temple's existence and which is revealed in the Gospels and in rabbinic traditions—is a cult-centered piety, which proposes to replicate the cult in the home, and thus to effect the Temple's purity laws at the table of the ordinary Jew, and quite literally to turn Israel into a "kingdom of priests and a holy nation." The symbolic structure of Pharisaism depends upon that of the Temple; the ideal is the same as that of the priesthood. The Pharisee was a layman pretending to be priest and making his private home into a model of the Temple. The laws about purity and careful tithing were dietary laws, governing what and how a person should eat. If a person kept those laws, then, when he ate at home, he was like God at the Temple's altar table, on which was arrayed food similarly guarded from impurity and produced in accord with Levitical revelation. By contrast, the rabbi was like God because he studied the Torah on earth, as did God and Moses "our rabbi" in the heavenly academy.

In order to trace the Pharisaic component of the rabbinic Judaism shaped at Yavneh after 70, let us turn to a major Yavneh authority, Eliezer ben Hyrcanus, because, as I shall show, he certainly represents in the period after the destruction the sorts of emphases characteristic of Pharisaism before that time. To be sure, Eliezer is represented in third-century C.E. rabbinic histories as a disciple of the founder of the Yavneh center, Yoḥanan ben Zakkai, but for our purposes, his legal traditions, which stand entirely independent of those of Yoḥanan ben Zakkai, are of greater interest than what later historians told about him as a person. Eliezer exemplifies the mentality of the Pharisaic component of the rabbinic synthesis, because his legal traditions correspond in a striking way to the agendum of legal themes assigned to the Pharisees before 70 both by the Synoptic Gospels and by the post-70 rabbis. At Yavneh Eliezer legislated, in theory if not in practice, primarily for people subject to Pharisaic discipline and mainly about matters important to Pharisaic piety, so his program for the post-Temple period concerned Pharisaism and little else. We simply do not know what, if anything, he might have had to say to non-Pharisaic Jews at Yavneh and in other parts of the country. Perhaps his saying, at that time, to repent before death would have seemed more important than it does now; but it hardly constitutes much of a program for a country which has just lost its autonomous government and capital and for a people suddenly without a sanctuary or a cult.

In general, the tendency of Eliezer's own rulings seems to have been in a single direction, and that was toward the rationalization and the liberalization of the application of Pharisaic law. What is asserted by the later tradition is absolutely correct: Eliezer really said nothing he had not heard from his masters. In an exact sense, he was profoundly "conservative." By attempting to reform details and to ease the strictness of the Pharisaic law, he hoped to conserve the Pharisaic way of piety substantially unchanged and unimpaired, essentially intact. This must mean that for Eliezer the destruction of the Temple did not mark a significant turning in the history of Judaism. Just as the destruction of the first Temple was followed, in a brief period, by the construction of the second, so he certainly supposed the same would now happen. He would see to it that the third Temple would be different from the second only in the more logical way in which its cult would be carried on, on the one side, and in the slightly simpler requirements of the application of the cult's purity rules to daily life and of the enforcement of the priestly taxes, on the other.

Eliezer's legislation, therefore, suggests he presumed life would soon go on pretty much as it had in the past. Issues important to pre-70 Pharisees predominate in his laws; issues absent in the rabbinic traditions about the Pharisees are—except the cult—mostly absent in his as well. Eliezer therefore comes at the end of the old Pharisaism. He does not inaugurate the new rabbinism, traces of which are quite absent in his historically usable traditions. Indeed, on the basis of his laws and sayings, we can hardly define what this rabbinism might consist of. The centrality of the oral Torah, the view of the rabbi as the new priest and of study of Torah as the new cult, the definition of piety as the imitation of Moses "our rabbi" and the conception of God as a rabbi, the organization of the Jewish community under rabbinic rule and by rabbinic law, and the goal of turning all Israel into a vast academy for the study of the (rabbinic) Torah—none of these motifs characteristic of later rabbinism occurs at all.

Since by the end of the Yavnean period (120 C.E.) the main outlines of rabbinism were clear, we may postulate that the transition from Pharisaism to rabbinism, or the union of the two, took place in the time of Eliezer himself. But he does not seem to have been among those who generated the new viewpoints; he appears as a reformer of the old ones. His solution to the problem of the cessation of the cult was not to replace the old piety with a new one but, rather, to preserve and refine the rules governing the old in the certain expectation of its restoration in a better form than ever. Others, who were his contemporaries and successors, developed the rabbinic idea of the (interim) substitution of study for sacrifice, the rabbi for the priest, and the oral Torah of Moses "our rabbi" for the piety of the old cult.

If so, we may take seriously the attribution of rabbinic ideas to others of his contemporaries. Where do we first find them? Clearly, Yoḥanan b. Zakkai stands well within the structure of rabbinic symbols and beliefs. It is in his sayings, admittedly first occurring in late compilations, that we find the claim of replacing the cult with something—anything—just as good. He is alleged to have told Joshua, his disciple, that deeds of loving-kindness achieve atonement just as satisfactorily as did the cult. He is further made to say that man was created in order to study the Torah. When Israel does the will of its father in heaven—which is contained in the Torah and taught by the rabbi—then no nation or race can rule over it. The cult is hardly central to his teachings and seldom occurs in his laws. The altar, to be sure, serves to make peace between Israel and the father in heaven, but is not so important ("how much the more so") as a man who makes peace among men or is a master of Torah. Yoḥanan's legal decrees are even better testimony, for they take account of the end of the cult and provide for the period of its cessation. The Temple rites may be carried on ("as a memorial") *outside* of the old sanctuary. The old priesthood is subjected to the governance of the rabbi. The priest had to pay the *sheqel* and ideally should marry anyone the rabbi declares to be a fit wife. Eliezer says nothing of the sort; what Yoḥanan has to say about the situation after 70 is either without parallel in Eliezer's sayings or contradicted by their tendency.

To be sure, we are scarcely able to claim that rabbinism begins with Yoḥanan or that Pharisaism ends with Eliezer. But Yoḥanan's tradition certainly reveals the main themes of later rabbinism, although these themes are more reliably attributed to later Yavneans and still more adequately spelled out in their sayings. And Eliezer's laws and theological sayings are strikingly silent about what later on would be the primary concern of the rabbinic authorities, the oral Torah in all its social and political ramifications, and are remarkably narrow in their focus upon the concerns of pre-70 Pharisaism.

If Eliezer stands for the old Pharisaism, for whom does Yoḥanan stand? I think he stands for the pre-70 scribes. The scribes form a distinct group—not merely a profession—in the Gospels' accounts of Jesus's opposition. Scribes and Pharisees are by no means regarded as one and the same group. To be sure, what scribes say and do not say is not made clear. One cannot derive from the synoptic record a clear picture of scribal doctrine or symbolism.

Having seen in Eliezer an important representative of the old Pharisaism, we find no difficulty in accounting for the Pharisaic component of the Yavnean synthesis. It likewise seems reasonable to locate in the scribes the antecedents of the ideological or symbolic part of the rabbinic component at Yavneh. Admittedly, our information on scribism in the rabbinic literature is indistinguishable from the later sayings produced by rabbinism. But if we consider that scribism goes back to much more ancient times than does Pharisaism, and that its main outlines are clearly represented, for instance, by Ben Sira, we may reasonably suppose that what the scribe regarded as the center of piety was study, interpretation, and application of the Torah. To be sure, what was studied and how it was interpreted are not to be identified with the literature and interpretation of later rabbinism. But the scribal piety and the rabbinic piety are expressed through an identical symbol, study of Torah. And one looks in vain in the rabbinic traditions about the Pharisees before 70 for stress on, or even the presence of the ideal of, the study of Torah. Unless rabbinism begins as the innovation of the early Yavneans—and this seems to me unlikely—it therefore should represent at Yavneh the continuation of pre-70 scribism.

But pre-70 scribism continued with an important difference, for Yavnean and later rabbinism said what cannot be located in pre-70 scribal documents: The Temple cult is to be replaced by study of Torah, the priest by the rabbi (= scribe); and the center of piety was shifted away from cult and sacrifice entirely. So Yavnean scribism made important changes in pre-70 scribal ideas. It responded to the new situation in a more appropriate way than did the Yavnean Pharisaism represented by Eliezer. Eliezer could conceive of no piety outside of that focused upon the Temple. But Yavnean and later scribism-rabbinism was able to construct an expression of piety which did not depend upon the Temple at all. While Eliezer appears as a reformer of old Pharisaism, the proponents of rabbinism do not seem to have reformed the old scribism. What they did was to carry the scribal ideal to its logical conclusion. If study of Torah was central and knowledge of Torah important, then the scribe had authority even in respect to the Temple and the cult; indeed, his knowledge was more important than what the priest knew. This view, known in the sayings of Yoḥanan b. Zakkai, who certainly held that the priest in Yavnean times was subordinate to the rabbi, is not a matter only of theoretical consequence. Yoḥanan also held that he might dispose of Temple practices and take them over for the Yavnean center—and for other places as well—and so both preserve them ("as a memorial") and remove from the Temple and the priests a monopoly over the sacred calendar, festivals, and rites. Earlier scribism thus contained within itself the potentiality to supersede the cult. It did not do so earlier because it had no reason to and because it probably could not. The latter rabbinism, faced with the occasion and the necessity, realized that potentiality. By contrast, earlier Pharisaism invested its best energies in the replication of the cult, not in its replacement. After 70, it could do no more than plan for its restoration.

Scribism as an ideology, not merely a profession, begins with the view that the law given by God to Moses was binding and therefore has to be authoritatively interpreted and applied to daily affairs. That view goes back to the fourth century B.C., by which time Nehemiah's establishment of the Torah of Moses as the constitution of Judea produced important effects in ordinary life. From that time on, those who could apply the completed, written Torah constituted an important class or profession. The writings of scribes stress the identification of Torah with wisdom and the importance of learning. Ben Sira's sage travels widely in search of wisdom and consorts with men of power. Into the first century, the scribes continue as an identifiable estate high in the country's administration. Otherwise, the synoptics' view is incomprehensible. Therefore, those who were professionally acquainted with the Scriptures—whether they were priests or not—formed an independent class of biblical teachers, lawyers, administrators, or scribes, alongside the priesthood.

Since later rabbinism found pre-70 scribism highly congenial to its ideal, it is by no means farfetched to trace the beginnings of rabbinism to the presence of representatives of the pre-70 scribal class, to whom the ideal of study of Torah, rather than the piety of the cult and the replication of that cultic piety in one's own home, was central. At Yavneh, therefore, were incorporated these two important strands of pre-70 times—the one the piety of a sect, the other the professional ideal of a class. Among them, as we have seen, Eliezer's teachings made for pre-70 Pharisaism an important place in the Yavnean synthesis.

Thus far, our definition of rabbinism has focused upon its central symbols and ideals. These seem to continue symbols and ideas known, in a general way, from "scribism"—if not known in detail from individual scribes, who, as I have stressed, formed a profession, not a sect. But what of the later, and essential, singularly characteristic traits of rabbinism: its formation as a well-organized and well-disciplined movement, its development of important institutions for the government of the Jewish communities of Palestine and Babylonia, its aspiration to make use of autonomous political instruments for the transformation of all Jews into rabbis? Of this, we have no knowledge at all in the earliest stratum of the Yavnean period. Clearly, Yoḥanan b. Zakkai worked out the relationship between the synagogue and the Temple. But the nature of the "gathering" at Yavneh—whether it was some sort of "academy," or a nascent political institution, or merely an inchoate assembly of various sorts of sectarians, professionals, pre-70 authorities, and whatever —is simply unilluminated.

So in all the "rabbinism" possibly present in Yoḥanan's corpus and remarkably absent in Eliezer's is simply the symbolic and ideological element represented by the study of Torah as the central expression of piety. The political institutions and social expressions of rabbinism make no appearance in the earliest years of the Yavnean period. They emerge, for the first time, in the development of the government under the patriarchate and its associated rabbinical functionaries, beginning with Gamaliel II—circa C.E. 90—and fully articulated, in the aftermath of the Bar Kokhba debacle, by Simeon b. Gamaliel II, circa C.E. 150. At that point, the rabbinical ideal produced serious effects for the political and social realities of Judaism.

By the end of the period of reconstruction after the Bar Kokhba War, the main outlines of rabbinic Judaism had been worked out, and their primary institutional embodiments were largely articulated. Then both the Torah-myth, expounded and exemplified by the rabbi, and the claim that that rabbinic Torah constitutes what is authentic and normative in Judaism were fully spelled out. From the middle of the second-century to the end of Talmudic times, two tasks were effected, first, the development of the literary and doctrinal corpus of rabbinic Judaism, second, the establishment, among the people, of the rabbis' claim to govern in the name of Sinai's revelation. The Babylonian and Palestinian Talmuds and related literature were the final outcome of the literary and doctrinal process. The institution of the rabbi, the school, and the autonomous government created by both, constituted the end-result of the political and historical process. The Jews, who in the first century C.E. and for a long time thereafter, were divided among numerous sects, by the end of the sixth century began to exhibit the traits of a single, unified and well-organized religious civilization. But, as we shall presently note, it was only much later on that the process of unification and harmonization was completed, so that the claim to normative status of rabbinic Judaism truly corresponded to the normal social and cultural realities of the Jewish people.

Rabbinic Judaism in Post-Talmudic Times

As is now clear, the purpose of this anthology is to point to the continuities of rabbinic Judaism from Talmudic to modern times. The proposition before us is that rabbinic Judaism laid the foundations for a mode of life, a pattern of organizing society and politics, a method of interpreting the meaning of both public history and private affairs, so comprehensive and so all-encompassing as to warrant the title, "civilization." Rabbinic Judaism supplied to Jews nearly everywhere a symbol so powerful and immediately meaningful that response, immediate and practical, was uniform. Whether a person was an ordinary fellow, living his or her life in private and concerned primarily for the here and now, or a religious virtuoso, possessed of great intellect or profound spiritual capacities, he or she found in "Torah" and all it meant a wholly satisfactory and exhaustive account of reality. What that means is this: wherever we turn, whatever evidence we examine, we shall time and again come back to the same simple conception of reality, the same abiding and enduring view that we are made to study Torah, that our duty is to carry out its precepts, that through Torah we come to, and serve, God. This uniformity of symbol and of the conceptions which explain and endow that symbol with meaning, this harmony of the individual and the community, of the private and the public, this total and world-surpassing conception of faith and destiny—these are the evidence that before us is a distinctive and single civilization, a way of living characteristic of a single group, the Jewish people, wherever they have lived. It is the enduring predominance of the rabbinic conception of Judaism and the rabbinic definition of what it should mean to be a Jew that justifies our calling the civilization of the Jews "rabbinic."

Our task now is to trace the main outlines of rabbinic civilization from Talmudic times. At the outset, therefore, we must ask, What are the primary traits, both cultural and theological, of the Talmudic Judaism which stands behind and generates the whole of rabbinic civilization? These introductory pages have simply meant to introduce some of the main cultural beliefs and characteristics, in historical context, of Talmudic Judaism. It remains to examine with some care the modes of Talmudic faith and law which would shape the minds of the later history of Judaism.

Once we have dealt with the Talmudic heritage, we must then face the inevitable outcome of the Talmud, which is law, and we therefore ask, What is the role of law in rabbinic Judaism? Why is law important? Of special significance, what are the effects of law in later times? Why is law—*halakhah*—regarded as central? Is this mere "legalism"—strict, literal, and excessive conformity to law? And does this "legalism" produce a kind of religious behaviorism? Or is the law meant to serve as a means of giving body and substance to a set of particular theological convictions? It goes without saying that we want to know not only about law in general, but about the specific legal writings which preserve and carry forward the Talmudic tradition. A final, and closely related, question is, What of the life of the people of the Torah? To answer this question, we turn to the synagogue, in which the Torah is revered and kept holy, and to which the people come to worship and hear the words of Torah.

We turn next to two great personalities of the legal tradition, Rashi, and the Vilna Gaon. To gain a clear picture not of law in the abstract, but of the sorts of heroes and leaders generated by the symbol and tradition of Torah, we consider two of the greatest figures in the two millenia before us, one at the middle, the other toward the end. Rashi, as we shall see, shaped the mind of the Jewish people more than anyone before or afterward, and he did so by making it possible for everyone to study Torah as the rabbis taught it, that is, both the written Torah and the oral tradition contained in the Talmud. He was the man for the masses, but he also educated the elite. The Vilna Gaon stood apart, a lonely man of the Torah, yet those privileged to study and reflect upon his interpretation of the Talmud and to follow in the strikingly original paths which he laid open know that his mind, in its way, is as formative for the rabbinic tradition, as revealing of the traits of that tradition, as Rashi's.

Everyone knows that "medieval" Judaism produced great philosophers and theologians, and that it was the task of these philosophers to "mediate" between "reason" and "faith." These are truisms in the minds of most informed people. Yet what is important, in my view, about the philosophers and the theologians is that they too were rabbis, in title and, even more important, in soul and spirit. The "faith" which they defended is that contained not only in the Hebrew Scriptures but also in the Talmud. The law which they rationalized is Talmudic law. The philosophy with which reason had to be harmonized was challenging because, if that philosophy was true (and they took for granted that it was), then it had, to begin with, to stand in some intimate relationship with Torah. We first ask about the main differences between the work of the rabbinic theologians and philosophers and that of the Talmudic sages. What are some specific points at which the former revised the heritage of the latter, and why did they do so? Then we turn to a philosopher who stands near the beginning of the philosophical and rational trend within rabbinic Judaism, but we focus as much upon his life as a rabbinic authority as upon his thought as a philosopher. Next comes a very different sort of philosopher, this time a poet, who gives us insight into a quite distinct mode of philosophical reflection, now not primarily through the analysis of general propositions but through the reflection upon specific events in the life of the Jewish people. Third is the quintessential rabbinic Jew, philosopher, lawyer, sage, community official, the religious genius of the rabbinic tradition, Maimonides. He better than anyone else demonstrates that Talmudic learning stands not only behind, but within philosophical modes of expression, which supply a new idiom for an essentially established message. Finally comes another sort of philosopher, this time a student of Scriptures and a mystic, but also a defender of Maimonides and of rationalism.

The second distinctive mode of religious expression in rabbinic Judaism is mysticism, which, from beginning to end, gave vividness and vitality to the life of Torah, including the keeping of the Torah's laws. To be sure, some mystics departed from the law, gave up the entire rabbinic structure. But most of them did not. Indeed, among the mystics are great lawyers, like Joseph Karo, who wrote the authoritative code of law, the Shulhan Arukh, and many of the mystics also were exceedingly erudite masters of Talmud itself. One cannot find a way meaningfully to distinguish between the disciplines of the law, which seem so routine and lacking in spontaneity, and the inspiration and imagination of the mystic, which, one might (wrongly) imagine would reject that routine and ordinary, everyday emphasis in favor of flights of the spirit. When the mystic in the rabbinic tradition reported on the vision perceived in his moment of exultation, it was in the symbols of Torah and the language of Talmud. Indeed, the Zohar, the great treatise of mystical doctrine, is attributed to the rabbis of the Talmud, just as the philosophers sought to harmonize philosophy with the rabbinic doctrines. We shall consider rabbinic mysticism in three ways, first, through a general account of its overall traits, second, through an ethical document produced by medieval mystics, and finally, through the life of a mystic figure still immensely influential in our own times.

Having seen as a single continuum the work of the lawyers, philosophers, and mystics, we turn to two classical rabbinic figures who lived at the beginning of the modern period in the history of Judaism. They are important in two ways. First, they are, in themselves, important exemplars of the rabbinic tradition, one as a major communal authority, the other as a formative force in the articulation of rabbinic ethics.

Second, both men stand for ways in which rabbinic Judaism, in its classic and traditional form, responded to the earliest challenges of modernity. What is important is that traditional Judaism, as distinct from Modern Orthodoxy, continues to follow policies laid down by each of these rabbis, and, it goes without saying, Modern Orthodoxy likewise draws upon their heritage. Nor are Conservative and Reform Jews oblivious to the meaning and message of the second of the two traditionalists who come at the end of our study.

In attempting this survey of the several primary traits of rabbinic Judaism, I have offered a single thesis and materials meant to illustrate that thesis. What I think not merely illustrative, but demonstrative, of the thesis is this: the several essays before us return, time and again, to a few very specific, very concrete matters: study of Torah, the centrality of ethics, the service of God through the ways laid forth in Talmudic tradition, the importance of learning, the significance of piety in the *halakhic* modes, and similar matters. Whether before us is a mystic, or a lawyer, or a philosopher, the center of interest remains one and the same: *Torah* as defined for the first time in the aftermath of the destruction of the Second Temple. The recurring motifs and themes, more than any facts asserted in the several papers we shall read, the tendency of the papers to repeat one another and to return to the same symbols and ideas time and again—these are proofs for the correctness of the theory offered here: rabbinic Judaism, from the beginning to nearly our own time, is a single, unified and harmonious religious-cultural structure, enduring change essentially intact, submitting to time, yet truly eternal, so far as nearly twenty centuries allow us to speak of eternity.

The Talmudic Heritage

The most important component of the Talmudic heritage is the Talmud itself. The Babylonian Talmud served in the history of Judaism from the time of its redaction, in about the sixth century, to the present time, as the primary authority in the formation and definition of Rabbinic Judaism. That well-established fact should not be taken for granted.

First, we might try to imagine the many other forms Judaism might have taken, had some other text—or no text at all, other than the Hebrew Scriptures—served as the authoritative source of all values. For the Talmud, despite its diversity, exhibits singular cogency. It is not simply a compendium of sayings, mindless and incoherent, about this and that. It is a remarkably consistent document, and through its discrete parts, expresses a single set of values. Talmudic sayings and laws lay particular stress, for example, upon mindful and thoughtful consideration of what one does. The Talmud's perspective on man is this: we think, therefore we and what we do are worth taking seriously. The Talmud moreover holds that we are what we do, and therefore it subjects to the closest possible scrutiny the definition, meaning, and motivation behind every right action. But the Talmud's analysis goes beyond the ascription of importance to trivial actions. It asks that these actions exhibit rationality and order, that they form a larger pattern and exhibit a deeper logic, that they in other words express in small ways a large rule for life. The Judaism shaped by the Talmud, therefore, exhibits three fundamental traits: first, belief in the rationality and order of existence, second, stress on the importance of reflection, study, and mastery of the laws which express that rationality and order, and finally, emphasis on concrete deeds. Rabbinic Judaism therefore will nurture people who respect the intellect and look for leadership to intellectuals, a society based on a sober appreciation for regularity and order, and a culture built upon practical concerns.

It did not have to be so. Had the Judaism adumbrated in the Dead Sea Scrolls prevailed, rather than that of the Talmudic rabbis, what sort of religious culture would have emerged? Clearly, we cannot imagine how the Dead Sea commune, or *yahad,* would have responded to the changing conditions of Jewish life. Yet we may be fairly certain, given what we do know, that the Judaism shaped by the ideals of the *yahad* would have stressed quite other matters, first of all, intense interest in the meaning and direction of historical events and search for the proper interpretation of great moments, second, emphasis on leaders deriving from the appropriate priestly lineage, and third, stress on ritual purity, and, by extension, other obsessive rituals. The sectarianism of the *yahad* surely would have left a less supple social policy than did the rabbis' eagerness to win over and make into rabbis all the Jews who could be reached. The intellectualism and stress on learning characteristic of rabbinic Judaism, to be sure, cannot be excluded from our hypothetical model, for the Dead Sea community possessed traditions as to the meaning and correct interpretation of Scripture. But it is difficult to imagine a stress on the intrinsic value of anyone possessed of learning, without regard to his origins, as against learned priests of appropriate lineage, in the emergent "Judaism" of the *yahad.*

So, as we observed, what the Talmud left behind was, to begin with, that vast and engaging document, the Talmud itself. Within the text, we have noted, are several predominant themes and central images. The first is the importance of Talmud-study. The second is belief in the divine origin of the substance of Talmudic teaching, that is, in the "Oral Torah," which, along with the Hebrew Scriptures, was alleged to have been revealed at Sinai. A primary image, therefore, will be "Torah." A further central concern of Talmudic Judaism, so obvious as to be taken for granted, is belief in the sanctity of Israel, the entire Jewish people, and not merely of a segment—a "saving remnant"—of the people, as at the Dead Sea commune. The rabbis of Talmudic times made every effort to persuade all Jews to accept their discipline and join in their undertaking. They sought to "rabbinize" all Israel and believed that when every Jew conformed to the paradigm of the rabbi, Israel would be saved. This social aspiration had far-reaching consequences for the formation of the civilization based upon Talmudic values. A third recurrent theme is the belief that man's task and the community's undertaking are to seek to sanctify this life, to serve God always and everywhere, and to do so in small as well as large matters. Talmudic literature is about justice and mercy, but it is, far more, about what is just in one particular setting, what is merciful in another. In the pages that follow are further references to the primary outline of the Talmudic legacy.

One question cannot be answered: at what point and in what way does the Talmud, which in its own day, at the time of its formation and composition, was the work of a handful of men, become the normal, not merely normative, for the entire Jewish people? When we reach the final evidences of Talmudic times, we still confront a small group, or estate, of teachers and bureaucrats, who evidently had some, circumscribed areas of authority over the masses, but who were not identical in values or behavior with the masses. That seems to be the state of affairs at the end of the fifth and the beginning of the sixth century C.E. Then our sources fall silent. When they speak again, three centuries later, they tell us of a quite new world, in which the Talmud is everywhere the source of Jewish law, and in which the Jewish people has accepted the task of shaping its life in accord with that law. In other words, the unattained aspiration of the rabbis who produced the Talmud three or four centuries later was in fact achieved, the 'rabbinization of all Israel,' so that we may accurately speak of Rabbinic Judaism as characteristic of nearly the whole people. Yet we do not have any information about how that remarkable transformation took place. While we may make some progress in tracing the formation of Talmudic Judaism, none at all seems possible in accounting for the acceptance, by the larger part of the people, of the values of the small group of rabbis represented in the Talmud itself. We do not, therefore, know how the ideals of intellectuals became those of the masses. But we know full well that that is what happened.

The religious outlines of the Talmudic heritage are described by Mordecai Kaplan. His *Greater Judaism in the Making* accomplishes two tasks, first, providing an account of the history of Judaism, and second, giving a Reconstructionist interpretation of that history. Kaplan's account in this area is perceptive and objective. His stress on the essential unity of rabbinic "civilization" is the natural beginning of our inquiry. He lays forth the primary traits of that civilization, in particular its emphasis upon the facticity of the Scriptures and of the Oral Torah of the rabbis, on the one hand, and upon the presence, the near-palpability of God, on the other. Kaplan's distinction between Torah's role in the life of the nation and in the life of the individual underlines the way in which private values and public ideals correspond and coalesce in Rabbinic Judaism.

Julius Guttmann then describes the primary religious ideas of Talmudic Judaism. He makes two important points. First, he outlines the main themes of Talmudic theology, expressed both in law and in theological sayings. Second, he underlines the particular ways in which rabbinic ideas are expressed, the modes of thought characteristic of the Talmudic, and later, sages. This prepares us to recognize the remarkable innovation represented by philosophical thinking later on. Guttmann has the merit, moreover, of stressing the centrality of the Bible in the Talmudic structure. But, as we have already suggested, we should not suppose that the Bible originally meant what the rabbis later claimed, or that the interpretation of the rabbis seemed obvious to those who stood outside their circle. Every group in ancient Judaism read the same Scriptures. The rabbis' understanding of those Scriptures was unique to them.

TORAH AND TALMUDIC JUDAISM

What do we mean by 'Rabbinic Judaism'? Mordecai M. Kaplan, whose philosophy is based on the view that "Judaism is a religious civilization," here tells us the central traits of the rabbinic structure in Judaism. He stresses what it means to live in the world shaped by the rabbinic literature. First, the Jew perceived a perfect and unbroken continuity between himself and Sinai. True, differing authorities had various opinions about details of the faith. But the pattern remained unchanged, it was alleged, from Sinai onward. Kaplan points out that that conviction was based upon the historical fact of uninterrupted persistence of the rabbinic value-structure from the first century to modern times. A tenth- or fifteenth-century Jew who saw himself within a perpetual continuum therefore did not err, except in chronology.

And it was a social continuum exhibited in his own times, for whoever lived in his day, whether rich or poor, learned or ignorant, was apt to share the same values and ideals. These common ideals centered on the symbol of "Torah," which encompassed all the religious ideas, values, themes, and experiences in modern times subsumed by the word "Judaism." "Torah" was the central image and the all-encompassing symbol for the Jews' perception of reality.

Above all, Torah meant three things: first, belief in the perfect correspondence between divine revelation and worldly life, between heaven and earth. Second, stress on continuing study of revelation as the means of understanding everything that happened and guiding all that was to be done. Third, confidence that through perfect loyalty to Torah, the Jew carries out God's will and purpose for both nature and history.

What is important is that these 'meanings' assigned to Torah, beginning with the pages of the Talmud and related literature, will everywhere predominate later on. No movement within the Jewish people from the Talmud until Zionism at the end of the nineteenth century took shape without a focus on the symbol of "Torah." The issues of philosophy, as we shall see, are fundamentally important primarily because defense of Torah required attending to them. The experience of the mystic

27

in like manner takes concrete form in the Torah's images and symbols. Heretical groups become heresies because they take issue with the central issues of Torah. In claiming that "Judaism" from the first to the nineteenth century, and thereafter as well, can only be the form of Judaism shaped by the rabbis of the Talmud, we adduce as evidence the fact of the centrality of Torah, both as a symbol and as a source of values, for all expressions and modes of Judaism.

1.

RABBINIC JUDAISM

Mordecai M. Kaplan

[*From The Greater Judaism in the Making. A Study of the Modern Evolution of Judaism,* by Mordecai M. Kaplan. N. Y., 1960: The Reconstructionist Press, pp. 5-13.]

Traditional Judaism is the religious culture, or civilization, of the Jews, as they lived it before they felt the impact of Western thought through the medium of Arabic culture in the Middle East during the tenth to the twelfth centuries of the common era. The salient character of Traditional Judaism was the pervasive awareness on the part of every Jew that his People had been covenanted to God, or committed to the task of making Him and His will known to the rest of mankind. The account of the enactment of the covenant and the duties that it imposed on the Jews were to be found in the Torah which God had revealed or dictated to Moses. Those duties, however, were spelled out with great detail in the patterns, ideals, institutions and norms of conduct formulated by the Sages of the Talmud.

"The Sages of the Talmud" is a term used to denote the *Tannaim* and the *Amoraim.* The *Tannaim,* all of whom were Palestinian Jews, were the authors of the various laws included in the *Mishnah,* which was adopted as an authoritative code by Rabbi Judah the Prince at the end of the second century. The *Amoraim,* some of whom were Palestinian and others Babylonian Jews, were the scholars whose interpretations of the *Mishnah* and the Bible, both legalistic and homiletic, are contained in the *Gemara* and the *Midrashim.* They flourished from about the beginning of the third century to the end of the fifth century, C.E.

That pattern of Traditional Judaism was maintained essentially intact until the invasion of Jewish life by modernism. The finality of Talmudic law formulated by the *Amoraim* was never questioned. "Rav Ashi and Ravina," we are told, "represent the consummation of authoritative teaching." That implies that no one has any right to change that teaching, "whether in substance or in form."

The sharply discerning eye of the scholar may perceive slightly different shades of belief and practice in the Rabbinic pattern, slight changes in emphasis under the influence of varying conditions. But by and large that pattern remained unchanged during the seventeen centuries that elapsed between R. Yohanan ben Zakkai and Moses Mendelssohn. The slight changes in outlook and in social structure of Jewish life which took place in the course of those centuries were so gradual as to be imperceptible. They certainly were not deliberate. To the ancient mind any deliberate change was considered subversive of tradition as a whole, and therefore dangerous.

To the generations of Jews whose mode of life was regulated by the Talmud, all the teachings of the Sages appeared inherently consistent. A considerable portion of the post-Talmudic writings is devoted to the reconciliation of contradictory statements in the tradition itself. Very seldom was a traditional text interpreted in the light of either literary or historical context. Whenever new conditions arose, it was tacitly assumed that they had been provided for in the tradition, since the tradition was assumed to have been revealed by God to Moses simultaneously with the written Torah. That is the assumption on which the entire Rabbinic literature is based. The discussions recorded in the Talmud were carried on in the Rabbinic academies of Palestine and Babylonia over a period of about five centuries. Their purpose was a twofold one; first, to arrive at an inherently consistent interpretation of the tradition as it had come down from the *Tannaim,* and as recorded in the *Mishnah, Tosefta* and other sources; and secondly, to relate that interpretation to the written Torah.

Except for the large-scale revolt against Rabbinic Judaism known as Karaism which flourished for a long time during the ninth to the twelfth century in the Middle East, and the extreme antinomian wing of the Shabbatean sect which arose in Smyrna in 1665, the Talmudic tradition was universally regarded as the norm of Jewish life. "The positive influence of this way of life (the Mosaic and Rabbinic Law) over the Jewish mind had been so great," writes G. G. Scholem, "that for centuries no movement, least of all an organized movement, had rebelled against the values linked up with the practical fulfillment of the Law."

During the three centuries between the tenth and twelfth inclusive, the rising tide of rationalism, which derived from Greek culture, had invaded the Moslem countries where most of the Jews then lived. It also seeped into Jewish life, and for a time jeopardized not only the authority of the Talmudic tradition but the very existence of Judaism, especially among the intellectual elite and the well-to-do. But before long, that threat was offset by a succession of writings which countered successfully the challenge of rationalist thought. Those writings were of two types, philosophic and mystic. Of the two, the mystic writings were by far the more potent in fortifying the Talmudic tradition. The mystic writings kept growing in scope and influence, while the philosophic writings remained limited in both. By the time Traditional Judaism began to feel the impact of modernism, there were but few extant copies of Maimonides' *Guide for the Perplexed,* and the interest in Medieval Jewish philosophy was at its lowest ebb, whereas the study of the *Zohar* received a new impetus with the rise of the Hasidic movement during the middle of the eighteenth century.

Another remarkable fact is that, in the pre-modern era, faith in Traditional Judaism was shared alike by all classes, regardless of their general educational background. Due to the fact that, with few exceptions, neither the philosophic nor the mystic writings seemed to challenge Traditional Judaism, there was little discrepancy in world outlook between the masses and the learned among the Jews. A Jewish woman like Glueckel of Hameln, though more literate than the majority of her kind, was nevertheless typical. Through the medium of the Judeo-German version of Rabbinic teachings she acquired a world outlook that contained virtually all the fundamental concepts and values articulated by the ancient Jewish Sages.

What Judaism as a whole meant to the Jews in the pre-modern era of Jewish history may be inferred from what the term "Torah" meant to them. There is, indeed, no Hebrew term for "Judaism" in the entire literature of that period. *Yahadut,* by which Judaism is designated in modern Hebrew, always meant in the past "Jewishness" or Jewish practice. The term used throughout that period as summing up the entire substance and import of Jewish life is "Torah." For the Jews before modern times *the* Torah consisted essentially of the Pentateuch as interpreted by the oral tradition, *Torah she-be-al-peh.* The authorship of the Pentateuch and of the traditional interpretations of its text was ascribed, in all literalness, to God. Unlike the other parts of the Bible, which were regarded as having been written under the inspiration of the Divine Spirit, but which also reflect the thought and personality of those who wrote them, the text of the Pentateuch was regarded as free from any human admixture. This assumption was so self-evident to the Sages that they did not hesitate to use a Pentateuchal text as source of verification or refutation, in the same way as we would use a logical or mathematical axiom.

The following passage from *Sifre,* a collection of Tannaitic interpretations of Numbers and Deuteronomy, is a typical illustration of that sort of reasoning: *"I, even I am He, and there is no God beside Me."* This verse is an answer to those who say, *"There is no Power in heaven,"* or to those who say, *"There are two Powers in heaven."* "One can imagine," C. G. Montefiore and H. Loewe comment ,"that this verse might be used against those who say that there are two powers, because such persons might also acknowledge the divine authority of Scriptures. But it is exceedingly curious that the Rabbis, who are not wanting in great acuteness when it comes to making legal distinctions or indeed to anything juristic, should not have seen that for those who deny that there is any God at all . . . the verse is valueless, as such people would obviously deny any authority to the book from which the verse comes."

Another example of how literally they took the tradition that the precepts in the Torah were authored by God is the following: Yehudah Halevi in his *Al-Khazari* has the Rabbi say to the Khazar king: "What is now your opinion of a select community which has merited the appellation 'people of God' and also a special name called 'the inheritance of God,' and of seasons fixed by Him, not merely agreed upon or settled by astronomical calculations, and therefore styled 'feasts of the Lord?' The rules regarding purity and worship, prayers and performances, are fixed by God, and therefore called 'work of God' and 'service of the Lord.' " It is not easy for a modern person to recapture that complete sense of acceptance of whatever was stated in the Torah as absolute truth. Such acceptance was possible only so long as Jews had implicit faith in the divine authorship of its contents.

Throughout the centuries of Traditional Judaism, the doctrine, or dogma, that the Torah had been dictated directly by God to Moses during Israel's sojourn at Sinai, was the cardinal principle to which every Jew had to give assent, or else he was read out of the fold. "He who says that the Torah is not from heaven forfeits his share in the world to come," that is, he is deprived of salvation. When the Sages said of the Torah that it was "from heaven," they were not speaking in metaphors. Heaven was to them a place actually above the earth. Just as literally as they believed in the existence of waters in the upper regions, so literally did they believe that the Torah emanated from the upper regions, that is, from God who dwelt in the heavens above.

Moses' relation to the Torah was nothing more than that of an amanuensis, according to Rabbi Meir, who used as an illustration the instance of Jeremiah's dictating his prophecies to Baruch. "Whoever says that Moses himself wrote even one word of the Torah, of him it is said that he holds God's word in contempt. He forfeits his share in the world to come." The only question was whether God dictated the contents of the entire Torah at one time, or in sections at different times. Some Rabbis maintain that it is forbidden to write the Pentateuch on the same scroll with the rest of the Scriptures, because of the superior sanctity of the former. For the same reason it is not permitted to place a scroll containing the writings of the Prophets and the Hagiographa upon one containing the Pentateuch.

If it were not for Israel's sins, we are told, only the Pentateuch and the parts of Joshua which indicate the boundary lines of Eretz Yisrael would have constituted the Sacred Scriptures. The benediction, *"Blessed art Thou . . . for having given us Thy Torah"* may not be recited before reading any section of the Scriptures outside the Pentateuch, though it may be recited before a passage from the *Mishnah*. In the future, according to R. Yohanan, when Israel's sins have been eliminated, the Pentateuch alone will continue to be studied, to the exclusion of the Prophetic writings and the Hagiographa.

The importance which Traditional Judaism attaches to the Oral Law may be gathered from the fact that it views the Oral Law not merely as coordinate with the Written Law, but as related to it organically. The Sage whose function it is to transmit the Oral Law is deferred to more implicitly than the Prophet. That is why the Oral Law is more authoritative than the Prophetic writings. The relation of the Oral Law to the Written Law is indicated in the story of Hillel and the would-be proselyte. The latter at first refused to accept the Oral Law. Hillel, however, convinced him by means of a lesson in the Hebrew alphabet that the Oral Law was as indispensable to the Written Law as was the tradition concerning the name and pronunciation of each letter of the alphabet to the letters themselves.

The Palestinian *Amoraim* of the third and fourth centuries advance the opinion that the Oral Law is that element of Torah which renders it the unique possession of Israel. This Amoraic conception of the Oral Law is, no doubt, intended to offset the claim of Christianity to the effect that, in adopting the Jewish Scriptures, including the Torah, as part of its sacred writings, it embraces all the revealed truth of which Judaism claims to be the sole possessor. The inclusion by non-Jews of the Pentateuch among their sacred scriptures was resented by the *Tannaim,* as is evident from the following passage in a Tannaitic *Midrash*: "The Torah is betrothed to Israel, and cannot therefore be espoused by any other people."

The Torah, in the sense of the Oral and the Written teaching and legislation, performed a twofold function in the life of the Jews: It served as an instrument of national and of individual salvation. The verse in Deuteronomy which reads: "That your days may be multiplied and the days of your children, as the days of the heavens above the earth" is commented upon in *Sifre,* as follows: 'That your days may be multiplied,' in this world; 'and the days of your children,' in the Messianic era; 'as the days of the heavens upon the earth,' in the world to come." Among the various petitions which the Jew has been wont to recite at the end of the prayer of thanksgiving after a meal is one which reads: "May the All-merciful make us worthy of the days of the Messiah and of the life of the world to come." This petition sums up in succinct fashion the two goals which Traditional Judaism sought to help the Jew attain. "The days of the Messiah" refers to national redemption, to freedom from oppression at the hands of other nations, and to the return of the Jews to Eretz Yisrael, their ancestral land. "The life of the world to come" refers to the life of bliss which awaits the individual Jew who, while in this world, lives in conformity with the will of God as expressed in the Torah.

The Torah, or Traditional Judaism, must therefore be understood as having made of the Jews both a nation (ummah) and an ecclesia (K'nesset Yisrael). As a nation, the Jews developed all those institutions which were essential to the conduct of everyday affairs in men's relations to one another and in their relations as a group *vis-a-vis* other groups. A nation is a political group. Before the modern era the Jews were a political group insofar as they always enjoyed a measure of autonomy. On the other hand, they were also an ecclesia or *K'nesset.* "Ecclesia" is a distinctly religious concept, religious in the *traditional* sense of being based upon some supernatural revelation of divinity. An ecclesia is a *corpus mysticum.* Its members are united by the common bond of allegiance to some specific instrument of a supernatural character. That instrument may be a sacred text, or it may be a sacred personality. By means of that instrument, it is assumed, men learn what God would have them do in order to achieve salvation.

Of the two functions of the Torah, that of maintaining the solidarity of the Jews as a People was expected to lead to the advent of the Messiah. The other function, that of uniting them into a holy nation, or ecclesia, designated as *K'nesset Yisrael* was expected to enable them, as individuals, to achieve salvation, or a share in the world to come. Those two functions were not inherently integral to each other, though, before Rabbinic Judaism became crystallized, they gradually fused into the one eschatological hope of a miraculously bright future for the entire People.

However, the belief in the hereafter, or in the world to come, because of its reference to the destiny of the individual, was bound to play a greater role in the Jewish consciousness during the centuries of exile than the Messianic expectation, which had to do with the destiny of the nation. This is apparent from the tendency of the Sages to reinterpret scriptural passages which unmistakenly refer to the future destiny of the nation as referring to the world to come. Thus the teaching of the Mishnah that "All who are of Israel have a share in the world to come" is based upon the statement in Isaiah which reads: *"Thy people are all righteous; they will inherit the land* (eretz) *forever."* Even if *eretz* means "the earth," it could mean that only in the same sense as in Psalm 37:11, where the poet wishes to affirm his faith in the ultimate survival of the meek and humble instead of the aggressive and violent ones. In any event, the Prophet is concerned with the destiny of the entire People and not merely with that of the individual. Moreover, the *Chapters of the Fathers,* which have as their central theme the importance of Torah study, and the reading of which is preceded by the foregoing *Mishnah* about the world to come, do not treat that study as a means to national redemption but to a share of the individual Jew in the world to come.

If we call to mind the difference between the origin of the belief in the advent of the Messiah and of the belief in the world to come, we sense the difference in the connotations of those beliefs. The belief in the Messiah stems directly from Biblical sources. It is indigenously Jewish. On the other hand, the belief in the world to come, with its concomitant belief in bodily resurrection, is an importation mainly from Zoroastrian civilization.

In the Bible, the People of Israel, after having undergone divine chastisement, is assured of its return to its land and of the attainment of bliss. Every such assurance became part of the pattern of hope in which the central figure was a scion of David, known as the Messiah. The prophecies of Balaam, the concluding verses in the farewell song of Moses, the prophecy in Isaiah and Micah concerning "the latter days," the description of the Messiah given in *Isaiah,* Chapter 11, the entire collection of consolatory prophecies in the second part of Isaiah, those in all the other prophetic books from Jeremiah through Malachi, the allusions in the book of Psalms, and the concluding chapter in Daniel— all were uniformly interpreted as referring to the Messianic era which awaited the Jewish nation.

On the other hand, the belief in bodily resurrection and the belief in the world to come stem from non-Jewish sources. It was accepted by the Jews to meet a spiritual expectation which had arisen during the period of the Second Commonwealth. That expectation was to find some correspondence between the merit and the lot of the individual. Experience seemed to refute the principle of reward and punishment stressed in the Torah. The Jews therefore had recourse to the same solution as all other religions which stressed the salvation of the individual. That solution posited another world wherein the inequities of this one were righted. Thus the belief in the world to come is essentially motivated by the desire to vindicate the principle of individual retribution Both the Messianic hope and the expectation of bliss in the world to come are voiced in the traditional liturgy, as in the following: "May it be Thy will that we keep Thy statutes in this world, and be worthy to live to witness and inherit happiness and blessing in the days of the Messiah and in the life of the world to come."

TALMUDIC THEOLOGY

The Talmudic legacy consisted of two main elements, a corpus of law, and a body of doctrine. Both the substance and the form of Talmudic Judaism were to exert a profound impact upon all later developments within rabbinic civilization. The form—pithy, brief statements—opened the way to considerable creative development, for what was stated briefly could be interpreted in many different ways, indeed, demanded further expansion and exposition. The substance—a distinctive set of laws and theological assertions based on laws—would require not only development, but radical revision in the light of new conceptions and different modes of thought. These latter developments could not be recognized for what they were, accretions and additions to the original body of the faith, but had to be subsumed within and shown to emerge from the potentialities of the original doctrine. Otherwise one would have to confess to the presence of innovation, and this, within a traditional, if supple, structure, was unacceptable.

What were the specific religious ideas laid forth in Talmudic Judaism? Julius Guttmann here spells out the dominant themes. At the basis of Talmudic Judaism is the Hebrew Bible, *Tanakh,* which was understood as a completely factual and entirely literal account of God's will for the world. But Talmudic Judaism entirely revised the historical meaning of the Scriptures to conform to its perception of reality. It was a "Talmudic" or "rabbinic" Bible which was handed down from ancient to medieval and modern times. For one thing, the rabbis accepted a human conception of God, that is, they found no difficulty in anthropomorphism, or in imagining God pretty much as they saw themselves. They further viewed God as demanding many things of man, as issuing *mitsvot,* or commandments, for every situation of ordinary life. These commandments were of various kinds, ritual, ethical, cultic, social, but all were of equal validity and laid an equal claim upon man's obedience.

If Israel, the Jewish people, proved itself loyal to the Torah, it could then look forward to the coming of the messiah. Prophetic predictions of such a messiah, an anointed man of God who would bring to a happy conclusion the distressing history of the nations and of Israel, in Talmudic times took many forms. For one thing, alongside a belief in the end of history developed the conception of the resurrection of the dead and the immortality of the soul. A further, related belief was in another world, besides and above this one, which would set the stage for the enjoyment by the pious of the presence of God.

The way in which the rabbis of the Talmud expressed these and related beliefs was profoundly unphilosophical and untheological. That is, the abstract and speculative modes of analytic thought characteristic of philosophy and theology in the Western setting were alien to the rabbinic way of discourse. The rabbis' sayings were just that, brief maxims or apophthegms, and no one worked out such sayings into elaborate systems of thought or tested the coherence of a group of such sayings with one another. That would be one of the primary tasks of later philosophy and mysticism.

2.

THE RELIGIOUS IDEAS OF TALMUDIC JUDAISM

JULIUS GUTTMANN

[From *Philosophies of Judaism. The History of Jewish Philosophy from Biblical Times to Franz Rosenzweig,* by Julius Guttmann. N. Y., 1964: Holt, Rinehart, and Winston, pp. 30-43.]

The dominant form of Jewish religion since the last centuries of antiquity—and the one that served as the foundation for the development of Judaism in the Middle Ages and modern times—was Talmudic Judaism, which developed in Palestine and Babylonia. Until the end of the first century of the Common Era, the most diverse religious tendencies flourished in Palestine, and many of the apocryphal books show the extent to which the Jews of Palestine were influenced by the religious syncretism of late antiquity. However, after the destruction of Second Temple by Titus (70 C.E.), all the religious currents that had competed with Pharisaic Talmudic Judaism quickly disappeared, and the latter achieved a unified form. The significance of the Talmud for coming generations resides mainly in religious law, which does not concern us here. The ritual, ceremonial, and legal provisions of the Talmud gave Jewish religious life its fixed and distinct form, which maintained itself until the end of the eighteenth century. The basic religious ideas of Judaism, on the other hand, were never given a similarly definitive form by the Talmud. The Talmud never attempts to formulate religious truths in fixed dogmatic expressions. The borderline between those binding doctrine and individual opinion is extremely fluid, and there is far greater variety between different generations and individuals than in the realm of religious law. The most diverse religious ideas were current between the last centuries B.C.E., when the development of the Talmud began to take place, and its final redaction at the end of the fifth century.

Many of the foreign doctrines which had penetrated into Judaism during the syncretistic period reappeared in Talmudic literature. Many of them, however, like those fantastic eschatological descriptions which we have already seen in the apocryphal literature, should be considered simply as the free play of imaginative fancy or the product of popular faith, rather than as doctrine in the precise sense. It is possible, after all, to detect a common and permanent pattern of basic ideas which proved of the greatest importance for subsequent developments.

The faith of Talmudic Judaism rests completely on biblical foundations. Central to it are the simple and sublime ideas of the Bible concerning a transcendent God, the Torah as the embodiment of his moral demands, the moral nature of the relationship between God and man, the wisdom and justice of divine providence, the election of Israel, and the promise of the coming kingdom of God. No theoretical reflection diminishes the living reality of God. Even speculations concerning hypostases and other mediating agencies could not affect his immediate presence to the world or remove him to an unapproachable distance. God acts as much in the present as he did in the past. It is true that prophecy and the miraculous events of biblical times belong to the past, and that the salvation announced by the prophets belongs to the future—the "end of days." This distinction between the present, on the one hand, and the mighty revelations of God in the past and future, on the other, is a necessary corollary of the historical character of the Jewish concept of revelation, and the expectation of a future (historical) salvation. Similar causes operated in Christianity and in Islam and led to similar distinctions between the present and the time of revelation—that is, the past. But even if the present was devoid of historic revelation, men still felt the immediate presence of God in their lives. Every individual Jew knew himself under the same divine providence which had governed the lives of his ancestors, and through some chosen pious persons, even miracles would be wrought—though these could not, of course, be compared to those wrought by the prophets. In order to express the consciousness of the presence of God, the religious imagination did not stop even before the most daring anthropomorphisms. In order to emphasize the value of the study of Torah, the Talmudic rabbis describe God himself as studying the Torah. The faith that the sufferings of Israel could not destroy the intimate bond between God and his people was expressed by saying that God not only lamented over the sorrows that he had brought upon Israel, but actually shared their exile.

But the Talmudists clearly recognized the nature of the anthropomorphisms of their own religious fantasy, as well as those of the Bible. They pointed out how God revealed himself according to the varying historical situations, and how the prophetic utterances were influenced by the individual personality of each prophet; in fact, they even suggested that every Jew standing at Sinai saw God in a slightly different fashion. These notions were never systematically developed; no attempts were made to distinguish between anthropomorphic forms of expression and the actual content of the idea of God, but their intention is quite clear. The idea of the personal and moral nature of God remains beyond all criticism, and provides the basic common core of the different concrete images.

The passionate violence of the religious ethos of the prophets had given place, in Talmudic times, to a quieter, more restrained, and in a way even sober piety, bound to history and tradition. However, the activist character of Jewish religion was preserved. Religious life was still centered on the divine "commands," in which God addressed himself to the human will, and showed the way of communion between man and God. Human destiny is conceived in different ways. Piety is not so much the mere observance of the divine commandments as the imitation of a divine model. The biblical commandment to be holy even as the Lord God is holy, and the injunction to walk in the ways of God, are interpreted as demands to imitate the divine qualities of love and mercy. Love of God and faithful trust in him are considered the foundation of the right observance of the commandments. The spirit of rabbinic religion is thus elevated above mere submission or obedience of the will. Its religious activity is rooted in the inner certainty of community with God, yet its piety remains one of precept and duty. Consequently, much stress is laid on moral freedom: man's actions are his own, even in relation to the divine omnipotence. The Torah is the embodiment of the divine will, and the observance of its commandments is the task given to Israel by God. The universality of the divine commandment is established by the notion of an original, pre-Israelite revelation, addressed to all nations and containing the foundations of morals.

However, the perfect divine revelation is the Torah given to Israel. As a divinely revealed law, all its parts—ritual as well as moral —are of equal validity, and equally constitute the religious duty of Israel. The idea of equal and unassailable validity—from a formal point of view—of all parts of the Torah follows as a logical consequence from the biblical notion of a divine legislation; at the same time the rabbis—from the material point of view—distinguished between central and marginal laws, between means and ends. The Talmud frequently interprets ceremonial and cultic items of the biblical legislation as means toward the ultimate moral ends of the divine law, subordinating the former to the latter in spite of their common divine origin. Psychologically of course, it is only to be expected that sometimes one, and sometimes the other of these two facets comes to the fore; at times the observance of the commandments is permeated by ethical attitudes; at other times, the distinction between ethics and ritual becomes blurred.

The messianic promises of the prophets were the mainstay of the Jewish community. We need not concern ourselves here with the transformation of the relatively simple expectations of the prophets into the more complicated notions of the later eschatologies developing in the last centuries of the pre-Christian era, or with the differences between the more national and the more universalistic versions of the messianic ideal, or with the changing ideas about the imminence or distance of the messianic coming. All these, though of considerable consequence for later times, are largely irrelevant to our present theme. Throughout all these variations on the messianic theme, the historical character of the prophetic hope for the future is preserved intact. An expectation of an entirely different sort is found in the ideas of the resurrection of the dead and the immortality of the soul. In a way, the resurrection of the dead still links up with the expectations of an historical fulfillment. It will take place at the end of time, and the resurrected will take part in the miraculous events of that age. The individual hope for an eternal life was thus combined with the idea that past generations, too, would share in the promise of the kingdom of God. The personal longing for eternal life is satisfied within the framework of collective historical eschatology.

These two elements are completely separated by the belief in the immortality of the soul. Frequently, the idea of immortality is overshadowed by that of resurrection. The Talmud, like the apocryphal literature, knows of a kind of intermediate state of the soul between death and resurrection; true retribution will be dispensed only after the resurrection of the body. But along with it, we also find the faith in a retribution coming immediately after death, and in a life of blessedness for the soul in the beyond. According to the latter view, the individual hope for the future has no connection whatsoever with history. "The world to come," the place of reward and punishment beyond, is distinct from the future "kingdom of God" even in its most eschatological form. "The world to come" does not succeed "this world" in time, but exists from eternity as a reality outside and above time, to which the soul ascends. This view faces a double opposition—on the one hand between the present reality of history and the future kingdom of God, and on the other, between life on earth and life beyond. The two orientations do not necessarily exclude each other. The original Jewish eschatology with its historical and collective hopes did not lose its power or intensity because of the belief in individual immortality, and the latter, as we have seen, could combine with the idea of the resurrection of the dead. Nevertheless, religious interpretation of the world had taken a new and decisive turn which provided starting points for the most diverse developments of Jewish thought in later periods.

The belief in another world, above and beyond time, led to a new evaluation of the present world. It was not enough that this world should find its perfection and fulfillment in a world to come, and that the wrongs of this earthly life should be made good there, but the ultimate end of man was shifted to the world to come. Our life in this world came to be conceived as a mere preparation, whether in terms of the resurrection of the dead or of the immortality of the soul. According to a well-known Talmudic saying, this world is like a vestibule in which man should prepare himself for entering the banquet hall of the world to come. The blessedness of the world to come is understood as consisting of the pious enjoying the radiance of the presence of God.

Nevertheless, this rabbinic view is very different from the dualistic contempt for the world of the senses exhibited, for example, by Philo, under Platonic influence. The Talmud emphatically repeats the biblical affirmation of this world and interprets the words of Genesis, "and God saw everything that He had made and behold it was very good," as referring to *both* worlds. The good things of this world, including sensual pleasures, may be enjoyed simply and naturally; only in rare instances do we find any ascetic tendencies. Even more important is the fact that asceticism plays no role in the understanding of ethics. Although the moral act was understood as a preparation for the future world, it lacked the negative connotation of separation from the world of the senses. Its meaning was rather wholly positive: to serve God in this world, to fulfill his will, and to build a social order in accordance with his will. The religious value of moral action is maintained even in the face of eschatological communion with God, since fulfilling the will of God in this world is no less communion with God than the state of blessedness in the hereafter. The same Talmudic teacher who described this world as only a vestibule to the coming world, also said that although one hour of blessedness in the world to come was worth more than all the life of this world, yet one hour of repentance and good deeds in this world was worth more than all of the life of the world to come.

What has been said regarding the rabbinic view of the world applies as well to the idea of man. The Bible had ascribed a divine origin to the human spirit, but now we find an explicit dualism. The body and the soul are seen in sharp contrast. Because of his soul, which is destined for eternal life, man belongs to the superior world of the spirit; in his body, he belongs to the earth. Thanks to his soul, he resembles the angels; thanks to his body, a beast. Following the Stoics and Philo, the relationship of the soul to the body is compared to that of God to the world. The idea of the pre-existence of the soul is also known to the Talmud. Man's higher powers, such as his reason and moral consciousness, are attributed to the soul; his lower passions are assigned to the body. The corollary of man's intermediate position between the higher and lower worlds is that by observing the divine commandments, he can rise to the rank of the angels, but by transgressing them he descends to the level of the beasts.

But this dualism is far from identifying evil with man's sensual nature. The body is not the ground of evil, and consequently man's moral task does not consist in his separation from the body. The warfare between good and evil is fought out *within* man's soul; it is there that good and evil impulses face each other. They represent two directions of the human will, and man must choose between them. As the source of temptation, sensuality occasionally is identified with the "evil impulse," but in itself it is ethically indifferent and has its legitimate sphere of existence. In spite of the Talmudic praise of the virtue of frugality as practiced by the pious, sensuality—provided it is kept under control—is considered unobjectionable, and the body is regarded as an essential part of man's God-given nature. Even the evil impulse is a necessary part of human nature, and the Talmud voices the remarkable demand to love God with both of our impulses—the good and the evil. Here again the end of ethics is seen not as separation from the world of the senses, but rather serving God within that world, with all available human powers. The body and the senses should be subordinate and subservient to the soul; they are not, of themselves, enemies of its heavenly destiny. Nonetheless, the whole complex of ideas described so far—the belief in a spiritual world above the world of the senses, the eternal destiny of the soul, and the dualistic conception of man, could easily be turned in the direction of an ascetic contemplative religion; it did, in fact, provide the opening through which the Neo-platonic type of spirituality entered Judaism in the Middle Ages.

Along with these speculative developments, there emerged another, more formal, though no less significant phenomenon: the growth of theoretical reflection on the contents of religion. Inquiry into fundamental religious questions is no longer an expression of the religious consciousness itself, seeking an answer to its doubts and anxieties (as in the later prophets, or in the book of Job), but acquires an independent value. The basic religious ideas of the Bible, as well as the commandments of the Law, become objects of theoretical reflection. Particularly in regard to ethical questions, a high degree of abstraction was reached. Of particular interest is the attempt to reduce the entire content of the biblical commandments to one principle. The Talmud, like the gospels, seeks to determine the "major principle" of the Torah. One Talmudic master finds it in the commandment, "But thou shalt love thy neighbor as thyself" (Leviticus 19:18); another finds it in the sentence, "This is the book of the generations of Adam. In the day that God created man, in the likeness of God made He him" (Genesis 5:1). Similarly, a well-known legend has Hillel, the greatest of the Talmudic sages, declare that the rule, "That which is hateful unto thee, do not do unto thy neighbor," was the "entire Torah," and everything else was only a commentary on it. By declaring love of one's neighbor to be the supreme ethical virtue, the Talmud does not make any material addition to the teaching of the Torah; the novelty lies in the theoretical formulations which describe the commandment of love as the greatest and most inclusive commandment of the Torah, or assert the whole Law to be merely a commentary on this superior ethical rule, to which both ethical and ritual laws are thus made subordinate. Elsewhere a comment on Leviticus 18:4, "Ye shall do my judgments and keep mine ordinances," emphasizes the difference between ethical and ritual commandments. These "judgments," which include the ethical commandments of the Torah, are defined as those laws that "ought to have been written" even if Scripture had not stated them.

The incomprehensibility of the ritual commandments is expressed in the saying that they were open to the objections of the "evil impulse and the nations of the world." The idea of the intrinsic self-evidence of the ethical commandments which God gave to man is essentially a biblical heritage; it is merely the theoretical formulation that is new. The self-evidence of the moral law, implied by the Bible, is emphasized in obvious imitation of the Greek notion of an "unwritten

law" in the pointed formulation that moral laws are laws that "ought
to have been written down." True, according to the Talmud, the biblical
laws which lack this intrinsic evidence possess the same unconditioned
validity as the self-evident "judgments of the Lord." The Talmudic
doctrine that the whole biblical law, by virtue of its divine origin, is
equally and unconditionally authoritative—although material distinctions
can be drawn between ethical and ceremonial precepts—appears here
in its utmost clarity.

The doctrine of retribution is strongly emphasized and elaborated
in considerable detail; yet the Talmud demands the disinterested observance of the divine commandments. It is not demand in itself, but
the theoretical precision with which it is formulated, that is of immediate relevance to our theme. In the saying to which we have already
referred—"Better is one hour of repentance and good deeds in this
world than the entire life of the world to come, and better is one hour
of blessedness in the world to come than all of the life of this world"
—the religious pathos employs conceptual language. Elsewhere the
same demand is stated in sober theoretical language.

In connection with the commandment to love God, the Talmud
discusses the difference between those who serve God out of love, and
those who serve him out of fear. The question is raised in the form
of a casuistical problem, whether an observance of the Law because
of a desire of reward or fear of retribution has any value at all. The
decision is that observance of the Law, even for ulterior motives, was
not devoid of value, for through it men could rise to a disinterested
observance. To this ideal of the observance of the commandments is
added the study of the Law. The latter was not only a divine commandment in itself but also gave full scope to the desire for education.
Discussing the primacy of "theory" (learning) over "practice" (the
observance of the commandments), the Talmud solves the dilemma on
one occasion by declaring that the study of the Law was equivalent
to the observance of all the commandments, and on another by concluding that not theory but deeds were what mattered. Elsewhere a
kind of compromise is reached: the dilemma is decided in favor of
study, but the reason given is that "study leads to practice."

Some of these ethical questions also led to theological discussions
of dogmatic problems. Belief in the freedom of the human will, which
in the Bible is an immediate religious certainty, becomes a doctrinal
proposition in the Talmud. Talmudic predilection for pointed formulations produces the paradox: "Everything is in the hands of Heaven,
with the exception of the fear of Heaven." The difficulty of reconciling

man's freedom with God's omniscience was fully realized, but was not resolved. Instead, the rabbis held fast to both horns of the dilemma: "Everything is foreseen, yet permission is given; the world is judged with mercy, yet the verdict is according to one's deeds." The second half of this sentence refers to a question which greatly preoccupied the Talmudic sages. Once we realize that even the righteous are not free of sin, and that there is no wicked man who has not done some good, what is the line of division between the righteous and the wicked? The answer, though somewhat primitive, states that man is to be considered good or evil according to the preponderance of his good or evil deeds. The biblical question "Why do the righteous suffer and the evil men prosper?" is treated in many and varied ways, and though faith in a future life dulled the point of this question to some extent, it did not solve it in principle. The meaning of human suffering remained a riddle. The Talmud stresses the purgative quality of suffering, and in some of its reflections on this subject it touches the most profound reaches of the religious consciousness. But in addition to such levels of insight we also find a mechanical explanation: the sufferings of the righteous in this world are punishment for those sins they have committed, and the prosperity of the wicked represents a reward for the good deeds that they have done; ultimate retribution for both is left to the world to come.

The rabbinic manner of thinking is seen in the form in which it is expressed. The terse and pithy formulations we have cited suggest its capacity for conceptual thinking. This appears at its best in those sentences and maxims in which the Talmudic masters enunciate with extraordinary concision fundamental religious and ethical doctrines. The art of coining such maxims was apparently cultivated in the schools of the Talmudic sages. One tractate of the Mishna—known as the *Sayings of the Fathers*—consists of a collection of sentences by some of the greatest Talmudic masters (some of which have already been quoted). Comparing these maxims with the proverbs or sayings in the biblical wisdom literature, one is immediately struck by the vast difference between them in regard to their subject matter, and perhaps even more, to their form of thought.

The Talmudic epigram is built on the pointed abstraction; its charm resides in its striking felicity and terseness of form. The epigram just quoted, concerning the relationship between divine providence and human freedom, may be taken as a complete theology in one sentence; in its power of compression it is not alone among rabbinic sayings. Even where the specific form of the epigram is not intended, rabbinic thought almost instinctively expresses itself in this way. The saying that certain precepts would have to be written down if they had not *already* been written down in the Torah, and the statement that everything is in the hand of God except the fear of God, are not less pungent than the maxims proper. A more precise formal analysis, which until now has never been attempted, would probably reveal, in addition to the characteristics described above, a whole series of typical forms of thought recurring again and again in rabbinic discussion of religious fundamentals.

These hints must suffice for our present purpose. They also enable us to recognize the limitations within which this type of thought moves. Its form of expression shows that the systematic treatment of religious problems is intended; it is satisfied with an individual maxim or comment on a scriptural verse, and at the utmost proceeds from there to the discussion of a particular question. This lack of system is characteristic of Talmudic discussions of theology. Problems are taken up one by one; there is never an attempt to combine isolated conclusions in a coherent framework. As our examples have shown, there are insights into the most basic problems of religion, with full awareness of their fundamental significance; but fundamentals are discussed in the same way as details, and no attempt is made to follow them systematically to their conclusions. The Talmud is content with the abstract statement that the love of one's neighbor was the supreme principle of the Torah, but it never attempts to trace the different moral laws to this supreme principle or to demonstrate concretely (apart from a few occasional examples) the moral purpose of the ceremonial law. The demand of completely disinterested worship of God does not in itself contradict the doctrine of retribution which occupies so important a place in Talmudic ethics; but the problems posed by the juxtaposition of these two ideas are never properly discussed.

All the most important ideas in connection with the problem of theodicy can be found in the Talmud; yet it is impossible to construct from them a systematic doctrine. This is especially true of the metaphysical aspects of theology. The Talmud repeatedly emphasizes that the anthropomorphic expressions of the Bible are only metaphors, but it never enquires into the criteria for delimiting metaphorical from literal utterances. We may therefore speak of a definite and consistent over-all religious viewpoint of the Talmud, but no correspondingly consistent and unified theoretical comprehension of the central questions of religion. What the Talmud has produced is not theology, but scattered theological reflections. This accounts for the sometimes strange

coexistence of ideas; next to insights of the utmost profundity there
are other pages which show a primitive thought wrestling laboriously
with its problems. Lack of theoretical maturity is often found in conjunction with sharp and pointed conceptual formulations.

The difference between the righteous and the wicked man consists, as we have seen, in the preponderance of good over evil deeds.
This atomistic conception of man characterizes not so much the moral
view of the Talmud as the adequacy of its conceptual tools, which can
measure the good or evil in man only according to the number of individual acts. Equally naive is the answer which tries to solve the profound question of theory versus practice by pronouncing in favor of
the superiority of learning because it leads to practice. Rabbinic
thought is struggling to master the content of religion, but seems still
unable to grasp it in its wholeness and unity.

. . . Nothing so well indicates the limits of theological reflection in
the Talmud as the absence of any dogmatic formulation of the substance of Jewish teaching. Attacks from the outside on certain doctrines, like the resurrection of the dead, are refuted, or those who deny
them are excluded from the fellowship of Israel. The Talmud nowhere
systematically attempts to fix the contents of the Jewish faith; hence
the impossibility of establishing with any precision the boundary between a generally valid doctrine and a teacher's individual opinion.
This proved of far-reaching consequence for the later development of
Judaism. The flexible form in which the faith of Judaism was cast
allowed the religious thought of later generations a great deal of
freedom. Medieval Jewish philosophy was able to reinterpret traditional religious beliefs with a freedom that was denied to Christian
scholasticism. Attempts were made in the Middle Ages to limit this
freedom by formulating articles of faith, but since Jewish spiritual
authorities could demand general recognition of their rulings only insofar as they acted as interpreters of the Talmud, such efforts could
at best have limited success. Nevertheless, the freedom with regard to
the tradition of faith had certain boundaries set to it from the beginning. The basic principles of the Jewish faith needed no dogmatic
systematization in order to be clearly determined. The belief in the
divine origin of the Bible as well as of the complementary oral tradition authoritatively bound the individual both in matters of belief and
religious law.

Religious truth had been given once and for all in the Bible and
the oral tradition, and it was the absolute norm for faith. All freedom
was merely a freedom to interpret this truth, which by its very nature

was valid for everybody. Also with regard to the material contents
of faith, this freedom was bound to certain fixed principles. Thus the
Jewish belief in revelation entailed a whole series of religious assumptions, sharing the authority of revelation and consequently not requiring
explicit dogmatic emphasis in order to assert their authority over the
faithful. The ideas of providence, retribution, and miracles were firmly
established as elements of the Jewish faith through their connection
with belief in revelation. Their factual truth was beyond doubt; only
in regard to their precise understanding was there freedom for philosophical interpretation. Other religious ideas, though they lacked this
close formal relationship to the notion of revelation, attained such
prominence in liturgy and public worship that their authority was un-
questioned. The whole complex of religious convictions that had grown
up in the Talmudic period served as an incontestable, valid norm of
faith for future Jewish generations and for their philosophies. Both
facts—the existence of a norm of faith and the absence of a systematic
formulation of dogma—are of equal importance for subsequent developments: both the freedom and constraint of medieval Jewish
philosophy derive from them.

PART II

THE FOUNDATIONS OF RABBINIC JUDAISM

What justifies the claim that the post-Talmudic history of Judaism constitutes a single, integrated cultural continuum, defined by the Talmud and its values, is the immense fact that all Jews everywhere lived under and by one law. The Talmud did not merely present beliefs and doctrines for peoples' contemplation. It laid forth patterns of behavior which both expressed and nurtured those central convictions. Most people in most places lived their lives in accord with Talmudic laws, and the impact of those laws upon the formation of their disparate culture and their varied lives was to give to all a single and ultimately uniform character.

At the foundations of Rabbinic Judaism, therefore, is law. We consider the law in several aspects. First, Mordecai Kaplan describes some of the main outlines of the law and the system of self-government which enforced it. But merely describing how the law works hardly does justice to the subject. We have to consider the way in which an authoritative representative of the rabbinic tradition in our own day, Eliezer Berkovits, argues that law not only is central, but should be normative, and explains why, in his conviction, it is law which determines what is "authentic." Clearly, a claim to define what is authentic is to be understood as a statement of theology, not merely of history. That is why in attempting to understand the predominant trait of Rabbinic Judaism, it is important to listen to an authentic spokesman of the viewpoint of that form of Judaism.

Mendell Lewittes then provides a rapid review of the main stages in the post-Talmudic history of the law and surveys the literature produced after the Talmud was completed. He introduces the facts which will become important in our later study.

Finally, Israel Abrahams describes the everyday life of the synagogue. The reason is that, while law is at the base of all else, it was the synagogue which embodied—and continues to embody—Jewish society. Even though other important institutions effected the application of law

51

to society—schools, courts, the rabbinate, for example—the synagogue provides the occasion for the realization and celebration of all else. In its walls the community takes physical form; then random individuals become "Israel" and receive and hear the Torah. There the life of the community becomes vivid.

Before us, therefore, are four disparate accounts of a single phenomenon, that cogent 'civilization' based upon the Talmud and shaped by the ideals of its rabbis and their heirs. One is descriptive, the next prescriptive; the third gives us important facts; and the last provides a sense of the humble center of the people described by historians, exhorted by theologians, and legislated for by lawyers.

TALMUDIC LAW

The reason we may confidently speak of Rabbinic Judaism without regard to the myriad of local beliefs, customs, and practices characteristic of the different Jewish communities, north, south, east, and west, which shared this international "civilization," is this: wherever Jews lived, whatever language they spoke, and however distinctive the particular traits of their mode of living, they shared a single, common law. That law was laid down in the pages of the Talmud. It was developed and applied by a single canon of rational principles, within a community of learned men who spoke a single language and thought in a single pattern. Talmudic law laid solid and sure foundations for Rabbinic Judaism, assuring its unity within diversity and establishing its stability and particular character under every circumstance.

This law, common to all Jews and built upon the principles laid down in the Talmud, dealt with not only narrowly religious questions but broad and socially relevant issues of all kinds. Civil litigations, personal status, the government of the community at large—these 'secular' matters were to be settled by the law of the Talmud, no less than the religious calendar or the order of prayer. Indeed, the larger part of Talmudic law deals with civil conflict and family affairs—inheritances and estates, on the one side, marriage and divorce on the other.

Local Jewish governments therefore were united in a vast international structure, because all affairs everywhere were referred to one law. Moreover, customarily Jews had resort not to Gentile, but to Jewish courts, and this was an important point. It meant that the government of the people lay in the hands of the learned, united masters of the law. So far as the Jews constituted a single nation, it was on the foundation of one law. But since the values of that law were essentially religious, based upon the rabbis' interpretation of the revelation of Sinai, the law which made Jewry into a nation also made them into a religion. It was law which made concrete and practical the highest ideals of revelation and prophecy, which brought down to earth and to the here-and-now the heavenly commandments to do justice and love mercy.

53

3.

THE LEGAL FOUNDATIONS OF RABBINIC JUDAISM

Mordecai M. Kaplan

[From *The Greater Judaism in the Making,* by Mordecai M. Kaplan, pp. 57-63.]

Throughout the centuries between the fall of their Second Commonwealth and the French Revolution, the Jews constituted a nomocracy, that is, a society held together and governed by laws which were enforced without the aid of a central government. The sense of common peoplehood among the scattered Jewish communities survived because of the effective system of decentralized self-government which the Jews had evolved. The particular function which a central government performs in the life of a nation was, in the case of the Jews, fulfilled by an autonomous legal system that was capable of being enforced wherever there was a quorum of ten Jews. That code laid down the procedure for collective self-discipline, thereby making possible the decentralized form of self-government which the Jews maintained throughout the centuries of enforced dispersion. The Jews possessed an adequate instrument of peoplehood in their autonomous system of civil and marriage laws. These laws provided the means of social control in the area of economic and sex relationships, where conflicts of interest were apt to wreak havoc.

To evaluate properly the significance of a common legal code for Jewish survival, we have to bear in mind that the Rabbis of old succeeded in formulating a code which fulfilled the following functions:

1) It provided the scattered communities of the Jewish people with a sense of unity and solidarity.

2) It called for the leadership of those who were expert in the knowledge and application of Jewish law, and who were authorized to use sanctions as means of enforcing their decisions.

55

3) It led to the establishment of courts of law which, being sufficiently flexible in structure, were able to adjust themselves to the various contingencies in the life of the Jewish People.

4) It helped to foster a conscious ethnic will which deprecated resort to non-Jewish courts as treason and sacrilege.

The Rabbis were on the alert against any tendency that might have led the Jews to avail themselves of the code law or of the common law by which their neighbors had their litigation adjudicated. In the second century (C.E.), R. Tarfon laid down the principle that Jews were not permitted to litigate in non-Jewish courts, even though those courts rendered decisions according to Jewish law. That principle was stringently enforced down to modern times. When Jews in thirteenth-century Spain showed a tendency to defy that law, Solomon Adret (Rashba) complained bitterly. "Of what use would the most holy writings then be to us, the Mishnah compiled by R. Judah, and after him the Talmud compiled by Rav Ashi and Ravina? Would Jews teach their children the laws of the Gentiles and build themselves altars of the uncleanness of the heathen? Far be it! It shall never be thus in Israel! Shall the Torah gird itself in sackcloth?"

"Any Jew," wrote Bachya ben Asher, toward the end of the thirteenth century, "who resorts to a civil court, thus evidencing greater esteem for secular ·than for divine law, is guilty of profaning God's name. . . . For a Jew to refuse to submit to the legal decisions of the Torah and choose to abide instead by the verdict of alien courts, is to proclaim his abandonment of the belief in its divine authority." On the other hand, the highest approval is accorded to those who function as judges: "When three sit and judge, the Shekinah is in their midst." That this norm survived until recently is borne out by the following: "The practice of appealing to the Russian courts for the settlement of cases between Jews," writes Shmarya Levin, "did not exist in those days (in the 70's of the last century). The appeal was made instead to the Torah, to Jewish law, as interpreted by the Rav of the town."

Due to the existence of Jewish self-government, the poorest was never without an opportunity for legal redress. This was made possible through a practice known as "the interruption of the Torah reading" during the Sabbath services in the synagogue. Any Jew, no matter what his station in life, who felt himself aggrieved could go to the synagogue and hold up the services, until he was promised that his grievances would be looked into. That practice is described by Shmarya Levin as follows: "The high officials of the synagogue make ready to bring out of the Ark the scroll of the Torah . . . . and suddenly a Jew appears in the pulpit where the scroll is to be laid down, delivers a resounding blow and cries out 'I forbid the reading.' The effect is electrical. First there is a gasp of astonishment; then a mutter of angry voices . . . . and then silence. The Jew in the pulpit waits, and when the silence is complete, he voices his complaint. He knows that he is secure. He is exercising an ancient privilege which it would be blasphemy to challenge."

Thus did the commonly accepted code of law serve as the basis of Jewish peoplehood during the many centuries after the destruction of the Second Commonwealth. "Since the time," says Solomon Maimon, "when the Jews lost their own national position and were dispersed among the nations . . . . they have had no national form of government but their religious constitution, by which they are held together and still form in spite of their political dispersion an organic whole. Their leaders, therefore, have allowed themselves to be occupied with nothing so much as with imparting additional strength to this, the only bond of union by which Jews still constitute a nation."

As an instrument of peoplehood, the legal code based on the Written and Oral Torah functioned in the double capacity of fostering culture and maintaining social order. This twofold function gave rise to the two main social institutions in Jewish life, the court and the academy. The rabbi, throughout the period of Traditional Judaism, likewise served in the twofold capacity of head of academy and judge in the civil court, enabling the academy and the court of justice to be mutually complementary. The Talmud itself is the product of this unique correlation of the theory and the practice of law.

Not long after the final redaction of the Talmud there arose the need for applying and organizing its laws. This led to the development of a vast legalistic literature consisting of legal *responsa,* of which there are about 1300 volumes, and codes of different types, ranging from monographs dealing with one or more branches of the law to all-inclusive compendia.

The Babylonian Talmud which received its final redaction about the end of the fifth or beginning of the sixth century C.E. was accepted by the Jews as the authoritative guide to Jewish belief and conduct. The principal codes which served Jewish life during the Middle Ages down to our own day were the *Yad ha-Hazakah* by Maimonides (1135-1204), the Semag (*Sefer Mitzvot Gadol*) by R. Moses ben Jacob of Coucy (circa 1250), the *Turim* by R. Jacob ben Asher (about 1269-1340), and the *Shulhan Aruk* by R. Joseph Karo (1488-1575). Of these the *Shulhan Aruk* was the most influential in molding the life of the Jews along traditional lines. The more recent codes not only facilitate the finding of the particular laws which apply to specific situations; they also indicate which opinion to follow in the case of conflicting views, and incorporate additional decisions and customs which have accumulated in the course of time.

From the standpoint of Jewish law as an instrument of Jewish peoplehood, the civil and marriage laws of the Talmud were most effective. These form the subject matter of the two orders of the Talmud known as *Nezikin* and *Nashim*. The Jewish civil law covers a wide range of problems, such as loans, property, obligations, inheritance, damages, torts, fraud and errors, assault and battery, hiring and letting, employer and employee, partnership, usury, taxation, trusts and trustees and agency. The marriage laws deal with subjects like the following: adultery, widow and *agunah* (the deserted wife or one whose husband's whereabouts are unknown), betrothal, divorce, dowry, *ketubah* (marriage contract) and seduction. The study of all this subject-matter in all of the Jewish academies produced in the Jewish consciousness an attitude of deference to the authority of the Talmud that was far more effective than any outward pressure which could be brought to bear even in a highly organized state.

Solomon Maimon in his autobiography states that it was usual in his day for a well-to-do merchant or farmer who had a daughter to make every possible effort to get a learned Talmudist as a son-in-law. It was customary for the father-in-law to make provision for maintaining his son-in-law from six to eight years, during which time the latter continued his studies. At the end of that time the son-in-law would either receive a call to the rabbinate or would continue his studies, while his wife not only attended to the affairs of the house but also ran a small store. Her reward consisted in sharing the reputation and the other-worldly bliss of her husband.

In the field of human relations, those which come under the category of "family" constitute the particular object of solicitude in any national system of law. Those relationships are basic to the character and welfare of the individual and to the health and integrity of the community. The main prerogative of a people is the power it exercises in giving status to the family. The family is not merely a group that exists by virtue of the consent of those who compose it; it is a cell in the context of the ethnic organism which holds it together, and which gives it social status. In return for such status, the family submits to the laws whereby the people exercises control over its individual members in their relations to one another. In these laws are reflected some of the most significant aspects of a people's individuality. "Judaism got its lofty moral tone," says Charles A. Ellwood, "from the projection, idealization and spiritualization of the values found in the ancient Jewish family. The concepts and phraseology of Judaism can indeed be understood only through understanding the Jewish family."

We can, therefore, understand why Traditional Judaism regarded the entire range of family relationships as entirely its domain, and resented violently any interference with them by non-Jewish authorities. It gave sanction to the marriage formula. The significant phrase "according to Mosaic and Jewish custom (*k'dat Moshe v'Yisrael*)" in that formula emphasizes that the validity of the marriage depends upon its being performed in accordance with the Jewish religio-ethnic practice. Thus did every Jewish home realize from the moment of its establishment that it owed its status and permanence to the authority of the Jewish People, which guaranteed the enforcement of the mutual obligations of its members. It is significant that the laws dealing with the family relationships take up practically as much space in the Talmud as the rest of the civil law.

The Jewish consciousness, in addition to being conditioned to submit to the authority of the civil and marriage laws formulated in the Talmud, was also conditioned to submit to the jurisdiction of the Jewish courts which put those laws into effect. The sanctions at the disposal of the Jewish court by means of which it could enforce its decisions consisted of "corporal punishment, outlawing by proclamation throughout the Jewish communities, complete religious ostracism by major or minor excommunication in which not only the culprit but all his family were involved, disqualification as witness, declaring one's oath as untrustworthy, and exile."

The communities throughout the Diaspora had organs of self-government with legislative assemblies and courts of their own. In Eretz Yisrael, under Roman-Byzantine rule, the Jews had their Sanhedrin, their academies and their Patriarchs. In Babylonia, they had their Exilarchs, *Geonim* and legislative academies. In Spain, they had their *Al-jamas* and Congresses of Communal Delegates. In Poland and Lithuania they had their *Kahals* or communities. Their *Vaadim* were Diets consisting of *Kahal* representatives.

Thus the stateless type of peoplehood which the Jews maintained was rendered feasible through their unanimous acceptance of the Torah, both the Written and the Oral, as a divinely given ethnic code. But it was the personality of the rabbi that actually made Jewish self-government possible. That had not always been the case. In the early stages of Traditional Judaism, as it existed in Babylonia, Spain and the Mediterranean countries, the tendency had been for the "goodmen of the town" to exercise executive authority and to utilize the services of the rabbi only for judicial purposes. He was merely a functionary. Thanks to the efforts of Rashi and his successors in Franco-German Jewry, the status of the rabbi assumed far greater importance. After being appointed by the "goodmen of the town," he was vested with full executive authority. That change in the status and function of the rabbi may have been due to the influence of the Roman Catholic Church environment.

The Rabbi of the Talmudic period, as described by Claude G. Montefiore, was a type of Jewish spiritual leader whose like one may still meet in densely populated Jewish neighborhoods, where as Talmudic scholars some of them still live the sequestered form of life of the Medieval ghetto. "Here were men," says Montefiore, "who had undoubtedly a tremendous love for God and for His Law: a complete readiness to sacrifice for God and for His Law, if need be, their very lives. Yet withal, these men were by no means anxious for martyrdom. On the contrary, they wished to avoid it wherever or whenever they legitimately could. They desired, if at all possible, to live their lives in peace and quiet, studying the Law, practicing as judges the most scrupulous justice, and showing in the intervals of study and as leaders of the Jewish Communities in Babylonia or Palestine charity, kindness, and consideration to those around them."

The knowledge of the Torah carried with it the moral duty of acting in the twofold capacity of teacher and judge, provided, of course, the scholar had received authorization to do so from one who himself enjoyed such authority. According to the *"Takkanot* of the Province of Moravia," every community that had thirty families or more was obligated to maintain a rabbi and a *Yeshivah* in which at least a dozen young men studied Torah. As late as the first part of the nineteenth century, it was customary in many instances to include among the duties of the rabbi, which were enumerated in the contract between him and the community, that he conduct a Talmudic academy or *Yeshivah*. The function of the *Yeshivah* was not to train rabbis, but merely to familiarize those who studied there with the teachings and practices of Judaism as set forth in the Torah, both Written and Oral. The notion of utilizing the knowledge of the Torah as a means to a professional career was strongly deprecated.

AUTHENTICITY IN RABBINIC JUDAISM

It is not sufficient merely to maintain that law laid the foundations of Rabbinic Judaism, for that claim does not do justice to the importance of law in Rabbinic Judaism. A single, common law not only provided the basis for the common religious civilization constructed by Talmudic Judaism. That law also provided the center and the focus for the life of Jewry.

To illustrate this matter we turn to a contemporary essay, one which is authentic to the spirit and substance of Rabbinic Judaism. Eliezer Berkovits argues here the proposition which has just now been stated and described, and he holds that what stands as the criterion for authentic Judaism, at any and every point in its history including the present day, is *halakhah,* the definitive axiom of Judaism. That is why law is central, not merely as a basis, but as the source of creativity and spiritual vitality, in Rabbinic Judaism.

To offer such a viewpoint, one needs also to illustrate it. It is not sufficient to claim the law is at the heart of matters. One has also, given the vastness and diversity of laws, to indicate what, within the law, is of primary importance. Berkovits shows that economic affairs may be made to conform to the divine image of man and society through the medium of *halakhah.* In like manner, society may be made more humane, people may be brought to a more wholesome and humanitarian relationship with one another, through *halakhah.* Every day life is made holy, set apart and sanctified, through law.

The main point is that "law" is abstract, an ideal, while *halakhah* is concrete and practical. As Berkovits will tell us, "We distinguish between the Law and *Halakhah. Halakhah* is not the law but the Law applied . . . in a given situation." That fact is what will render supple and highly textured the fabric of rabbinic civilization. For nothing can have been cut-and-dried, obvious and clear. To ask a question of law is not merely to seek information, but to elicit judgment, responsible opinion. The law exists in the abstract, but life is lived in the concrete and here-and-now. Therefore the central task of rabbinic civilization will be not to profess generalities, but to locate in the specific setting of ordinary life the requirements of those generalities.

61

What makes Rabbinic Judaism interesting is the specificities, the people who made the law, the documents which contain it, the courts which applied it, the philosophers who sought its rationality, and the rabbis and disciples who learned and reflected about it. The generalizations about the importance of a common law and about the centrality of law in the articulation of Rabbinic Judaism must give way to the details of *halakhah*. To put it differently, while Rabbinic Judaism exhibits certain continuities, to understand the working of Rabbinic Judaism requires constant attention to particularities, and, especially, to the specific individuals who both mastered and distinctively embodied the generalities. The tension between the general—the law, the Talmud—and the specific—the communities which embodied the law—is what makes the study of Rabbinic Judaism compelling.

4.

THE CENTRALITY OF HALAKHAH

ELIEZER BERKOVITS

[From "Authentic Judaism and Halakhah," by Eliezer Berkovits. *Judaism,* Vol. 19, No. 1, Winter, 1970, pp. 66-76.]

For those who take their stand on the ground of Halakhah, our theme may appear tautological. For is not authentic Judaism adequately defined as the Judaism of the Halachah? Such a definition may, indeed, be theoretically adequate, but it is also much too general to throw sufficient light on what constitutes authentic Judaism in a given situation. By itself, it could help us only very little in our search for determining the nature of authentic Judaism in the specific historic situation in which Judaism and Jewry find themselves today.

Jewish history has known a succession of different types of Judaisms as well as Jewries. There is a Judaism understood rationalistically, as by Maimonides and Gersonides. There is another type, historically interpreted, as it is found in the *Kuzari* of Yehuda Halevi. There is also the Judaism of the mystics. These various types do not always live in peace with each other. Ever since Sinai we have witnessed an entire series of Jewries, all based on Torah and Halakhah, yet differing from each other in outlook, attitude, and their understanding of Judaism. Babylonian Jewry was not Spanish Jewry; and the Spanish Jewry of Gabirol, the Ibn Ezras, of Hasdai Ibn Shaprut, Halevi and Maimonides, was not the Central European Jewry of the authors of the *Tosafot.* Nearer to our own times, the Halachic Jewries of Eastern Europe were not the Halachic Jewries of a Samson Raphael Hirsch or an Ezriel Hildesheimer. There were vast differences between them in the understanding of the Halakhah, in the philosophical interpretation of the teachings and the faith of Judaism; considerable divergencies in their respective attitudes to the outside world, far-reaching ideological disagreements concerning secular studies and professional pursuits. Nor could they have been identified in the areas of ethical valuation and aesthetic taste. They were different branches of the same stem.

Were the numerous different Jewries and their differing interpretations of Judaism authentic? We like to think so. What constituted their authenticity, notwithstanding the obvious differences between them? The importance of the question for us may be readily recognized. All the historic Jewries collapsed in our times. Everywhere we have relatively new settlements of Jews. Note that I speak of new settlements of Jews, not of new Jewries. In America, in Europe, in Israel, all over the world, we have "melting-pot Jewries," conglomerates of remnants, survivors of former Jewries everywhere. As yet, we do not have new Jewries. Our task is to establish them.

Because of this task and its historic responsibility, it is of vital importance that we understand what constitutes Jewish authenticity. There are at least two clearly definable considerations that underline the problem that confronts us. To all of the countries of new settlements Jews have come from varied backgrounds, traditions, and memories. Which one of the trends shall the "melting-pot Jewries" continue? The Lithuanian? But why not the Polish? The Polish? But why not the Hungarian or perhaps the German? The Sephardic or the Ashkenazic? The Hasidic or the rationalistic?

Such and similar questions lead us directly to the other consideration. In our entire history, after great catastrophes, we never just continued as before. After every *hurban* something new emerged. After the first destruction of the Temple we created the synagogue in its classical meaning. After the destruction of the Second Commonwealth we created the Talmud. The new that followed upon each of these catastrophes was not a mere repetition of the old in a new land under different conditions, but a truly new creation. Our reading of Jewish history tells us that every historic Jewry is unique and, thus, inimitable. We have to understand the nature of Jewish authenticity because once again we find ourselves after a *hurban,* at a turning point in Jewish history; once again we are at the beginning of the road. We shall not succeed in resurrecting, on this continent or in the State of Israel, or anywhere else in the world, either Polish or Lithuanian, or Hungarian, or German Jewry. Such resurrection never happened before; nor can it happen now. No Jewry is repeatable. This is so determined, not only by historic conditions, but even more by the very nature of the Halakhah. It is the nature of the Halakhah that determines the authenticity of a Jewry; and it is the essential quality of the

Halakhah which also brings it about that each authentic Jewry is different from every other authentic Jewry.

What is the nature of the Halakhah? Needless to say that within the scope of this essay it cannot be answered definitively. But some examples of Halachic teaching chosen at random may help us to concentrate our attention on some of the major concerns of classical Halakhah.

Rather interestingly, Halakhah is deeply concerned with the effective functioning of the economic segment of society. In a number of cases where the Biblical law would have made it difficult for people to obtain a necessary loan, the Halakhah decided on a deviation from the original Biblical principle in order that "the door not be closed before a borrower." For the same reason the original Biblical requirement for the qualification of the judges who could adjudicate in cases of monetary disputes was relaxed and the procedure itself, in deviation from the Biblical law, simplified. It was necessary to make the conditions for obtaining a loan more favorable for a would-be borrower. There was, of course, a Halakhic principle at hand whose application rendered such changes in the original law possible. Significant, however, is the reason that induced the Halakhic teachers to apply that principle. Most known, of course, is the institution of the *prusbol* by Hillel, the declaration in court that protected a loan against forfeiture in the Sabbatical year as provided in Biblical law. Here, too, it was the desire to render the economic life of the community capable of functioning within the frame of the Torah which motivated the great sage to introduce his *takanah*.

Some post-Talmudic examples which belong in the same category are also worth considering. We present only two. According to one of the teachers of the Talmud, a Jew was not allowed to enter into a business partnership with an *akum* (a Gentile). The reason was that in case of a disagreement between the partners, the Gentile partner could be required to affirm something in court with an oath. He would, of course, swear by his god. In this manner the Jew would have contributed to the enhancement of respect for a false deity. Now, in the Middle Ages, in certain parts of Europe, such business associations between Jew and Christian were not unusual. The question arose whether these partnerships were permitted, or should they be dissolved. Rabbenu Tam gave his famous decision that Christians were not to be considered *akum* in the sense of the Talmud. The *akum* were idol-worshippers, whereas Christians worshipped the God of heaven and earth. When they associate another person with Him, such association was not forbidden for non-Jews.

Our second example concerns the Talmudic prohibition to sell certain kinds of animals to Gentiles. This was a Rabbinic, not a Biblical, law. There is no need for us to discuss the reasons for this law, which were purely religious. What interests us here are the economic consequences of the prohibition. Again the situation arose in the Middle Ages in Europe when trade in such animals became a significant source of Jewish livelihood. What was to be done about it? A very simple solution was found. The authoritative Halakhic decision maintained that the prohibition was valid only in Talmudic times, when large Jewish communities were closely settled in the Land of Israel as well as Babylon. In such a situation, "if a Jew had an animal which he did not need, he could sell it to a fellow Jew. But in our days, what can he do?" Under conditions of a Jewish settlement not at all conducive to this kind of trading, economic necessity was sufficient to set aside a ruling of a previous generation. The purpose of these post-Talmudic examples is still the same.

Even more impressive are, of course, the humanitarian concerns of the Halakhah. We shall illustrate our point by some rules in the area of marriage and divorce laws. As is well known, according to Biblical law only a husband can divorce his wife; but not the wife the husband. It is also required that the divorce be given by the husband freely, without any compulsion. A *get* given under coercion invalidates the divorce. Yet, there were cases when one could not expect a woman to remain with her husband. A certain kind of skin disease or a sickness which brought about a severe case of an ill odor of the mouth or the nose, or even when a bad odor was inseparable from the person of the husband because of the work in which he was engaged—in all such cases a divorce was deemed to be objectively justified. If the husband refused, the Halakhah stipulated that "one compels him until he says that he is willing to grant his wife a divorce freely." Maimonides provides us with an interesting explanation of the procedure, how, notwithstanding the coercion, the divorce may be considered as having been given freely. What is important for our consideration is the fact that because on the basis of the original law problems arose, solutions were found so that the law may function meaningfully.

Another interesting example in a related field deals with a modification of the Biblical law of witnesses. According to the Bible, the judicial establishment of a fact as a fact has to be based on the testimony of two witnesses: the testimony of one person is not enough.

The Talmudic interpretation of the law held that women or slaves were not admitted as witnesses; nor could one such testify on the basis of testimony heard from an eye-witness. The problem that challenged these provisions of the law was the case of a woman whose husband disappeared and whose death had to be established in order to allow her to remarry. In such a situation the Talmud ruled that the woman was allowed to remarry on the strength of the testimony "of a witness from the mouth of another, from the mouth of a woman, a slave, or even the testimony of only one witness." Very good reasons were given for allowing such far-reaching departure from the original law. The discussion of the matter is concluded with the statement that, in order to protect the wife against being "the widow of a man who is assumed to be alive," the Rabbis were lenient in the case. Their boldness in certain other cases where the situation required that problems be met was so far-reaching that they even conceived a formula by which a marriage could be annulled by Rabbinical authority.

Most revealing is the concern of the Halakhah with the practical requirements of every-day life. In the arrangement of the calendar the Rabbis had the authority to institute a "leap year" by inserting an additional month into the current year. All kinds of circumstances may call for a "leap year." Among them we find: the need to repair the roads, the bridges, and the ovens (in which the paschal lambs were to be roasted). All this was necessary in order to enable the people to reach Jerusalem in time and to offer the paschal sacrifice. Moving, however, is another reason for the postponement of the Passover festival. Had news been received that a group of Jews living in Exile had left on the journey to Jerusalem in order to celebrate the festival in the holy city, but that they could not arrive in time, the additional month of Adar was inserted and the festival delayed by one month. Of course, in those days the Sanhedrin had the authority to determine the particulars of the calendar. Significant, however, is that purely practical considerations, or the desire not to disappoint some people who were looking forward to Passover in Jerusalem, were sufficient for them to invoke their authority and thus bring about a change in the dates on which all the festivals of the year were to be celebrated.

Into a similar category of Halakhic concern with the amenities of man's day-by-day existence belong the following two examples. Both are intended to render a woman more pleasing to her husband. Among the five forms of self-mortification which are prescribed for the observance of the Day of Atonement one also finds the prohibition to wash on that day. There are two exceptions to this rule. One is that of the bride, i.e., the woman during the first thirty days after her marriage. The reason given for the exception is most simply humane consideration: "that she should not appear unattractive before her husband."

Furthermore, according to the Talmud, the "elders of a former generation" taught that, in order to eliminate temptation, a woman "should neither paint nor rouge herself nor clothe in attractive garments" during her monthly period. This was the rule until Rabbi Akiba came and abolished it, saying: "This way you render her unattractive for her husband, who may even divorce her." As to the Biblical verse on which the ruling of "the former elders" was based, Rabbi Akiba gave it a new interpretation. Here Rabbi Akiba determined the interpretation of the Biblical law in the interest of preserving material conditions tending to enhance marital happiness.

We also find that ethical considerations elucidate Biblical meaning even in cases of purely ritual law, where an obligation obtains not "between man and his fellow," but "between man and God." The Talmud discusses the exact nature of "the branches of palm trees" and "the boughs of thick trees" that are used together with the *ethrog* and the willows in "the rejoicing before God" on the Succoth festival. After all the definitions of these two plants have been given, two questions are asked. The first refers to the *lulav,* the branches of the palm tree: Could it not be *kufra?* (*Kufra* are younger twigs on a palm tree which would satisfy all the requirements of the law.) The answer is that *kufra* could not have been meant by the Bible; for it is said of the Torah that "all her ways are ways of pleasantness." To us *kufra* would not be a pleasant way of fulfilling a commandment of the Torah, for the twigs of *kufra* are spiked, and the spikes could easily hurt the hand. Thus, it could not have been the intention of the Bible to use *kufra.*

The second question deals with "the boughs of thick trees": Could not *hirduph* serve the same purpose? It would meet all the requirements. Two answers are given. The one, as before, rules out its leaves as stinging, which, therefore, do not qualify for "the ways of pleasantness." The second answer is based on a verse in *Zechariah* that enjoins man: "Therefore, love ye truth and peace." According to Raba's comment, *hirduph* would be a poor symbol for loving either truth or peace, for it is used for producing a lethal poison from its leaves. In such interpretation of the Biblical intention the concern of the Halakhah was to render the Torah meaningful with reference to its own all-embracing purpose of establishing life's discipline as ways of pleasantness and paths of peace.

Rather revealing, and pertinent for our analysis, is a discussion between the teachers of the Mishnah on the subject of capital punishment. The Bible, of course, does provide capital punishment for certain crimes. Yet Rabbi Tarphon and Rabbi Akiba maintained that, had they been members of the Sanhedrin at the time that it functioned as such, they would have seen to to it that no one should ever be executed. They would have conducted the court procedure in such a manner that the Biblical law on capital punishment would never have been applicable. We have here the case of an individual conscience interpreting the applicability of a Biblical law in accordance with its own Torah-imbued ethos. In a similar instance in another Mishnah it is the ethos of peace which determines a law of Sabbath observance. Since on the Sabbath it is forbidden to carry any burden, the question is discussed whether a man is permitted to carry arms on the Sabbath day. The majority opinion is that it is forbidden. Rabbi Eliezer, however, disagrees. According to him, arms are ornaments for a man and not a burden. To which the Sages replied: They are a disgrace for any man to carry, for does not the prophet look forward to the time when men will beat their swords into ploughshares and their spears into pruning-hooks, when "nation will not lift up sword against nation, neither shall they learn war any more." Arms are a denial of the ideal of peace. To carry them can only be a shameful burden on man; therefore, one must not go out with them on the Sabbath. Here, too, it is an ethical conscience that determines the application of the law.

We recall these examples at random—and they could be multiplied manifold from the vast domain of the Halakhah—in order to give substance to our thesis. We distinguish between the Law and Halakhah. Halakhah is not the Law but the Law applied—and by the manner of its application rendered meaningful—in a given situation.

The purpose of the Halakhah is to render the Torah in a given historic situation a) practically feasible; b) economically viable; c) ethically significant; d) spiritually meaningful.

Authentic is a Jewry that is based on Halakhah. But a Jewry is based on Halakhah if indeed Halakhah applies Torah to the contemporary situation. Halakhah is the bridge over which Torah enters reality, with the capacity to shape it meaningfully and in keeping with its own intention. Halakhah is the technique of Torah-application to a concrete contemporary situation. But while the Torah is eternal, the concrete historic situation is forever changing. Halakhah therefore, as the application of Torah in a given situation, will forever uncover new levels of Torah-depth and Torah-meaning and thus make new facets of Judaism visible. It was for this reason that we said earlier that Halakhah determines not only authenticity but also the uniqueness of each authentic Jewry. No Jewry is imitable or repeatable, because each authentic Jewry represents a single application of Torah to a specific constellation of conditions in which Jews find themselves at one time in their history.

RABBINIC WRITINGS

Just as the law did not exist in abstraction, but took many concrete forms, so too the law produced a varied literature in the aftermath of the conclusion of the Talmud itself. This literature, described by Rabbi Lewittes, was shaped in response to the particular needs of the day. We discern three major types of legal writing.

The first form was commentaries, composed upon specific ancient texts, primarily the Babylonian Talmud. The form of the commentary is dictated by its purpose: to elucidate particular sayings found in the Talmud itself. A commentary is, by definition, not a sustained essay, it is not well-organized according to a given agendum, and it is not going to produce important generalizations. It is meant to attach itself to the specific sayings of the Talmud and to clarify the meanings of these sayings in their own context.

The second type of legal literature was the code of laws, in which the given text was transcended, and the principle of organization was the logic of the substance of the law itself. Codes of law would prove useful to both lay people and rabbinic authorities in locating the law pertinent to a particular issue without recourse to the far-ranging pages of the Talmud itself. The code thus made it possible to bypass extended research in quest of a specific point of law.

The third type of legal writing was the responsum, the answer to a specific question addressed to a major, international authority. Collections of such answers—responsa—would then be developed, so that the legal opinions of that authority would be made available not only to the individuals who addressed questions to him but to a considerable audience. In time these responsa, themselves based upon the interpretation of particular Talmudic passages, thus a sort of commentary, and at the same time constitutive of a systematic account of practical law, thus a sort of code, would be gathered and circulated.

Rabbi Lewittes furthermore lays out the stages in the development of legal literature. He begins with the Geonim, the Talmudic masters of the early Middle Ages. He turns next to the "rishonim," the classical authorities, and names the more important figures, some

71

of whom we shall meet again. At the same time he records the development of the two great groupings within rabbinic civilization, Ashkenazim, in Europe, and Sepharadim, in North Africa and the Middle East, and shows how they came into existence. He speaks, moreover, of particular centers of legal creativity and tells us in a brief way about the main authorities. He ends with an account of the most influential set of legal codes, the "Four Rows" which stand behind the everywhere authoritative code, the *Shulhan Arukh*. Thus in his brief essay he provides a remarkably comprehensive account of the legal literature of Rabbinic Judaism.

5.

THE LITERATURE OF LAW

MENDELL LEWITTES

[From "The Nature and History of Jewish Law," by Mendell Lewittes. In *Studies in Torah Judaism,* edited by Leon D. Stitskin. N.Y., 1969: Yeshiva University Press, pp. 237-316. Excerpt: pp. 273-288.]

The Geonim

The final editing of the Babylonian Talmud in the generation following R. Ashi and Rabina (2nd half of 5th century C.E.) did not mark—as it did in the case of the Palestinian Talmud—the closing of the Yeshivoth, or, as they were called in Aramaic, the Methivtoth. Sura and Pumbeditha—after closings of short duration—continued to flourish as centers of learning and seats of halakhic authority for some 500 years. The heads of the Academies were now given the title *Gaon* (Excellency), and therefore this period is designated in the history of the Halakhah as that of the Geonim. It was during the earlier half of this period that the rise of Islam took place. The followers of Mohammed swept from the Arabian desert all through the Middle East, conquering all of North Africa and crossing over into Spain. Jews were swept along with this movement, establishing new communities in these lands and adopting Arabic as their household language.

Uncertain as to the religious practices which should be instituted in these new settlements, and no longer conversant with the Aramaic of the Talmud, the leaders of these communities addressed their questions to the Geonim, inquiring after the exact manner in which to perform a ritual, or the exact text of a prayer, or the precise meaning of a Talmudic statement. In fact, the very first *Siddur* (Prayer Book), *Seder Rav Amram Gaon,* was a *teshubah* to an inquiry from the community of Barcelona in Spain. The Geonim responded directly and to

73

the point, invariably stating that, "this is the practice or custom of our Methivta." In the course of the centuries, these *teshuboth* no doubt numbered in the thousands, and frequent reference is made to them by the *Rishonim,* the halakhic authorities of the period succeeding that of the Geonim. Hundreds of them have been found in manuscript, edited and published, constituting the first section of the vast halakhic literature now extant in the form of *she'eiloth uteshuboth,* a literature constantly growing and serving as an important—indeed, indispensable —basis for decisions in Jewish Law.

Halakhic Codes

Teshuboth are not the only literary heritage of the Geonim. There are collections of *halakhoth,* or digests of Jewish Law, which serve as handy references for the layman as well as for the halakhic authority. Most prominent among these are the *Halakhoth Pesukoth* of Rav Yehudai Gaon and the *Halakhoth Gedoloth,* ascribed to both Rav Yehudai and Rav Shimon Gaon Kiara. Again, these works are frequently cited by the *Rishonim* and constitute the prototype of another genre of halakhic literature, the Codes or Digests. Somewhere in between the *teshuboth* and the *halakhoth* are the *She'iltoth* of Rav Aha of Shivha, which—a modern scholar maintains—incorporates material of Talmudic times.

From the literature of the Geonim, we see that they regarded themselves as the legitimate successors of the Sages of the Talmud, exercising their prerogatives as halakhic authorities in much the same manner as the Sanhedrin of old. They instituted many *takkanoth,* largely reflecting the changed economic conditions in which Jews now found themselves.

Ashkenaz and Sepharad

Centuries before the spread of Islam in North Africa, Jewish communities had been established in all the lands of the Roman Empire. The imperial capital, Rome, was a large center of Jewish life, maintaining frequent contact with the Palestinian authorities. Beyond Rome, Jewish life took root in Italy, Spain, France and Germany, reaching over as far as England. These countries fell under the hegemony of the Church, and the Occident became divided into two antagonistic cultures, the Christian and the Moslem. The Jews in Christian lands came to be known as Ashkenazim, and their halakhic tradition derived mainly from the Palestinian schools; whereas the Jews in Moslem lands came to be known as Sephardim and followed the tradition of the Babylonian schools.

The Rishonim

By the year 1000, Jewish communities in both Ashkenaz and Sepharad had developed to such an extent that they could boast of famous schools of Torah learning of their own, with noted scholars as their religious leaders. After the death of Rav Hai Gaon in the year 1038, the Jews of Sepharad were no longer dependent upon Babylonia for halakhic instruction, and the glorious history of the Academy of Sura came to an end. Two late contemporaries of Rav Hai were heads of famous schools which attracted students from many parts. Though one was a Sephardi and the other an Ashkenazi, their contributions to Halakhah were very similar, and they both mark the transition from the period of the *Geonim* to that of the *Rishonim*. The Sephardi was Rabbenu Hananel of the North African community of Kairawan, and the Ashkenazi was Rabbenu Gershom of the Rhine (Franco-German) community of Mainz. Both distinguished themselves by being authors of a new division of halakhic literature, *peirushim* or commentaries on the Talmud, paying particular attention to the proper *girsa* or correct textual reading. R. Gershom's commentaries are extant today only in fragments, but his fame is enduring because of his well-known *takkanoth* against polygamy and divorcing a woman without her consent. These are known as *"herem* of R. Gershom," because—as mentioned before—the means of enforcing such regulations was the *herem* or excommunication. The ban against polygamy was accepted only in those lands recognizing the spiritual leadership of R. Gershom, namely in Ashkenaz, but was not accepted by Sephardic Jewry, which permitted the practice of polygamy until the present day.

The Influence of the Environment

The difference between Ashkenaz and Sepharad with respect to polygamy—and with respect to many other laws and customs—leads us to acknowledge another characteristic of Halakhah. Ashkenazic Jewry lived in Christian lands where polygamy was not sanctioned by the general community, whereas Sephardic Jewry lived in Moslem countries where polygamy was tolerated and practiced. Thus Halakhah —as Jewish life in general—was not immune or impervious to the influences of the non-Jewish environment. Though Jews in the Middle

Ages lived largely in self-contained communities and followed religious teachings and practices basically different from those of their neighbors, they nevertheless assimilated many features of the ambient culture, such as language and dress and even modes of thinking. The *Sefer Hasidim* of 12th-century R. Yehudah Hehasid went so far as to say—though in a no way approving tone—that "in every city, as is the custom of the Gentiles so is the custom of the Jews." Parallels can even be found between the halakhic literature of the medieval Ashkenazim and the scholiasts of the Church; as well as between the religious literature of the early Sephardim and that of the Muslims.

The social milieu in which medieval Jewry found itself did affect certain areas of the Halakhah. The Rishonim ruled, for example, that the Talmudic requirement for a mourner to cover his head and face and to overturn his bed is no longer obligatory, since it does not conform to the custom of the times and might appear ridiculous in the eyes of our non-Jewish neighbors. Similarly, a change from Talmudic times in the manner of Torah study led a medieval authority to rule that the manner of fulfilling the Scriptural mitzvah which bids each Jew write a Sefer Torah for himself also has to change. He argues as follows: The purpose of the mitzvah is to promote the study of the Torah, and since we no longer use the Torah scroll for purposes of study—which they did in Talmudic times—we fulfill the mitzvah nowadays by purchasing *humashim* and *mishnayoth* and the other texts currently in use. Furthermore, the fact that European Jewry no longer spoke Aramaic—the language of the Targum—led to the abandonment of the ancient practice to translate each verse of the Torah into that language when reading the Scriptural portion in the Synagogue. Nevertheless, one should not always assume that every halakhic decision or religious attitude is a result of such environmental influence. We must always bear in mind the unique sources, as well as the unique development, of Jewish law and life. And where such influence is apparent, we must recognize the peculiarly Jewish stamp which Jewish thinking imprinted upon it.

Provence

A third center of Jewish law and learning, in addition to the centers of Ashkenaz and Sepharad, arose in Southern France. There is a long roster of distinguished halakhic scholars, known as *hakhmei provincia,* who lived in the Provence. The beginnings of this prolific Torah center date back from the reign of the Emperor Carl, who invited R. Makhir of Bagdad to become the spiritual leader of the Jewish community in Narbonne at the close of the 8th century. This community of Torah, and a cluster of communities in its environs, flourished for 400 years, culminating in the work of that great commentator of the Talmud, R. Menahem Hameiri, whose works are only now being published for the first time.

Giants of the Halakhah

It is beyond the scope of this monograph to list all the bright stars of the Halakhah whose brilliance illuminates the myriad facets of Jewish Law to this day. We can record only those outstanding teachers whose works served as the core—we might say, as the bright suns—of numerous satellite works or the commentaries of hundreds of scholars of lesser brilliance, and thus indicate the main course of the stream of Halakhah which refreshed and energized Jewish life in so many climes and epochs. In the period of the *Rishonim,* the first of these luminaries is R. Isaac Alfasi, known in halakhic parlance as the RIF. He was born in North Africa in the year 1013 C.E., a disciple of R. Hananel; and his *halakhoth,* in itself a digest of the Talmud, became a prime source of both halakhic commentary and decision. Towering high above all others is a disciple of a disciple of the RIF, the illustrious Moses b. Maimon, the RAMBAM, whose contributions to Jewish thought in general are almost without par. His monumental Code of Jewish Law, the *Mishneh Torah* or *Yad Hahazakah,* stands out in the history of the Halakhah as preeminent because of both its comprehensiveness and its systematic arrangement, in addition to its lucid style. To this day, most halakhic discourses contain one or more references to the decisions of Maimonides; and his Code is surrounded by a veritable host of commentaries, second in number only to those which surround the Talmud itself.

Peirushim and Hiddushim

Older by a generation, and living not in Sepharad but in Ashkenaz, is the commentator *par excellence,* R. Shlomo b. Isaac, familiar to all as RASHI. His commentary to the Talmud made the Talmud accessible to all subsequent generations; and it gave rise to a super-commentary that is a compilation of the teachings of a score of scholars over a period of a century; namely, the *tosafoth.* The *ba'alei hatosafoth* may be said to have introduced a new *genre* of halakhic literature, the *hiddushim.* Their work is not merely commentary; it is critical analysis.

They not only advance novel interpretations of the text; they establish the correct reading, and they reconcile its seeming contradictions by positing new assumptions and distinguishing between cases which at first glance appear to be identical. Their *hiddushim* are important sources of halakhic decision, together with the many concise digests or handbooks of Jewish Law which were composed by them during this period. Foremost amongst the *tosafists* is the noted grandson of RASHI, R. Jacob b. Meir or Rabbenu Tam. His boldness in asserting opinions contrary to those of his predecessors is testimony to the continuing vitality of the Halakhah.

Mysticism vs. Philosophy

In the early period of the *Rishonim* there was little contact between the *hakhmei Ashkenaz* and the *hakhmei Sepharad*. RASHI did not know of the RIF; the RAMBAM did not know of RASHI; and the *tosafists* knew very little of the RAMBAM. As a consequence of their particular environment, the Ashkenazim were unfamiliar with classical philosophy and concentrated exclusively on the study of Talmudic law. They displayed little interest in the study of Nature or Physics, except where it impinged upon the Halakhah, accepting the Talmudic concept of this world and the hereafter unquestioningly. As a concomitant of this exclusiveness, there arose a group of pietists called *Hasidim* whose view of life was more mystical than rational. Such a circumscribed course of study led to much theoretical discussion unrelated to the actual demands of life. This in time developed into a system of study known as *pilpul,* about which we shall hear more later.

All this contrasted with the more logical and practical approach which prevailed among the Sephardim, where Jewish culture and creativity was not confined to the Halakhah. This could not fail to have its bearing on the Halakhah itself. Maimonides went to the extreme in this regard, including in his *Mishneh Torah* a description of the universe more Aristotelian than especially Jewish. In fact, there arose among the French scholars a great deal of violent opposition to the Maimonidean recognition of non-Talmudic wisdom, an opposition which persists down to our own times, as halakhic scholars continue to differ concerning the importance and relevance of scientific knowledge to Jewish Law.

The Last of the Rishonim

Because of the frequent persecutions and expulsions in France and Germany during the 13th century, the period of the *baalei hatosa-*

foth was coming to an end. By this time, however, their works and mode of study were familiar to the Sephardic scholars of Christian Spain. The scholars of Provence, who were closer to Spain but maintained contact with their correligionists in France, served as the intermediaries, bridging the gap between the Torah of Sepharad and the Torah of Ashkenaz. Thus, the outstanding scholar of the latter half of the 13th century, R. Moses b. Nahman or the RAMBAN, though a Sephardi, accepted many of the decisions of the *tosafists* and was more of a mystic than a rationalist.

The scholar who brought this merger to its climax, and who may be designated as the last great luminary of the *Rishonim,* was R. Asher b. Yehiel or the ROSH. He was a disciple of the last of the *tosafists,* R. Meir of Rothenburg, and left his native Germany to escape the persecutions. He finally settled in Toledo, and was acclaimed by Spanish Jewry as a scholar of renown. He brought with him the teachings of *hakhmei Ashkenaz,* affirming that their interpretations and customs were valid for all Israel. He is known primarily for his digest of the Talmud, which followed the style of the *halakhoth* of the RIF but included the opinions of the scholars of the intervening two centuries.

The Geonim had regarded themselves as the direct heirs of the *hakhmei hatalmud* and exercised their religious authority for all Israel, even challenging the authorities residing in Eretz Yisrael. Their appointment as official heads of the Yeshivoth was sanctioned by the chiefs of the Diaspora (*resh galutha*) who, in turn, found sanction for their own hegemony in Scripture. " 'The scepter shall not depart from Judah' (Gen. 49:10) refers to the chiefs of the Diaspora in Babylonia who rule the people by virtue of their office." After the decline of Babylonia as the center of Jewish life, however, no religious authority received formal appointment to an office which could be construed as authoritative for all Israel. Thus religious authority in the Middle Ages was confined to a spiritual leader's own community; or spread beyond those confines only by virtue of his personal repute as a scholar of outstanding erudition. As a result, the Rishonim, in contradistinction to the Geonim, hesitated to exercise any jurisdiction equivalent to that of the rabbis of the Talmud.

This hesitation can be illustrated by their attitude towards the power of the Rabbis to confiscate property (*hefker beth-din hefker*) and to annul marriages. In the Middle Ages it had become necessary for many communities, in order to eliminate certain abuses, to institute certain conditions for the marriage ceremony. The question then arose, could a marriage be declared annulled if those conditions were not complied with? Though theoretically the Rishonim felt that such power was not restricted to the rabbis of the Talmud and could be exercised by any communally-appointed rabbi, they were loath to declare so without reservation. As a result, such powers were eventually abandoned by succeeding religious authorities.

The Arba'ah Turim

In addition to the Codes and Commentaries, scholars were constantly adding to the *Teshuvoth* or Responsa literature, as individuals and communities turned to them from near and far for religious guidance. Halakhic literature was now becoming so bulky that the time had come to make some compendium that would collect the opinions of the *Rishonim* in an organized fashion. This task was accomplished by the son of the ROSH, R. Jacob b. Asher, the author of the *Arba'ah Turim* or Four Rows. In place of the Six Orders of the Mishnah, which included many laws in effect only in Temple days, R. Jacob divided Jewish Law into four major divisions, as follows:

1. *Orah Hayyim* or Way of Life, comprising the laws concerning prayer and the observance of the Sabbath and Festivals.

2. *Yoreh De'ah* or Teacher of Knowledge, comprising the dietary laws and other prohibited matters and the laws of mourning.

3. *Eben Haezer* or Rock of Help, comprising the laws of marriage and divorce.

4. *Hoshen Mishpat* or Breastplate of Judgment, laws concerning the processes of judgment and all matters concerning property. In his introduction the *ba'al haturim* states, "My purpose is to gather halakhic decisions, and where there are differing opinions I shall cite them, but then I shall cite the conclusions of my father the ROSH."

The Talmud avers, "The study of the Torah never ceased all the days of our fathers." No matter the precarious conditions of Jewish life, despite the frequent expulsions and uprooting of time honored Jewish communities, Torah always accompanied our forefathers in their wanderings from land to land. By the end of the 15th century the map of Jewish life had changed considerably. Sephardic Jewry was now dispersed in Italy, Turkey, Greece, North Africa and Palestine; while Ashkenazic Jewry traveled eastward to Bohemia and Poland. Indeed, the need for religious instruction became even greater as new communities sought to transplant the traditional practices of the old. Rabbis were constantly being solicited as to the proper *minhag,* and the responsa literature grew apace. Among the many respondents who enriched the Halakhah in this period of transition there stand out the following: R. Jacob Moellin (MAHARIL), who transmitted the German *minhag;* R. Israel Isserlein of Austria, whose decisions are recorded in his *Terumath Hadeshen;* R. Joseph Colon (*Maharik*) of Italy; and R. Simon b. Zemah Duran (TASHBAZ) of North Africa. The latter followed in the tradition of the eminent Sephardi respondents R. Solomon b. Aderet (RASHBA) of Barcelona in the 13th century and R. Isaac b. Shesheth (RIBASH) of the 14th century.

The Shulhan Arukh

The *Arba'ah Turim* "suffered" the fate common to all Codes. Before 200 years passed by it was subjected to the critical analysis of a cluster of commentaries. Outstanding among these are the *Beth Yoseph* of R. Joseph Karo, a Sephardi, and the *Darkhei Moshe* of R. Moses Isserles, an Ashkenazi. Out of these two commentaries, following the historic pattern of halakhic literature, a new Code was crystallized, the *Shulhan Arukh,* which was published for the first time in 1564. R. Karo, a Spanish refugee who finally settled in the city of Safed, Palestine, initiated this project. He patterned his *Shulhan Arukh* after the four divisions of the *Turim,* but he did not cite any conflicting opinions. He rather followed the example of Maimonides' *Mishneh Torah* and set down the law in terse and decisive statements. He was guided primarily by the opinions of the RIF, the RAMBAM, and the ROSH, but also took into consideration the opinions of more recent Responsa.

It was the intention of R. Karo, as it was that of the previous codifiers, to provide a handy, though comprehensive, digest of Jewish Law which could serve even the layman, who had to apply the manifold injunctions of his faith to daily life. However, the *Shulhan Arukh* of a Sephardi could not serve very well the Ashkenazi Jew, who felt obliged to follow decisions and customs of his own authorities. Consequently, R. Moshe Isserles (RAMOH) of Cracow added to practically each paragraph of the *Shulhan Arukh* notes setting forth the Ashkenazic practices. It was not long before this combined work achieved universal recognition among a widespread Jewry as the authoritative Code of Jewish Practice. It continues to serve as such to this day, 400 years after its first appearance.

An examination of the differences between Karo's decisions and those of the RAMOH will reveal some of the basic differences be-

tween the Ashkenazi approach to the study of Jewish Law and that
of the Sephardim. By the time of the RAMOH the system of study
known as *pilpul* had become the norm for Polish Jewry. The Mishnah
as a branch of study preliminary to the Talmud was skipped over, and
children were introduced to the Talmud at a very early age, learning
more by rote than by real understanding. The number of works known
as *hiddushim* multiplied, as scholars displayed their intellectual prowess
in constructing speculative systems of interpretations (*hilukim*) which
could not very well be applied to actual halakhic decisions. In general,
there was great hesitancy in making clear-cut decisions where earlier
authorities had expressed contrary opinions, and the rule adopted was
always to follow the more stringent opinion. This hesitancy reflected
itself, for example, in declaring as forbidden slaughtered animals whose
kashruth could be ascertained only after an examination of its organs,
because of a categorical assumption that we lack today the competence
to make such examination. Ashkenazic *minhag* gave the force of law to
many other additional restrictions which the Sephardim did not follow.
The RAMOH himself recognized the limitations of such a system when,
in the section dealing with the obligation to respect one's teacher, he
says, "In these times, the chief quality of a rabbi is not in teaching the
pilpul and *hilukim* which are now customary, but in teaching the *pesak
halakhah* and in setting before his pupil the truth." Despite this frank
appraisal and the criticism of a few contemporary scholars, this mode
of study continued in full force in Central and Eastern Europe. Even
amidst the appalling pogroms that took place in the 17th century, when
Cossack hordes under Chmielnicki devastated dozens of Polish Jewish
communities, no brute force could extinguish the love of Israel for the
divine gift of Torah and Mitzvoth.

THE PEOPLE AND THE LAW

It is one thing to contemplate the achievements of the legal geniuses. It is quite another to ask about the affairs of the ordinary people, those who kept the law, but did not make it. To gain a picture of the everyday life of common folk, we turn to an account of the synagogue.

Israel Abrahams here draws upon the records of commonplace and workaday life to describe the life of the synagogue. What is important for our purpose is to locate in his account evidences that the elevated values of the rabbis indeed permeated and shaped the practical life of the folk. If the law, for its reasons, required attention to cleanliness, for example, then the people, loyal to the law, would make themselves clean, even without a clear understanding of the law's higher motivations. If the law, faithful to prophetic ideals, required the limitation of differences in wealth, so that rich and poor would be subject to one Torah and one standard of justice, the people, keeping the law, would dress in a way respectful of the feelings of people who could not afford rich clothing. Clearly, the law would impose a certain standard of behavior upon everyone. For example, it would make it customary for people to come to the synagogue and would legitimize the use of coercive measures against those who did not attend. In like manner the law required that people study Torah, and in the synagogue this was carried out through systematic instruction, for example, in sermons.

The synagogue for Jewry carried out functions which a wide range of institutions effected in other societies. It was the center of communal life. Therefore it was the natural place for collecting necessary funds. It also was a kind of gathering place for the sharing of information and common concerns, also for gossip. Since people met regularly in the synagogue, they found it natural to chat together and to share the information which, in modern times, will find its way into newspapers or media of other kinds. Since the synagogue was the primary public building, it also would, through its art and architecture, express the aesthetic sense of the community. The women and children would

83

find their place there; young men would first appear before the community, to take their place in the ranks of responsible authorities, within the synagogue walls.

So far as one may speak of Rabbinic Judaism, then it becomes important to pay close attention to the one institutional expression of the whole, the synagogue, Israel's distinctive 'homeland' in every country and the setting for, the occasion of, all that Rabbinic Judaism knew as life.

6.

LIFE IN THE SYNAGOGUE

Israel Abrahams

[From *Jewish Life in the Middle Ages,* by Israel Abrahams. Philadelphia, 1958: Jewish Publication Society of America, pp. 15-34.]

The attitude of the medieval Jew towards his House of God was characteristic of his attitude towards life. Though the Jew and the Greek gave very different expressions to the conception, the Jew shared with the Greek a belief in the essential unity of life amidst its detailed obligations. It is not enough to say that the Jew's religion absorbed his life, for in quite as real a sense his life absorbed his religion. Hence the synagogue was not a mere place in which he prayed, it was a place in which he lived; and just as life has its earnest and its frivolous moments, so the Jew in synagogue was at times rigorously reverent and at others quite at his ease. In this respect no doubt the medieval Church agreed with the Synagogue. "Be one of the first in synagogue," writes a fourteenth-century Jew in his last testament to his children. "Do not speak during prayers, but repeat the responses, and after the service do acts of kindness. . . . Wash me clean, comb my hair as in my lifetime, in order that I may go clean to my eternal resting place, just as I used to go every Sabbath evening to the synagogue." This writer's sensitiveness was by no means exceptional. Medieval Europe was insanitary and dirty, and the Jewish quarters were in many respects the dirtiest. Epidemics made havoc in the Jewries just as they did in the other parts of the towns. The ghetto streets were the narrowest in the narrow towns of the middle ages. But all these disadvantages were to a large extent balanced by a strong sense of personal dignity. It was not until three centuries of life in the ghettos had made their Jewish inhabitants callous to the demands of fashion, indifferent to their personal appearance, careless in their speech and general bearing, that

85

this old characteristic of the Jews ceased to distinguish them. In the middle ages, however, the Jews justly prided themselves on their regard for the amenities of clean living and gentle mannerliness.

This cleanliness in person and speech, this—unique for its age—complete sense of personal dignity, was a direct consequence of the religion, and it was the synagogue again which enforced a valuable social influence. Cleanly habits were in fact codified, and, as we shall see in a later chapter, the medieval code-books of the Jewish religion contain a systematized scheme of etiquette, of cleanly custom, and of good taste. The codification of these habits had the evil effect of reducing them to a formality, and later on even the ritual hand-washing, essential in many Jewish ceremonies, became a perfunctory rite, compatible with much personal uncleanliness. But in the middle ages this was not yet the case. A quaint detail or two must suffice here. Jacob Molin had a bag suspended on the wall near his seat in synagogue, containing a pocket-handkerchief for use during prayer, an article of attire unknown in the ordinary life of the middle ages. A medieval Jew had, as already remarked, a special synagogue coat, called in some parts a *Sarabal*. It was a tunic which hung down from the neck, and formed part of the gifts bestowed by parents on their sons when the latter married. Gloves were forbidden in prayer because humility was essential to a proper devotional demeanour, and much vexing of spirit was caused by young men and old who would carry walking-sticks with them to synagogue. There was an iron scraper at the synagogue doors so that worshippers might wipe their feet on entering. Indeed, special synagogue shoes were *de rigueur,* for a regard to decent footgear was a very old Jewish characteristic. He who yawned in synagogue or during prayers was ordered to place his hand in front of his mouth. Men did not go to synagogue with the small cap worn in the house, but changed it for a more costly one.

With regard to the feet, it was customary to pray barefooted or in light slippers on the ninth of Ab or on the Day of Atonement, on the "eve" of which many passed the night in the synagogue. Talmud students in the thirteenth century often went barefooted in the streets —from poverty, however, rather than from piety; but there are indications that in the East Jews habitually prayed with bare feet. At all events the wooden sandals of the fifteenth century in Germany were forbidden except to keep the feet clean, and in some places Jewish worshippers were forced to leave their shoes in the vestibule before entering the House of God, under penalty of excommunication. From reverential motives a space was left unprinted on the wall facing the

synagogue door, to recall the glory of Zion trailing in the dust. In many
private homes a similar custom prevailed.

But there was another motive at the back of the prohibition
against a few worshippers using cushioned seats while the others sat
on the bare wood. "It is unseemly to make such distinctions, but the
whole congregation may use cushions." So, too, we find whole congregations denying themselves the luxury of wearing the *Sargenos*—
or white surplice—on the Day of Atonement, for fear of putting to
the blush the poor who were unable to provide themselves with the
attire. This regard for the feelings of the poor was extended to the
unlearned. In Palestine the worshipper who was called to the Law
read his section from the scroll. But very early there were many Jews
who were unable to do this, and though the practice continued in force
right through the middle ages, it had already been modified in Babylon,
where the *Chazan,* or officiating reader, always helped in the reading
whether the individual were learned or not, in order to avoid putting
the unlearned to the blush. There is indeed some evidence that the
general level of Hebrew knowledge among Jews was higher in the
middle ages than it is to-day. There were more professed students of
Hebrew, but some of the general Jewish public seem to have been
unable to understand any but the most familiar prayers.

To these details must be added the general principle that in the
synagogue the worshipper was to be at his best, dignified, simple-
hearted, respectful, and attentive. But the inroad of the wider conception of the functions of the synagogue, to which allusion has
already been made, inevitably produced breaches of decorum, which,
however, were not tolerated without vigorous and often effective protest. To some extent the more educated classes were to blame. The
Rabbis themselves were not regular attendants at public worship, and
only preached at rare intervals. This was due to their habit of holding
semi-public services in their own houses, primarily for the special benefit of their pupils. But the custom of praying at home naturally led
to late arrival at synagogue, or total abstinence from it.

Attendance at synagogue was enforced by penalties in some
places, but they were ineffective in preventing late arrival. When there,
learned men would often prove inattentive, for they had already
prayed, and they would while away the time over their learned books
while the *Chazan* trilled his airs. It was not unusual for the whole congregation to talk while the Precentor sang or read the Pentateuch, or,
what must have been equally disturbing to decorum, the worshippers
recited their prayers aloud, going their own way while the Precentor

went his. Praying aloud was a long-standing grievance of the synagogue authorities, and has never been quite eradicated. Coming late was a source of disturbance which it was also hard to remove, for no food might be eaten in the morning until after the morning prayer, and many must perforce pray at home and breakfast before going to synagogue. In synagogue, on the other hand, the service could not be begun late, because the rubrics required that the chief part of the prayer be recited within three hours after early dawn. Late arrival was thus so far an admitted necessity that a special chapter in the codebook provides for the case. This feature was more marked on the Sabbath; on week-days, when the synagogue service was held at a very early hour, workmen would take their breakfasts with them to synagogue, and, after praying, would eat their meal in the courtyard before proceeding to their work. Still, a large number of worshippers went to prayer early on Sabbaths, and waited till the close of the service before taking any food. This class had claims on communal recognition which seriously interfered with one of the chief elements of divine worship, *viz.* the homiletical discourse. Throughout the later middle ages the sermon falls into the background. In the Talmudic and Gaonic eras the sermon invariably formed part of the morning service, but in Europe the sermon gradually sank into the low position from which the Mendelssohnian revival raised it at the end of the eighteenth century.

Sermons were not given every week, were transferred as a luxury to the afternoon, and the place in which they were delivered became the school and not the synagogue, a fact which tended to convert the homily into a learned lecture. The sermon was spoken in the vernacular, but was far from popular, especially in Germany. The preacher was frequently interrupted by questions, as was indeed the custom in some medieval churches. It is interesting to contrast the effect of suffering on Jews and other sects in regard to the sermon. With, say, the Covenanters, persecution gave a new point to the homily and placed in the preacher's hand a sharpened two-edged sword. The German Jew was too overwhelmed by his fate to listen patiently to hopeful prophecies of peace. Yet the contrast is more formal than real, for the Covenanter could be roused to armed revolt, a resource denied to Jewish victims of oppression. Hence to the Covenanter the love of homilies was political rather than religious; and just because the Jew had no political hopes, so he placed less reliance in the religious consolation provided by homiletical discourses. Never ceasing to be the teacher, the Rabbi ceased almost entirely to preach, and the delivery of sermons was left to a class of itinerant preachers known as *Maggidim,* of considerable eloquence and power. With emancipation came a considerable outburst of Jewish pulpit eloquence; the Rabbi resumed his old role of preacher. . . .

One of the noblest principles of Judaism was its insistence on *effort* in well-doing. A Jew of the middle ages would thus be as anxious as the Jews of Temple times to expend his means in the service of God. He would always value more highly an act that needed a sacrifice of his time and money than one which made no such claim. Hence it came that he would buy the right to participate in the synagogue service, since he could no longer spend his means at the Temple celebrations in Jerusalem. The Jewish layman, if the term can be used when there was no clerical caste, performed certain of the religious rites in the synagogue, and the privilege was so coveted that though, in later times, occasionally apportioned by lot, in the middle ages it went literally to the highest bidder. The *mitsvoth,* as these coveted rites were named, were sold by auction in synagogue, and each congregation had its fixed rules regulating the method and time of sale. Sometimes the *mitsvoth* were sold once or twice a year, sometimes once or thrice a week, most often once a month. Disputes occasionally arose as to these auctions, and the function led to considerable disorder. Moreover, the poorer members of the congregation were debarred from the coveted honour, though these sometimes made special efforts and sacrifices to secure the privilege.

Again, the announcement in synagogue of money offerings for benevolent or religious purposes gave opportunity for gossip and comment. In the early Church, the offerings of Christians were made publicly, not privately. The presiding officer of the church received the gifts, and solemnly dedicated them to God with words of thanksgiving and benediction. Yet it must be remembered that a free and easy attitude in worship was associated with a very sincere piety. The same authority who applauds the sale of *mitsvoth* enforces the strictest rules for reverent behaviour during prayer. Pray with head bent, with soft utterance, with feet placed neatly together. Spend an hour in the synagogue in silent meditation before venturing to pray—and so forth. Other sources of disturbance, especially among Oriental Jews, were the custom of utilizing the synagogue for inviting guests to semi-religious festivities, the putting on and off of the *sargenos,* laving the hands of the *Cohanim,* or descendants of Aaron, previous to their recitation of the Priestly Benediction. Yet, on the whole, the abuses of the great principle that the Jew was at home in his place of worship, did not appreciably lessen devotion. It was only at the close of the eighteenth

century, when the Jews hovered between the old and the new, that
this familiar attitude towards God became indecorous; for the old sense
of ease was retained, but there was a loss of the thoroughgoing piety
which, seeing God everywhere and in all things, looked upon him as
a partner in the business of life, rather than as a superior Being to be
approached with formal etiquette. In Oriental lands the sense of in-
congruousness does not strike the observer so strongly as it does in
Europe, and this difference in itself amounts to a justification of the
synagogue of the middle ages, especially in France and Germany,
where the warmth of Oriental emotion was retained. In Italy and
Spain there was, perhaps, a more stately demeanour in synagogue;
there was unquestionably less warmth and religious intensity.

Gossip was inevitable in synagogue, for the latter was the chief
meeting-place of Jews. The licensed conversation, however, occurred
in the courtyard, not in the synagogue itself; and, perhaps to encourage
the people to congregate there rather than in the sacred building, the
courtyard was sometimes laid out as a garden. It became a fashion,
even with the most punctilious Jews, to reassemble after the service
for the purpose of talking over the news of the hour, military and political. But those were forbidden to join the concourse to whom such
gossip proved tedious, for as "the Sabbath is a delight," says my
authority, "none should participate in the function if it wearies or
bores them."

Probably the most serious difficulty in maintaining decorum arose
from the children. The Jews were not the only sect so troubled, for
one frequently meets with Puritan diatribes against the "wretched boys."
In New England churches the tithing-man used to rap the knuckles of
boys (and even of elders) to wake them up or keep them well-behaved
during divine service. Occasionally a similar measure was resorted to in
synagogue, and, especially with the Sephardic Jews (i.e., those using
the Spanish Jewish ritual), the children were kept in order by an official,
stick in hand. Some authorities resented the intrusion of young children
into the synagogue at all; indeed the trouble must have been increased
by the separation of the boys from their mothers.

In the separation of the sexes, the synagogue only reflected their
isolation in the social life outside. The sexes were separated at Jewish
banquets and home feasts not less than in the synagogue. If they did
not pray together neither did they play together. The rigid separation
of the sexes in prayer seems not to have been earlier, however, than
the thirteenth century. The women had their own "court" in the Temple, yet it is not impossible that they prayed together with the men in

Talmudic times. Possibly the rigid separation grew out of the medieval custom—more common as the thirteenth century advances—which induced men and women to spend the eve of the Great Fast in synagogue. By the end of the thirteenth century, and perhaps earlier, Jewish women had their own prayer-meetings in rooms at the side of and a little above the men's synagogue, with which the rooms communicated by a small window or balcony. Or if the women had no separate apartments, they sat at the back of the men's synagogue in reserved places, screened by curtains. There were no galleries for women as at present. In their own prayer-meetings, the women were led by female precentors, some of whom acquired considerable reputation. The epitaph of one of them, Urania of Worms, belonging perhaps to the thirteenth century, runs thus:—

"This headstone commemorates the eminent and excellent lady Urania, the daughter of R. Abraham, who was the chief of the synagogue singers. His prayer for his people rose up unto glory.
"And as to her, she, too, with sweet tunefulness, officiated before the female worshippers to whom she sang the hymnal portions. In devout service her memory shall be preserved."

The tender regard for woman, despite her inequality as regards legal and religious status, was shown in one or two features of which considerations of space cannot justify the omission. Women, when away from home, were allowed to light their Sabbath candles in the synagogue. It was not an unknown thing even in the seventeenth and eighteenth centuries, when the exclusion of women from active participation in the public worship was most rigid, to use a woman's gold-embroidered cloak or silver-braided apron as a curtain for the ark, a mantle for the scroll of the Law, or a cover for the reading-desk. The decoration of the synagogue was not severely simple. "The Jews may not enlarge, elevate, or beautify their synagogues," enacted Alfonso X in 1261. Thus the Talmudic prescription to elevate the synagogue beyond the highest building in the town was impossible in Spain. The difficulty was evaded by making a small symbolical addition to the height of the synagogue whenever a higher house was newly built, and it is barely possible that this cause, besides imitation of the ancient Jewish temple and of the medieval mosque, tended to preserve the old custom of leaving the synagogues in the East without roof as late as the fifteenth century. Occasionally, however, European synagogues were very high; and a complaint is recorded that the synagogue at Sens in the time of Innocent III was higher than the neighbouring church. Complaints are also recorded in London that, owing to the proximity of the synagogue, the church prayers were interfered with by the noise of the Hebrew hymns. But in Rome in the fourteenth century churches were erected quite close to synagogues and the relations between the two sets of worshippers were not strained by any such recriminations.

The number of windows in a synagogue was by preference twelve, but this feature was neither common nor general. More regard was paid to the Orientation of European synagogues. The decorations of the synagogue were often costly; and legend has recorded many wonders of the Alexandrian synagogue, among others. Separate parts of that building are said to have been reserved for special trades, and in the middle ages synagogues for Jews of different nationalities were common especially in Italy and on the Mediterranean coasts. Spanish and Italian synagogues were noted for their beauty, and even elsewhere the floors were often of stone or marble. The doors of the ark were sometimes ornamented with figures of vines or candlesticks, or stone lions graced the steps leading to it. The lion was, indeed, a favourite Jewish decorative ornament. It appears in the modern synagogue in every available place, on the ark, whether in relief or painted, in precious metal on the plates which adorn the scrolls of the Law, and in gold embroidery on the mantels and curtains, and even as supports to tables designed for semi-religious use.

The lamp, burning constantly in front of the ark, was of gold or silver, but burnished brass, "such as is found only in the houses of princes" was not excluded. So popular was the presentation of such gifts to the synagogue that it became necessary to restrict the liberality of individuals, and no lamp was admitted as a gift without the special permission of the council. The privilege of supplying lights for the Sabbath was even inherited. That the synagogue was not Puritanically averse to sensuous attractions, may be seen from the fact that rose-water was, later on, used for washing the hands of the "Priests" on public festivals. On semi-private festivities rose-leaves were strewn in the ark among the very scrolls of the Law. On the "Rejoicing of the Law" the "Bridegroom," as the layman selected to read the last section in the Pentateuch was named, held a reception in synagogue and his guests were sprinkled from scented sprays. These remarks apply more to the East than to Europe: but on the subject of artistic decoration in synagogue one general remark must suffice. There grew up a strong feeling against ornamenting the synagogue with representations of animals other than lions. Some authorities applied the restriction only to the human figure, or to designs in relief, or to the decoration of the side of the synagogue which worshippers faced during prayer. Others forbade all representations of natural objects. Still, as we have seen, these sentiments were not universal, and in the twelfth century the Cologne Synagogue had painted glass windows, and it was not an unknown thing for birds and snakes, probably grotesques rather than accurate representations, to appear on the walls of the synagogue without the Rabbinical sanction. But these grotesques, like the seal of a thirteenth-century Jew, cannot, as Tovey wittily says, "be thought a breach of the second commandment, for it is the likeness of nothing that is in heaven, earth, or water." Prayer-books were illuminated and pictorially embellished, and after the invention of printing, wood-cuts depicting the signs of the Zodiac and the ten plagues of Exodus appeared in many an edition of the Hebrew prayer-book used in synagogue. On the feast of Pentecost, again, the synagogue was deco-rated with flowers. Grass was strewn on the synagogue floor on the Day of Atonement, less however as an ornament than to serve as a softer ground on which the worshippers might prostrate themselves.

As to the shape of synagogues, no special form can be called Jewish. A famous authority of last century maintained that no Jewish law, old or new, restricted the fancy of synagogue architects in this respect. He himself authorized the choice of an octagonal form, and this shape is now rather popular on the continent. . . .

The synagogue music does not seem to have been very ornate or refined; volume of sound being ascribed to it rather than delicacy. The singing Precentor (*Chazan*) was not tolerated without a struggle, though he eventually became a marked feature of the synagogue. Much conservatism prevailed regarding synagogue tunes; and each locality possessed its own melodies. No serious compunction was felt, however, against introducing popular airs into the synagogue, though there was no doubt some feeling against it. The congregational singing was vigorous and probably general, for we find in later times some resentment at the introduction of boy choirs.

This leads us back from our digression. The boys had their rights in the synagogue long before they attained their thirteenth year, after which they were accounted, from a religious point of view, as adults. The Barmitzvah rites, which accompanied the completion of a boy's thirteenth year, cannot be clearly traced earlier than the fourteenth century. From early times, however, young boys were encouraged to recite in synagogue the Hallel and the weekly lesson from the Prophets; boys sometimes lit the synagogue candles on the eve of the festivals;

in the fifteenth century boys read part of the regular service to congregations of adults. Boys sometimes made announcements in synagogue,
a function afterwards filled by the shamash or beadle. Flags in hand,
boys headed the procession of the bearers of the scrolls on the "Rejoicing of the Law," they ascended the reading-desk *en masse* on
that occasion during the reading of the Pentateuch lesson, some of
them even bare-headed. On every Sabbath they stood by the steps of
the Almemor (reading-desk) and reverently kissed the sacred Scroll.
When they were nine or ten years old, they fasted a few hours on the
Day of Atonement, and some authorities included them among the ten
adults requisite for *minyan,* the ritual quorum for public worship.

The boys were even allowed to preach; and, as some authorities
assume, were admitted to administrative honours. An epitaph of the
third century describes an eight-year-old Roman boy as an *Archon* of
the synagogue. But the title of Archon seems to have been hereditary
at Rome, and this particular boy may have borne the title in virtue of
his descent. Boys were taught to show the greatest respect to their
parents in synagogue; they carried their fathers' prayer-books for them;
they never occupied their fathers' seats; they stood while their fathers
stood, and their fathers blessed them after the reading of the Law, or at
the close of the Sabbath eve service. Fathers refrained from kissing
their boys in synagogue, but when the service was over the children
kissed the Rabbi's hand, which he raised to the children's heads, uttering meanwhile a prayer for their welfare. The mother was not excluded
from these tokens of respect, and on Friday, in the interval between the
afternoon and evening services, the boys were sent home to their
mothers, to intimate that the Sabbath was about to begin, and that
the Sabbath candles must be kindled. For the children's sake certain
verses from the book of Esther were sung in chorus on Purim, and,
despite the trouble they caused there, the young were treated as though
the synagogue was their second home. Indeed, up till the ninth or
tenth centuries, Asiatic synagogues were homes for travellers, who
lodged in the synagogues and took their meals there. The Kiddush or
Sanctification over the wine which has, quaintly enough, survived in
the modern synagogue ritual, was thus in its origin part of the Sabbath
meal, which was spread in the synagogue itself or in its immediate pre-
cincts for passing strangers. In the European synagogues no such
meals took place; the Sanctification over the wine became a symbol
rather than part of the meal, and, instead of the Precentor, a boy sipped
the wine from the full cup handed to him.

No doubt there was, as the middle ages closed, a tendency to specialize, and subtract from the synagogue some of its functions. Yet the association between the school and the synagogue always remained an intimate one. It was a very old custom for pious worshippers to repair to synagogue early before the services, with the object of studying the Bible and the Rabbinical writings. Still, the school and the synagogue were independent institutions, though praying was usual in the school, and learning took place in the synagogue.

PART III

MASTERS OF LAW

It is exceedingly difficult to give an account of the achievement of the great legal authorities, those who wrote codes, commentaries, and responsa. Their life-stories have remarkably little to do with their legal accomplishments, unlike the philosophers, whose lives and thought exhibit a close correspondence. Perhaps embedded in the legal thought and expression of commentators and codifiers is a perception of life based upon what they saw and experienced, but it is difficult to demonstrate it in detail.

More likely, the discipline of the law, carrying forward its inexorable logic and normative rules, made it impossible to give expression through more than episodic decisions in particular cases to individuality. To put it differently, the function of law is to make objective and general what is, to begin with, private and subjective, for law pertains to everyone everywhere. It would be contrary to the nature of law in the rabbinic system for one's private experiences and particular perceptions to play a major role.

When, therefore, we come to the towering figures, Rashi and the Gaon of Vilna, we should not be surprised to discover that the biography of each plays little role in his creative life. Indeed, in the case of Rashi we have remarkably slight biographical information, and for the Vilna Gaon, what we know is a repertoire of fairly routine stories of prodigious learning at an early age. These may well be true—there are no grounds to doubt it—but they do not serve to differentiate young Elijah from others of whom similar stories are told. Yet with little biography, both masters before us made a distinctive and highly particular impact upon the legal tradition.

Though we know little about Rashi's life, his creative work as a commentator tells us all we could hope to know about his mind and personality. He exemplifies the ways in which the objective system of the law made possible highly subjective and individual modes of creativity. On the one hand, the raw material was the Talmud and

97

the Bible, the common property of everyone. On the other, what Rashi did with these holy books is entirely of his own making. Possessed of remarkable erudition, he was able to bring to bear upon the explanation of a given sentence of Bible or Talmud the whole of the antecedent tradition of learning. Endowed with exceptional taste and judgment, he selected from all that he knew precisely what one had to be told for a full comprehension of the matter. Enjoying exceptional powers of expression, he did so in a graceful and lucid, succinct and very personal style. His importance in the legal tradition therefore is to illustrate the range of creativity available to those subject to the disciplines of the law.

The Gaon of Vilna opposed Hasidism, opposed the changes in Judaism beginning to make their impact in the West, opposed the efforts at secular 'Enlightenment' within East European Jewry, opposed the accommodation of the tradition to changing circumstances, and single-handedly effected the most profound and far-reaching revision of the mode of legal study most particular to traditional circles. He reformed the structure of the law from within, and his reforms were far more radical in spirit and in substance than anything achieved outside the pale of learning. For he proposed nothing less than an entire revision in the curriculum of the law, including documents, such as Tosefta and the Palestinian Talmud, neglected for many centuries. He introduced an entirely new mode of thinking and legal analysis, which involved attention not to the games and conceits of superficial logicians, but to the careful, close, and learned exegesis of what the Talmud itself had to say. When he had completed his work, the world of the Talmud would never again be the same. Only a master of the Talmud, such as Louis Ginzberg, could give us so penetrating an account of the full weight and meaning of the Vilna Gaon's new critical mode of thought.

THE PEDAGOGUE

Rashi—Rabbi Solomon b. Isaac—laid open the treasures of Talmudic and Biblical literature to the Jewish masses. His great commentaries to the Bible and the Babylonian Talmud, extraordinarily succinct, pedagogically brilliant, encyclopaedic in their scope and highly selective in taste and fine judgment, are the beginning of rabbinic wisdom. With the help of Rashi, one may read the Hebrew Scriptures in the light of the Talmudic interpretation. With his unfailing assistance, one may study the Talmud, secure in the knowledge that words, phrases, larger concepts and directions of argument—all are going to be clarified. Rashi is the pedagogue of the Jewish people.

When teaching Scriptures, Rashi stresses the plain meaning. He only sparingly imposes on the biblical text the rich lore of stories and narrative elaborations available from Talmudic literature. At the same time he brings to bear the rabbinic perspective. He explains both the words and what they mean.

In explaining the Talmud, he addresses the intellectual elite, but his intention is to make entry into that elite open and accessible. A person may be justifiedly assured that he or she understands the Talmud when he or she finds Rashi's commentary a help and not a burden. Rashi is brief and purposeful, always addressing himself to the explanation of specific words and concrete phrases. It is a commentary intended not to distract the reader or to impose alien ideas upon the text, but aimed at giving a simple and lucid explanation of what is before the student. Because of his genius, Rashi gave to the whole Jewish people the opportunity to take up and study the source of rabbinic values, to make their own the literature itself. It would no longer be necessary to turn to experts or to take someone's word for what is in the difficult Talmudic discussions. With one's own guide and teacher, each person could find out for himself.

Interestingly, Abraham Joshua Heschel accounts for the widespread popularity of Jewish learning among the masses of Eastern Europe in terms of Rashi's success: "It was ... Rashi who brought intellectual emancipation to the people. Without a commentary, the Hebrew Scripture and particularly the Talmud are accessible only to the enlightened few. The old commentaries offered interpretations of isolated passages and were mostly limited to single sections of the Talmud. Rashi's Commentary, explaining with exquisite simplicity almost every word of the immense text . . . is a faithful companion who attends the student to whatever part of the text he may turn . . . he communes with the student, conveying by a minimum of words a maximum of meaning." That is why not only rabbinic values and patterns of action but also rabbinic teachings and the actual texts in which Rabbinic Judaism is preserved became available to, part of the everyday life of, wide circles of European Jewry.

7.

RASHI

ALEXANDER MARX

[From *Essays in Jewish Biography,* by Alexander Marx. Philadelphia, 1947: The Jewish Publication Society of America, pp. 61-86.]

Before turning to a discussion of Rashi's great literary achievements, we shall consider the little we know of the great man's life.

His full name was R. Solomon ben Isaac, and so he signed some of his responsa. A German authority of the thirteenth century maintained that Rashi generally signed his name *Shin Yod,* i.e. Shelomo Yitshaki, and this abbreviation sometimes occurs in our sources. From a letter of R. Nathan, author of the *'Aruk,* and his brothers, who were the heads of the Academy of Rome, we learn that Rashi signed a letter he sent to them "Shelomo ha-Yitzhaki." His pupils generally referred to him as *ha-Moreh,* the teacher, or *Rabbenu,* our master. . . .

We do not know the exact date of Rashi's birth. Tradition has it that, even as "the sun also ariseth and the sun goeth down" (Eccl. 1.5), so Rashi was born in the year of the death of the great pioneer of Jewish learning and culture in the Frankish empire—Rabbenu Gershom ben Solomon, the "Light of the Exile." The latter's death occurred, according to the same tradition, in the year 1040. Some sources, however, date R. Gershom's death in the year 1028. And as if to tease us, his tombstone, which was discovered towards the end of the last century and correctly deciphered two decades ago, no longer shows the date of the death of the great leader in whose memory it was erected. . . .

We are better informed about the date of his death; several sources record that the great man passed away on Thursday, the 29th of Tammuz, 4865 (July 13, 1105). And the fact that literary tradition has preserved this date is striking evidence that his contemporaries realized the outstanding merit of the scholar; for it is altogether exceptional, exact dates transmitted by medieval Jewish literary sources for the lives of scholars being very rare.

These dates and the fact.that Rashi was born at Troyes, the capital of the duchy of Champagne, are about all the direct information we have about him. There are half a dozen compilations by Rashi's pupils, but they were interested in transmitting to us the opinions and interpretations of their great teacher; the "facts" (ma 'asim) which they record are his legal decisions, but never incidents of his life. Only by the way, here and there, do some points of personal interest occur in these works and in the master's own writings. With their help a few bare facts of his biography can be pieced together.

Nothing is known about his parents. We cannot even tell whether his father was a scholar. He never refers to him in his writings; he may have died while his son was still very young. Twice he mentions a brother of his mother—R. Simon the Elder, a pupil of Rabbenu Gershom—but we do not know where he lived and whether he exercised any influence on his nephew's education.

It was the merit of my revered teacher, Professor Abraham Berliner, whose publications on Rashi have thrown much light on his personality and work, to have pointed out for the first time that the city of his birth gave the young man an opportunity to become familiar with many aspects of practical life and that he made good use of this opportunity. Rashi's commentaries indicate that he was not a man of books alone, removed from problems of everyday life; they show an unusual familiarity with practical matters which he could not easily have acquired anywhere but in Troyes. For the capital of the Champagne was a mercantile and industrial center of importance, an importance which it maintained until the expulsion of the Jews in 1306. The great fairs arranged twice a year at Troyes were attended by merchants from France and Germany, Flanders, England and Italy. From visitors to these fairs Rashi learned about the city of Venice and its wonders, where one had to travel by boat from house to house, or about a great wall in Hungary. Conversations with seafarers and perhaps inspection of their ships were helpful for an understanding of Ezekiel's prophecy on Tyre (ch. 27), and it was from them that he learned about tides. In connection with Tyre he states that the foreign visitors were not permitted to deal directly with one another, but had to call in the services of the inhabitants as brokers; evidently Rashi transferred the experience of his own day to biblical times. He became familiar with the Cologne standard of coinage, which was used in Western Germany, saw tokens without engravings and learned about the procedure of coining, which, he tells us, followed certain practices of the blacksmiths. He knew of soldering and of engraving, of weaving figures into the material and of embroidering silk with gold. He evidently had observed these processes at the workshops of Troyes. He also speaks of the import from Lucca, Italy, of expensive taffeta interwoven with silver, of gold buckles and other jewelry, of belts worn by noble ladies when on horseback, and of many other items. He mentions buffoons who appeared during the fairs to entertain the people. What is of particular interest to us is that he knew of the preparation of parchment, manufactured in the tanneries of Troyes, which thus made available the indispensable material for a scholar of his type. Berliner informs us that owing to the high price of that material the scribes of the eleventh and twelfth centuries utilized every strip and corner of the skin. There are two manuscripts in the Jewish Theological Seminary Library which illustrate that old custom—one is a thirteenth-century copy of Rashi's commentary on the Prophets.

From his own experience—for Rashi earned his livelihood as a vinegrower—he describes to a son-in-law the difference between the wine-presses then in use and those formerly employed. In one of his responsa he apologizes for the briefness of his letter on the ground that he and his family were all busy that day with the vintage.

Thus Rashi went through life with his eyes wide open and was able to utilize the observations he made in his own day for the interpretation of practical matters in Bible and Talmud. He frequently gave the equivalent of these things in the French vernacular in his glosses, about which we shall have more to say later on.

In Troyes, Rashi could not find any teachers to give him a deeper understanding of Bible and Talmud; he therefore decided, after his marriage, to turn to the great academies which, in the preceding generation, had been established on the Rhine by the scholars of Lotharingia, as they are called in Jewish literature.

In Mayence, R. Judah ha-Kohen, also called R. Leontin, had opened the first academy in northern Europe (10th century). Under the leadership of his pupil, the aforementioned Rabbenu Gershom, the school quickly grew and developed; it trained a large circle of prominent scholars who continued the work of the Mayence academy and established similar schools in Worms and other cities.

In these academies the study of the Talmud was cultivated with great zest and devotion. There the interpretations of the great master, Rabbenu Gershom, and of other scholars were eagerly collected by groups of younger scholars who preserved them in writing. The

"Mayence Commentary" (*Kuntres Magenza*)—a product of this activity—enjoyed considerable fame and was excerpted by Rashi's contemporary, R. Nathan of Rome, in his *'Aruk*. In Italy it was ascribed
to R. Gershom himself; it is under his name that the commentary on
several treatises has been preserved and was so printed half a century
ago in the great Wilna Talmud. A similar compilation originated in the
Worms academy.

The Jews of the Frankish empire, like their Italian brethren, had
been dependent on the Palestinian academies, and in the tenth and
eleventh centuries they still turned to Palestine for decisions in difficult
cases. The Spanish Jews, on the other hand, looked up to Babylonia for
centuries and received their inspiration from the Babylonian center. As
Dr. Louis Ginzberg has shown, the Babylonian Talmud had replaced
the Yerushalmi even in Palestine as the main subject of study; in
Europe, so far as we know, it had been the textbook of the academies
from the very beginning. Somehow Babylonian traditions also reached
northern Europe and were incorporated into the German commentaries on the Talmud.

These great schools of Mayence and Worms now attracted Rashi,
and here, he felt, his thirst for knowledge could be quenched. It was
generally assumed that he first attended the Worms school; but recently
Dr. V. Aptowitzer has brought forward good reasons for the assumption
that Rashi first directed his steps to the academy of Mayence, where
R. Gershom himself had taught and where prominent pupils of his
carried on the work of that great master. R. Jacob ben Yakar, who
died in 1064, and R. Isaac ben Judah were the heads of the academy
while Rashi attended it, and he refers to the former as his "old
teacher" and his "teacher in Bible and Talmud." Incidentally, among
Mayence tombstones recovered in recent years has been found that of
R. Yakar, the father of R. Jacob, but, like that of Rabbenu Gershom
already mentioned, it lacks the date. The other teacher, R. Isaac ben
Judah, was related to Rashi, as was R. Isaac ha-Levi, the head of the
Worms academy to which he went from Mayence.

We do not know when and at what age Rashi went to these academies, nor how many years he studied at each. From a note in one
of his letters we learn that from Worms he went home—we do not
know whether just for a visit or for a longer period—and later returned
to the academy. He tells us that he had received instruction from his
teacher on a certain point, but that when he came back to Troyes and
studied the subject thoroughly he became convinced that his master
had been wrong; on his return he had an opportunity to point out his

error to him. Even after Rashi's final return to Troyes he probably
intended to go back to his school in Worms; for on another occasion he
expressed the hope that, although he had failed to prove his point by
correspondence, when he saw his master again he would show him
that he was correct. It is from such casual notes that we gather the
few facts about Rashi's biography.

About his family the sources are very scanty, too. He had no son,
but two or three daughters who were married to prominent scholars.
One of them, Jochebed, was married to R. Meir ben Samuel who
attended the Mayence academy together with Rashi. Four sons were
born to them and they all became famous scholars: Isaac, Samuel,
Solomon, and the youngest and the greatest of them, Jacob, called
Rabbenu Tam. All but Solomon, who was forgotten until recent times,
belonged to the outstanding French scholars of the following generation; they were the founders of the great school of Tosafists, who
contributed so much to the interpretation of the Talmud and its practical application to the changed conditions of European life. Rabbenu
Tam, indeed, outshone his grandfather Rashi himself as an authority
on practical decisions.

Another daughter, Miriam, was married to R. Judah bar Nathan,
a famous commentator on the Talmud, whose commentary on the last
pages of the treatise Makkot is included in all editions. Large parts
of his commentary on Ketubot, which were heretofore considered as
belonging to a first version of Rashi's own commentary, were shown a
few years ago by Professor J. N. Epstein of the Hebrew University to
be the work of Rashi's son-in-law, R. Judah bar Nathan; they were
collected together with some remnants of his commentary on Nedarim.
This couple also had a learned son, Yom-Tob, and a daughter.

Whether Rashi had a third daughter, Rachel, is rather doubtful.
R. Tam, in a responsum to his cousin, the Yom-Tob just mentioned,
speaks of the divorce of their aunt Rachel, called Belle-Assez, from
Eliezer, called Joseline. But is is possible, as several scholars assert, that
dodah here does not mean aunt, but cousin, relative. Accordingly,
the information given by Italian authorities of the sixteenth century
that Rashi had three daughters cannot be verified, and the matter will
have to be left in doubt unless new sources of information come to
light. Incidentally, we learn from this case that among the French
scholars it was quite common for a person to have a French name
besides the Hebrew one.

When Rashi returned to Troyes he opened a talmudic academy
of his own, and many students flocked to the teacher who evidently

very quickly succeeded in gaining recognition and fame. Although he was the rabbi of Troyes, he did not receive a salary but earned his living from his vineyard which, as mentioned before, he cultivated with the help of his family.

Turning now to the literary activity of Rashi, we come to his commentaries on the Bible and, in the first place, to that on the Pentateuch. No other Bible commentary ever had greater success and influence. It is noteworthy that it is the first edition of Rashi on the Pentateuch which bears the earliest date for a Hebrew book printed in Italy, namely February 1475, though the printing of a larger work had probably started a little earlier. A year later, in 1476, printing in Spain, too, began with an edition of this commentary. And still a third edition preceded the text of the Hebrew Pentateuch itself, which appeared in print for the first time in 1482—accompanied by Rashi. . . .

Its popularity was richly deserved. It is a masterpiece in every respect. Rashi's aim was to offer a literal interpretation of the text. Up to his time homiletical interpretation based on the Midrashim—works that originated from the first or second to about the tenth century, mostly in Palestine—had predominated among the Jews. These books, containing the comments of the great authorities of Mishna and Talmud, include many a simple explanation, but these are almost lost in the mass of homiletical interpretations. A desire for a proper understanding of the Bible made itself felt in France at that time, and Rashi had at least one predecessor there. But it is his great merit to have succeeded in combining the two methods in masterly fashion and, with unerring instinct, to have selected such explanations from the rich storehouse of midrashic literature as fitted the biblical text best, without forcing its sense. He was aware of the homiletical character of these works, and at times expressly stated that there are many haggadic interpretations which the rabbis collected in various Midrashim; but it was his purpose to give *peshat,* the literal explanation of the Bible, and to combine it with "the haggadah which explains the words of the Bible." He emphasized that many of the midrashic interpretations actually offer an exact understanding of the biblical word. But he fully realized the fundamental difference between literal and homiletical exegesis, and not infrequently rejected interpretations which did violence to the text.

This happy blending of the two methods was responsible for the unique success of Rashi's efforts. His pupils and successors in the schools of northern France carried the desire for literalness much farther than the great master and even criticized his method. Perhaps the best of them, Rashi's grandson, R. Samuel ben Meir, called Rashbam, related in his commentary to the Pentateuch that Rashi had intended to revise his own work and adapt it to the new literal interpretations which were turning up every day. Rashbam's own commentary was a high achievement in this field and has found generous appreciation in modern times. It certainly was considered an advance over Rashi in his time, but it is dry and lacks the warmth so characteristic of Rashi's work. It is sufficient to record that his commentary had to wait for publication till 1705, when innumerable editions of Rashi had appeared and a whole literature had been written about it. . .

Rashi's commentary is thorough and deals with the narrative portions in the same way as with the legal ones, including even minute descriptions of the Tabernacle and its vessels. Here his practical sense and his observations of daily life, to which I have referred above, proved most helpful. He sometimes even added drawings to his explanations of Bible and Talmud; which, however, have been omitted by copists and printers, and only the indication "like this," followed by a blank space, has remained in our texts.

Grammatical studies had made great progress, by the time Rashi began his literary activity, through the efforts of the great Spanish scholars; but their works, written in Arabic, were inaccessible to Western Jewry. Rashi only knew the first groping steps in this field, the Hebrew dictionary of Menahem and its criticism by Dunash. He quoted these frequently, but his fine sense and intuition led him in many instances to avoid their mistakes so that, compared with these early Spaniards, Rashi's linguistic explanations, to which he gave considerable space, represented real progress. A grammarian like Abraham de Balmes (1523) rated these grammatical notes in Rashi's commentaries very highly and stated that Rashi revealed the true nature of the Hebrew language. His occasional remarks on the shades of meaning of various synonyms are still of real value. Many a Jewish scholar in former centuries owed his grammatical training to his study of Rashi.

A characteristic of Rashi in all his commentaries is his use of the vernacular for the interpretation of difficult words. It has been noted that about 3,000 French words occur in his works. These words are of the highest value for the study of old French, for they belong to the very oldest remnants of that language.

Rashi generally followed the *Masorah* in the interpretation of the Bible, and only rarely did he deviate from the accents of the text. He treated the *Targum,* the official Aramaic translation of the Pentateuch

and the Prophets, with the greatest respect, constantly referring to
them, for he considered them of the highest importance for exegesis.
He was not so much concerned with the anthropomorphisms which
the *Targumim* are at great pains to avoid; apparently such locutions
offered no serious problem to the people of his time. He occasionally
referred to them, however, and once he stated that it was the method
of the Bible to speak of Divinity in human terms in order to facilitate
understanding. He paid as much attention to the interpretation of the
single word as to the context, subject matter and order of the verses.

Rashi's commentary on the Pentateuch is a truly popular work. It
offers instruction to the scholar and to the layman; even children can
easily follow its simple language. It earned him the honorary title
Parshandata, "the interpreter of the Torah." His language is quite remarkable; clear and simple, it avoids all unnecessary phrases, always
uses the right word and displays great felicity in explaining one Hebrew
word by another.

The Rashi commentary on the other parts of the Bible is not as
popular as that on the Pentateuch; the midrashic interpretations do not
occupy quite so prominent a place and more emphasis is laid on pure
literalness. Otherwise it has the same characteristics. We find here
occasional polemics against Christian interpretations, with which Rashi
evidently was familiar.

There was a flourishing Christian school in Troyes in Rashi's days.
As his relations to his Christian neighbors seem to have been friendly—
to judge from various expressions in his works which suggest great
tolerance towards Christians—he may have heard such interpretations
from the clergymen of Troyes, who probably cultivated the allegorical
interpretation of the Bible so prevalent at that time.

We find in the later books a few references to suffering and persecution of the Jews; and we may be justified in assuming that these
passages, like some of the *Selihot* he composed, were written after the
first crusade which cast a gloom over the last decade of Rashi's life.
But of that we shall have to say more later on.

Theological ideas rarely occupied Rashi, but a well-known saying
in his commentary on Psalms (49.11) may be mentioned: The term
mitah, death, is there employed in reference to scholars, for only their
bodies die in this world; for the foolish and ignorant, however, the
Psalmist uses the term *abedah,* perishing, indicating that both their
bodies and their souls perish.

Rashi always began with the interpretation of the text, without any
preliminary remarks; in two instances only did he write short prefaces—

to the Song of Songs and to the Book of Zechariah. In the former he points out that a biblical text has more than one meaning, but ultimately always retains its plain sense; and although the prophets speak in allegories, we have to explain them properly according to context and order of verses. This he proposes to do for the Song of Songs, though with constant references to the midrashim. He then goes on to speak of the reason why King Solomon composed the book in the prophetic spirit. In the case of Zechariah, the difficulty of the prophecy causes him to remark: "The prophecy of Zechariah is very mysterious, for it contains visions which, like dreams, require interpretation; but we cannot understand their real meaning until the teacher of truth (the Messiah) comes. I shall try to expound every verse in accordance with fitting interpretations and the explanation of the *Targum.*" In the course of the commentary he says (11.13): "I have seen many interpretations of this prophecy which I cannot understand." In all his commentaries, Rashi, with his customary modesty and love of truth, never hesitates to admit that he does not know the solution to a problem or does not understand a certain passage.

He is also ready to admit an error without any effort to defend his original interpretation. Thus he states on one occasion that he has reconsidered his explanation of a passage in Ezekiel and now, having gone over the book once more with one of his pupils, Shemayah, and found that he had contradicted himself, offers a more acceptable interpretation. This pupil, Shemayah, who, like one of his grandsons and several other persons in his entourage, occasionally served Rashi as secretary, inserted quite a number of explanations into his master's works, even during Rashi's lifetime. Of another pupil—the excellent exegete Joseph Kara—Berliner collected over eighty such additions to the commentary on the Pentateuch; in some instances Kara states expressly that they met with the approval of the master. . . .

Rashi occasionally quotes his sources by name; more often he refers to them in general terms: "I have found," "some say," "some explain," or similar expressions. Frequently we read that he "heard" or, more definitely, that he "heard [or received a tradition] from his teachers." As against such explanations by others, he expressly states in some instances: "I have not heard or found," or, more definitely: "I say," "I explain," "it seems to me," etc., thus emphasizing his originality on the points at issue. . . .

But it is not only his new suggestions which make Rashi's work on the Bible of outstanding importance; his judicious selection from the works of his predecessors and his restatement of their opinions in his own classical diction are deserving of just as much recognition.

Such recognition Rashi's biblical commentary found from the very beginning, not only among his co-religionists, but also among Christian scholars. One of the most famous Christian exegetes, Nicolas de Lyra, a French Franciscan of the first half of the fourteenth century, quoted Rashi constantly, and this commentary was one of the main sources used by Luther in his translation. The collaborators in the King James version of the Bible also made ample use of Rashi.

If the commentary on the Pentateuch is the book that made Rashi famous among wide circles, that on the Talmud is of no lesser importance. So far as we know, only two or three parts of the Talmud were ever printed without this indispensable work.

The widespread influence of the Talmud commentary may likewise be illustrated by the fact that the Seminary Library has forty-four editions of the complete Talmud and some two hundred and fifty individual treatises, and all but one of them are accompanied by Rashi. Even when an enterprising publisher decided, half a century ago, to print a one-volume edition of the Talmud, in small type, he did not dare omit Rashi. The few Spanish and Portuguese incunabula, with one exception, also added the commentary of the French scholar, though they did not print the *Tosafot* by Rashi's pupils which appear in all the Italian, German and Polish editions.

We do not know whether Rashi had already conceived the plan of the commentary on the Talmud when he went to the Rhenish academies; but undoubtedly the commentaries of the Mayence scholars and the direct instruction received from his teachers there were of a very material help to him. It has been shown that he generally follows the interpretation of the teacher under whom he had studied the part of the Talmud in question, adding divergent explanations he had received from one or another teacher, or found in earlier works, with the introduction: "some explain," or "another interpretation." Often he states that either the first or the last interpretation is preferable.

He collected, during his years of study, all the material available in the academies, that is, the Mayence and Worms *Kuntresim* which may be compared to notebooks of Talmud students recording the instruction of their masters. Only thus can we understand why some serious errors have been discovered in these early works. Whatever geonic interpretations were accessible in the Rhenish schools were carefully copied. At the same time, Rashi looked for all available material for the text of the Talmud, which in the course of transmission had suffered corruption and unauthorized additions before it had reached the academies of Western Europe. Scholars had made free with the text and had corrected and interpolated it. R. Gershom, therefore, had with his own hand prepared a careful copy of this fundamental work and had issued a prohibition against any change or correction. Rashi naturally used this autograph, which probably was considered normative in the schools. He, however, was not satisfied with this work, but collated all the other manuscripts he could procure. His numberless notes on the text in his commentary, which he introduces with the words "we should read thus," are undoubtedly based on the authority of some manuscript or perhaps on a parallel in one of the *Baraita* collections. It is unlikely that he often resorted to mere conjecture to emend this book for which he had such great respect, as in his modesty he hardly would have trusted his own judgment without some such authority.

His pupils, on the other hand, permitted themselves great freedom in the matter of emendation. Rashi's grandson, R. Tam, complained bitterly about the rashness of his elder brother, R. Samuel, whom he otherwise greatly respected, in changing the readings of the Talmud. He says that, unlike his grandfather, R. Samuel changed the texts themselves, whereas Rashi had merely noted his corrections in his commentary without touching the text.

We cannot tell whether Rashi merely collected material for his work at Mayence and Worms or actually started there on his great task. Nor do we know in what order he commented on the various treatises. In two of them his commentary stops in the middle in our editions and manuscripts—Baba Batra 29b and Makkot 19b. In that on Makkot, *tahor,* "pure," is one of the last words, and we read: "Our master with his pure body, whose soul expired in purity, did not comment any further; here begins the commentary of his pupil and son-in-law R. Judah bar Nathan." But Berliner found in one manuscript merely "Up to this point is the commentary of the master, from here on we read the words of the pupil"; and explanations of his on later passages of these treatises are quoted in comments of the French school. The commentary on five treatises printed under Rashi's name has been the subject of much discussion, and their authenticity has been doubted with good reason. It is not impossible, as Lipschütz, the latest comprehensive biographer of Rashi, suggests, that we have here an early, unrevised version of Rashi's commentaries, which therefore do not show all the characteristics and the excellence of the rest of the work. This question deserves further study.

Rashi worked constantly on the revision of his commentaries. We have a curious description of his autograph by a German scholar, written a century after his death. He relates how Rashi crossed out words, wrote and corrected between the lines and made additions on the margin. There are a few such references to Rashi's holographs with author's corrections, but unfortunately not a line from his own hand has been preserved. . . .

Rashi's commentary on the Talmud is extremely brief and to the point. Often he answers a question that might occur to a student by the insertion of a single word. The Tosafists, who carried on his work, at times did not realize this and added discussions which more careful attention to the wording of his comments would have made unnecessary. One of the greatest German Talmudists of the last century, R. Jacob Ettlinger, occasionally calls attention to such cases. Rashi is interested in establishing the general methodological rules which the Talmud follows; he is careful about the chronological succession of the generations of tannaim and amoraim and tries to interpret points of archaeology. His attention is generally directed towards the details. He always finds the points which require elucidation and expounds them briefly; what is easily understood he passes over. He never tries to show either his vast knowledge or his acumen; he keeps his personality entirely in the background and considers nothing but the text and the need of the student.

There is a great and basic difference between Rashi and all his predecessors. They all tried to facilitate the understanding of the Talmud by giving a brief outline of the talmudic discussions while adding relatively few explanations of details. Rashi, on the other hand, refrained from doing so. He left it to the student to find the context and the logical development of the discussion, of which, however, he never lost sight and to which he occasionally pointed with a brief remark. His main aim was to give the necessary help without ever distracting the reader from the text for any length of time. He thus created an indispensable and incomparable tool for the study of the Talmud, which became the basis for practically all work in this field. The simplicity and lucidity of his interpretations—a rare gift which he possessed to an unusual degree—made his work as valuable to the scholar as to the beginner. It has been justly asserted that his commentary restored the Talmud to us, that without his masterly interpretation it would have remained a closed book to the majority of students, that it was his commentary alone which made possible the great development of tal-mudic knowledge by the northern French scholars. It is the work of a genius and a master craftsman who, penetrating into the very struc-ture of the Talmud, enables us to see its growth and evolution. It is only thanks to Rashi's commentary that the proper study of the Talmud did not gradually cease, as Maimonides had feared. Maimonides tried to save the subject matter from oblivion by a marvelous digest, since he saw no real hope for the revival of its study. Rashi, however, forged a key to the treasure-house of the Talmud which enabled an easy entrance into it and thus made it again the cornerstone of Jewish learning and culture.

The commentary on the Talmud is gigantic in size, and there is still a possibility that parts of it may have perished. Who can tell what wealth of ancient and medieval literature was lost to us when twenty-four carloads of Jewish books were consigned to the flames in the market place of Paris around the year 1240?

Rashi's commentary is a phenomenal piece of work, which hardly has its equal in any other literature. It has become almost an institu-tion. We cannot imagine the study of the Talmud without this indis-pensable guide. All of us, like countless generations before us, have been introduced to it by his help; and, although modern scholarship may occasionally interpret the Talmud more scientifically, it recognizes its indebtedness to the genius of Rashi and still stands on his shoulders.

A little over a century after Rashi's death, a member of the later Babylonian schools, Daniel ha-Babli of Damascus, referred to Rashi as the "greatest commentator who enlightened the eyes of the people in exile." The members of the Babylonian schools considered themselves the true successors of the geonim and looked with disdain on the results of Western scholarship; they refused to recognize the great Code of Maimonides and bitterly attacked it. The praise of a critic from this circle is therefore a rare recognition of Rashi's outstanding merit.

It is a curious phenomenon that in the eleventh century, after the close of the geonic period and the decline of the Babylonian schools, there arose three contemporaries who summed up the work of the five centuries after the conclusion of the Talmud: Rashi, by his commen-tary; R. Nathan of Rome, by his talmudic dictionary; and R. Isaac Alfasi, of Lucena, Spain, by his great code. Of the three, all of whom died within a space of four years at the beginning of the twelfth cen-tury, Rashi was the greatest genius.

There is only one side of talmudic study to which Rashi, again in contradistinction to his predecessors, paid little attention in his commentary—the practical application of the talmudic discussions to legal decisions. In his capacity of rabbi, however, he was naturally deeply concerned with questions of Jewish law. Some brief legal summaries of his are incorporated in the legal compilations composed by his pupils which go under his name and which have mostly been published only during the last century. These books also give us information about Rashi's opinions and decisions on numerous legal questions. They include a large number of his responsa, some of which have been found separately in manuscripts and were also published during the last century. An edition of the about two hundred and sixty responsa of Rashi has been published by Dr. Israel Elfenbein. Through these letters, which contain more personal references than all the other, greater writings of our sage, we get a clearer perspective of the beauty of his character and personality. He corresponded with his teachers, his colleagues and his pupils. To all of them he wrote with the same modesty and loving interest. It would be tempting to discuss these utterances of Rashi in greater detail, but space permits the mention of only a very few characteristic points. They show Rashi's independence of judgment; he does not follow his teachers when his own study of the sources leads him to different decisions. They give evidence of his love of peace and of his great tolerance, which finds expression especially in his dealings with the victims of the first crusade. Though French communities had suffered very little, the crusade had caused the destruction of the ancient Jewish communities of the Rhine, so dear to Rashi since his student days. Many Jews had embraced Christianity to save their lives, and most of these returned to their ancestral religion as soon as circumstances permitted. Rashi insisted that these unfortunate persons should be treated with the utmost consideration, since they had not given up Judaism of their free will but only to save their lives and in many instances had been baptized by force and under direct compulsion. He permitted men of priestly descent to function in their communities as before, declared a marriage entered into during the period of conversion valid and strictly forbade reminding these unfortunate victims of their lapses. He was guided in this by Rabbenu Gershom, whose attitude we know through a responsum of Rashi.

Time and again we are struck by the ideal relationship between master and pupils. His teachers address Rashi with love and admiration as an "honored and great scholar"; they show their deep concern over his well-being and inquire after him from every foreign visitor.

"The generation to which such a man belongs is not orphaned," one of them writes to him; another asks him to pray for him. Rashi shows the same loving concern for his own pupils, whom he addresses as: "my brother," "my beloved."

I may quote one of his most characteristic utterances: "It is not my custom," he writes, "to consider myself chief judge and to pass final decisions; far be it from me to consider myself a prominent court of law (to decide for other communities). If I were in your midst, I would vote with you to permit this matter; but who am I to take for myself authority elsewhere, a little man like myself whose importance is slight, an orphan of orphans."

Let us in conclusion compare his modest self-appraisal with the remark of a competent judge, one of the great German scholars of the following generation, R. Eliezer ben Nathan of Mayence. Speaking of a responsum of Rashi, he says: "His water we drink, and from his mouth we live . . . We must try to understand the perfect teaching of R. Solomon, who searched and explored the Torah and, so to speak, provided it with handles . . . The words of that Gaon are straightforward for the learned, correct for those who know the law; his lips guarded understanding and the interpretation of the law was asked and requested and renewed from his mouth; true learning was in his mouth, in peace and in righteousness he walked, established for the world one of its three pillars (the truth) and enlarged and glorified the Torah."

Few facts, as we have seen, are known about Rashi's life, but as he somewhere remarks: "The true biography of a man is the record of his deeds."

THE MASTER

If Rashi spoke to the masses, Elijah of Vilna addressed the elite. His exegetical achievements are so sophisticated and difficult to fathom, his mind so full of high abstraction, his mastery of the profound issues of the law so complete, that only a few of the best Talmudists follow him to the depth of his thought. Their reward is rich indeed. Yet if Rashi stands at the beginning of the democratization of Talmudic learning, Elijah Gaon stands at the height, for his name, no less than Rashi's, is a household word in the rabbinic world.

His prodigies of learning, his mastery of Talmudic law and lore as well as mystical literature, carried him to the far reaches of the rabbinic tradition. Yet he was for the most part a hermit until the age of forty, and even after that time remained an essentially private person. He held no position of power in Lithuanian Jewry; his learning was his power, and his prestige was enormous: he could make a great many things happen. He was a reformer of synagogue worship and of Talmudic study alike. His stress on gaining the widest range of pertinent learning for the interpretation of the literature stood against the ignorant obscurantism, accompanied by mumbling erudition, characteristic of lesser minds. He truly wanted to know the meaning of the text, truly believed it important to use the mind, not merely to go through ritual processes accompanying essentially rote learning, characteristic of others before and after his day. He therefore took a close interest in texts not ordinarily studied before his time—the Palestinian Talmud, the compilations of exegeses attributed to second-century authorities called Tannaitic Midrashim, and the Tosefta. Moreover, he showed through the greatness of his intellectual achievement that mere *pilpul,* that endless spinning out of unbridled dialectics, was of severely limited value. One need not make the Talmud into a precious sport for obscurantists, when so much was to be found there.

Ginzberg, himself a great Talmudic master, explains the achievement of the Gaon. The *pilpul* which the Gaon opposed ignored the text of the Talmud: "Like a wax nose, the interpreter could shape and twist it as he pleased." The Gaon created a new mode of Talmudic learning and through the prestige and power of his learning, established its predominance. He stressed reason, not authority, and so reopened the long-closed Talmudic conversations and discussions, gaining entry through the power of his clear logic and establishing his presence through the force of his criticism. His was an amazingly independent sort of criticism. First, he sought an accurate picture of the actual words of the text. Second, he was willing to allow his own reason to guide him to a view of what the text, by every canon of logic and reason, ought to say.

What is surprising in the achievement of the Gaon is that, after so many, many centuries of learning, the rabbinic tradition had not exhausted itself or entered a state of irrevocable decadence, but produced so fresh and original a mind. That fact strongly suggests that within the pages of the Talmud lies a power, a regenerative force, reproduced from one generation to the next through the puissance of reason and the power of logic. So long as the new generations would produce men of intelligence and learning, the Talmud would renew itself.

8.

THE GAON, RABBI ELIJAH OF VILNA

Louis Ginzberg

[From *Students, Scholars and Saints,* by Louis Ginzberg. Philadelphia, 1928: The Jewish Publication Society of America, pp. 125-144.]

R. Elijah Vilna, called the Gaon par excellence, came of a family celebrated for the learning and piety of its members. Students of heredity might find it highly interesting to study the stock from which the Gaon sprang and to ascertain what it contributed to the extraordinary qualities of his soul and intellect. I shall refer to but one of his ancestors, Rabbi Moses ben David Ashkenazi, around whom arose a large cycle of legends which are current among Lithuanian Jews to this very day and were told to the young Elijah as he in turn told them to his children.

Rabbi Moses was a small shopkeeper, and when appointed Chief Rabbi of Vilna about 1670, he refused to accept any remuneration from the community, being satisfied to eke out a living from his shop, and hence he became known as Rabbi Moses Kraemer, that is, Rabbi Moses, the shopkeeper. The members of the community thought that the least they could do for their beloved Rabbi was to patronize his shop. However, when he noticed an unexpected increase in business, he insisted that his wife, who of course was managing the shop, should keep a careful record of the profits and as soon as she had enough for her weekly expenses, should close the shop for the rest of the week. "It would be," he said, "unfair competition on my part to take advantage of my being a Rabbi." That such a poor business man should have been called "Kraemer" (merchant), is not without a touch of humor.

Rabbi Moses Kraemer was, according to the testimony of his contemporaries, one of the greatest Talmudists of his time. Nothing, however, is known of his literary activity. Characteristic of the man

119

is the witty remark made by him in reply to those who criticized him because he attempted to change an old established custom. He said: The words of Scripture *al tifnu el ha-obot* are usually translated, "Seek not after the wizards," but they might also be rendered, "Seek not after the ancestors"—a play on the words *abot* "ancestors" and *obot* "wizards." Scripture thus teaches us that one must use his own judgment as to what is right or wrong and not exclusively depend upon custom established by ancestors. This remark reminds one of his great descendant, the Gaon, whose principle was, use your own eyes and not the spectacles of others. R. Moses Kraemer's son, R. Elijah, was one of the leaders of the Vilna community distinguished for his learning and piety. He was known as R. Elijah "the Saint" at a time when the Jews were still very chary of epithets of this kind. His grandson was R. Solomon, described in a contemporary document as one whose profession is the study of the Torah, and—one is almost inclined to say therefore—living in straitened circumstances. R. Solomon and his wife, Treine, lived in Seltz, a small town near Brest, Lithuania.

On the first day of Passover of the year 5480, that is April 23, 1720, there was born to them a boy, their first child, whom they called Elijah after his great-grandfather, R. Elijah the Saint. The child had an unusually beautiful face, "as beautiful as an angel" are the words of his biographers, and to see him was to worship him. When the child grew older, people marvelled no less at the lad's beautiful soul and his mental gifts than they had done at the infant's angelic beauty. Even if we discount heavily the stories told about the Gaon's youth, there can be no doubt that he was a real prodigy. At the age of six he was advanced enough in his studies of the Bible and the Talmud to dispense with the assistance of a teacher. When six and a half years old he delivered in the great Synagogue of Vilna a learned discourse taught him by his father. Put to the test by the Chief Rabbi of Vilna, the lad showed that he possessed sufficient knowledge and acumen to enable him to deliver such a discourse without the assistance of others.

Lively feeling and clear thinking accompany each other much oftener than is commonly supposed. The combination of mysticism and criticism, of which the Gaon is the best example, was inherent in his nature and discernible no less in the young child than in the ripe man. The tussle of the dialectic athletes attracted the phenomenal mentality of the young child, and his imagination was nourished with the delicious fruits of the Haggadah. The Haggadah of the Talmud led him to the mystic literature, and we have the Gaon's own words to the effect that he had studied and mastered this branch of literature before he was thirteen. Notwithstanding these occasional flights, he remained on solid ground. His main studies centered about the Talmud, and his mathematical genius led him early to recognize the deep truth that to understand a literature dealing with life, one must consider facts and facts only. He studied at a very tender age mathematics, astronomy and anatomy. He even contemplated taking up the study of medicine, but was prevented from doing so by his father, who apprehended that as a physician his son would not be able to give all his time to the study of the Torah, since it is the physician's duty to assist suffering humanity. The study of botany he was forced to abandon because he could not stand the uncouth life of the Lithuanian farmers, from whom he attempted to acquire the knowledge of plants. It was a principle of his that to understand the Torah one must be well versed in secular knowledge, and he tried to live up to it. One may state with certainty that he was in possession of all the knowledge he could derive from Hebrew sources. However, not satisfied with these materials, he encouraged the translation of Euclid into the Hebrew language, and what is still more characteristic of his wide vision, he wished to see the works of Josephus made accessible to Hebrew readers that they might be helped by them in their study of the Talmud.

The sphere of the scholar is circumscribed by the walls of his study, while the realm of the saint is limited to his soul. The outer life of the scholar and saint is briefly told. He married early, in accordance with the rule laid down in the Mishnah, "At eighteen the age is reached for marriage." His wife was Hannah, the daughter of a certain R. Judah from the town of Kaidan, and it is said that for a time the Gaon lived in this town, returning to Vilna at the age of twenty-five. A document of the year 1750 informs us that R. Elijah the Saint was granted a small weekly allowance from the legacy left by his ancestor, R. Moses Rivke's, for the maintenance of those of his descendants who would devote themselves to the study of the Torah.

Though living in complete retirement, his fame spread rapidly. When comparatively a young man, thirty-five years old, he was approached by the greatest Talmudist of the day, R. Jonathan Eybeschuetz, to state his position with regard to the controversy that was then raging among the Jews of Germany and Poland. I have no intention of entering even into a brief account of the controversy between Eybeschuetz and his cantankerous opponent, Emden. The interest of the student of history ought to be in the flower which history puts forth and not in the muck in which it grew. For our purpose it will suffice to quote a part of the Gaon's reply to Eybeschuetz. He writes: "Oh, that I had wings like a dove, then would I fly to restore peace and quench that strange fire, the fire of contention. But who am I that people should listen to me? If the words of the Rabbis, the heads of the holy congregations, are not listened to, who would care about the opinions of a young man hidden in his study?"

A few years later, at the age of forty, the Gaon seems to have partly given up his seclusion, and though refusing up to the end of his life to accept the position of Rabbi, for all practical purposes he became the spiritual head not only of the community of Vilna but also of the entire Lithuanian and Russian Jewry. He changed his mode of life in compliance with the injunction of the old sages that the first forty years of one's life should be devoted exclusively to acquiring knowledge and the years following to imparting it. The first step in his changed attitude towards the public was the establishment of a model synagogue. The changes introduced by him as, for instance, the abolition of a goodly part of the Piyyut and the introduction of congregational singing, were certainly intended to give decorum to the service and intensify the devotion of the worshippers. The synagogue served at the same time as a house of study where a select number of prominent scholars sat at the feet of the Gaon, and though they were a handful only, they succeeded in causing the influence of the master to spread far and near. Especially the community of Vilna, the metropolis of Lithuania, felt such reverence for the Gaon that a word of his sufficed to annul the most solemn resolutions of a powerful board of Parnaism. When, for instance, the Board of Jewish Charities in Vilna in a fit of efficiency decreed that no one should be permitted to solicit contributions, all of which should go directly to a central body, the Gaon maintained that philanthropy must never lose all sense of humanity, which would be the case if all the needy were required to apply in person to the administration of charities. He therefore not only annulled the decision of the Board, but made them put at his disposal a certain sum of money to be distributed by him to those who in his opinion deserved to be spared the humiliation of appearing before the officers of the community.

The incident which more than anything else brought the name of the Gaon before the great masses of Jewry, not only of Lithuania and Russia but also of Poland and other countries, was his bitter fight against Hasidism. That the rush of the flood of this movement stopped at the gates of Vilna and that even in countries like Galicia and Poland the large communities, the seats of Jewish intelligence, were not swept away by this flood, is mainly due to the Gaon. The Gaon issued his decree of excommunication against the Hasidim on the night following the Day of Atonement of the year 1796. On the eve of the next Day of Atonement he became very ill and died a few days later, on the third day of the Feast of Tabernacles, October 17, 1797, at the age of 77 years and six months. The Feast of Joy was turned into days of mourning for the community of Vilna, for they felt that their greatest intellectual and spiritual light had been put out.

To one concerned with the study of Jewish mentality the works of the Gaon will furnish very interesting material. They consist of commentaries on nearly all the books of the Bible; treatises on biblical geography, chronology and archaeology; commentaries on the Mishnah and Talmud of Jerusalem, critical notes and annotations to the Tannaitic Midrashim, the Mekilta, Sifra and Sifre, as well as to the Babylonian Talmud; commentraies and notes on the classical works of the mystic literature like the Sefer Yezirah and the Zohar; treatises on astronomy, trigonometry, algebra; a grammar of the Hebrew language; and, last but not least, his most important work, the commentary on the Shulhan Aruk.

To give an adequate estimate of the Gaon's phenomenal mentality and his lasting contribution to the different branches of Jewish learning would require more than a dozen lectures. Here I shall merely attempt to make clear his claim to originality.

Most of the biographers of the Gaon maintain that his importance consisted in having abolished or, to be accurate, in attempting to abolish the dialectical method of studying the Talmud, i.e., the Pilpul. However, one must not overlook the fact that the Talmud in its main contents is a structure of dialectics. One might as well study calculus without applying the mathematical laws of equation as the Talmud without using dialectics. It is true that Gaon had only words of scorn for those who build the roof before laying the foundations, but the study of the Talmud was not for him any more than it was for his predecessors a matter of a purely archaeological-historical nature, having no bearing upon life. The development of talmudic law in all of its departments but especially in the domain of civil law would have been an impossibility without the application of dialectics, and the Gaon was the last one to decry its importance and justification.

Of course, there are dialectics and dialectics, there is legitimate use and there is pernicious abuse thereof. Many a great Talmudist before the Gaon saw the evil of unbridled dialectics, but none of them recognized its cause, and hence they were unable to remedy it. The originality of the Gaon consists in the fact that he not only diagnosed the disease but also established its cause and found its remedy.

Book infallibility without authoritative interpretation is no better than a mighty sword without a mighty hand to wield it. It hangs on the wall as a glorious memory; it cannot do its work. In the long run the rule-of-thumb infallibility will not serve. If the dogma of book infallibility is to play an efficient and enduring part in history, there must be an authoritative body to translate the book into law. The infallibility of the Bible necessitated during the second commonwealth the authority of the Sanhedrin, whose legitimate heirs were the Patriarchate in Palestine and the Academies in Babylonia. The conception of the Talmud as infallible arose in a time when the Babylonian Geonim possessed a practical monopoly of spiritual prestige. With the extinction of the Gaonate about the middle of the eleventh century, the last authoritative body disappeared from among the Jews. The great danger confronting the spiritual life of the Jews in the Middle Ages lay in the difficulty of continuing Jewish tradition. In other words their problem was how to maintain the authority of the Talmud in the absence of any authoritative interpretation, and the result was the endless multiplicity of authorities. For the views of every competent scholar, especially if they were written down, came to be considered authoritative. Multiplicity of authority, however, is identical with no authority, and hence the rise of the Pilpul, by means of which the differences among the authorities were as far as possible explained away.

Now dialectics is a system whereby the interpreter can first put into a text any given set of ideas and then with a grand air of authority take it out of the text. Under a bold dialectical method the text of the Talmud lay helpless. Like a wax nose, the interpreter could shape and twist it as he pleased. The attempt to maintain the authority of the Talmud by upholding the authority of all its interpreters by means of dialectics could not but lead to exegetical abuse of the worst kind, and in the long run it endangered the very authority which the Pilpul wished to safeguard, the authority of the Talmud. The tacit proviso was that dialectics must be kept within the bounds marked out by authority. But the leopard does not change his spots when he is put into a cage. It is true, behind the commentators and the codifiers stood the Talmud, but it stood behind them and could not be reached save through them.

After these preliminary remarks we may be in a better position to understand the originality of the Gaon, the father of the criticism of the Talmud. The first condition of criticism is the emancipation from tradition, and the Gaon was bold enough to declare that the interpretation of the Talmud must be based on reason and not on authority. Yet the Gaon did not belong to those whose motto was, to quote a witty Frenchman, *Les grands pères ont toujours tort,* or in homely English, "Whatever was good enough for our fathers is not good enough for us." His admiration and reverence for the post-talmudic scholars was boundless, but to use his own words, "No personal regard where truth is involved." Criticism involved, according to him, two elements, religious conscience and reason. If the Talmud is the great treasure of the Synagogue, then it is an act of conscience to bring it forth from behind tradition into direct touch with everybody. Again, if conscience insists upon a first hand knowledge of the Talmud for the man who needs it for his guidance in life, reason insists upon the same thing for the sake of the object to be known. For the scientific mind guarantees to every object, great and small, the right to be seen as it is.

With the shaking off of the yoke of authoritative interpretations, the critical principle was conceived. But it might have taken centuries before it came clearly to the light. Criticism was a lost art for the last centuries of antiquity and the entire Middle Ages, and was rediscovered in comparatively modern times. The genius of the Gaon, however, was so great that he not only conceived the critical principle but also showed the way it should be applied. Living as he did in an isolated world without being in the least influenced by the spirit of the eighteenth century, he nevertheless evolved the essential canons of criticism which it took the best minds of several centuries to attain.

The contribution of the Gaon to external and internal criticism of the Talmud—for obvious reasons I prefer these terms to those commonly used, "lower and higher"—are numerous and of lasting value. He was the first Jewish scholar to see clearly that ancient documents, copied and re-copied as they have been for centuries with very little care and exposed at every fresh transcription to new risk of alteration, were bound to reach us full of inaccuracies. He, therefore, before using a written source, set about to find out whether the text was sound, that is, in as close agreement as possible with the original manuscript of the author, and if the text was found to be corrupt, he undertook to emend it. Many a law, many a view of the later authorities was thus shown by the Gaon to have been based on passages of the Talmud corrupted in transmission, and they collapsed as soon as the true readings were discovered or restored. It would be easy to fill pages with lists of happy emendations by the Gaon. One may say without exaggeration that a great part of the tannaitic literature would have remained words of a "writing that is sealed" if not for the ingenious emendations of the

Gaon. No one down to our day has equalled him in the art of conjectural emendation.

External criticism, however, is only a means to an end, leading to internal criticism which deals with interpretation and examines the accuracy of authors, thus enabling us to gain a profound insight into past ages. The Gaon was no less the founder of internal criticism of the Talmud than of external. Plato, comparing the power of a book with that of a living teacher, declared that the book is helpless at the mercy of the reader. The truth of the statement is best seen in the lot that befell the books of Plato himself. Students have misread them, carrying into them their own wisdom and ignorance, making Plato speak a language widely different from his own. The same may be said of the Talmud. So long as the talmudic scholars studied the Talmud only, they could not help misunderstanding it. The Talmud or, to be accurate, the Babylonian Talmud, is only a part of a very vast literature, and a knowledge of the whole is indispensable for the understanding of the part. The Gaon did not limit his studies to the Babylonian Talmud but extended them over the entire field of cognate literature, to the tannaitic sources that form the basis of this Talmud as well as to the Yerushalmi, its twin brother. Accordingly, the Gaon had historical-critical problems to solve. So long as the old form of Talmud studies reigned, there could be no critical problems connected with the Talmud because the real facts in the case could not force themselves into notice. For the Gaon, however, it became necessary to ask for an explanation of the striking likeness between the Mishnah and the Tosefta or between the Babli and the Yerushalmi and their almost equally striking diversity. Following his healthy instinct for facing facts boldly, he could not but come to the conclusion that as the interpretation of the Talmud must be independent of post-talmudic authorities, so must the interpretation of the pre-talmudic literature be independent of the authority of the Talmud.

The Gaon was described above as the last great theologian of classical Rabbinism. The central thought of his theology is that self-perfection or, to use his own words, the perfection of character is the essence of religion, and that the Torah is the only medium through which this purpose can be achieved. "The Torah," I give his words literally, "is to the soul of man what rain is to the soil; rain makes any seed put into the soil grow, producing nourishing as well as poisonous plants. The Torah also helps him who is striving for self-perfection, while it increases the impurity of heart of those that remain uncultivated." Self-perfection cannot be achieved without hard training, and hence there is a strong current of ásceticism in the Gaon's theology. But it ought to be pointed out that his asceticism is essentially of a different nature from that taught by the predominating religion of the Middle Ages. He does not see in the material world the seat of evil; he does not even teach us to despise the enjoyment of this world. What he maintained is that asceticism is a necessary means to self-perfection. Men's desires must be purified and idealized but not done away with. In the severe struggle between the ideal and the material world it is the Torah and its commandments that give man the weapons which if used properly assure him of victory. I have quoted these few theological remarks of the Gaon because they throw light upon the fundamental principles of rabbinic Judaism. It may be said of the Gaon's theology that the old became new, appropriated and applied by a great original mind.

Torah, of course, means for the Gaon as for any Jewish theologian the written word and the unwritten tradition. The Gaon, however, more than any Jewish theologian before him, strained the claim for the binding power of the Talmud, the depository of the unwritten Torah, to the utmost. So-called historians point to this as a proof of the re-actionary tendency of the Gaon's theology. They fail to see that he set up the authority, almost the infallibility of the Talmud as a bulwark against the authority claimed for many of the post-talmudic codifiers and interpreters. The Gaon's directions to his disciples were, "Do not regard the views of the Shulhan Aruk binding if you think that they are not in agreement with those of the Talmud." In this statement the novel feature is the denial of the authority of the Shulhan Aruk and not the emphasis laid upon the authority of the Talmud, which was never questioned by rabbinic Jews.

The earliest documents in which the Gaon is mentioned, one dating from a time when he was thirty, the other from a time when he was thirty-five, call him Rabbi Elijah the Saint, and to this day his synagogue in Vilna is known as the synagogue of the Saint, the "chosid's klaus." It is true that Gaon strongly protested against the epithet "Saint" being conferred upon him, maintaining that he merely attempted to fulfil the duty incumbent upon every Jew, to live in accordance with the Torah, and that he only should be called "Saint" who does more than is ordinarily expected of man. However, the greatness of the Gaon rests on the wonderful concentration with which he gathered up all the most significant elements in rabbinic Judaism, the inwardness and depth with which he realized the thought of pre-ceding ages, and on the magnetism of his personality which streamed forth from him to others. The last great representative of classical Rabbinism is the most classic type of the man in whom deep inner experiences, energetic thought and absolute faith in authority united in a close and characteristic union. The ideals of rabbinic Judaism thus became realized in him.

There was a certain kind of spiritual chasteness in him which made it impossible for him to draw out his innermost treasures even for his own inspection, still less for the inspection of others. For under inspection the stamp of inwardness is apt to tarnish. We must be silent on our own internal life or it may cease to be internal. Accordingly the Gaon was extremely reticent about his inner experiences, and it is therefore very difficult to get a clear conception of them. Their main feature is that in the study of the Torah and the fulfilment of its commandments he experienced the prophetic fervor, the joy and the inspiration of personal communion with God as well as the high privilege of serving Him. The service of God was everything to him, and he used to say, "Elijah can serve God without any rewards," the joy of serving Him being sufficient reward in itself. Notwithstanding his austerity and asceticism, he never experienced a depressed or sad state of mind. He always was, as we are informed by his biographers, in a joyful mood and in high spirits, though his trials were not few. For several years he and his family had to suffer actual hunger and other privations by reason of the dishonesty of a petty official of the community who kept for himself the weekly allowances granted to the Gaon from a legacy administered by the community. The Gaon preferred to suffer rather than to inform the authorities of the dishonesty of the official, being of the opinion that according to the Torah it was his duty to suffer silently. He argued that putting a man to shame is declared in the Talmud to be equal to bloodshed, and one must not cause bloodshed even to save one's life. He was not at all conscious of the heroic element in his suffering, but believed that he only did his duty and he enjoyed his suffering as a service to God. He often sold all his furniture to assist the poor or gave away his last meal. He did it joyfully, holding that a man's duty is always proportionate to his capacity, and he quoted the Talmud to show that in ethics there must always be progressive taxation.

PART IV

RABBINIC JUDAISM IN THE THEOLOGICAL IDIOM

The theologians before us mastered Talmudic literature, and many of them made important contributions to its study. They would not have been taken seriously in their own day had they stood apart from Talmud-learning, which was the first qualification of any person of eminence. It is quite natural, therefore, that Rabbinic Judaism laid forth the agenda for their philosophical and theological studies, but only in part. The other part derived from the Hellenistic-Islamic philosophical inheritance.

To appreciate the importance to the theologians of that inheritance, we have to regard it as the equivalent, in prestige and common-sensical acceptance, to modern science. If modern Judaism were to claim that the laws of gravity do not apply to the scroll of the Torah, it would be no more absurd to modern ears than the claim that the truths of Aristotle, in particular, or of reason, in general, came into conflict with the equally ineluctable truths of the Torah. In one way or the other, the men before us had to come to grips with the correlation between revealed Torah and reason.

Two main theories emerge. First, Saadia and Maimonides show us how those to whom a conflict between reason and religion was unthinkable managed to think their way through to harmonization. They took as part of their task the demonstration of the compatibility between the one and the other. Saadia, for example, dealt with the nonrational claim of revelation and the rational claim that through reason all truth is to be uncovered. Revelation and reason come to the same propositions, but the former is both more efficient and more impressive for the masses, those who cannot in any case find their way by reason to truth. Maimonides' perfect appropriation of philosophical reason and lucidity is even more impressive, for it permeates all of his work, on the law as well as on philosophical issues. The power of

129

his fine mind made it inevitable that what he attained in philosophy would shape his legal thought, and even more, the way in which he shaped and expressed that thought. The elegance and clarity of his legal thought found appropriate form in the equally elegant and lucid language and form in which he expressed that thought.

Judah Halevi and Nachmanides (Moses b. Nachman), by contrast, squarely faced the issues of philosophy and declared them irrelevant to faith. The truth derives from Scripture. But the truth which they sought concerned issues more pressing than the perfection of the Godhead or the relation of reason to faith. For they had, in their times and in their own lives, to confront the troubled condition of Israel, the Jewish people, and the trying fate of ordinary folk. They had no leisure to wonder about what lies beyond this world, for the world itself pressed too heavily upon their conscience. Both therefore found their way back to the history of Israel and sought to interpret the meaning of the present age in terms of the biblical account of Israel's past and future.

They turned in times of trouble to the holy land and made their way to Jerusalem, hoping to find what they could not discover in the countries of their birth, a serene and peaceful life. But both were to be disappointed. Judah Halevi expressed his thought in the form of a disputation about the faith, in which he represented a Gentile king as seeking to evaluate the claims to truth of the great religions of the day. Yet in that disputation he had the rabbi maintain the most particular and private propositions of faith, about the uniqueness of Israel and the Israelite capacity to apprehend God. This paradox will occupy us again.

None of the philosophers before us was primarily a philosopher. All were men of varied careers and many parts. Maimonides and Saadia were deeply involved in public life. Saadia's engagement in the politics of the Jewish community, far more than his philosophical essays, occupied his best efforts. I have deliberately chosen an account of Saadia's life and politics, in preference to accounts of his thought, to stress the worldliness of the rabbinic philosopher. But Maimonides' tempestuous life and his activities as a physician left him no more leisure for reflection and contemplation than was enjoyed by Saadia. Judah Halevi and Nachmanides, facing the need to defend the despised faith and the people that held it, in like manner cannot be said to have lived the contemplative life. Both expressed their faith in many modes and ways, only one of which was philosophical in form.

It has already been stressed that the theologians were also Talmudists. But at least three of them did more than study Talmud; they also wrote commentaries, or responsa, or codes, or all three. The striking unity of Rabbinic Judaism—its law, philosophy, and, as we shall see later, inner mystical life—is illustrated in the persons of these philosopher-lawyer-community officials. One simply cannot abstract the "philosophical" Maimonides from his legislative and legal-exegetical role, or show how to distinguish the Saadia who wrote on religion and reason from the Saadia who opposed the Karaite heresy, on the one side, and vigorously contested the control of the Jewish community's institutions, on the other. Judah Halevi, the poet, and Nachmanides, the mystic and biblical exegete, cannot be readily separated from their philosophical and theologial persons. Not only their several roles cannot be distinguished. Of greater importance, the single set of values— rabbinic values—which they carried through and expressed in each of their life's tasks, have to be understood as integrated and integrative. The fundamental unity and coherence of Rabbinic Judaism is best perceived in the persons of the protean figures in the philosophical movement.

RABBINIC RATIONALISM

Alongside the pursuit of the classical disciplines of Talmudic learning in essentially the established modes of thinking, rabbinic civilization accomodated and made its own a quite different approach to thought. This is the philosophical way of thinking, an approach to inquiry which seeks generalization and abstraction, well-organized and well-criticized propositions of thought. Rationalism—the search for a reasoned understanding of things—was a quite novel approach in rabbinic thought. Talmudic thinking, while full of logic and reason, is essentially episodic and unsustained, moving rapidly from point to point, rarely systematically facing an essentially separate and even alien corpus of ideas. With the encounter between rabbinic beliefs and Hellenistic modes of thinking, which, for Rabbinic Judaism, took place with the rise of Islamic rationalism, Talmudic thinking was confronted with an intellectual crisis of far-reaching dimensions.

For the issue was not solely or primarily the way in which one would think through a problem. Hellenistic-Islamic rationalism also contained numerous specific propositions about reality and metaphysics, derived from Aristotle and other Greek thinkers, and the rabbinic thinkers not only had to think in a new way, but also faced a quite new agendum. Their task therefore required both thinking in a rational, reasoned way, and thinking about the specific, propositional results of an earlier rationalism. It was, for example, not sufficient to explain the Torah's commandments in accord with the dictates of reason. It also was necessary to draw upon specific ideas which people agreed were reasonable.

Philosophy was important to a learned few, but since these few also were the intellectual leaders of the community, capable of changing the mind of the many, it was important to show the congruence of reason and Torah. For this purpose, the best available means was the reinterpretation of Torah in the light of reason. The Torah, which had accepted within itself so many new ideas and shown its susceptibility to so many different interpretations, exhibited the suppleness and openness required in the new age. Since it was taken for granted that philosophy was true, and since Jews equally believed that the Torah was revealed truth, the accomodation of the one to the other was absolutely necessary.

In that accomodation, rabbinic ideas were critically reexamined. But the primarily reform lay in the imposition of a distinctive, rationalist perspective on all that went before, so that the prophet, for example, came to be regarded as an intellectual paragon, and so that the commandments had to be interpreted in intellectually meaningful ways. Rabbinic anthropomorphism had to be rejected or reinterpreted out of existence. Miracles, which testify to the changefulness, therefore the imperfection, of God's will, had to be "understood" in a new way. God's perfection had to be harmonized with the specific attributes assigned to him, for it was thought less than perfect to exhibit specific affirmative traits, which were thought to imply limitations on God's being. Fore-knowledge and free will had to be shown in harmony. The biblical stories had to be reinterpreted in the light of reason.

What is important in the philosophers we are about to consider is the fact that they took up this considerable intellectual agendum. The Judaism they accomodated to reason was Rabbinic Judaism, the problems they faced were raised solely within that structure, and the answers they posited were entirely directed toward the rabbinic community. Philosophy and theology spoke in a new idiom, but they spoke the enduring language of Rabbinic Judaism. No philosopher was ignorant of the Talmud, as I said, and some of them were great Talmudists indeed. None was indifferent to the Talmudic values and laws, which, for them as for the masses, were held to be sacred and eternal. That is why philosophy and theology were to be brought into relationship to Talmudic and later Rabbinic Judaism and seen as integral in the civilization founded upon the teachings of the Talmudic rabbis.

9.

MEDIEVAL JEWISH THEOLOGY

Mordecai M. Kaplan

[From *The Greater Judaism in the Making,* by Mordecai M. Kaplan, pp. 112-123.]

It is impossible to have a proper understanding of the Jewish tradition as it has come down to us without taking into account the two distinct trends that developed in it during the Middle Ages, namely, rationalism and mysticism. Gershon G. Scholem does not exaggerate in the least when he says: "Undoubtedly both the mystics and the philosophers completely transform the structure of ancient Judaism; both have lost the simple relation to Judaism, that naïvete which speaks to us from the classical documents of Rabbinical literature." Both philosophy and mystic lore were esoteric disciplines. Nevertheless, insofar as they permeated the teachings of many outstanding leaders in Jewish life, they exerted a powerful, even if indirect, influence on their followers. Only in the recent East European Hasidic movement did mystic lore, known as Kabbalah, come to have a direct bearing on the lives of the Jewish masses.

Rationalism invaded Rabbinic thought with R. Saadia's *Emunot ve-Deot* (The Book of Beliefs and Doctrines), in the tenth century. It had its heyday in what is known as the "Golden Era" of the Jews in Spain, during the period between the twelfth and fifteenth centuries. It flourished to a limited extent in Italy during the Renaissance of the sixteenth century and in Holland in the eighteenth century, but was either ignored or referred to only disparagingly by East European Jews before the rise of *Haskalah.*

The Jewish rationalist writings were intended to fortify the loyalty to Judaism of those Jews whose knowledge of the writings of some of the Greek philosophers tended to shake their religious faith. Those writings were based on the assumption that mankind could have arrived at the truth concerning God by way of the intellect as well as by way of revealed tradition. Revelation was a short-cut for what was intellectually a long and difficult pursuit which only a gifted few were capable of undertaking.

As far as the Jews were concerned, the Torah which God had revealed to their ancestors was for them an adequate and unfailing source of salvation. There were, to be sure, many teachings in that Torah which were evidently in conflict with those of reason, as expounded by the great philosophers. Theologians, like Saadia and Maimonides, regarded such conflict as only apparent. They were certain that both Torah and reason originated from the same divine source, and therefore concluded that a proper method of interpreting the teachings of the Torah would eliminate the seeming conflict.

It is certainly far easier to bring the teachings of the Torah into harmony with the conclusions of reason than vice-versa. Only a bold thinker like Isaac Albalag (second half of the thirteenth century) ventured to suggested that Torah and philosophy belonged to different universes of thought. In any event, the recognition of philosophy as a possible source of salvational truth gave validity to the ideas or beliefs which certain great thinkers had arrived at as a result of rational reflection. Such validity, however, was likely to weaken the Jews' sense of complete dependence upon the Torah and their adherence to its precepts. The theologians, it is true, did all in their power to reinterpret the statements in the Torah that were in conflict with reason. Maimonides went even further in catering to the demands of reason; he tried to justify the ritual laws in the Torah on rational grounds, by stressing their practical value. But the more plausible became the attempts of Jewish theologians at harmonizing tradition with reason, the greater grew the prestige of reason at the expense of tradition.

Men render unswerving loyalty to tradition so long as they lack confidence in the ability of the human mind to help them find the true way of life. As soon, however, as they begin to rely on their own thinking, they are inclined to challenge the tradition in which they have been brought up, especially when it is the tradition of a minority group. In the Diaspora, Jews have always been outnumbered in power and influence; hence, they suspected the tendency to defer to reason as likely to undermine loyalty to their tradition. That suspicion inhibited the development of philosophic studies.

That accounts for the at best merely grudging reception accorded by the main body of the Jewish People and its spiritual leaders to philosophical or theological writings. It is true that some of the most important results of the rational approach to the conception of God ultimately found their way into the normative Judaism of pre-modern times. The negation of all human attributes applied to God in sacred scriptures and the deprecation of literal rendering of spiritual concepts became an integral part of the Jewish theology. That was indirectly due to the influence of Philo's writings. Those writings were known only in Christian theological circles, but their influence reached the Jewish theological writings of the Middle Ages. It is interesting to note the difference between Judaism and Christianity, from the standpoint of how they assimilated Greek philosophic thinking. Whereas the synthesis of the early Christian tradition with Aristotelianism, effected by Thomas Aquinas in the thirteenth century, became the official and authoritative doctrine of the Roman Catholic Church, the synthesis of Jewish tradition with Aristotelianism effected by Maimonides never received official sanction, and was for the most part resisted rather than welcomed.

Jews first encountered philosophy in Alexandria. They lived there in considerable numbers during the four centuries between 200 B.C.E. and 200 C.E. Though they retained their Jewish identity and group life, they were completely Hellenized. Their vernacular was Greek. The most intellectually alert among them came into contact with Greek culture, which was then dominant in Alexandria. The Bible and the observance based on the laws in the Torah were all that bound those Jews to Judaism. For the Bible to function in their lives, it not only had to be translated into Greek; its teachings had also to be made compatible with the assumptions concerning God and man which they had acquired from Greek culture. Thus began the process of reinterpretation of traditional values in terms of the dominant world outlook of the Hellenist world, a process which culminated in the writings of Philo.

That process of reinterpretation of the Jewish tradition contributed perhaps more than any other factor to the spread of early Christianity beyond Jewish circles, and to the viability of that tradition in the Gentile world. It also laid the foundation for the synthesis of early Christianity with Greek philosophic thought for mankind. For when the Arabs conquered Syria, the part of the world where this synthesis had been achieved, they took over the entire scientific and philosophic heritage of the Greek and incorporated it into Moslem culture. From there Greek philosophy passed on to the Jews.

The majority of the Jews happened to live then in the Moslem empire. Before long they found themselves so adjusted to the life of their Arab neighbors that they gave up the Aramaic language they had been using for centuries and adopted Arabic as their vernacular. Their cultural and spiritual leaders acquired the philosophic learning which had become part of the Arabic culture. During those centuries (800-1200), the foremost men in Jewry wrote most of their important works in Arabic. But what is more significant is that they had to reconcile once again the teachings of Judaism, as Alexandrian Jews before them had done, with the teachings of Greek philosophy and ethics.

The outstanding thinker whose writings were regarded as authoritative, second only to divinely revealed teachings, was Aristotle. He was referred to as "the philosopher." According to Maimonides, all that Aristotle had taught concerning the sublunar universe was unquestionably true. The four outstanding works in Jewish theology which are a product of the contact with Greek thought through the medium of Arabic culture are Saadia's *Beliefs and Doctrines,* Bahya's *Duties of the Heart,* Halevi's *The Kuzari* and Maimonides' *Guide for the Perplexed.* These four works, written originally in Arabic, were later translated into Hebrew for the Jews who lived in Provence during the thirteenth century.

The awareness of having drawn on non-Jewish sources for his philosophic ideas is clearly indicated in the statement of Maimonides. "You will find that, in the few works composed by the Geonim and the Karaites on the unity of God and such matters as are connected with this doctrine, they followed the lead of the Moslem Mutakalimun. It also happened that at the time when the Moslems adopted this method of Kalam, there arose among them a certain sect called Mutazila." Maimonides himself, though as much influenced by non-Jewish thought as the other Jewish philosophers, speaks rather contemptuously of the tendency among the latter to adopt the first philosophy they came upon.

The purpose of Jewish philosophic thought during the Middle Ages was to effect a *modus vivendi* between two such apparently incompatible approaches to reality as those of Greek philosophy and Rabbinic Judaism. The two outstanding arguments whereby the Medieval Jewish philosophers justified the need for revealed truth, without implying that such truth in any way conflicted with reasoned truth, were the following: In the first place, revelation makes accessible to the multitude, in a form adapted to their understanding, such truth as, in its reasoned form, would be capable of being grasped only by a few intellectuals. Secondly, revelation supplies the knowledge of truths which the most intellectually gifted could arrive at only after arduous study and reflection.

To what extent Rabbinic Judaism underwent metamorphosis when synthesized with Greek philosophy may be seen from the following teachings of Medieval Jewish theology:

1. According to Rabbinic Judaism, salvation (or the fulfillment of human life) can be achieved only through the study of Torah and the practice of the *mitzvot*. According to Medieval Jewish theology, it can be achieved only through contemplation of the truth concerning the nature of reality or of the Divine government of the world; this is what the Jewish theologians understood by study of Torah in its esoteric sense. They accepted Aristotle's view of the moral virtues as being, in the words of Matthew Arnold, only "the porch and access to the intellectual, and with these last is blessedness." At the hands of the Jewish theologians, also the conception of prophetism underwent a radical change. In Rabbinic writings, the prophet is conceived merely as the "messenger of God," or *malak,* whose intellectual powers had nothing to do with his being selected by God to exhort and instruct. In philosophic writings, however, the prophet is viewed as a great thinker whose intellectual powers were so extraordinary as to render him qualified for his prophetic mission.

2. Rabbinic Judaism is not troubled by the anthromorphic conception of God. But Medieval Jewish theology's principal task is the vigorous deprecation of anthropomorphism. It explains away the anthropomorphisms in the Bible as purely metaphorical, on the Rabbinic principle of "the Torah speaks in human idiom." That principle was intended originally to apply only to the legalistic rendering of the Torah text. As such, its purpose was to offset the tendency to derive legal conclusions from what appeared to some *Tannaim* to be verbal redundancies; it had nothing to do with questions of theology.

3. Rabbinic Judaism was not in the least disturbed by the problem which miracles presented from a philosophic point of view. Now, philosophically, miracles imply changes in God's will in accordance with circumstances occasioned by man. That conception of miracles is incompatible with the assumption that God's will is immutable. Those statements in Rabbinic writings which have a bearing on the miracles of the Bible are not motivated, as is wrongly assumed, by the foregoing consideration. To the Rabbis, the miracles are part of their Israel-centered view of the world, and their comments on miracles have to be understood in that light. For the theologians, however, the philosophic considerations are primary. Maimonides, therefore, treats the miracles as having been built into the structure of the world when God created it. Gersonides, who tries to steer a middle course between tradition

and reason, arrives at a highly sophisticated explanation of miracles which seems to satisfy the demands of neither.

4. Rabbinic Judaism sees no contradiction between the conception of God's infinite power and the many attributes ascribed to Him such as those in Exodus 34:6-7, which imply that He is influenced by factors outside Himself. On the other hand, Jewish theology, finding it necessary to describe God in negative terms, gives a negative meaning to the attributes ascribed to God in the foregoing verses in Exodus, since their affirmative meanings imply limitations on God's being and power.

5. Rabbinic Judaism is unaware of any contradiction between God's foreknowledge and man's free will. The usual interpretation given to R. Akiba's statement in *Abot* III, 19, as implying an awareness of such contradiction is incorrect. The phrase *Hakol teafus* in that statement does not mean "everything is foreseen," but "everything is beheld." Hence what R. Akiba says is not "Everything is foreseen, yet freedom of choice is given," but "Everything is beheld *and* freedom of choice is given." What he wishes to emphasize is not God's foreknowledge but God's *knowledge* of whatever man does or thinks. Jewish theology, on the other hand, never wearied of seeking a solution for the apparent contradiction between God's foreknowledge and man's freedom to choose between obeying and disobeying the will of God.

6. Rabbinic Judaism sees no need for attaching any meaning other than a literal one to biblical stories in which human traits are ascribed to God. Jewish theology either interprets those stories allegorically, or it considers them as visions or dreams. It does not regard them as accounts of objective events. This applies especially to stories like those of Creation, the Garden of Eden, the Tower of Babel, the three divine visitors to Abraham, and Jacob's struggle with the angel. In the case of the theophanies recorded in the Bible, Medieval Jewish theology resorts to the novel concept of *kavod nivra,* a kind of visible being created for the occasion, or an existing light too dazzling for human eye to behold, except after it has passed. The basis for this novel view is the biblical term "the glory of the Lord" and the Rabbinic term "*Shekinah.*"

7. Rabbinic Judaism recognized only one kind of authoritative law, namely, the supernaturally revealed law contained in the Torah. It regarded that law as intended to help the Jew attain his well-being in this world and bliss in the hereafter. Jewish theology, on the other hand, as represented by Joseph Albo in his *Ikkarim,* which is a kind of abbreviated Jewish *Summa Theologica,* accepts the classification formulated by Thomas Aquinas of three kinds of law—namely, natural

law (the medieval equivalent for our term "moral"), positive law (formulated in some human code), and divine, or supernaturally revealed, law. According to this classification, the Torah as supernaturally revealed law is contrasted with moral and humanly formulated law. This classification has given rise to the modern distinction between religious and secular, a distinction which has only helped to confuse thinking and darken counsel.

8. Rabbinic Judaism deprecates the interpretation of the *mitzvot* as having a purpose other than that of affording the opportunity to serve God. It insists on their being observed as divine decrees, or as means of teaching man to obey God's will without any ulterior purpose. Jewish theology, on the other hand, takes it for granted that ritual practices have the additional purpose of improving man's character. Ritual practices which seem devoid of such purpose are regarded as inferior in sanctity or importance.

Rabbinic Judaism has a special category for duties pertaining to interpersonal relations. It assumes, however, that the Torah lays down in each case what is right and what is wrong. Jewish theology introduces an additional ethical norm which emanates from reason. That norm is usually the one suggested by Aristotle's "Golden Mean." According to Maimonides, who makes a point of stressing the "Golden Mean," it is identical with whatever conduct the Torah prescribes. He considers it the principle underlying the Mishnaic treatise of *Abot.*

9. Rabbinic Judaism sees no difficulty in conceiving God as exercising individual providence over the life of every human being. Jewish theology regards such providence as being exercised in accordance with the intellectual development of the individual. If the individual has failed to develop his intellect, divine providence knows him only as a member of the general species "man." To be an object of God's special care, a human being must develop his intellectual powers.

10. Rabbinic Judaism accepts the principle of reward and punishment. Jewish theology finds it necessary to retain the belief in divine retribution, but, in doing so, it draws a sharp distinction between the body and the soul, insofar as they are objects of reward or punishment. The soul is conceived in philosophical terms suggested by Aristotle. According to him, man possesses three souls—the vegetative, the animal and the human. Of these, the human soul, which is synoymous with the intellect, is the only one that survives the body. But its survival consists in being united with what is termed the Active Intellect of the world, third in the order of spiritual beings, of which the first two are God and the Separate Intelligences. Maimonides, Hillel

ben Samuel (1220-1295) of Verona, Italy, in his *Tagmule ha-Nefesh,* and Hasdai Crecas (1340-1410) of Barcelona, Spain, in his *Or Adonai,* explain allegorically the statements in Rabbinic writings concerning *Gan Eden* and *Gehinnom.*

11. Rabbinic Judaism assumes that in the world to come the human body will be so perfected as not to be subject to the hunger, ailments, and deterioration which mark its present life. We seldom meet in Rabbinic writings any attempt to describe in detail the process of bodily resurrection. Otherwise, that belief is accepted as a matter of course. The theologians, on the other hand, find resurrection a troublesome belief. Admitting that it has to be accepted on faith, they recognize that it calls for stretching that faith. Maimonides, however, is the only one who refuses to accept unqualifiedly the traditional idea concerning the resurrection. Though he accepts that part which affirms the reunion of the soul with the original body, or with a new body, at some time after death, he cannot accept the traditional assumption that this reunion is to be eternal. The body, being a compound substance, must ultimately disintegrate and fall away from the soul.

All of the foregoing deviations from Rabbinic Judaism show that Medieval Jewish theology evolved a radically different universe of thought from that of the Rabbinic tradition. Medieval Jewish theology was based on an attempt to reconcile authoritative tradition with the conclusions of reasoned thought. The Jewish theologians themselves were unaware how radically different their own point of view was from that of tradition. This unawareness was due to their lack of historical perspective. One has only to read Maimonides' Introduction to his Commentary on the Mishnah and the one to his Code, for his account of the transmission of the Torah from Moses to his successors, to realize how uncritical of tradition Maimonides was, from the standpoint of objective history.

In contrast with the Jews who lived in Moslem countries, those who lived in Christian countries did not have the opportunity to come in contact with philosophic thought. The reason for this was that the medium of philosophic thought was not any of the vernaculars of the populations in those countries, but Latin, which was the language used by the functionaries of the Church. Those vernaculars were the incipient languages of modern Europe, and were also familiar to the Jews, but they were not used as a means of philosophic discourse or writing. Hence, in Christian Europe, prior to the Renaissance, the Jewish authorities did not encounter the challenge of philosophy. That accounts for their resistance to philosophic studies, as exemplified by the ban against them issued by R. Solomon ben Adret of Barcelona in 1304.

The influence of the early opponents to the study of philosophy went beyond their own original intent. What they combatted was mainly the attempt to deal with the belief in God from a metaphysical standpoint. But more recent imitators have banned all secular studies. "What matters it," said R. Ezekiel Landau (1713-1793) of Jampol, Poland, "that logic is necessary for acquiring the wisdom of the Torah? Since the original purpose of logic was to aid one in acquiring secular knowledge, one should have nothing to do with it." The theological writings of the Jewish thinkers in the Western world fell into neglect and would have been completely forgotten were it not for Maimonides' Code known as *Yad ha-Hazaka* and his Commentary on the *Mishnah*, and the Medieval exegetical and homiletical commentaries on the Bible, which contain philosophic material. Even those commentaries, however, were not always viewed with favor. R. Nachman of Bratzlav (1770-1811) said of *Akedat Yitzhak*, which is a collection of philosophic homilies on the Pentateuch by R. Yitzhak Aramâ, a Spanish rabbi of the fifteenth century, that although it is a *sefer kasher*, it should not be studied because it contains statements by philosophers and the questions they raise.

An incident which illustrates how antagonistic Jews were to the study of philosophy during the sixteenth century is the following: In the course of a response to a question pertaining to *kashrut*, R. Moses Isserles (1520-1572) happened to quote Aristotle's opinion concerning a certain disease to prove that it was not fatal. For this he was roundly denounced by R. Solomon Luria. R. Moses Isserles found it necessary to appease his disputant with profuse apologies for having introduced Aristotle's name into a question of Jewish law. "Although I have quoted some words of Aristotle, I take heaven and earth to witness that I have never in all my days busied myself with any of his books."

R. Joel Sirkes (1561-1640) of Poland, the author of a famous commentary on the *Arbaah Turim* of Jacob ben Asher, characterizes philosophy in the following words: "Philosophy is the essence of heresy and 'the strange woman' against whom King Solomon warned man." R. Solomon Luria (1510-1573) of Lithuania assails Maimonides for having advised his own son to study the writings of Ibn Ezra. Solomon Maimon (1754-1800) was not admitted into Berlin, because the rabbi of the Jewish community of that city refused to vouch for his character. The reason for this refusal was that Maimon had written a commentary on Maimonides' *Guide for the Perplexed*. When the commentary was published, it appeared anonymously. "The Rambam," said R. Elijah, the Gaon of Vilna, to his disciples in a fit of anger, "was allured by the cursed philosophy. Its sophistry misled him into interpreting the *Gemara* as though it were a jest, and tearing away the aggadic passages from their literal meaning." In Russia during the middle of the nineteenth century there were many large Jewish communities where not a single copy of Maimonides' *Guide* was to be found.

It is not necessary to give more than a brief sketch of those philosophic problems and conceptions which, despite the prejudice against philosophy, were kept alive in the various writings that shaped the Jewish consciousness before the end of the eighteenth century.

First and foremost was the problem of explaining the anthropomorphic allusions to God. The creed of Maimonides had found its way into the daily prayer book. So did some of the religious poetry of Ibn Gabriol and of the anonymous author of the "Song of Unity." These reminders of the importance of having the right conception of God helped to keep alive the doctrine that it was sinful to conceive God as having bodily form, or as subject to human emotions. Despite the many naïve-minded authorities in Rabbinic Judaism who voiced their opposition to Maimonides, he did succeed to a large degree in impressing upon the Jews the idea that to think of God as though he were a magnified man was to be a heretic and to forfeit one's salvation. Despite that prohibition, however, the average Jew found it necessary to form some mental image of Deity. Only in intellectual circles was the anthropomorphic conception of God taboo.

Related to the problem of anthropomorphism is that of the numerous passages in the Bible where God is represented as harboring such emotions as pity, anger, delight, or regret, and acting as though he possessed human traits. All these are explained away by means of the principle that "the Torah spoke in human idiom."

Another principle which survived from Medieval Jewish theology was *creatio ex nihilo*. Insistence upon the doctrine that the world was created out of nothing was due mainly to its pragmatic significance. For only on the assumption that God had created the world out of nothing was it possible to understand how He could suspend the routine order of the world from time to time for the sake of Israel. To assume with Aristotle that matter was eternal was to ascribe limited power to God, since the existence of primeval matter necessarily put a limit to what God might want to do. The need for stressing the historicity of the miracles may have been felt because the increasing awareness of a fixed order of nature tended to undermine belief in the religious tradition. Besides reenforcing the belief in the historicity of the miracles recorded in Scriptures, the assumption that God created the world out of nothing was necessary to fortify one's faith in the resurrection of the dead—a miracle, as it was then believed, essential to the future redemption of Israel.

A third principle which survived from the philosophic age in Judaism was that the text of the Torah was intended to convey more than the surface meaning, or *Peshat*. Not even the Rabbinic interpretation, or *Derush*, was regarded as exhaustive of the significance of the text. There was, in addition, the allegorical meaning, or *Remez*, which could be ascertained only after one had developed his intellect and acquired a need for a rational approach to tradition. And finally, there was *Sod*, the mystic or esoteric significance, which was reserved for those who were spiritually qualified. The first two types of interpretation were exoteric, i.e., intended for everybody; the last two were esoteric, i.e., intended only for the intellectual élite.

More important, however, than those specific principles which came down from Medieval Jewish theology to modern times was the basic assumption that the demands of reason must not be disregarded, and that the traditional beliefs and practices have to be interpreted in compliance with those demands.

THE RABBINIC PHILOSOPHER AS STATESMAN

It is ironic that the land in which the Talmud was created, Babylonia, also was the place in which the first great rabbinic philosopher-theologian, Saadia, did his work. Saadia's work was provoked by the challenge of Islamic rationalism. His response was to lay the foundations for rationalism in Rabbinic Judaism. At the outset, we have to keep in mind that Saadia himself was a master of Talmudic literature and law. Not only so, but he was head of a major Talmudic academy, which traced its ancestry back to the school from which the Talmud had gone forth in the first place. His contribution was not limited to philosophical rationalism, moreover, for he founded the science of Hebrew philology, that is, another mode of rational inquiry, this time into the logic and meaning of language. He furthermore wrote a commentary on parts of the Pentateuch, indeed translating it into Arabic for use by the larger part of the community which did not know Hebrew.

A measure of the philosophical interest infusing all he did was the exclusion, from his translation, of anthropomorphic language. He wished to show that everything in Scriptures is clear and open to reason. His major philosophical work, *The Book of Philosophic Doctrines and Religious Beliefs,* centers on the first issue before rabbinic philosophy, the relationship between reason and revelation. If man can achieve truth through rational processes, then what need does he have for revelation? If reason is the road to truth, why did God make use of prophecy? His reply is that reason and revelation supplement one another. Both are valid ways to the truth. Reason is the more difficult of the two, however, and revelation makes it easy to reach what through reason is far less accessible. Further important problems include the unity of God and the immutability of the Torah.

What makes Saadia even more revealing of the central traits of Rabbinic Judaism is his public role. He was not a cloistered thinker, but an active politician in Jewish community affairs, a controversialist and a partisan. This combination of intellectual power with political and social concern is characteristic of rabbinic civilization, which

147

looked for its leaders to men of attainments in Talmudic learning, but expected them to derive from the Talmud and related tradition wisdom for the guidance of the community at large. When in Western Jewry the leadership of Jewry passed out of the hands of men of learning and fall to men of merely political cleverness, on the one hand, or of wealth but no learning and wisdom on the other, the end of Rabbinic Judaism as the normative expression of Judaism in the community's life was at hand.

10.

SAADIA GAON

Alexander Marx

[From *Essays in Jewish Biography,* by Alexander Marx, pp. 3-38.]

The Babylonian Jews were a well organized group, guided in spiritual matters by the geonim. Politically, however, the exilarch, a scion of the royal family of Judah, ruled over them as an autonomous, recognized minority in the caliphate. He represented them at court, where the exilarch held a very high position. The office had flourished throughout the Persian period by appointment of successive Persian rulers, and later, after the Muhammedan conquest of Babylonia, was continued by the caliphs. After designation by the Jewish representatives, the exilarch was inducted into his office with great solemnity by the heads of the two academies.

Relations between the political and the spiritual heads of Jewry were not always pleasant. Our sources inform us of a number of bitter quarrels between the two. Even in the academies, peace and goodwill did not always prevail. Several times the academies were split between contenders for the Gaonate, and two opponents presided simultaneously over factions of the membership of the same school. Most of the Geonim of both academies belonged to the same few leading families which opposed the election of anyone from the outside. Sherira Gaon, the historian of the academies, refers disdainfully to one of his predecessors, Aaron ben Joseph ha-Kohen, i.e., Kalaf ben Sarjado, of whom I shall have to speak later. Sherira states that originally Aaron did not belong to the scholars of the academy, but was the son of a merchant.

During the five centuries of the geonic period, only one of the heads of the academies was not a native Babylonian. Rab Saadia ben Joseph al-Fayyumi,—i.e., from the Egyptian district of Fayyum—had come to Babylonia as a recognized scholar. The mere fact that such a man attained this outstanding position which made him one of the world-leaders of Jewry is sufficient to indicate that we are dealing here with a towering personality, a man of such outstanding qualifications that all notions of local pride, of petty objections, were silenced by his merits. What the particular merits were which brought to him this unique distinction, we shall discuss later.

Saadia was born in 882, between the 27th of June and the 5th of July, and died in the night between Sunday and Monday, May 16, 942, about 2 o'clock in the morning. This information we owe to his two sons who, eleven years after his death, compiled a list of his works in which they also gave the date of his death and a statement that he died some forty days before his sixtieth birthday.

Saadia was a man of strong convictions as well as of a pugnacious nature and was often involved in controversies. Some of the data on his personal life are derived from remarks made by his opponents in bitter attacks on his personality. From such sources we gather that his native place was Dilaz in the Fayyum and that his father followed him to Palestine and died in Jaffa. In order to disparage him, his opponents claimed that his father was a butcher, a barber, and even a muezzin in a mosque! While Saadia claims descent from Shelah, the son of Juda, his enemies maintained that he was descended from converts. Sherira, in the epistle in which he traces the history of the oral tradition, refers to Saadia's father as a scholar, and there is thus good reason to disregard the charges of evil-tongued adversaries.

Saadia was reared in Egypt, where he received his education. There he started his literary activity and gathered a group of pupils around him. We conclude from this that the Muhammedan conquest had greatly improved the condition of the Jews in Egypt, too, and had caused a revival of spiritual activity after the oppression by the Church.

About the teachers who inspired the young genius to devote his great gifts to the furthering of Jewish learning, we know nothing. The Arabic historian Masudi mentions the name of the Tiberias scholar, Abu Kathir Yahya al-Katib, as Saadia's teacher. But Saadia probably came under his influence at a later period, when he had emigrated to Palestine.

We know that at the age of twenty Saadia composed his dictionary, *Agron,* which he later revised, and that at the age of twenty-three he inaugurated his polemical writings with a refutation of the work of Anan, the founder of Karaism.

Again our sources do not permit us to state whether the sectarian movement of the Karaites, which at that time had its center in Palestine, had spread to Egypt. Possibly Saadia had become acquainted with Anan's work and considered it necessary to write against it, although Karaism had not as yet extended its influence to his homeland.

The Egyptian period of Saadia's life is shrouded in darkness. We cannot tell when he left Egypt for Palestine. The only allusion to a definite date is found in a letter to his pupils whom he left in Egypt. In this letter, written in 921 or 922, he says that he had not heard from them for six and a half years and that he was separated for this length of time from his wife and children. Accordingly, it is stated that he left Egypt in 915. But a description is extant of a trip through Palestine and Syria by a young man in his early twenties, which Schechter thought might possibly have been written by Saadia. If that hypothesis is correct, we should have to conclude that Saadia left his home about ten years earlier and perhaps returned again to Egypt. However that may be, we may assume that there was no challenge to his abilities in Egypt, and that he decided to turn to one of the centers of Jewish spiritual life to find for himself a wider sphere of activity. But success was slow in coming.

What his activities were in the various cities of Palestine and Syria that he visited, and how long he stayed there, we cannot tell. As stated above, he probably enjoyed for some time the instruction of a scholar at Tiberias, but the Palestinian academy did not offer an opening to the gifted foreigner. There, as in Babylonia, all the important positions were held by the members of a few families. Undoubtedly, he wrote some books during these years and made a name for himself. Only thus can we understand his being in correspondence with one of the Babylonian geonim, R. Judah, the head of the Pumbedita academy, who died in 917.

A recently discovered responsum of Sherira Gaon mentions the questions which Saadia, while still in Palestine, directed to this Gaon Judah, Sherira's grandfather. One of these questions dealt with a point of the Jewish calendar which was to play a decisive part in Saadia's life.

The announcement of the new moon and the determination of the date of the holidays was an ancient privilege which the Palestinian schools maintained for many centuries. Though it is generally assumed that the calendar was published in the middle of the fourth century by Hillel II, it seems that it was not automatically followed without official announcement by the Palestinian authorities. As late as 835, a Babylonian exilarch expressly stated in a letter that, in the interest of the unity of Israel, he, the geonim, the scholars and the public at large follow the calendar announcement of the Palestinian scholars. About the same time, it seems, the Babylonian schools sent a group of scholars to Palestine to study and discuss the problem of determining the calendar and, probably soon afterwards, they emancipated themselves from the ancient custom of relying on Palestine for the calendrical announcement. Yet less than a century later the Babylonian scholars already claimed that even the oldest among them did not recollect that they had ever waited for Palestinian guidance in this matter. At the time, however, there was no difference between the two countries as to the dates of the holidays.

A new situation arose when an energetic head of the Palestinian schools, Aaron ben Meir, a scholar of high standing, decided to announce a rule which would prevent the postponement for two days of Passover and New Year in the year 921. The Babylonian academies refused to recognize this rule.

Ben Meir hoped to be able to carry this point, and he made careful preparations to do so. He had been having great difficulties with the Karaites. This sect which denied the authority of the Oral Law had grown very powerful in Jerusalem. To gain the support of the central government, Ben Meir traveled to Bagdad and obtained the assistance of Aaron ben Amram, one of the great bankers at the court of the caliph. Through the banker's influence, he succeeded in getting a favorable decree against the Karaites.

The exilarch, David ben Zakkai, probably did not cooperate with him and kept aloof. Ben Meir, however, made contacts with the head of the school of Pumbedita, Rab Mebasser, who had been appointed by the members of his school in 917 after the death of Saadia's above-mentioned correspondent, the Gaon Rab Judah. There had been a bitter quarrel between the previous exilarch, Ukba, a cousin of his successor, and the academies. Ukba had been removed from his position and exiled from the country. Rab Mebasser and the members of the Pumbedita academy were afraid to see his cousin, David ben Zakkai, take his place, and refused him recognition. The exilarch thereupon appointed one of his adherents, Rab Kohen Tsedek, counter-gaon of Pumbedita. But only a smaller group of the scholars recognized the new appointee.

During his stay in Bagdad, Ben Meir made contact with the Gaon Mebasser and his partisans, and on his return promulgated a decree of excommunication against the exilarch and his appointee, Kohen Tsedek.

He was confident that these friends he had made in Bagdad would support him in his calendar scheme, which, he claimed, was not to institute a reform, but to follow ancient tradition. He proceeded to make his announcement and it caused a split in Jewry.

A Christian Syrian chronicler of the eleventh century records that in 921 the Western (Palestinian) Jews started their New Year on Tuesday; those of the East (Babylonians) on Thursday. This statement, first brought to the attention of Jewish scholars by Dr. Cyrus Adler, as well as a remark of a Karaite zealot of the tenth century about a controversy on the calendar in Saadia's time, can be properly understood now on the basis of the documents which were brought to light from the treasures of the *Geniza*.

In the summer of 921, Ben Meir sent circular letters to various countries, stating that in the fall of that year the months of Marheshvan and Kislev would have only 29 days, while according to the Babylonian calculation they would be full months of 30 days. At the annual solemn convocation which took place on Hosh'ana Rabba on Mount Olivet, he ordered his son to make a public announcement to that effect. Thus the struggle between Palestine and Babylonia was started.

Saadia was traveling that summer from Aleppo to Bagdad. He heard rumors of Ben Meir's plans and sent him letters advising him that he was mistaken in his method of fixing the calendar and urging him to desist from his plan. When Saadia arrived in Bagdad, he learned that he had been wrong in his assumption that Ben Meir would accept his reasons and give up his new plan. The exilarch and the heads of the academies thereupon issued letters denouncing Ben Meir's proceedings and insisting that their calculation of the calendar be followed. Neither side was ready to yield, and thus the Passover and the following New Year's Day were observed on different days by the adherents of the contending parties. How far the influence of the two sides extended we cannot tell, but we learn from the above-mentioned Karaite that both sides had adherents in Palestine as well as in Babylonia.

Saadia seems to have become the leader of the Babylonian party immediately upon his arrival. Of a militant nature and powerful personality, his great superiority over the other participants was evidenced at once, and they recognized him as the natural champion of their cause.

It was of the utmost importance to create a united front in Babylonia, and the exilarch was prevailed upon to make peace with the rebellious faction of the Pumbedita academy. While his appointee, Kohen Tsedek, retained his income and title, the exilarch, David ben

Zakkai, now recognized Rab Mebasser, the choice of the members of the academy. The majority of the academy had joined him from the beginning, and their number probably increased in consequence of the exilarch's recognition, only a few adherents remaining faithful to his opponent.

Ben Meir resented the change of mind of his former partisans. He pleaded with them; he voiced bitter recriminations; but to no avail.

Only a small part of the writings of the contending parties has been discovered so far, but we get a general picture of the course of the controversy. The details of the struggle are too technical to be presented in a popular essay. What interests us in particular is the part Saadia played in this fight and the influence it had on his life.

Naturally it was his task to see to it that his old home, Egypt, should side with the Babylonian authorities. Some letters of his to his former pupils in Egypt have been preserved. In two of them he urges these pupils to take steps so that Passover should be observed in Egypt on the right days and that they should not eat leaven on the holidays. The first letter was evidently written towards the end of the year 921 and included a proclamation by the exilarch and the heads of the academies. This is the letter already mentioned, in which he tells them that he has not heard from them directly for six and a half years. In the second letter, written in the beginning of 922, he emphasizes that in Babylonia all the scholars stand together and maintain the same point of view on the calendar question. By that time unity had been restored in the academies.

A third letter of Saadia to Egypt, in Arabic and evidently to the same pupils, is dated Friday, January 3, 922. They had written that Egyptian Jewry had followed Ben Meir's calendar. Saadia implores them to change their attitude and not to cause him further mortification.

The controversy raged for some time and both sides sent appeals to the Jewries in and outside their countries for support. Direct communications between Ben Meir and his opponents seem to have ceased after a while and, as far as we can judge, unity was restored in Israel after two years. Babylonia prevailed over Palestine.

Saadia undoubtedly had the lion's share in this triumph. It brought him at last an adequate position and ended the years of his restless wanderings. For shortly after his arrival in Babylonia, he was rewarded for his energetic stand by an appointment to a high post in one of the academies.

He signs the first letter to his Egyptian pupils, the one written towards the end of 921, "Said ben Josef, Ras al-Kal." Five or six months later, in Tammuz 922, he signs one of the documents on the controversy as "Saadia ben Josef, *Alluf.*" *Alluf*, or *Resh Kalla*, was a title given to the first seven members of the academy after the gaon and the *ab-bet-din*. Which of the two academies honored itself by adding this new member to its staff cannot be determined. Thenceforth Saadia was an outstanding member in a most exclusive group of scholars in one of those ancient schools which were reluctant to admit an outsider into their midst.

After the conclusion of the controversy, Saadia, at the request of the exilarch, recorded the facts for future generations in a book called *Book of Festivals.* Only fragments of this book have been preserved and contribute to the reconstruction of this interesting chapter of Jewish history.

We may assume that in the following years Saadia devoted himself to teaching in the academy and to literary pursuits. We hear that one of the powerful court-bankers, Sahl ben Natira, became his pupil.

Two of Saadia's poetical compositions bear his name in the acrostics, with the title *Alluf* and *Resh Kalla* respectively, and must have been composed in the years following his settlement in Babylonia.

His most comprehensive work against the Karaites was written in 926. Many other works for which we lack such indications undoubtedly came from the pen of the indefatigable scholar during the years he was a *Resh Kalla* at one of the academies.

But Saadia was destined for a much greater distinction. By his valiant and successful fight against Ben Meir, he had placed the exilarch under deep obligation. This brought him, a few years later, the fulfillment of an ambition of which he might hardly have dared to dream.

The Academy of Sura, founded by Rab in the third century, which for centuries had enjoyed considerable privileges over the rival Academy of Pumbedita, had fallen into a very precarious state. Perhaps it was the fact that the Academy of Pumbedita, though retaining its name, had been transferred to Bagdad, the capital of the Caliphate. This may have given it new prestige and attracted the best scholars, even from the rival academy. At any rate, Sura had declined to such an extent that serious consideration was being given to closing the famous seat of learning and merely maintaining its name by appointing a member of the Pumbedita school as titular Gaon of Sura, a gaon *in partibus*. But the man designated for this distinction, an uncle of the later Gaon Sherira, died before the plan was carried out. His sudden death was taken as an omen that this step was wrong. A new gaon, therefore, was to be appointed who should be able to restore the old luster of Sura. The exilarch first turned to one of the scholars of Sura who had been instrumental in terminating the fight between Rab Mebasser of Pumbedita, the leader of the opposition, and the exilarch, David ben Zakkai. But this old scholar, Nissi al-Naharwani, a blind man, did not feel equal to the arduous task and refused the honor.

Thereupon the exilarch asked his advice as to which of two other candidates was preferable. One of these was Tsemah ben Shahin, a descendant of Babylonian scholars. The other was none other than Saadia. Nissi, though recognizing the eminence of Saadia, advised against him, for, although a scholar of outstanding merit, he was difficult to get along with. His great learning and piety would never permit Saadia to take personal considerations into account.

But the exilarch had made up his mind beforehand that Saadia was the only person who could be expected to restore the Sura academy to its ancient glory, and he determined to appoint him. The objection of the wise old scholar, however, made an impression on him and, before appointing Saadia, he exacted a formal promise from him never to oppose him, conspire against him, or join a counter-exilarch. He claimed later that Saadia accepted these conditions and confirmed them by an oath. It is to the credit of David that, in spite of the warning, he made the choice which in his judgment was the only proper one in the interests of the academy.

Saadia must have been deeply gratified with this appointment to the highest and most dignified office to which a Jewish scholar of that time could aspire. To fill the position which Rab, the greatest Babylonian leader, the founder of Jewish learning in that country, had created seven centuries before, must have given him the greatest satisfaction possible. The appointment was probably unexpected, for he applied to it the verse, "And Hezekiah rejoiced, and all the people, because of that which God had prepared for the people; for the thing was done suddenly" (II Chron. 29.36). The passage occurs in one of the two letters announcing his election to his friends in Egypt.

Of the first of these letters only the beginning and the end have been preserved. He asks the Egyptians to turn to him for any support they may need from the Bagdad government. He will present their wishes to the court-bankers, the sons of Netira and of Aaron, who will ask the ruling powers to grant their requests. He is aware of the great responsibility that has been placed upon him. He is anxious to hear from his pupils regularly, for there cannot be a king without a people and there is no honor for scholars without pupils.

In this "letter of good tidings" he promises a second "letter of warning and advice." This one also has been discovered in recent times, although not in the *Geniza*. Here he speaks of the sessions of the academy over which he had presided and of the prayers he directed to the Lord for the remnant of Israel. The letter contains thirty short paragraphs addressing the readers as "Sons of Israel." He urges them to watch and reprove one another, to fulfil every *mitsva* wholeheartedly. He exhorts them to expect the redemption every day. He asks them, possibly in view of the Karaite attacks, to maintain every part of the Oral Law.

For two years Saadia devoted his tremendous energy and his great gifts to the re-establishment of the Sura academy and injected new life into the old school. The relations between the gaon and the exilarch were most friendly. How the head of the rival school of Pumbedita felt about the newcomer who outshone him and restored its old privileges to the Sura Academy, we cannot tell. But we may assume that there were many who envied the outsider, and some who would have preferred the Sura school to decay so as to bring about a merger between the two institutions.

The harmony between Saadia and David ben Zakkai came to an abrupt end in 930 or thereabouts. As Nissi had foreseen, the two strong and unbending personalities were bound to clash sooner or later; and the occasion came more quickly than expected.

Certain decisions by the exilarch in important civil matters required endorsement by the two geonim. By chance, one such decision by David ben Zakkai, with Saadia's endorsement, has been preserved. A similar case caused the clash between the two men. About the year 930, the exilarch was asked to decide on the distribution of an inheritance, estimated to amount to 70,000 gold pieces, of which he, possibly in his official capacity, was to receive ten percent. He rendered his opinion and asked the parties to submit it to the geonim for their approval. Saadia did not agree with some points; however, he did not want to raise any questions and asked the men to submit the document to his older colleague, the Pumbedita gaon, Rab Kohen Tsedek, who signed it without hesitation. When it was returned to him, he tried to avoid a quarrel by saying that one endorsement was sufficient. But the people insisted that he should give the reason for his refusal and, after being repeatedly adjured to reveal his opinion, he finally had to explain his objections. The exilarch naturally was incensed over this action and sent his son to tell Saadia: "Don't be a fool; sign the document." The young man politely urged him to avoid a quarrel. The gaon replied that one must show no respect to a person in matters of law. The young man was repeatedly sent to and fro, and in the end he lost patience and threatened the gaon with physical force. Thereupon Saadia's adherents unceremoniously threw the son of the exilarch out of the house. The exilarch now put the gaon under excommunication and appointed in his place Joseph ben Jacob ibn Satia, a more pliable man, a scholar of no consequence, but a descendant of geonim. Saadia's fighting spirit was now aroused. He was not a man to yield easily to a powerful opponent. He in turn excommunicated the exilarch and appointed the latter's brother, Hasan, or as they called him in Hebrew, Josiah, as a counter-exilarch. Thus began the battle between the two headstrong leaders, the issue of which remained in doubt for several years.

Besides the gaon and the exilarch, a third power had developed in Bagdad during the tenth century—the court-bankers. Two rich and powerful merchants, Joseph ben Phineas and Aaron ben Amram, both from the Persian province Ahwaz, had joined forces and founded a firm which exerted great power and influence at the court of the caliph. Arabic sources, which have been investigated recently by Dr. Walter Fischel, supplement our information and shed much light on that period. The two bankers are mentioned for the first time in 908, when they had business dealings with one of the viziers. In 912 or 913, they were officially appointed court-bankers and for many years they carried on large-scale operations. Their names occur in the records till 924, and we are informed that they retained their position until their deaths. Their clients were mainly high officials and viziers. One of the latter had deposited with one of these bankers not less than 160,000 dinars by the time he was deposed. These were public funds which the vizier had turned over to his own secret account, and the Caliph al-Muktadir compelled the bankers to return the money to the royal treasury. The bankers were employed to transfer money from one place to another by means of letters of credit, thus avoiding the risk of robbery which the transport of large sums to distant places would involve. By this method the taxes from the provinces were transmitted to the capital. Sometimes the bankers had to make large advances to the payrolls of the army, or for other urgent needs. They were reimbursed by income from the taxes. For a period of sixteen years the firm advanced loans of 10,000 dinars on letters of credit for taxes which were not yet due, and they received a monthly interest of 2,500 dirhams. Once they were compelled to make an advance of 150,000 dirhams a month under duress by one of the viziers.

These bankers were deeply interested in the welfare of their co-religionists and seem to have been particularly concerned with the affairs of the academies. It was through their good offices and international connections that the contributions collected abroad, in the various communities of Northern Africa, Spain, and elsewhere, for the sustenance of the Babylonian schools were transferred to Bagdad. In all likelihood, they also transmitted the correspondence between the geonim and these foreign Jewish centers.

We can well imagine that these men, because of their daily contacts with the highest government officials, had greater influence and that their opinions carried more weight than the word of the official head of the Babylonian Jewry, the exilarch, in spite of the august rank of the latter at court.

It was the support of these bankers which had enabled the geonim to succeed in their fight against the previous exilarch, Ukba, and to have him banished from the caliphate. One of these bankers, Aaron ben Amram, had lent his support to Ben Meir and procured for him a favorable decree against the Karaites. He had, at least for some time, supported him in his calendar scheme. Ben Meir in his letters repeatedly refers to this support.

By the time Saadia had been elevated to the gaonate, the two founders of the firm were no longer among the living. But some years before they passed away, they had taken into the firm Natira, the son-in-law of Joseph ben Phineas, the one partner, and the sons of Aaron ben Amram, the second partner. Natira must have passed away before his father-in-law and was succeeded by his two sons who carried on the business with their grandfather. The sons of Natira and the sons of Aaron enjoyed the same influence which had been exerted by their father and grandfather. During the crisis produced by the quarrel between the gaon and the exilarch, they were divided in their sympathies.

The sons of Natira were staunch adherents of Saadia. One of them had been, or still was, his pupil and the proud owner of copies of Saadia's literary works, while their partners favored Saadia's opponents. The daughter of one of the latter was married to a scholarly man, Kalaf ibn Sarjado (in Hebrew—Aaron ben Joseph ha-Kohen). Kalaf was not a member of the old families from which the dignitaries of the academy were commonly chosen, but a newcomer, a member of a rich merchant family whom the Gaon Mebasser had appointed to a high place in his academy, perhaps to gain influential support in his fight

against David ben Zakkai. As a matter of fact, Aaron ben Amram, one
of the court-bankers, had sided with him. Kalaf was a scholar of standing and a man of burning ambition who was intensely jealous of the
foreign scholar who had attained so high a rank. He spent a fortune
to have Saadia deposed and published a very scurrilous pamphlet against
him. An abstract of this pamphlet has been preserved in a work of a
Karaite who gloats over these undignified squabbles among his Rab-
banite opponents.

Because of the division between the partners in the bank, and because they could not afford to work at cross-purposes at court, they
refrained from using their influence. The two opponents thus had to
carry on their fight without political support. An Arabic writer tells us
that the quarrel was once considered by the state council, but, since he
does not mention the result, we may assume that the government also
washed its hands of these internal Jewish affairs.

The documents pertaining to this controversy, which came down
to us, are in a very fragmentary form and do not permit a clear view
of its various stages. We are not even properly informed about the
charges of the two sides. In Kalaf's pasquil Saadia is charged with
having taken bribes in law suits which came before him, and it is likely
that the same charge was raised by the other party against the exilarch.
We are told that Saadia appealed to high officials and bribed them on
a Sabbath, as witnessed by many Jews of Bagdad. In this connection
he also was held responsible for the fact that many Jews suffered corporal punishment on Sabbaths and Holy Days.

In the beginning it seemed as if Saadia would triumph over his
powerful opponent. He published an intensely interesting document, his
"Open Book" (Sefer ha-Galui) which unfortunately has been lost; only
a few fragments of it have been recovered in recent years, but these
are very revealing. Of the seven chapters, the third, according to
Saadia's statement, describes the misfortune which befalls a people
ruled by a despot (like the exilarch); the fourth states that God sends
to every generation a sage whom He inspires and enlightens to lead
the people in the right path. He points to his own providential mission
as leader and defender of the Jewish faith. In the sixth chapter, he
gives an account of his sufferings at the hands of his unjust enemies.
The final section of the book is meant as a warning to his opponents,
since, as he points out, the Bible teaches us that the wicked who oppress
the innocent are severely punished.

This book, written in poetic form, was provided with vowels and
accents, a point for which his opponents attacked him as placing his

work on a par with biblical books. It was by no means merely a polemical pamphlet. The other chapters of the book deal with general subjects, and even those mentioned above contain much more than attacks on the exilarch and his adherents. But Saadia's tone must have been very sharp. He makes bad puns on the names of his leading opponents, calling, e.g., Kalaf, *Keleb met,* the "dead dog." It is evident that, when he published this work, Saadia felt sure of the downfall of his enemies and had faith in his own victory.

His attack called for a rejoinder, and it was Kalaf ben Sarjado who undertook this task in a scandalous document which, to quote D. S. Margoliouth, "in virulence and obscenity exceeds anything of the sort I have ever seen." As I said before, we owe the preservation of these filthy charges against the great gaon to a Karaite opponent of Saadia who did a service to historical research, although that was far removed from his thoughts. It has been suggested that he may have garbled the original text. If he intended to besmirch the memory of the great foe of Karaism, he did not succeed. It is the enemies of Saadia who appear in a most unfavorable light.

Saadia answered again in a new edition of his "Open Book" to which he added an Arabic translation and a lengthy introduction, also in Arabic, wherein he outlines the contents of the entire work.

For a number of years, Babylonian Jewry was split: there were two exilarchs and two geonim of Sura, both of whom had their adherents and both of whom claimed to be the only rightful incumbents of their respective offices. Such a condition had existed before, and it certainly did not help to raise the standard of the exilarchate and gaonate. Nobody could foresee how long this struggle would last and how it would end, when conditions were changed by the murder of the Caliph Al-Muktadir in a rebellion in October 932. His brother, Al-Kahir, succeeded him, but was in turn overthrown by the army which, after a year and a half, placed the son of a former caliph, Al-Radi, on the throne in 934.

It seems that the sons of Natira, Saadia's strongest supporters, lost their influence in the course of these events and returned to Ahwaz. Now there was no reason why their former partners should not use their power in the interest of David ben Zakkai and his devoted adherent, Kalaf, a member of their family. Hasan, the counter-exilarch, was banished to a remote province, and Saadia had to retire and even go into hiding for some time. But he must have retained many prominent and influential men among his adherents, while he lived as a private man in Bagdad, pursuing his literary plans and enriching Jewish literature with many more important works.

His life was not to end in eclipse. Even in the darkest hour, he was not without influence and many people looked up to him as their leader. By a curious trick of fate, it was a litigation which was to bring about his rehabilitation, just as a litigation had been the cause of his removal.

Two men decided to have their dispute arbitrated by judges of their choice: one chose the exilarch, the other chose Saadia. The exilarch was greatly incensed over this. In his formal excommunication of Saadia, David ben Zakkai had declared that anyone who would appear before the deposed gaon in a litigation, would direct a legal question to him, or would recognize him in any other way, should likewise be excommunicated. He therefore saw in this choice by one of the litigants a defiance which he bitterly resented. Accordingly, he had the recalcitrant apprehended by his guards and badly manhandled. This proceeding aroused general resentment in Bagdad, since any man not belonging to the exilarch's jurisdiction had the right to choose whomever he pleased. A group of notables approached the banker Bishr ben Aaron, father-in-law of Kalaf ben Sarjado, and urged him to bring to an end the long struggle for which his son-in-law was largely responsible. Bishr, who evidently had retained his influence at court, was prevailed upon to take the matter up. He invited the leaders of Jewry to his house, summoned the exilarch, and told him plainly that the people were tired of the protracted struggle and that he had to make peace with Saadia.

We may assume that David, on his part, was tired of the drawn-out quarrel which evidently, as he must have realized, did not strengthen his position. We hear, for instance, that his son was once shown scant regard when on a mission from his father to a province under his jurisdiction. Through his influence at court, the exilarch took bitter revenge on these opponents who were, perhaps, partisans of Saadia. Such events must have convinced him that it was in his own interest to end these internecine fights. Thus the request of the notables of Bagdad found a willing ear. Saadia, who was approached next, certainly had been made to feel that it was to his advantage to come to terms with his powerful opponent.

Bishr brought the two men to different rooms of his residence and acted as the go-between to arrange the terms of reconciliation. When an agreement had been reached—it is noteworthy that neither of them was asked to take the first step in approaching the other—they came forward, embraced and made peace with each other. This took place on the Fast of Esther, and Bishr wished to crown his efforts by having both as his guests at the reading of the *Megilla* and at the succeeding Purim festivities. But they refused and decided that one of them should be the guest of the other. In the spirit of Purim, the matter was settled by drawing lots. Saadia, accordingly, was for two days the exilarch's guest, and the old friendly relations between them were fully restored.

As far as Saadia's position was concerned, he was reinstated as gaon of the Sura academy, while Joseph ben Jacob retained his income and was designated as Saadia's successor—just as had happened previously in the Pumbedita academy when David ben Zakkai had made his peace with Rab Mebasser, and Rab Kohen Tsedek had to yield his place, retaining his income.

For about five years longer, Saadia adorned the gaonate of the Sura academy, and gave it new luster. But that was too short a time to re-establish it permanently. A few years after Saadia's death, his insignificant sucessor gave up the struggle against the rival academy which now was presided over by Kalaf ben Sarjado, Saadia's bitter opponent, who, Sherira tells us, had by force and intimidation finally attained the goal of his ambition. The gates of the Sura academy were closed for half a century, not to be reopened until about the end of the tenth century. The third gaon, after its reopening, was Saadia's son, Dosa (1013-1017).

To return to Saadia, we know very little about his activity after his restoration to his position. There is only one interesting and characteristic record: David ben Zakkai died some time after the reconciliaton, and his son and successor, the man who had threatened Saadia with physical violence, followed him to the grave seven months later, leaving a young son of twelve. Saadia took upon himself the education of the child of his former enemies and befriended him in every way.

The space devoted to the interesting life story of Saadia is justified by the tremendous contributions he made to many fields of learning. Both quantitatively and qualitatively, his literary work is astounding. We can place him side by side with Maimonides. In several fields, the latter brought to fruition what Saadia Gaon had started; and without his pioneer work, Maimonides might not have been able to accomplish what he did. Saadia, moreover, was more versatile in his activity than the later sage of Cairo.

Abraham ibn Ezra characterized Saadia aptly as "the first speaker in every field" among the Jewish mediaeval scholars, a characterization which is by no means to be taken merely chronologically. Saadia's work was epoch-making in the true sense of the word—in his work on Hebrew grammar and exergesis; in his translation of the Bible into Arabic; in his study of the Hebrew calendar; in his defense of tradition against the onslaughts of the sectarian Karaites as well as against Hiwi, the sceptic and early Bible critic of Balk.

Even in the subject of Halaka, to which his predecessors in the gaonate had devoted their literary and teaching activity almost exclusively, we find him hewing new paths and making original contributions of the first order.

To the modern mediaevalist, his first serious effort to reconcile religious tradition with the philosophy of his time, is of the greatest interest. It was granted to few scholars to be pathfinders in so many subjects, and we cannot but admire the originality, profoundity and lasting quality of the work accomplished by this genius as these characteristics are reflected even in the incomplete form in which many of his important works have come down to us. How he could find the time, during his full and active life and during his extended travels, to write so much is hard to understand, the more so if we remember that he also had to devote a great deal of time to practical affairs.

To do justice to his important original contributions to learning would require more space than we have devoted to the sketch of his life. I must therefore limit myself to a very brief outline of his literary activity in all fields of Jewish learning.

Hebrew philology did not exist before Saadia. Only crude beginnings can be discerned in the work of the Masorites. Saadia was the first to realize the necessity of investigating the phenomena of the language in order to reach a clear understanding of its literature. Only little of his twelve *Books on the Language* or the *Book on the Elegance of the Language of the Hebrews* has been published, though a considerable fragment was discovered half a century ago. Of his dictionary, *Agron,* which he composed at the age of 20, a few specimens have appeared, aside from the incomplete introduction. We see that this earliest attempt at writing a Hebrew grammar was comprehensive in its scope and dealt with many of the linguistic phenomena in a systematic way.

Naturally, Saadia's philological insight must not be measured by comparison with his great successors in Spain. Its shortcomings are considerable, but his conscious effort to get behind the formation of the language is remarkable. His dictionary, again the first in the field, is very brief and contains also a part arranged by the end letters. One

of its purposes was evidently to serve as an aid to the poet who wished
to arrange his verses with acrostics and rhymes as Saadia did himself.
A short treatise on seventy (actually ninety) hapax-legomena in the
Bible is remarkable as the earliest tentative trial of comparative lin-
guistics. He applied the later Hebrew of the Mishna and the Aramaic
to the interpretation of biblical Hebrew.

More important is Saadia's contribution to the understanding of
the Bible. Here the attacks of the Karaites against the rabbinic interpretation may have given him the impetus. His lengthy commentary on the
first part of Genesis, on Exodus and Leviticus, which seems to have
been one of his early works, contains linguistic, philosophic and halakic
discussions as well as attacks on the Karaites. Only fragments and
quotations of this work have reached us. We know even less about his
glosses on the whole Pentateuch to which he gave the title *Garden
Flowers* and his *Questions and Solutions* on the same book.

Of far greater significance in his translation of the Pentateuch,
which was printed in the first Jewish polyglot (Constantinople, 1546),
together with the Aramaic Targum and a Persian translation. It became
the standard Arabic translation for the Jews and even the basis of the
Arabic translation of the Samaritans. The Jews of Yemen use it in their
services to this day, and, at the end of the last century, they published
an edition in Jerusalem. This monumental work, the first translation
from Hebrew into Arabic, aimed simply to give a clear rendition of the
text. It is a free translation, not a paraphrase, but it sometimes contains additions of single words and tries to bring the parts of the verses,
and occasionally the verses of a section, into a syntactic context which
enables the reader to get a picture of the content, although it loses
thereby some of the color of the text.

Under the influence of the Aramaic Targum, the authoritative interpretation of the old synagogue, Saadia avoided anthropomorphic
terms and expressions. It was his purpose to show that there is nothing
in the Bible which is uncertain and which we do not understand. Therefore he did not hesitate to render technical words with definite Arabic
terms, although he had no tradition as to their meaning. He also identified geographical names of the Bible with Arabic ones which were
known to his readers, identifications which often have no real basis.
Curiously, he sometimes used Arabic words which phonetically resemble
the Hebrew ones, although they do not have the same meaning in
Arabic.

It seems that Saadia wrote this translation in Arabic characters in order to make the Bible available to Muhammedans as well as to Jews, although in general he wrote all his Arabic works in Hebrew characters, as the Jews were wont to do in Arabic-speaking countries. However, the few manuscripts of the translation in Arabic characters which have come down to us, do not contain his original text but are later revisions by other hands. None of our texts offers a faithful reproduction of Saadia's version.

The Jews immediately transcribed the work into the more familiar characters, and the very numerous manuscripts in this form are closer to the authentic work of the gaon. Besides the Pentateuch, we have his translation of Isaiah, Psalms, Job, Proverbs, Daniel, Esther, Lamentations, and perhaps Canticles as well as fragments of Samuel and Ezekiel. To Esther he added a translation of *Megillat Bene Hashmonai* with an introduction. Some of these books are accompanied by shorter or longer commentaries and provided with introductions.

To the Minor Prophets he composed a commentary in the form of questions. His interpretation of the Books of Kings is mentioned in a book list, but not in the list of his works. It is curious that Hebrew commentaries on Daniel and Ezra were published under Saadia's name, though they are undoubtedly not his work. Perhaps a later man by the same name is responsible for them.

The calendar was a subject in which Saadia was deeply interested. In his polemics against the Karaites, he deals again and again with questions pertaining to the calendar and, as I have already stated, he carried on a correspondence on this subject with the gaon of Pumbedita before 917. The objections of the Karaites to the Jewish method of calculating the calender may have given the impetus to take up this study and thus he was especially well prepared to defend the method of these calculations by the Babylonian academies against the attack on Ben Meir which I have discussed at length. A special work dealing with the calendar is recorded, but since nothing of it has come down to us, we cannot determine its character. Whether his *Kitab al-Aflak* ("Book of the Spheres" or "Heavenly Bodies," or "Astronomy"), which is recorded in book lists of the *Geniza,* refers to this subject, also must remain doubtful.

Polemical works by the great gaon fill an important part of his literary activity and are particularly characteristic of his fighting nature. The centuries preceding our author were filled with religious unrest. Numerous sects arose in the East and, while most of them were of ephemeral character, they inaugurated a movement which finally led to the rise of Karaism, a sect which was founded in the second half of the eighth century and is still in existence. Like the other movements that preceded it, it was directed against the authority of official rabbinic Judaism and threatened to undermine and overthrow it. Curiously, the earlier geonim, as far as we know, paid no attention whatever to these opponents, and we have only a single reference to them in a geonic work of the ninth century.

Saadia was the first to realize the dangers inherent in the movement, and as a young man of twenty-three he already wrote against the Karaites. He devoted numerous works to the subject during the four decades of his literary activity. That Saadia's attacks on the Karaites made a deep impression on his opponents may be seen from the violent abuse they heaped on him down to the nineteenth century. Poznanski has collected such attacks by forty-nine *Karaite Literary Opponents of Saadia Gaon.* His first work was a criticism of Anan, the founder of Karaism; but only a few quotations from this book, which he wrote in 905, in all likelihood in Egypt, have been preserved.

I shall limit myself to those books of which fragments have been recovered in recent years.

The most comprehensive was probably his *Book of Distinction,* which discussed in eight treatises nearly all the subjects of controversy between Karaites and Rabbanites. It is not written against any individual and, in contrast to the rest of his polemical works, is distinguished by its calm tone. It was composed in 926, after his appointment as a *Resh Kalla* of one of the academies.

While these works were written in Arabic, about a third of a Hebrew polemic by Saadia, in poetic form, *Esa Meshali,* has been recovered in the course of the last decade. In twenty-two chapters of twenty-six stanzas each, the author gives praise to the talmudic authorities and deals with some of the differences with the Karaites. This book with its highly complicated technique of poetic composition was perhaps directed against Ben Asher. Its language is very difficult and not always clear. It is one of the works against which a younger contemporary, Salmon ben Yeruhim, wrote a sharp answer in poor Hebrew verses. His book of the *Wars of the Lord* was published by Davidson in 1934, almost exactly a thousand years after its composition. The editor suggests, with good reason, that Salmon followed this work with an Arabic treatment of the same subjects in two books of prose, one about the talmudic literature, which he called the *Book of Shameful Things,* the other concerning the rest of the differences. Against these Saadia wrote two of his treatises: *Refutation of Ibn Sakaweihi* and

Refutation of the Unfair Aggressor—of both of which fragments have been published. Thus we know at last who this Ibn Sakaweihi was. It was the Arabic name of Salmon ben Yeruhim.

The latter also attacks some statements in Saadia's *Open Book,* which, as has been pointed out above, was directed against the Exilarch David ben Zakkai. In writing against the gaon, first in Hebrew verse and then in Arabic prose, Salmon followed Saadia's example in that book. Limitations of space do not permit me to discuss this most interesting and most personal of Saadia's writings in greater detail. Mention need only be made here of Saadia's reference to his defense of Jewish tradition against the Karaites and against Hiwi of Balk as especially meritorious actions.

The polemic against Hiwi, about one-sixth of which was discovered and published by Dr. Davidson, throws light on a very curious movement among the Jews of the East in the second half of the ninth century. Hiwi, in contradistinction to the Karaites, not only denied the validity of the Talmud, but also that of the Bible. He wrote his *Two Hundred Questions on the Bible* with an absolutely destructive tendency, pointing to inconsistencies in the biblical narrative. Deeply influenced by an early Pehlevi work of polemics against the Bible, he even denied the unity of God, His omnipotence and omniscience. He claimed that the teachings of the Bible led to dualism, like that of the Persian religion, and to trinity. He believed in the eternity of the world. He denied free will and the possibility of miracles, and he objected to circumcision. These heretical ideas spread widely and were even taught in schools for children.

It was the great merit of Saadia that he put an end to this movement which disappeared in consequence of the refutation which he wrote in verse and with acrostics. Since he called himself *Alluf* and *Resh Kalla,* we see that the book was written in Babylonia before he became gaon. Many more polemical works are recorded, but we know them only by title.

As pointed out above, the heads of the Babylonian academies had centered their activities for three centuries on the study of Talmud and rabbinic law. New contributions of fundamental, even epoch-making importance in this field could only be the work of a genius. Without going into details, suffice it to state that Saadia was the first to write an "Introduction" on the methodology of the Talmud, of which five passages were translated into Hebrew by a famous Talmudist of the sixteenth century; commented on the Thirteen Rules of Interpreting the Bible; and composed a number of halakic compendia in which he, for the first time, discussed these laws systematically without regard to their sequence in the talmudic sources. Theretofore, all the geonic codes had followed the unsystematic order of the Talmud with only slight deviations. It is hard for us to realize what courage this new departure required. In some of his early works in this field he did not even give the sources for his statements, a procedure in which Maimonides followed his example and for which he was subjected to violent criticism. Whether such criticism was directed against Saadia also, and whether it was for this reason that he followed a different method in some of his codificatory work, we do not know.

He probably also wrote commentaries on Mishna and Talmud which, however, dealt mainly with lexicographical explanations. It goes without saying that, like all the geonim, he answered questions directed to him from various countries even as far as distant Spain. In the Jewish Theological Seminary Library I came across a torn leaf of an introduction to a series of such questions which have not reached us.

Saadia's *Siddur*—the *Collection of Prayers and Hymns,* as he calls it—also partly belongs to the field of law. It was preceded by a short treatise, the *Obligation of Prayers,* composed somewhat earlier, which he, or perhaps some copyist, placed in front of the *Siddur.* Here he discusses the necessity of prayer on the basis of Bible, reason and tradition, and enumerates the various categories of prayer occurring in the Bible.

The *Siddur* is not the first in this field. One of his Sura predecessors, Rab Amram, in the middle of the ninth century, had composed such a prayerbook, and the comparison between the two works is enlightening.

Saadia's *Siddur* is a work of quiet different caliber and shows the pronounced individuality of the author. He does not merely codify the current customs, but uses his judgment in selecting the prayers, declares what is proper and valid, and criticizes and omits what he considers wrong.

He tells us that it was the lack of uniformity, the corruption of prayers, improper additions and omissions which he had observed in the course of his travels through the various countries, which induced him to undertake this work. He differentiates between the individual prayers and those recited with a quorum of men in the synagogue. His arrangement is very interesting. He does not hesitate to deviate from the old custom of the academies and, although one of his contemporaries raised objections against some of his changes, we are informed that he exerted a deep influence on the ritual even in Babylonia.

The text of the prayers is naturally Hebrew, but the rubrics are given in Arabic, briefly and without sources since he intended it as a handbook for the layman. The influence of Egypt, the land of his birth, is strongly evident in Saadia's *Siddur,* though it was composed in Babylonia. Only one manuscript has been preserved, and that one is not complete and does not bear his name. It was identified by Steinschneider in 1851 and published in 1941 in Jerusalem through the initiative of the late Israel Davidson, in collaboration with Professor S. Assaf and Dr. B. I. Joel. For this edition they consulted thirty-four *Geniza* fragments of the *Siddur.*

The *Siddur* includes a selection of later hymns, partly from his own pen. As an appendix, Davidson collected all the poetic compositions of a religious character by Saadia as far as preserved. In the spirit of the period, Saadia excelled in the artificial technique which was then considered the essential of poetic compositions. Rare expressions and difficult word-formations abound here as in the polemical treatises in verse form. They often make it hard to understand the meaning. While very objectionable to our taste, they were considered highly poetic in his time. But Saadia could also write in a prose which compels admiration. His two *Bakkashot* reveal him as a true master of Hebrew style and gained him the praise of so severe a critic as Abraham ibn Ezra, who, after a sharp condemnation of the early *payyetanim,* stated that the Gaon Rab Saadia avoided all these mistakes in his two *Bakkashot* the like of which no other author had composed.

Philosophy had occupied Saadia's attention since his youth, and philosophic discussions occur in his early commentary to the Bible and elsewhere in his work. His main philosophic books were composed towards the end of his life.

In 931, while he was engaged in the struggle with the exilarch, he wrote his commentary on the enigmatical *Sepher Yetsira,* the "Book of Creation." He did not consider it a mystical work but a philosophic attempt to express the process of the world's generation by the will of the Creator. The theory current at the time, that its author was the patriarch Abraham, he accepts with some reservation. The commentary contains important points of grammar, but is devoted mainly to philosophic problems.

Two years later he composed his chief work—the *Book of Philosophic Doctrines and Religious Beliefs,* which marks the beginning of the history of Jewish philosophy. With an exposition of his point of view he combines a continuous discussion of ideas opposing his own.

Saadia himself was a rationalist and belonged to the same school of thought as the Muhammedan school of the rationalistic Mutazilites. But he often discusses philosophic problems in an independent manner. His main problem is the relation between Reason and Revelation. To him, as to all religious thinkers, Scripture is of revealed divine origin. And this divine Revelation is identical with Reason. Philosophy and religion therefore do not contradict but supplement one another in making known the truth.

He discusses the problem of creation at great length, giving a survey and criticism of all the theories as to the origin of the world known in his time. He defends the theory of *creatio ex nihilo*. He further discusses the unity of God, at which point he touches on the doctrine of trinity. In his chapter on the revelation of law he also defends the eternity and immutability of the Mosaic law. The other problems which he discusses in special chapters are: freedom of the will, the value of obedience to the law, the immortality of the soul, resurrection, Messianic times, and reward and punishment in the world to come. He concludes the book with a lengthy section on ethics.

Saadia's book was the first comprehensive effort to take up the fundamental problems of Jewish philosophy and has had a deep influence on all later Jewish writers in this field. Some of his conceptions occur again even in Maimonides' *Guide to the Perplexed*.

THE RABBINIC PHILOSOPHER
AND ISRAEL'S DESTINY

The mood of Judah Halevi's writings—poetry and philosophy alike—differs in a distinctive way from that of Saadia's. The latter, confident and fresh, does not exhibit the Messianic obsession and the apocalyptic vividness of Judah Halevi, who lived not in times of vigorous conflict within Jewry, but in an age of acute political difficulties. The Jews, caught between the Islamic and Christian struggle for Spain, could not emerge unscathed from the struggle of the nations. "Whenever they fight their fight, it is we who fall." For him, therefore, the central issue of the day was not the serene pursuit of philosophical reason, but the struggle for meaning in interesting history. Is there a pattern in the endless movement of events? Does Israel, the Jewish people, face a history of unceasing struggle for existence? When will salvation come?

Judah Halevi's answer was the return to those convictions in the rabbinic heritage which would endure, come what may: the revelation of God, the election of Israel. The weak and inconsequential people in fact possessed within itself the power to master history. In the *Kuzari,* Halevi argues that those who are despised are supreme. What makes the condition of Israel seem contemptible is reason, for by the canons of worldly rationality, Israel indeed is weak and unimportant. But revelation already has shown otherwise. Abstract propositions, rational truth, do not contain the meaning of Israel's history, which is revealed from Sinai. Israel's fate seems unimportant. In fact what happens to the Jewish people is what lends significance and imparts meaning to what happens to the nations. For from the perspective of eternity, the important events are revelation at Sinai—to Israel—and the coming of the Messiah at the end of time—to Israel.

These assertions, based upon biblical and Talmudic perspectives, therefore begin with the paradox that the weakest is strongest, the most despised the most honorable, the least important the most significant. Philosophy teaches otherwise, and philosophy is therefore to be rejected. Reason is not the way to the true interpretation of matters, for, when reason contradicts revelation, it is revelation which will prevail. Reason, after all, does not lead to communion with God. Prophecy, not philosophy, is the way to his presence. God makes himself known; man's reason without God's grace achieves nothing. Since God addresses his teachings to Israel, Israel enjoys the power to accomplish what is denied others. The nations are subject to reason and natural law; Israel has a direct inheritance, a religious faculty unavailable to others, lives a supernatural existence and is above the laws governing the history of the nations.

Yet these arguments are laid before a gentile king, in the hope of converting him to Judaism. Life with God is open to all men. The paradox of Talmudic and later rabbinic particularism alongside universalism—the fact that one may enter into the highly distinctive life of Israel through conversion—is herein brought to its fullest expression.

11.

JUDAH HALEVI

Henry Slonimsky

[From *Judah Halevi. The Kuzari. An Argument for the Faith of Israel.* Introduction by Henry Slonimsky. N.Y., 1964: Schocken Books, pp. 17-31.]

Judah Halevi (b. ca. 1080) is the greatest poet and one of the profoundest thinkers Judaism has had since the closing of the canon. He plumbed depths in religion and reflection on history, and he made claims for Israel so strange and inordinate, that he would be merely an anomaly unless profoundly related to his time and viewed centrally from that history and destiny in which he was rooted and of which he is clearly the deepest expression and interpretation. The over-shadowing event of his time was the struggle of Christian and Moslem for Spain; and, farther afield, for the mastery of the Holy Land. In Spain, the community of Israel was ground between upper and nether millstones; and in Palestine, the last spark of hope seemed finally extinguished with the advent of the Crusaders. Israel appeared to be doomed. Judah Halevi's poetry and prose are the response evoked by that world situation.

The general setting was the *reconquista,* the gradual reconquest of Spain by the Christians from the north, where they had been pushed in the first great Moslem irruption into Europe four centuries earlier. And, though Judah Halevi's life span was marked at its beginning and end by two fierce counterattacks from the south—the Almoravides in the 1080's and the Almohades in the 1140's—the victorious advance from the north remained unchecked.

The *reconquista* was a curious fusion of crusading religious fanaticism with astute political realism. While the Arab ruling classes were ruthlessly eliminated and the peasantry allowed to remain, the Jews, so politically innocuous and economically valuable, were treated with in-

175

dulgence at the insistence and special pleading of the Jewish court grandees and permitted to take refuge in the north. But their condition remained forever precarious, and that is the crux of the matter. The court Jews who dominated Jewish policy, the *gevirim* and *nesiim* to whom Judah Halevi as Moses ibn Ezra and others before him tirelessly addressed poems and hymns of praise, and who were hailed each in turn by the trusting masses as the final savior of Israel, were capable of nothing better than parleying and maneuvering for position with the powers that be.

Judah Halevi belonged by birth and tradition to this upper stratum of court Jewry, and his material existence may have been linked up with this group. Its attitude toward life—its views on love, religion, philosophy, politics, and the future of Israel—Judah Halevi undoubtedly shared for the first half of his life. And the radical break with this outlook on life constitutes the secret of his power, clears the way for that efflorescence in poetry and thinking which makes of him the unique figure he is.

The shock which brought about this complete inner change in him, this reversal of all the values he and his class had lived by, led, among the masses, to the revival of a Messianic mood and apocalyptic hopes. As an aftermath of the great struggle of which the Jewish masses were witnesses and victims caught between two fires, minor Messiahs began to appear among them, old apocalypses dealing with the "end" once again emerged, and calculations as to the exact date of that "end"—as the coming of the Messiah is usually designated among Jews—were made by consulting signs and stars. And, while Judah Halevi shared to the full these moods and hopes, he knew better than any of them, better than the practical politicians whose principle was opportunism, better than the eschatological astrologers who calculated ends, better than the vague votaries of Messianic enthusiasm, how truly to interpret the great events of the times.

Born in Toledo while it was still Mohammedan, he went south for his education to the old seats of learning. Those were his happy *Wanderjahre,* and they were spent, according to the fine civilization of the age, not merely in absorbing Jewish learning in the regular Talmudical schools, but in assimilating everything he could of the science and philosophy which Arabic culture had to offer; cultivating the poetic arts in both Arabic and Hebrew; fraternizing with young men of like gifts and inclinations; and frankly enjoying life. The love poems of his youth, it may be said in passing, are certainly not academic exercises in imagined passion. Love was in the mores of his time for the members of his class, and, while native fastidiousness may have led him to avoid the profligacy characteristic of the rich of his class, the tenderness and sensuousness of his love poems are too authentic to allow any doubt of the realness of the experience.

He returned to Toledo, then in Christian hands, to practice medicine, but he speaks ironically of his patients and his profession. "Thus we heal Babylon, but it cannot be healed." His work as a physician did not fill his life. His contacts with the south continued unabated, despite the fluctuation of arms, and his literary activity increased. Besides his love songs, this period of poetic production was marked by poems addressed to friends and court functionaries, poems of praise and homage to court Jews in either Christian or Mohammedan service, possibly patrons of the poet, certainly men whom he regarded as the leaders of his class and of Jewry.

As the years went by, however, and he witnessed one Jewish community after another going down in destruction as it was caught between two fires in the advance of the Christian armies, a new light dawned on him to which he gave expression in a new type of poetry— an insight which found mature and conscious formulation in his later and most powerful poems and the great prose work of his closing years. This insight—that whoever won in the struggles of the *reconquista*, Israel was bound to lose, that, although some powerful court Jew might find protection for his people in the north as they fled their burning homes in the south, such asylum would be merely a refuge built on quicksand—slowly ripened into conviction.

There came a point where Judah Halevi's poems of homage to Jewish grandees ceased, and another type of writing, another way of thinking, came into predominance. In a poem which still trembles with the concrete detail of death and murder recently witnessed, our poet sums up its final meaning for him. "Between the armies of Seir and Kedar (i.e., Christian and Moslem), my army is lost. Whenever they fight their fight, it is *we* who fall, and thus it has been in former times in Israel." And so again in another poem of this period: "The enemies battle like wild beasts, the princes of Eliphas and the rams of Nevayot (i.e., Christians with Moslems), but between the two the young sheep (of Israel) are undone."

The new poems dealing with the destiny of Israel begin to follow a definite pattern: they are marked by grief over the loss of God's proximity which was Israel's distinction of old; they depict conditions in Spain; they lament the loss of Jerusalem to the Crusaders; they raise questions as to the future. And, while the older poets dealing with the same themes had followed a similar pattern, namely, the triadic scheme of the lost ideal of the past, the hopeless present, and the prospect of salvation in some future, Judah Halevi differs from them in his definiteness and concreteness, in his realistic treatment of the present, and in his interpretation of the struggles of the time as the actual birth-pangs of the imminent Messiah. His poems do not end on a vague note of hope, but are charged with new resolution and conviction. His espousal of the Messianic hopes current in his day assumes an almost political character, and the belief itself is merely the index of an entire change of viewpoint.

What is this change of heart? It is the rejection of the entire basis on which the existence of Spanish Jewry rested: culture of the senses and the mind, love-making and philosophy, economic dependence on the princely courts and political security that hinged upon the favor of the princes, the building up of this life in the north as rapidly as it was being destroyed in the south. Judah Halevi saw that it could not go on.

It was not merely the eternal political opportunism which he rejected as inadequate and which he realized must be replaced by a far more radical cure, but all the things that went with it and were part and parcel of the same scheme, above all, the evaporation of religion in the intelligentsia. The enlightenment which came in the train of philosophical studies had led not to a higher and freer faith on the basis of pure reason, but merely to a decay of the inner sanctions of the old religion, and even to a readiness on occasion to forsake Judaism—as if Christianity were any the less subject to the same rationalistic critique.

Judah Halevi saw that, if the return to Zion must be the political remedy at a time when all seemed lost, the return to God must go along with it, the return to traditional Judaism with all its transcendent claims, as a means of renewing power; the return, therefore, to Revelation and Election. He realized that the Jewish religion shares the fate of the Jewish people, that when both seem doomed, the moment has come for supreme re-assertion, that the political and the religious go hand in hand for the Jews.

However, such changes of heart are never easy, and again and again he falters. In poems of intense personal pathos he records these trepidations and fluctuations of his heart. The process means uprooting, from country, language, home—therefore, a kind of death; and in his case it did lead to death, but to death and transfiguration. For, in the drama of his personal life, he enacted, on a kind of ideal stage, the deepest drama of Israel.

The Kuzari, Judah Halevi's philosophical masterpiece, written between 1130–1140, is a book of defense, as the full Arabic title expressly states, and as that title goes on to say, a defense of a despised religion; despised, we may add, not merely by the world, by the two great religious powers who between them divide the inhabited globe, but secretly also by the educated and powerful among its own adherents. So that with hardly a place to stand, pushed so to speak to the edge of things by enemies from without and by doubt within, Judah Halevi still opposes to that world a philosophy of history (as we should say today) or more strictly a theology of history, whereby a supreme place is vindicated for his people and for its religion in the economy of world events. Everything of "pure" philosophy which the book contains is entirely subservient to this main purpose and is invented *ad hoc*. That purpose is the eminently practical and life-giving one of asserting a primary place in history for his people chronically threatened with external annihilation and internal disruption. The time and the scene could hardly have appeared more fraught with doom and disaster: Judah Halevi picked that moment as precisely the time for grandiose self-assertion.

The anti-rationalist tone of the book which makes it unique among all the products of Jewish mediaeval thinking is not just a new fashion in philosophy but is to be understood from an entirely different motivation. It is directed against the enemy within the gates. All the Jewish magnates and intellectuals of the day had gone through the school of Arabic philosophy. The educated, enlightened and superior people of that generation had insensibly substituted a set of metaphysical propositions for the ancestral religion. In any case its old vigor had slackened and relaxed; its great texts and images allegorized and symbolized. Judah Halevi's idea of defending the Jewish religion was not by showing its identity with rational truth, as all his predecessors and his successors after him tried to do. He did not have that ambition. He sees that the Jewish religion is not reducible to a sum of abstract propositions. Propositions in philosophy can always be debated both ways; and even at their best they never pierce deeper than the plane of argument. He tries to vindicate for it a securer place, a place beyond all reason. As against the influences of Arabic philosophy he re-asserts the original historical character of the Jewish religion, constituted by historic fate and historic election. The great scene at Sinai puts it in possession of the truth. And as the doctrine there imparted is the sole source of religious truth, so the people chosen to be its bearer is alone capable of realizing the religious life, and is therefore the core and heart of mankind. Sinai being the one authentic event in religious history, Christianity and Islam are inevitably derivative and imitative. But with all that they are assigned a high place. Israel has indeed a central position in history, but Judah Halevi robs the idea of chosenness of all hate and intolerance, and in the broad humanism of his Messianic conception he leaves far behind him the limitations of Mediaeval feeling. The two world-religions perform a function in their place and time, and in the end will be converted to the truth. The seed in the ground, Israel among the nations, though apparently disrupted and dying, transmutes the surrounding earth and loam by a magic alchemy into its own higher life. And towards his own people there is polarity of attitude manifest throughout—the polarity furnished by its high promise and its miserable present. His book is an elaborate theory of an innate superhuman distinctiveness inhering in the Jewish people and amounting to a special soul-form; but the actual fact which confronts him, and which his poet's eye made him perceive all the more unflinchingly, was a condition of shabbly dilapidation, an outer and inner disarray. What helps him to overcome the discrepancy is unbounded love and faith. Judah Halevi's steadfast belief in the meaning of Jewish history enables him to overarch the present by spanning Sinai with Messiah.

Two great themes dominate the book, the one culminating in the other; the first deals with the difference between an historical religion and a religion of reason, and the second gives a theory of the Jewish people. As for the first, he is not opposed to philosophy as such; he merely contests its claim to supplant religion, to be a religion in its own right. And he makes his point by an amazingly modern and valid analysis of the God-idea offered by each. But the climax towards which everything converges is the notion of Election, and of the unique and supernatural character of the Jewish people and its history. There is of course a touch of irony, deliberate or implicit, in every elaborately maintained extreme, in every soberly defended audacity of thought. But Judah Halevi is dealing with extremes; he is dealing with a people living in a chronically desperate situation, a people every element of whose life and history is so extreme that living for it becomes plausible and tolerable only on the basis of transcendental assumptions. In any case this is Judah Halevi's thesis and he adheres to it throughout.

Judah Halevi's apology for Judaism arises out of a polemic with the prevailing power of the day; that power was philosophy—the educated beliefs of his contemporaries. He insists that metaphysics does not yield truth in the higher reaches. There may be a preliminary area in which the light of reason gives us sure guidance both in questions of God and in the field of ethics, but for ultimates the real source of religious truth is Revelation.

Philosophy indeed appears as a Promethean undertaking. It is an attempt to reach God through man's unaided efforts, through his will to know. Man's intellect, by appropriating the great truths of metaphysics, fuses (so we are told) with the "Active Intellect" which presides over this earth from its seat in the lunar sphere and, through the Active Intellect, with God. The human mind becomes as eternal as the truths which it assimilates, as the objects which it comprehends, chief among them being God. And there is a point where knowledge and understanding become contemplation and emotion, and philosophy takes on the character of religion for the higher man, and the philosopher at the peak of vision is the true prophet, the seer of God.

Judah Halevi denies this power of the intellect to establish communion with God. For one thing the actual historic fact refutes the claim made for philosophers: they do not figure in any special way among great religious leaders or prophets. On the contrary, and unreasonable as it may appear, prophets and men of religious power seem to be chosen from ranks outside the class of philosophers.

Moreover communion with God seems to be a gift of God, not a product of the efforts of men. And here precisely is the difference between real and apparent religion. Attainment of God, living contact with him, cannot be achieved by man's reason out of its own resources. The point of departure is always with God; the genuine religious experience or event is always due to the spontaneity, the free grace, the self-revelation of God. It is he who reaches out and seeks man. Revelation alone then establishes the true, the real religion. This real or historical religion is basically different from the intellectual religion of the philosophers and God is a radically different being in both. The God of philosophy remains the far-off unmoved goal towards which man aspires and towards which he raises himself by his own cognitive efforts. The God of religion does not remain at rest in self-sufficiency but reaches out actively and with solicitude to call and raise man to himself.

The opposition between the two may be expressed in a somewhat different way. For philosophy God is an object of knowledge, standing in exactly the same relation to the theoretic faculty as any other object we set out to know. God is indeed a supreme object in the sense of being the first cause, but that is merely a logical pre-eminence, not a supremacy of concern or value. And this is reflected in the contemplative character of the Aristotelian religiosity, in the note of theoretic peace and imperturbability which pervades it. But while philosophy is primarily the knowing of God, religion is living with God. The religious man is impelled to God not by a desire to know but a yearning to be with him, by love; bliss and misery coincide, in the Psalmist's phrase, with being near to God or cast from him. The whole relation is a dynamic of longing, entirely different from the serenity of the theoretic attitude. The God of Abraham and the God of Aristole are two different gods.

This superiority of the religious experience over the theoretic understanding finds psychological expression in the assumption by Judah Halevi of a separate religious faculty, higher than the understanding, whereby union with God is achieved. The Hebrew term employed is the strange *ha-inyan ha-elohi;* it is used indifferently to indicate the double direction which obtains here, objectively the revelation coming from God, subjectively the power to apperceive it. It thus replaces intellect or rational soul which had till now served the philosopher to establish the relation with the unseen world. And one might suppose that in all this Judah Halevi is being motivated by a disinterested desire to distinguish the religious experience for its own sake, as something superior to the study and meditation of the philosopher. But his real intention is to provide a rationale for Israel's supernatural place and function.

For the religious faculty has been granted only to Israel. Israel has it by direct inheritance from the first man. Adam coming from the hand of God himself had it in full measure, and it was bequeathed in each generation to one or a few who were the "heart" or "treasure" of mankind in that generation—by a divine insistence on a hierarchy of being, which subordinates plant to animal and animal to man and among men the "husk" to the "treasure." When it finally passed on to Jacob it became the peculiar heritage and the common possession (though in endless degrees of variation) of the whole household of Israel, which by virtue of this is the "heart" or "treasure" of mankind. In all other respects, in understanding and moral qualities, there is no distinction between Israel and the nations, but this faculty constitutes the specific difference between them. In itself a mere disposition or potentiality, the religious faculty is brought to full fruition through the efficacy of the ritual and ceremonial law. The ceremonial law is thus not the opaque and irrational appendage which it seemed to the Jewish rationalists, but rather the agency prescribed by God to serve the superrational purpose of achieving living contact with Him. And along with the superrational efficacy of the ritual a similar religious pre-eminence inheres in the Holy Land, and a similar virtue resides in the Hebrew language. This is to be understood in a precise manner. As certain precious vines can grow only in a definite place and only through specific cultivation, so religion, the highest life of man, the constant communion with God, can come to full fruit and flower only through the union of all the requisite elements— the chosen people residing in the Holy Land, speaking the first and noblest tongue of men and performing the prescribed ordinances of ritual. The magic of exact co-ordination of elements is as necessary on the highest plane of creation as on the lower plane of nature in the production of orchid or peacock.

Particularism could seem to go no further with this concentration of religion on one people and the exclusion of the rest of the world. But the bare fact that the theme of the book is the conversion of a heathen king to the Jewish faith should be enough to indicate the true intention of the author. Mankind is not to be excluded from the life with God; nothing could be further from the spirit and intention of the book. But it is primarily a theory of first and last things and of the place of Judaism in this scheme; and it was written to remind the Jewish people of that supreme fact in the moment of deepest danger and decline. Jews and Judaism may be the least of these now; they were and shall be first—but this in a world-embracing scheme involving all men. Meanwhile those among the nations who observe the moral law given by God to all men shall have their reward from God, and if they join the Jewish faith they shall be accounted equals in all respects except the highest one of eligibility for prophecy. And even that invidious distinction shall disappear in the coming of the Messiah, when all peoples will have attained *ha-inyan ha-elohi,* and the seed in the ground will have assimilated all the earth to its own higher substance. Judah Halevi makes express use in this highest connection of the most tragic and beautiful of all symbols—the death and resurrection of the seed in the dark earth.

But that is the end, the final light. For the present the immediate concern is with the long hard road, and for that the Jews must have their courage renewed. Judah Halevi is impressed and overwhelmed with the one idea that the Jews are in a pre-eminent and unique sense the God-bearing people of history. He devotes his life to recalling them to that one thought. His poetry, his philosophy, his journey to the Holy Land, his whole personality in which the very soul of the race seems embodied, all serve to inculcate and impress the one idea.

To us as well as to his contemporaries, he gives two answers, a lived life and a book. He provides the exemplar or archetype of the tragic-heroic life of high resolve, return to faith and active endeavor. And he writes an apology for Judaism designed, first, to prove its world historic mission as against the two world powers who between them seem to fill the entire stage; and, second, to restore and reopen the sources of religious power in a people despised, discouraged, and depressed.

As for the man himself, he seems to be Israel's own answer to its problem. Only one profoundly rooted in his people and its substance could produce such an answer. In Judah Halevi the genius of Judaism comes to consciousness.

THE QUINTESSENTIAL RABBI

The fundamental unity of Rabbinic Judaism, through all of its modes of expression, whether legal, or philosophical, or literary, or mystical, is best demonstrated in the person of Moses ben Maimon (Rambam or Maimonides), who stands at the pinnacle of Jewish theology, who mastered the whole of Talmudic and cognate literature and law, who presented a code of the entire corpus of law for ready access, who through his code and his commentary to the Mishnah, also provided an authoritative exegesis for the bulk of rabbinic literature, and who exercised practical authority in his own day over much of the Jewish world—a truly protean figure, and the quintessential rabbinic Jew.

He pursued his studies through every difficulty, finding in them a secure haven in a time of troubles. Indeed, no one better illustrates the centrality of study in Rabbinic Judaism. He did his work wherever he might be, in exile and at home, when preoccupied with the affairs of state and when on board ship. The results are commensurate with the continuous effort.

His first mature work was a commentary on the Mishnah, which, for the first time, treated that keystone of rabbinic literature in its own terms and in accord with its own agendum, not solely as the Mishnah was interpreted in the pages of the Babylonian Talmud. But even while this work was underway—it took a decade—he also began to issue responsa in answer to legal questions and to write extended epistles to various communities on major issues of the day, for example, on the status of people forced to convert to Islam who later wished to return to Judaism, on the one hand, and on the ultimate meaning of the history of Israel, on the other.

His four great works are, first, the afore-mentioned Mishnah-commentary, second, the Book of Commandments, third, the Mishnah Torah, a massive code of rabbinic law, and, finally, his philosophic treatise, the Guide to the Perplexed.

The Book of Commandments is a study of the enumeration of the hundreds of commandments. Maimonides proposes fourteen guiding principles on how these are to be organized.

It is the Mishnah Torah which is the center-piece of his creative achievement. In it Maimonides accomplishes the union, both in form and in spirit, of the law and rationalism. The form of the work is a masterpiece of lucid organization and careful expression, in which reasonable principles of arrangement, which always are apparent to the student, bring sense and order to the entire corpus of rabbinic law. The law's substance, moreover, is laid forth in an entirely rational spirit. It is all-inclusive and therefore pays attention to the principles and fundamentals of the law, as much as to its details. As Twersky stresses, "Maimonides tried to bring about the unity of practice and concept, external observance and inner meaning, visible action and invisible experience, law and philosophy." This achievement, which is one both of philosophical learning and legal erudition, is the high point in Rabbinic Judaism, embodying the result of both Talmudic rationality and philosophical reason.

12.

MAIMONIDES

Isadore Twersky

[From *A Maimonides Reader*. Edited, with Introductions and Notes, by Isadore Twersky. N.Y., 1972: Behrman House, pp. 1-29.]

Maimonides' biography immediately suggests a profound paradox. A philosopher by temperament and ideology, a zealous devotee of the contemplative life who eloquently portrayed and yearned for the serenity of solitude and the spiritual exuberance of meditation, he nevertheless led a relentlessly active life that regularly brought him to the brink of exhaustion. A harassed physician and conscientious leader of his community, he combined an arduous professional routine with unabated scholarship, vigorous creativity, and literary productivity. Maimonides' life was a mosaic of anxiety, tribulation, and, at best, incredibly strenuous work and intellectual exertion. This is perhaps the first matter worthy of attention for the modern reader, accustomed for the most part to comfort, leisure, and even affluence.

Maimonides was born in 1135 in Cordova, at one time the greatest center of Jewish learning and general Islamic culture; his father was a prominent judge and respected scholar. His entry into adolescence— just as he was becoming a bar mitzvah (1148)—was filled with gloom and despair because of the invasion of Spain by the Almohades, fanatical, puritanical Muslims who presented all non-Muslims with the radical choice of conversion or death. Some Spanish Jews chose martyrdom, others fled, while many reluctantly took upon themselves a life of duplicity and ambivalence, creating a searing gap between their public Muslim-like behavior and their private adherence to Judaism. The colorful history of the Jews in Islamic Spain, which reached unusual heights in its material and intellectual development, was coming to an abrupt, inglorious end.

The Maimonidean family, uprooting itself from its ancestral home, where eight generations of scholars had served as rabbis and judges, entered into a turbulent decade of flight and nomadism, wandering through southern Spain and northern Africa (ca. 1148-1158) and finally settling for several years in the city of Fez (c. 1159-1165) where the Almohades also ruled with Spartan rigor and inquisitorial zeal. Life continued to be filled with apprehension, pretense, and defamation, theological indictment and physical harassment.

In 1165, heeding the advice which he had given to his perplexed, despairing fellow Jews—and which he would repeat to the distraught Jews of Yemen some years later—to flee the land of persecution at all costs, "without considering separation from family or loss of wealth," Maimonides undertook a hazardous sea voyage from Morocco to the land of Israel, which was then the scene of the crusades. During this particular period, the Latin Kingdom of Jerusalem, momentarily triumphant, was enjoying politico-military ascendancy over the Muslims; since its religious fanaticism equaled its political power, Maimonides found no haven in the Holy Land. His wanderings continued. It may even be that he regarded his trip primarily as a pilgrimage. His journey from Morocco to Palestine, as described in a statement quoted by a sixteenth-century writer (R. Eleazar Azikri), ended in prayer at the Western Wall:

> On Sunday evening, the fourth of the month of Iyar, I went to sea; on Sabbath, the tenth of Iyar, in the year 4925, a heavy gale arose, the sea was turbulent and we were in danger of drowning. I vowed to observe these two days as strict fast days for myself, my family and all my household, and to order my descendants to keep these fasts also in future generations and to give charity in accordance with their means. I further vowed to observe the tenth of Iyar in complete seclusion and to devote the day to prayer and study. On that day, God alone was with me on the sea; so upon the anniversary of this day, I wish to be alone with God and not in the company of man, unless I am compelled to.
>
> On Sunday evening, the third of Sivan, I landed safely in Acre and thus escaped persecution. The day on which we set foot in the land of Israel I vowed to observe as a day of festivity and joy accompanied by the distribution of gifts to the poor, I as well as my offspring in future generations.
>
> Tuesday, the fourth of Marheshvan, in the year 4926, we arrived in Jerusalem from Acre after a dangerous journey. I entered the site of the great and holy Temple and prayed there on Thursday, the sixth of Marheshvan.

In any event, this experience of terrified flight from the lands of

Islam and implacable hostility on the part of the powers of Christianity is in some respects reminiscent of the general fate of the Jews caught between the fierce rivalries of Christian and Muslim.

His extraordinary difficulties in pursuing his studies during these years of instability and exile and the profound sense of uprootedness and precariousness which permeated his thought are poignantly portrayed in several of Maimonides' writings from this period. In the epilogue to his *Commentary on the Mishnah* (c. 1168), he writes:

> In concluding this work according to my plans, I pray to God that He save me from errors. Whoever finds occasion to criticize me, or knows of a better interpretation of any of the laws, should call my attention to it and graciously forgive me. Every righteous and intelligent person will realize that the task I undertook was not simple or easy of fulfillment. In addition, I was agitated by the distress of our time, the exile which God had decreed upon us, the fact that we are being driven from one end of the world to the other. Perhaps we have received reward for this, inasmuch as exile atones for sin. God knows, there are some laws which I explained while on the road; some matters I collected while on board ship. Besides, I also devoted myself to the study of other sciences. The reason that led me to describe my situation in detail was my desire to justify my critics; they should not be blamed for criticizing me. May God reward them, and I will regard them as friends, for they do godly work. The description of the conditions under which I wrote this commentary will explain why its completion required such a long time.

The prologue to his *Epistle to Yemen* (1172) echoes a similar refrain:

> Verily, I am one of the humblest of scholars from Spain whose prestige was lowered in exile. Although I always study the ordinances of the Lord, I did not attain to the learning of my forebears, for evil days and hard times overtook us; we did not abide in tranquility. We labored and had no rest. How could we study the law when we were being exiled from city to city, and from country to country? I pursued the reapers in their paths and gathered ears of grain, both the rank and the full ones, as well as the withered and the thin ones. Only recently have I found a home. Were it not for the help of God, I would not have culled the store I did and from which I continually draw.

After making his way southward from Acre through Jerusalem to Hebron, Maimonides settled in Cairo, an important, strategically located center of the Arab world, with a large, heterogeneous Jewish community. The first years in Egypt were punctuated by the death of

his father, his own prolonged illness, intermittent strife—personal and
communal—instigated by both Jews and Muslims, and, in 1173, the
crushing blow: the death of his younger brother David, a well-to-do,
enterprising merchant who had been supporting the entire family, and
who was drowned in the Indian Ocean while on a business trip. Maimonides could not be consoled in his mourning. A letter written several
years later (c. 1184) evokes the mood of agony and anguish and notes
the residue of grief:

> In Egypt I met with great and severe misfortunes. Illness and mate-
> rial losses came upon me. In addition, various informers plotted
> against my life. But the most terrible blow which befell me, a blow
> which caused me more grief than anything I have experienced in my
> life, was the death of the most perfect and righteous man, who was
> drowned while traveling in the Indian Ocean.
>
> For nearly a year after I received the sad news, I lay ill on my
> bed struggling with fever and despair. Eight years have since passed,
> and I still mourn, for there is no consolation. What can console me?
> He grew up on my knees; he was my brother, my pupil. He was
> engaged in business and earned money that I might stay at home
> and continue my studies. He was learned in the Talmud and in the
> Bible and an accomplished grammarian. My one joy was to see him.
> Now my joy has been changed into darkness; he has gone to his
> eternal home, and has left me prostrated in a strange land. When-
> ever I come across his handwriting or one of his books, my heart
> grows faint within me, and my grief reawakens. In short: "I will go
> down into the grave unto my son mourning." Were not the study of
> the Torah my delight, and did not the study of wisdom divert me
> from my grief, "I should have succumbed in my affliction."

Soon after, he began to practice medicine and, thanks to his erudition, skill, and conscientiousness, became the house physician of Saladin's
vizier and one of the most respected court physicians. Simultaneously,
he emerged as the untitled leader of the Jewish community, combining
the duties of rabbi, local judge, appellate judge, administrative chief
responsible for appointing and supervising community officials, and
overseer of the philanthropic foundations—to which he was especially
dedicated. His professional and communal commitments—resulting in
working hours which present-day scholars and professionals would find
appalling—were not unrelated, for Maimonides was absolutely determined to guarantee his independence and self-sufficiency. He received
no financial aid or official remuneration from the Jewish community;
as a matter of fact, he violently opposed and condemned those scholars
or religious functionaries who relied on communal support. Some of

his most passionate and animated prose was elicited by his distaste for
this practice, which he tried—unsuccessfully—to eliminate. His own
painful consistency in this regard lends all the more pathos and determination to his writing.

Maimonides apparently married twice. His first wife, about whom
we know very little, died in Egypt, and he later remarried. His only son
Abraham, who was to become the official head (*nagid*) of the Jewish
community in Egypt and the zealous defender and interpreter of the
total—*halakhic* and theological—Maimonidean legacy, was born in
1187. Maimonides lavished fond attention on his son, whom he described as possessing modesty and integrity as well as a fine intellect.
Although only seventeen at the time of his father's death (1204), Abraham was able still to absorb an impressive amount of his father's teaching and in his own works he cites many interpretations and opinions
transmitted to him orally by his illustrious father. The son's commentary
on the Bible, his voluminous *Complete Guide for the Pious* (*Kifayat
al-'Abidin*), the *Treatise on Aggadot,* and numerous letters and responsa
are thus important sources of Maimonidean doctrine. All his duties and
commitments notwithstanding, Maimonides must have found time to
"teach his son Torah." Indeed, we have here a good example of a sustained aristocracy of the intellect and spirit, and it is interesting to follow
the literary history of this family, starting with R. Maimon's Letter of
Consolation, over many generations.

Aspects of Maimonides' medical practice and intellectual preoccupations are described in a candid letter (1191) to Joseph b. Judah, the
favorite and trusted disciple for whom he composed the *Guide of the
Perplexed:*

> I inform you that I have acquired in medicine a very great reputa-
> tion among the great, such as the Chief Qadi, the princes, . . . and
> other grandees from whom I do not ordinarily receive any fee. As for
> the ordinary people, I am placed too high for them to reach me.
> This obliges me continually to waste my day in Cairo visiting the
> [noble] sick. When I return to Fostat, the most I am able to do,
> for the rest of the day and night, is to study medical books, which
> are so necessary for me. For you know how long and difficult this art
> is for a conscientious and exact man who does not want to state
> anything which he cannot support by argument and without know-
> ing where it has been said and how it can be demonstrated. This has
> further resulted in the fact that I find no time to study Torah; the
> only time I am able to read the Bible is on Saturday. As for other
> sciences, I have no time to study them at all and this distresses me
> very much. Recently I received all of Averroes' commentaries on

Aristotle . . . and my impression is that he explicates the author's views properly, but I have not yet found the time to read all his books.

The most revealing piece of personal testimony about Maimonides' professional and communal schedule is to be found in his letter of 1199 to Samuel ibn Tibbon, the Hebrew translator of the *Guide of the Perplexed:*

Now God knows that in order to write this to you I have escaped to a secluded spot, where people would not think to find me, sometimes leaning for support against the wall, sometimes lying down on account of my excessive weakness, for I have grown old and feeble.

With regard to your wish to come here to me, I cannot but say how greatly your visit would delight me, for I truly long to commune with you, and would anticipate our meeting with even greater joy than you. Yet I must advise you not to expose yourself to the perils of the voyage, for beyond seeing me, and my doing all I could to honor you, you would not derive any advantage from your visit. Do not expect to be able to confer with me on any scientific subject, for even one hour either by day or by night, for the following is my daily occupation. I dwell at Misr [Fostat] and the Sultan resides at Kahira [Cairo]; these two places are two Sabbath days' journey [about one mile and a half] distant from each other. My duties to the Sultan are very heavy. I am obliged to visit him every day, early in the morning; and when he or any of his children, or any of the inmates of his harem, are indisposed, I dare not quit Kahira, but must stay during the greater part of the day in the palace. It also frequently happens that one or two of the royal officers fall sick, and I must attend to their healing. Hence, as a rule, I repair to Kahira very early in the day, and if nothing unusual happens, I do not return to Misr until the afternoon. Then I am almost dying with hunger. I find the antechamber filled with people, both Jews and Gentiles, nobles and common people, judges and bailiffs, friends and foes—a mixed multitude, who await the time of my return.

I dismount from my animal, wash my hands, go forth to my patients, and entreat them to bear with me while I partake of some slight refreshment, the only meal I take in the twenty-four hours. Then I attend to my patients, write prescriptions for their various ailments. Patients go in and out until nightfall, and sometimes even, I solemnly assure you, until two hours and more in the night. I converse and prescribe for them while lying down from sheer fatigue, and when night falls, I am so exhausted that I can scarcely speak.

In consequence of this, no Israelite can have any private interview with me except on the Sabbath. On this day the whole congregation, or at least the majority of the members, come to me after the morning service, when I instruct them as to their proceedings

during the whole week; we study together a little until noon, when
they depart. Some of them return, and read with me after the afternoon service until evening prayers. In this manner I spend that day.
I have here related to you only a part of what you would see if you
were to visit me. Now, when you have completed for our brethren
the translation you have commenced, I beg that you will come to
me but not with the hope of deriving any advantage from your visit
as regards your studies; for my time is, as I have shown you, exces-
sively occupied.

His physical infirmity and all these apparently stultifying conditions notwithstanding, Maimonides was constantly studying, teaching,
and writing. He may have chafed under the tensions and pressures,
but he never fell to brooding and self-pity; he sometimes described his
difficulties in elegaic prose but did not allow them to paralyze his work.
He began writing early—with zeal, almost with a sense of mission—
and continued writing prodigiously to the end of his life. His writing,
in essence, was a work of art and a labor of love. Even if he had enjoyed optimal conditions of comfort and security, unlimited research
and secretarial assistance, it would still be hard to understand how he
could have produced what he did.

In 1158, at the age of 23, he began writing his pioneering commentary on the Mishnah, a task which was to engage his attention for
the next ten years. During the same period he also completed two other
works which, for a variety of reasons, remained marginal in the later
history of Talmudic literature and interpretation: a brief commentary
on those three sections of the Babylonian Talmud which were regularly
studied in the Spanish schools, and a compendium of laws found in the
Palestinian Talmud. The first represented a conventional preoccupation
of rabbinic scholars, while the purpose of the second was more original:
to cull all those sections of the rather neglected Palestinian Talmud
which would shed light on the normative Babylonian Talmud, explain
obscurities, fill in *halakhic* details, and by such use automatically enhance the importance of the Palestinian Talmud. In common with other
scholars of North Africa (primarily in Kairwan) and Spain, Maimonides
was devoted to the study of the Palestinian Talmud and eager to extend
its popularity and influence.

Throughout his life, Maimonides was to write hundreds of responsa,
decisions concerning the interpretation or application of the law, letters
of advice, comfort, or arbitration to all parts of the world: Yemen,
Baghdad, Aleppo, Damascus, Jerusalem, Alexandria, Marseilles, and
Lunel. Some were curt answers providing the authoritative opinion re-

quired; others were balanced expositions of moot points; still others were small monographs which Maimonides himself considered as treatises which would henceforth be available for all to consult. In other words, the writing and despatching of a comprehensive responsum was equivalent to publication of a book, for important responsa were customarily copied, collected, and widely circulated. Maimonides' responsa are significant not only for presenting an X-ray picture of a creative mind at work but also for illuminating through frequent cross-references the method, motivation, or meaning of his major legal and philosophical works. The most notable of the early letters and occasional pieces are the *Epistle on Conversion* (*Iggeret ha-Shemad*) and the *Epistle to Yemen* (*Iggeret Teman*).

Iggeret ha-Shemad (c. 1161-2) is a broadside, a real polemical treatise. It was not written in answer to a specific inquiry or request for guidance, but was rather Maimonides' passionate reaction to the *halakhic* decision rendered by a certain scholar who, totally insensitive to the plight of those tormented Jews under Almohade rule who succumbed to inexorable pressures and feigned acceptance of Islam, had unqualifiedly read them out of the Jewish community and, by his insensitivity and practically clinical detachment, had greatly increased their anguish and despondency. Maimonides, following in the footsteps of his father who had previously written a highly emotional Letter of Consolation for the same audience, sought to bolster the sagging spirits of his brethren and to save the Jewish community from total demoralization and disintegration. The letter is unique in that Maimonides reacted viscerally as well as intellectually; he did not limit his response to rigorous *halakhic* reasoning and interpretation but went out of his way to marshal every possible argument, legal, theological, and rhetorical, and cited a profusion of *aggadic* passages in order both to discountenance his opponent and to discredit the views which he had propounded.

The *Epistle to Yemen* was written in response to a specific inquiry from the Jews of Yemen concerning the religious persecutions in that country (begun about 1165) which were compounded by the seductive, conversionary preaching of a recent apostate and the unsettling pronouncements of a self-proclaimed messiah. In this responsum Maimonides reviews among other things the entire history of persecutions of the Jews, the special animosity which Christianity and Islam, the derivative monotheistic systems, feel toward Judaism, and the inviolable unity of the Bible and rabbinic tradition. He tries especially to cope with the "problem of history," to confront the recurrent facts of catastrophe and decimation, to explain the ubiquitousness of suffering:

"people witnessed our feebleness and noted the triumph of our adversaries and their dominion over us." As a result, "the hearts of some people have turned away, uncertainty befalls them and their beliefs are weakened." Maimonides writes in order to mitigate this distress and supply comfort and counsel stemming from a long-range, philosophical view of history. Punishment does not mean repudiation by God. Faith in God's promises to Israel must be as firm as faith in His existence. "As it is impossible for God to cease to exist, so is Israel's destruction and disappearance from the world unthinkable." The letter—eloquent and philosophical on the one hand, sensitive and emphathetic on the other—won for Maimonides a special place in the hearts of Yemenite Jews who, as a token of gratitude and reverence, included the name of Maimonides in the recitation of the kaddish. The Yemenites remained ardent students, copyists, and commentators of Maimonidean writings through the ages.

Maimonides' major works—major by dint of their unfailing originality, impressive size, and abiding influence—are: the *Commentary on the Mishnah* (*Perush ha-Mishnah*), *Book of Commandments* (*Sefer ha-Mitzvot*), *Mishneh Torah* (also known as *Yad ha-Hazakah*), *Guide of the Perplexed* (*Moreh Nevukhim*).

The *Commentary on the Mishnah* should be seen in light of the fact that although the Mishnah was prior to the Talmud in point of time, it gradually became subservient to and assimilated in the Talmud as a unit of study. Consequently, while several, practically complete commentaries on the Talmud were in existence by the end of the eleventh century, commentaries on the Mishnah were rare and fragmentary. In an effort to rehabilitate the Mishnah as a legitimate, self-sufficient unit of study, Maimonides intended his commentary to serve both as an *introduction* to the Talmud—this follows from the nature of the Mishnah—and as a *review* of the Talmud—this follows from the nature of his commentary which summarizes different interpretations and indicates the normative conclusions. He here combines minute textual study, even lexicographical annotation, with conceptual analysis, both of which are necessary for a comprehensive commentary. He often digresses in his commentary in order to elaborate a theological principle or elucidate a philosophic issue, for, as he confesses, "expounding a single principle of religion is dearer to me than anything else that I might teach."

Similarly, he is already preoccupied here with a problem that was to engage him intermittently for the rest of his life and was also becoming a staple, central theme of Jewish intellectual history: the metaphorical interpretation of the *aggadic,* or non-legal sections of the Talmud. Apparently implausible passages of *aggadic* literature had to be made reasonable and meaningful. As a matter of fact, most medieval scholars were convinced that *aggadah*—in common with certain Biblical passages —could not and should not be taken literally, for it was initially intended to convey metaphysical insights and basic truths, which could be uncovered and identified only by judicious interpretation. Non-literal interpretations were indispensable companions to literal understanding; *aggadic* texts had an intrinsic multiplicity of meanings, and a simple literalism would not do them justice.

We should note, of course, that the process of interpreting or deriving insight *from* texts and the habit of reading apriori, firmly grasped doctrines *into* the texts have to be carefully and honestly balanced. In the history of textual interpretation, one is not always sure whether something is being cleverly inferred from a text or whether it is being subtly read into the text. Both, to be sure, keep the text vibrant and relevant and provide continuity where discontinuity might have appeared. In any event, to borrow a phrase from Lovejoy, we might say that the problem of *aggadic* exegesis for Maimonides was "to disengage its serious philosophic content from the poetic imagery." Maimonides informs us in the *Commentary on the Mishnah* that he was planning a special commentary which would classify, explain, and rationalize the *aggadah*. He later abandoned the idea of composing such a commentary and, he tells us, the *Guide of the Perplexed* which was devoted in great part to matters of exegesis and allegory was intended as partial replacement for this work. This statement raises the history of *aggadah* to a higher level than is usually accorded to it and also puts the *Guide* in a different perspective, suggesting that the *Guide* is part of the *aggadic* as well as of the philosophic tradition.

Embedded in this pioneering commentary on the Mishnah are a number of independent monographs which have their own focus and integrity and can be—indeed have been—studied independently. First is the general introduction which may properly be described as the first comprehensive, sophisticated inquiry into the theoretical, historical, and doctrinal foundations of the Oral Law—the act of revelation and, particularly, the process of transmission and on-going interpretation. Maimonides emphasizes that the Oral Law is a completely rational enterprise, subject to its own canons of interpretation, and brooking no suprarational interference. It follows that even prophecy is of little relevance to the juridical process. Only the prophecy of Moses was legislative—and, therefore, unique; all subsequent prophecy was ex-hortatory, based on moral persuasion, and could not create new laws (see also *Guide*, II, ch. 39). A thousand prophets would not, therefore, outweigh a thousand and one jurists, for the juridical principle of majority rule, absolutely indifferent to claims of special inspiration or heavenly instruction, would prevail. The Torah "is not in heaven" (Deut. 30:12).

Maimonides here addresses himself, for systematic as well as, apparently, for polemical reasons, to a question which is at the very core of any authoritative system, be it law or philosophy: how is one to reconcile diversity of opinion with authority and certitude? How can divergent views—in which the Talmud abounds—crop up in a legal system which claims to derive from relevation and uninterrupted tradition? Maimonides' answer introduces a sharp distinction between two components of the Oral Law: tradition, which is complete, absolute, and never subject to dispute; and the laws arrived at by accepted canons of interpretation.

The first group contains laws which have no foundation what-soever in the Biblical text but are based solely on tradition—for example, the requirement that the *tefillin*, phylacteries, should be square and black. It also includes laws which are ascertainable by independent reasoning and which can be related to a Biblical text by careful exegesis but whose validity and authority are based on tradition, on direct, continuous practice—for example, the interpretation of "beautiful fruit" in Leviticus 23:40 as referring to the *etrog*, the citron, or the interpretation of "an eye for an eye" in Exodus 21:24 as meaning monetary compensation. Such laws have always been unequivocal and apodictic.

The second group, which accounts for the bulk of the Oral Law, is based on interpretation, inference, and analogy, on judicial review, and becomes part of authoritative tradition only after its conclusions have been agreed upon, after the norms have been established by majority decision or other principles of the juridical process. Only this area, which is in the hands of man, is subject to dispute and open to divergence; consensus of interpretation could not always be expected and was not necessary. The core of tradition thus remains free of controversy.

The section of the Mishnah commentary concerned with the methodology of text interpretation and the explanation of the term "world to come" also stands as an independent monograph. The chapter (*Perek Helek*) in the Talmudic tractate Sanhedrin beginning "All Israelites have a share in the world to come . . ." provides Maimonides with the pretext for a lengthy excursus on Jewish belief. After debunking crude, materialistic concepts of the world to come and identifying the religious concept of the world to come with the philosophical notion of the immortality of the soul, Maimonides defines the term "Israelites" by formulating the famous thirteen principles or articles of faith which every Israelite is expected to endorse. The thirteen principles may conveniently be reduced to three basic categories: (1) God—His existence, unity, incorporeality, and eternity, and the prohibition of idolatry; (2) the Law—prophecy, uniqueness of Mosaic prophecy, divine origin of the Written and Oral Law, and the eternity and immutability of the Law; (3) beliefs relating to reward and punishment—God's omniscience, divine compensation for good and evil, coming of the Messiah, and resurrection.

It seems most probable that this dogmatic structuring of Judaism was not undertaken in order to formulate a creed or catechism but was part of a philosophical-theological program which reflected Maimonides' intellectualism. It said, in effect, that there is a minimum of theoretical insight and true conceptual knowledge which even an unsophisticated, philosophically-innocent believer must possess. The difference, consequently, between such a person and the philosopher would be in the mode of acquiring true beliefs: blind conformity and unquestioning acceptance versus intellectual perception and rational demonstration. Both, however, would have a common set of beliefs. This discussion, in turn, becomes the point of departure for *all* subsequent investigation of Jewish dogma (*e.g.,* by Crescas, Albo, and Abarbanel), and indeed for the very question of whether Judaism has dogma, whether it has a distinct creed or consists solely of deeds—a question which has been at the center of modern theologies and critiques of Judaism from Spinoza and Moses Mendelssohn on the one hand to Kant and Hegel on the other.

A third, self-contained unit of this commentary is the introduction to *Pirke Avot* (Ethics of the Fathers), usually entitled *Eight Chapters.* This may be described as a psychological-ethical treatise; its basis is psychology while its goal is ethics. It contains the fullest presentation of Maimonides' theory of the golden mean, which defines virtues as psychological dispositions between extremes of excess and deficiency. The "good deed is equibalanced, maintaining the mean between two bad extremes." For example, generosity is seen as the median point between stinginess and extravagance; courage is the mean between recklessness and cowardice. The last chapter contains an unequivocal affirmation of human freedom and, concomitantly, the rejection of all views (e.g., astrology or divine predestination) which would undermine free will. Without freedom to choose and act there would be no ethics. As Maimonides says in the *Mishneh Torah*, freedom is the "pillar of the law and the commandments" and "every human being may become righteous like Moses our Teacher, or wicked like Jeroboam, wise or foolish, merciful or cruel, niggardly or generous." Man has the power and freedom to chart his own course.

Maimonides' *Book of Commandments* belongs to a conventional genre of rabbinic literature, inaugurated in the eighth century, which was based on the Talmudic reference to 613 divine commandments. While there has been general agreement on the number of 613, there has been no agreement on which commandments deserve to be included in the enumeration. Dismissing his predecessors with a few lines of devastating critique, Maimonides suggests fourteen guiding principles which should help bring about a consensus. These principles contain provocative assumptions as well as profound insights. For example, Maimonides contended that laws derived from Scripture by use of the traditional means of exegesis are not to be included in the enumeration, for they are considered rabbinic rather than Biblical in origin. The ninth principle introduces an interesting classification of laws: (1) beliefs and opinions—*e.g.,* to acknowledge the unity of God; (2) actions—*e.g.,* to offer sacrifices; (3) virtues and traits of character—*e.g.,* to love one's neighbor; (4) speech—*e.g.,* to pray. What is especially significant about this fourfold classification is its all-inclusiveness and its repudiation—intentional or incidental but clear and convincing —of a narrow "legalism" in the pejorative sense that is often attached to the term as a description of Judaism. This ambitious attempt to add rigor and objectivity to the enumeration by classifying Jewish law, defining the differences between Biblical and rabbinic commandments, differentiating between general exhortations and specific commands, is the novel and original part of the book. The enumeration itself was preparatory to his code and was designed to insure its comprehensiveness. He needed an exact, exhaustive list of commandments in order to guard against forgetfulness and omissions in his *Mishneh Torah*.

The *Mishneh Torah* was completed about 1178 after a decade of painstaking work. Its novelty and importance may best be understood by noting five features, to which Maimonides himself called attention in various places and which he considered as the distinctive characteristics of this work.

(1) Language. Maimonides chose the Hebrew of the Mishnah rather than the Hebrew of the Bible or the Aramaic of the Talmud. Biblical Hebrew was inadequate and Talmudic Aramaic was too difficult, and he wanted his work to be easily intelligible to as large an audience as possible. This meant, incidentally, that we find here substantial portions of the Talmud translated into a fluent, rather felicitous Hebrew. Maimonides took great pains with his style; his use of Hebrew and his development of a rich, flexible style that enabled him to write with precision, brevity, and elegance were exacting, novel undertakings, for we know from the plaintive testimony of such writers as Judah HaLevi and Moses ibn Ezra that contemporary Hebrew was in a sad state.

(2) Arrangement and classification. Maimonides abandoned the sequence of the Mishnah and created a new topical-pedagogical arrangement—one that would not do violence to the subject matter and that would also be educationally sound. Classification is, of course, a prerequisite for codification and necessitates interpretation, sustained conceptualization, a large measure of abstraction, and a synoptic view of the entire body of material. Classification deals not only with clear, given data but with latent assumptions and relations that must be rationally perceived; for in order to group *a* and *b* together, their common denominator, which is not always explicit, must be established. Legal classification concerns itself not only with the sum total of individual laws but with the concept of law per se. John Gray quotes the saying "that he who could perfectly classify the law would have a perfect knowledge of the law." There is neither antecedent nor sequel in rabbinic literature for such an ambitious attempt at classification. If, as Aristotle said, "it is the business of the wise man to order," Maimonides displayed great wisdom in his ordering and structuring of *halakhah*.

(3) Codificatory form. Maimonides chose to present the massive material in crisp, concise form, moving at a quick tempo, eliminating indeterminate debate and conflicting interpretations, and formulating as a rule unilateral, undocumented decisions. He emphasized that he wanted to write a code, not a commentary. The fact remains, however, that the *Mishneh Torah* is not a monolithic, cut and dried code in the conventional sense, but is in many respects a commentary cast in codificatory form, abounding in interpretations, bits of exegesis (Biblical, *halakhic,* and *aggadic*), historical surveys, explanations of tricky phrases and subtle concepts. It occasionally cites sources, mentions names of authorities, and describes personal views and practices. It

not only summarizes normative patterns of behavior but expounds in capsule form the entire Law. It is a manual of study as well as a guide to practice.

(4) Scope. One of the truly revolutionary aspects of the *Mishneh Torah* is its all-inclusive scope, obliterating accidental distinctions between the practical and the theoretical. Maimonides opposed the pervasive tendency, reflected in his own youthful commentaries, to study only those parts of the Talmud which were of practical value and immediate relevance. He insisted that the abstruse, "antiquated" sections of the Talmud—*Zeraim* and *Kodashim*—were not inferior to *Moed* and *Nashim* and should receive equal time and consideration. Maimonides knew that many of these treatises were "bristling with fundamental difficulties and even the greatest masters find it hard to comprehend them," but this was no justification for continued neglect. Laws momentarily impracticable because of historical or geographical circumstances—*e.g.,* laws concerning sacrifices or the Land of Israel—and laws relating to the messianic period should be studied and known, and were accordingly codified as precisely and minutely as laws of prayer, holiday observance, and marital relations. Maimonides aimed at comprehensiveness, at producing an all-embracing corpus of Jewish laws so that "discerning students . . . will have no need to roam and ramble about in other books in search of information." His intention was to codify everything concerning "that which is forbidden or permitted, clean or unclean, and the other rules of the Torah," but he also included statements "that have only an academic value"—such as rules governing the visibility of the new moon—"in order to make the Torah great and glorious" (Is. 42:21).

(5) Fusion of *halakhah* and philosophy. As part of the overall unity of learning, Maimonides tried to bring about the unity of practice and concept, external observance and inner meaning, visible action and invisible experience, law and philosophy. This unification of the practical, theoretical, and theological components is actually underscored by Maimonides in a letter to a student in which he describes the twofold objective of the *Mishneh Torah:* to provide an authoritative compilation of laws and also of "true beliefs." This aim is not confined to Book I, which briefly summarizes the metaphysical and ethical postulates of Judaism, talks about improvement of the moral qualities, and encourages learning and teaching, for "if knowledge is not achieved, no right action and no correct opinion can be achieved." There are also pointed philosophic comments, rationalistic directives, ethical in-

sights and theological principles incorporated into other parts of the *Mishneh Torah*. Maimonides' systematization of the *halakhah* includes a good measure of ethicization, spiritualization, and rationalization. Ethical assumptions are spelled out and made explicit. Ideals concretized in a particular law are articulated. While not too many laws are actually rationalized, the mandate to engage in rationalization, to penetrate to their essence and their real motive powers, "to meditate upon the laws of the Holy Torah and to comprehend their full meaning" is clearly issued in the *Mishneh Torah*. It takes within its purview, in other words, not only the laws but the theological stimuli and ethical underpinnings which suffuse the legal details with significance and spirituality. A law code which instructs as well as commands, it is an instrument of education and edification, for law itself is an educative force leading to ethical and intellectual perfection. Law must, therefore, be understood and appreciated as well as obeyed and implemented.

The *Guide of the Perplexed,* Maimonides' philosophic testament par excellence, was composed (sometime between 1185 and 1190) for a special kind of reader, described by him as follows:

> It is not the purpose of this treatise to make its totality understandable to the vulgar or to beginners in speculation, nor to teach those who have not engaged in any study other than the science of the Law—I mean the legalistic study of the Law. For the purpose of this treatise and of all those like it is the science of Law in its true sense. Or rather its purpose is to give indications to a religious man for whom the validity of our Law has become established in his soul and has become actual in belief—such a man being perfect in his religion and character, and having studied the sciences of the philosophers and come to know what they signify. The human intellect having drawn him on and led him to dwell within its province, he must have felt distressed by the externals of the Law and by the meanings of the above-mentioned equivocal, derivative, or amphibolous terms, as he continued to understand them by himself or was made to understand them by others. Hence he would remain in a state of perplexity and confusion as to whether he should follow his intellect, renounce what he knew concerning the terms in question, and consequently consider that he has renounced the foundations of the Law. Or he should hold fast to his understanding of these terms and not let himself be drawn on together with his intellect, rather turning his back on it and moving away from it, while at the same time perceiving that he had brought loss to himself and harm to his religion. He would be left with those imaginary beliefs to which he owes his fear and difficulty and would not cease to suffer from heartache and great perplexity.

Maimonides also indicates a second function:

> . . . namely, the explanation of very obscure parables occurring in the books of the prophets, but not explicitly identified there as such. Hence an ignorant or heedless individual might think that they possess only an external sense, but no internal one. However, even when one who truly possesses knowledge considers these parables and interprets them according to their external meaning, he too is overtaken by great perplexity. But if we explain these parables to him or if we draw his attention to their being parables, he will take the right road and be delivered from his perplexity. That is why I have called this treatise the *Guide of the Perplexed*.

The concern of the *Guide* is thus, on the face of it, hermeneutical, methodological, and interpretive; its raw material consists of knotty, often disconcerting passages from Biblical and rabbinic literature, aligned with concepts and images drawn from philosophic and scientific literature. In essence, however, the *Guide* covers a wide spectrum of staple philosophic problems such as the claims of reason versus revelation; the existence, unity, and incorporeality of God (*i.e.*, the theory of attributes, the problem of anthropomorphism, cosmological and ontological proofs for the existence of God); the freedom of God's action; creation of the world; problems of physics; miracles and natural law; prophecy; evil; providence; the reasons for the commandments of the Torah and the insistence that divine commandments are not arbitrary. Maimonides' views on basic problems of religious philosophy are not very different from those of his predecessors (*e.g.*, Saadyah Gaon or Bahya ibn Pakuda, Abraham ibn Ezra or Abraham ibn Daud) whom he sometimes criticizes or else simply ignores. All medieval religious philosophers shared basic principles, had common characteristics, and agreed on fundamental conceptions of metaphysics, physics, and ethics —in other words, God, the universe, and man. The main difference lies in his form of argumentation and methods of demonstration, in a more rigorously scientific approach based on what were considered to be unimpeachable Aristotelian doctrines. For he was convinced that "the works of Aristotle are the roots and foundations of all works on the sciences" and that "Aristotle's intellect represents the extreme of human intellect." He would not, therefore, settle for a shoddy defense of, or rickety apology for, religion—and that explains why Maimonides, in common with Muslim philosophers such as Al-farabi (whose philosophical acumen Maimonides admired), mercilessly exposed the inadequacies and inconstancies of the Kalam, the system on which Muslim theology was erected. The Mutakallimun, practitioners of this unsound and unsatisfying philosophy, are repeatedly upbraided by Maimonides. He sought a candid confrontation with philosophy and an honest demonstration of the importance and supremacy of religious tradition. He addressed himself to the implicit antagonism between religion with its insistence upon the necessity and value of action, and philosophy with its insistence upon the excellence and superiority of contemplation—the "ultimate perfection" which consists only of rational opinions without "actions or moral qualities" (*Guide,* III, ch. 27). He was concerned with but not stymied by the difficulties involved in transferring philosophic concepts to religion or identifying religious notions with philosophic postulates. It is in this sense—and notwithstanding Maimonides' recognition of the fallibility of reason as a guide to truth. of the necessary limitations of philosophy as a body of knowledge and the resultant need to criticize or revise certain philosophic conceptions in light of religious belief—that the *Guide* marks the peak of medieval Jewish rationalism.

Actually, Maimonides was caught on the horns of a painful dilemma. He was fully aware of the dangers, and indeed of the limitations, of philosophy, of the need for prudence and discretion in the dissemination of rationalistic views, of the fact that the philosopher would always be part of an intellectual elite far removed from—and often suspect by—the mass of simple believers. This accounts for the dialectic of the *Guide,* which aims to enlighten some people without disconcerting others. Maimonides warns the reader that the *Guide* contains premeditated, carefully wrought contradictions. In common with the Biblical allegories and *aggadic* parables, the *Guide* must manage to communicate with different people on different levels. But despite these difficulties, he remained unswervingly committed to the supremacy of speculative theology, convinced that all people should pursue it "to the extent of their ability" and "according to the measure of their apprehension." Any esotericist, convinced of the validity and usefulness of his doctrine, eventually has to evangelize his cause and face the dangers of popularization. Maimonides emphasized his attitude with the following homiletical flourish:

> One of the parables generally known in our community is that comparing knowledge to water. Now the sages, peace be on them, explained several notions by means of this parable; one of them being that he who knows how to swim brings up pearls from the bottom of the sea, whereas he who does not know, drowns. For this reason,

no one should expose himself to the risks of swimming unless he
has been trained in learning to swim (Guide, I, ch. 34).

Like swimming in deep water, the pursuit of philosophic knowledge demands multiple skills, patient preparation, and extraordinary tenacity.
The training is long and hard but indispensable if one is to achieve the
goal and enter the palace (see *Guide,* III, ch. 51).

Maimonides' philosophic posture may thus be seen as reflecting
his innate conviction that "it is through wisdom, in an unrestricted sense,
that the rational matter that we receive from the Law through tradition,
is demonstrated" (*Guide,* III, ch. 54), and this real wisdom is the goal
toward which every person must strive. "The opinions [of the Torah]
should first be known as being received through tradition, then they
should be demonstrated." Belief is not just assent to a body of truth,
but "belief is the affirmation that what has been represented is outside
the mind just as it has been represented in the mind" (*Guide,* I, ch. 50).

It is important that his intellectual position, however, which may
be presented as typically rationalist, should be seen also from the historical perspective. It arose from a specific milieu and was an answer
to the perplexity of the times. Maimonides must be seen against the
background of Muslim philosophers (from Al-farabi and Avicenna to
Averroes) who either provided his immediate sources or determined the
general climate of philosophic opinion and its characteristic tendencies.
Philosophy was widespread, and rationalism was a common modality of
thought, almost a way of life. Left alone, unharnessed and untram-
meled, it could destroy positive religion and produce skepticism,. agnosticism, and relativism. Heresy and antinomism became real dangers.
Muslim theologians were agonizing over this problem and Christian
scholastics would soon have their prolonged confrontation with it.

The beliefs of Judaism had to be expounded systematically and
with sophistication while the practices of Judaism had to be endowed
with rationality and significance. R. Bahya ibn Pakuda, anticipating
Maimonides' very phraseology, submitted that his *Hovot ha-Levavot*
(Duties of the Heart) was designed "to show the way to the perplexed."
R. Saadyah Gaon's description of the circumstances that motivated the
composition of his *Emunot ve-Deot* (Beliefs and Opinions), although
written in Baghdad, is also pertinent: "I saw men sunk, as it were, in a
sea of doubt and overwhelmed by the waves of confusion and there was
no diver to bring them up from the depths and no swimmer to come to
their rescue." Maimonides' summation and evaluation of R. Saadyah
Gaon's activities (in the *Epistle to Yemen*) is noteworthy: "For the

Jews of his time were perplexed and misguided. The divine religion might well nigh have disappeared had he not encouraged the pusillanimous and diffused, disseminated, and propagated by word of mouth and pen a knowledge of its underlying principles. He believed, in all earnestness . . . that he would inspire the masses with hope for the truth." One is tempted to discern autobiographical allusions in this panegyric; the paragraph might well have been written with regard to Maimonides' own activities.

We should add that this projection of Maimonides against the backdrop of twelfth-century science and rationalism is not merely a result of our modern historical sense. Maimonides was sensitive to the challenges and complexities of his time, was aware of the essential universality of philosophy, and stressed the need to present Judaism within such a general framework. There is, in other words, a conscious sense of "outer-directedness" in his philosophizing, an awareness of the profile of the Jews "in the eyes of the nations" and a need to project continuously the image of a "wise and understanding people" (Deut. 4:7). Literalism and unphilosophical thinking will only result in the other peoples' saying that "this little people is foolish and ignoble."

Although religious rationalism did not begin with Maimonides, it came to be totally identified with him. Protagonists and antagonists would draw the lines of their positions in relation to Maimonides. To a great extent, subsequent Jewish intellectual history may be seen as a debate concerning the wisdom and effectiveness of the Maimonidean position. Adherents of philosophy unequivocally asserted the primacy of the intellectual experience and cognitive attainment in Judaism and, consequently, this indispensability of philosophy. Philosophic knowledge as a duty was the nuclear notion of their program. Man is duty bound to realize his intellectual potential, for "his ultimate perfection is to become rational in actu, I mean to have an intellect in actu; this would consist in his knowing everything concerning all the beings that it is within the capacity of man to know in accordance with his ultimate perfection" (*Guide,* III, ch. 27).

There is, furthermore, a religious dimension to intellectual attainment. There is a religious obligation to apply one's intellect to the study of the world. "It is known and certain that the love of God does not become closely knit in a man's heart till he is continuously and thoroughly possessed by it and gives up everything else in the world for it; as God commanded us, 'with all your heart and with all your soul' (Deut. 6:5). One only loves God with the knowledge with which one knows Him; according to the knowledge will be the love. If the former be little or much, so will the latter be little or much. A person ought therefore to devote himself to the understanding and comprehension of those sciences and studies which will inform him concerning his Master, as far as it lies in human faculties to understand and comprehend" (*Mishneh Torah,* Book I, Laws of Repentance, ch. X). The protagonists of philosophy did not conceal the fact that they found perfunctory piety or unexamined traditionalism uncongenial and that routine Talmudism divorced from spiritual animation was not at the top of their scale of values. A prominent component of the philosophic apologia is also the desire to show the world (*i.e.,* fellow intellectuals) that Judaism has not forfeited its claim to, or skill in, philosophy and science. In common with their first-century coreligionists of Alexandria, they were deeply conscious, in H. A. Wolfson's words, of "the social significance of the philosophical interpretation of Scripture either as a means of satisfying the inquiring minds among the Jews or as a means of defending Judaism against the attacks" of antagonistic non-Jews. In their view, it was one of the lasting achievements of Maimonides that he helped restore lustre and dignity to Judaism by commanding the respectful attention of Christians and Moslems.

Opponents of philosophy vigorously condemn the development of rationalism and its detrimental consequences, are hostile to studies tainted by foreign origin and philosophical associations, and view the indiscriminate spread of allegorism as potentially disruptive of the Jewish tradition. The rationalization of the commandments and the reduction of the law, in some cases, to pragmatic-utilitarian categories were considered to be the prelude to antinomism, and contempt for traditional Jewish practices. They feared the victory of the "God of Aristotle" (as defined by Judah HaLevi) who is removed from and unconcerned with human affairs, who is not accessible in prayer, who would not and could not intervene miraculously in the natural course of events. In short, the reasons for opposition to philosophy and religious rationalization as articulated in the introduction to the *Emunot ve-Deot* remained valid: "there are people who disapprove of such an occupation, being of the opinion that speculation leads to unbelief and is conductive to heresy." Maimonides also reproduces the view of those who contended that philosophic inquiry "undermines the foundations of law" (*Guide,* I, ch. 33). Some—Hasdai Crescas in the fourteenth century is a good example—simply wanted to disentangle religion from philosophy, to extricate faith from the clutch of reason, and establish the complete independence of religion, even when philosophy purported to be in agreement with it. Religion should not be dependent on or subservient to anything.

The whole debate revolved around Maimonides—and, in many ways, still does. For Maimonides represents a type of mentality and suggests a direction of thought concerning which neutrality is impossible. In the final analysis, two conflicting ideal types were juxtaposed: a traditional puritanism which is distrustful of secular culture and insists on the absolute opposition between divine wisdom and human wisdom; and religious rationalism which is convinced of the interrelatedness and complementarity—indeed the essential identity—of divine and human wisdom, of religion and culture, and strives doggedly for their integration.

A synoptic view of Maimonides' work attests to its remarkable unity and systematic progression. In spite of changes, evolution of thought, allusive presentation of certain ideas, and outright contradictions, his work adds up to a judicious interpretation and systematic presentation of Jewish belief and practice. As it moves from one literary form to another, from textual explication to independent exposition, and from one level of exposition to another, one would think he had had a master plan from the very beginning to achieve his overarching objective: to bring law and philosophy—two apparently incongruous attitudes of mind, two jealous rivals—into fruitful harmony. We see him consistently espousing a sensitized view of religion and morality, demanding a full and uncompromising but inspired and sensitive observance of the law, openly disdaining the perfunctory, vulgar view of the masses, searching for the ultimate religious significance of every human action, and urging a commitment to and quest for wisdom and perfection. He wanted to unify mood and medium, to integrate the thought of eternity with the life of temporality, to combine religious tradition with philosophical doctrine. He knew that this could not be done easily or indiscriminately but he was convinced that the very attempt, though fraught with danger, was indispensable for true religious perfection. It may be said that Maimonides allowed religious rationalization, which had led a sort of subliminal existence in earlier rabbinic writing, to claim and obtain legitimacy and dignity.

Such an integrative view of Maimonides has significant repercussions for the study of his writings and warns against the widespread, misleading tendency on the part of students to fragmentize Maimonides' works. Throughout the ages, scholars have often set up a dichotomy between Maimonidean law and Maimonidean philosophy, or have even isolated different components of his legal legacy (i.e., have studied the code without the commentary or responsa). This failure to see and study Maimonides in his totality has often obscured the historical vision, blurred the real forms of his intellectual achievement, and erased his individuality.

There are, moreover, certain pre-eminent traits which are common to all of Maimonides' writings and these should be boldly underscored. Maimonides never tired of emphasizing that he wrote with great care and precision, that his ideas were rigorously reasoned, his balanced sentences were meticulously formulated, and the sections of his various writings were thoughtfully organized. He disclaimed anything haphazard or incidental, writing only "after reflection and deliberation and careful examination of true opinions as well as untrue ones." Concerning the *Guide* he said: "The diction of this treatise has not been chosen at haphazard, but with great exactness and exceeding precision, and with care to avoid failing to explain any obscure point." His rigorous attitude in general was described in the *Epistle on Conversion:* "It is not proper to speak publicly unless one has rehearsed what he wants to say many times and studied it well. This is how the rabbis interpreted the verse in Job 28:27-28. 'Then did He see it and declare it; He established it and searched it out.' And only after this punctilious preparation did He speak: 'and He said to man.' "

The compliment which the French encyclopedist Diderot paid to the German philosopher Leibniz is applicable to Maimonides: "He combined two great qualities which are almost incompatible with one another—the spirit of discovery and that of method." His writings are marked not only by ordered intelligibility and terse summation but also by creativity and originality. Sometimes he himself called attention to the "spirit of discovery" which permeated his work, as when he declared the *Mishneh Torah* to be a work of unprecedented scope and arrangement, for not since R. Judah the Prince redacted the Mishnah had anyone undertaken to rework and reformulate the entire *halakhah*. In the introduction to the *Guide* he claims to write about topics "which have not been treated by any of our scholars . . . since the times of our captivity." He did not engage in popularization in any conventional sense; he was a molder and architect of ideas.

Another outstanding feature of Maimonides was his intellectual honesty and courage, unintimidated by pressure, dissatisfaction, or potential censure. In his *Commentary on the Mishnah* he addressed himself to a certain problem even though he knew that his views would be uncongenial to most—or even all—of the great scholars; he proceeded "oblivious of predecessors or contemporaries." Elsewhere in that work he repudiates the method of R. Saadyah Gaon who used obviously fallacious arguments, which he himself did not accept, just for the purpose of vanquishing his opponents. In the *Eight Chapters* he asserts: "Let what others have said be compared with our opinion, and the truth will surely prevail." He was sensitive to the fact that his innovating code of law would give rise to abundant and vehement criticism—he even listed the kinds of critics that would rise against him—but this awareness did not deflect him from his course. Concerning the *Guide,* Maimonides says:

> I am the man who when the concern pressed him and his way was straitened and he could find no other device by which to teach a demonstrated truth other than by giving satisfaction to a single virtuous man while displeasing ten thousand ignoramuses—I am he who prefers to address that single man by himself, and I do not heed the blame of those many creatures.

Maimonides also felt the need to resist the tyranny of the published word. Most readers tend to dismiss something as obviously erroneous if it contradicts an earlier book; even scholars do not always examine a work critically in an effort to establish its intrinsic worth and plausibility but merely compare it with older books. Maimonides opposed the pervasive mood of intellectual conservatism which accepts anything published as authoritative, anything old and familiar as correct, and anything novel as suspect. Independent judgment and honest criticism must play an important role. In the Letter on Astrology, Maimonides exclaims:

> The great sickness and the grievous evil consist in this: that all the things that man finds written in books, he presumes to think of as true—and all the more so if the books are old.

A special aspect of this radical honesty and courage is his determination to "accept the truth from whatever source it proceeds." In other words, non-Jewish sources are equally relevant and valid. This inflexible determination is formulated early in the *Eight Chapters:*

> I have gleaned [the ideas] from the words of the wise occurring in the Midrashim, in the Talmud, and in other of their works as well as from the words of the philosophers, ancient and recent, and also from the works of various authors, as one should accept the truth from whatever source it proceeds.

It is repeated emphatically in the *Mishneh Torah,* where Maimonides extols the wise men of Greece and insists upon the indispensability of their scientific writings:

> . . . all this is part of the science of astronomy and mathematics, about which many books have been composed by Greek sages— books that are still available to the scholars of our time. But the books which had been composed by the sages of Israel, of the tribe of Issachar, who lived in the time of the Prophets, have not come down to us. But since all these rules have been established by sound and clear proofs, free from any flaw and irrefutable, we need not be concerned about the identity of their authors, whether they were Hebrew prophets or Gentile sages. For when we have to do with rules and propositions which have been demonstrated by good reasons and have been verified to be true by sound and flawless proofs, we rely upon the author who has discovered them or has transmitted them, only because of his demonstrated proofs and verified reasoning.

The importance of this principle for his philosophical and medical works is quite transparent.

While much of his writing has—or has been invested with—the quality of timelessness, Maimonides did not write in an historical vacuum, and it would be wrong to uproot him from his moorings in time and place. Explicitly and implicitly he addressed himself to the socio-political realities, spiritual problems, and intellectual challenges of his generation. To be sure, he left his imprint on his age and on future ages, but his age left its imprint on him as well. We may, in other words, learn a great deal from his writings about the intellectual and religious confrontations of his period: about the decline and fall of the Gaonate, the nature and seriousness of the Karaite attack on rabbinic tradition, the divisiveness within the Jewish community, the demands and problems of contemporary rationalism, the posture of Judaism vis-à-vis Christianity and Islam, the history—accomplishments and lacunae—of rabbinic and philosophic literature, the prevalent forms and methods of Biblical and Talmudic study, the varieties of Jewish and non-Jewish intellectual and religious experience.

A strong pedagogic sense, finally, motivates his writing. Starting with his youthful works on logic and astronomy, he shows himself eager to teach, to transmit knowledge, and to guide his readers. Failure to share one's knowledge with others would be tantamount to "robbing one who deserves the truth of the truth, or begrudging an heir his inheritance" (*Guide,* III, introduction). His own words in the *Guide of the Perplexed* (II, ch. 37) best express this: "A man endowed with knowledge does not set anything down for himself in order to teach himself what he already knows. But the nature of that intellect is such that it always overflows and is transmitted from one who receives that overflow to another one who receives it after him. . . ."

FROM PHILOSOPHY TO MYSTICISM

Impressive as are the range and substance of Maimonides' achievements, he was not the only master of biblical and Talmudic tradition, philosophy and metaphysics. Others exhibit in their person the same unity of tradition and perspective, modes of thought and ·expression within Rabbinic Judaism. Nachmanides is of special interest because he gives us an insight into how Rabbinic Judaism confronted the claims to truth put forward by other, very present religious communities, in his case, the Christian one. He shows us that rabbinism exhibited keen awareness to the alternatives in the Scriptural traditions and the capacity to argue in behalf of its own.

The dramatic moment in his life was his disputation in 1263 with Pablo Christiani, a convert from Judaism to Christianity. The purpose of the disputation, imposed by royal decree, was to argue the contested claims to truth of Judaism and Christianity. The setting was hardly neutral: the court of a Christian king, in whose territories the Jews lived by sufferance. Under such circumstances, discretion rather than forthrightness was called for.

No wonder, then, that Nachmanides, like Judah Halevi, found his way to the land of Israel. In a time of trouble, it was natural for thoughts to turn to the holy land and to the imagined blessedness of life there. But, as in the exilic community, so in the holy land was to be found ample evidence that the redemption had not yet come.

Nachmanides' works are, as is to be expected, devoted both to law and to theological and homiletical problems. In the manner of the rabbinic sage, he composed glosses to the Talmud. But it is in the theological works that he struck out in new directions. He did not phrase the central issue as had Saadia and Maimonides, the reconciliation of revelation and reason, but, in accord with the dilemmas of his own day, the need to "reconcile man with religion," in Schechter's words. The center of interest in his thought, therefore, is the nature, not of reason or rationality, but of man. For the exploration of human nature, Aristotle provides little help. Human destiny is to be resurrected and to stand in judgment. But this is not a source of fear. God is con-

213

cerned for mankind and judges man with mercy and love. That God knows man means that he loves man. Israel's loyalty to the Torah is a mark of the inseparable attachment between God and his people, a sign of reciprocal love.

Nachmanides' greatest literary achievement is his Commentary on the Pentateuch, which is meant to explain the Scriptures in response both to the best philology of his time, and to the situation of the Jewish people. The Torah is turned into a source of solace and comfort for the troubled day. The work is full of mystical hints; Nachmanides forms a bridge between the world of the philosophers and that of the mystics, uniting in his person the legal, exegetical, philosophical, and mystical elements characteristic of rabbinic Judaism.

13.

NACHMANIDES

Solomon Schechter

[From *Studies in Judaism,* by Solomon Schechter. London, 1896: Adam and Charles Black, pp. 120-172.]

R. Chayim Vital, in his *Book of the Transmigrations of Souls,* gives the following bold characteristic of the two great teachers of Judaism, Maimonides and Nachmanides. Their souls both sprang forth from the head of Adam—it is a favourite idea of the Cabbalists to evolve the whole of ideal humanity from the archetype Adam—but the former, Maimonides, had his genius placed on the left curl of Adam, which is all judgment and severity, whilst that of the latter, Nachmanides, had its place on the right curl, which represents rather mercy and tenderness.

I start from these words in order to avoid disappointment. For Nachmanides was a great Talmudist, a great Bible student, a great philosopher, a great controversialist, and, perhaps, also a great physician; in one word, great in every respect, possessed of all the culture of his age. But, as I have already indicated by the passage quoted by way of introduction, it is not of Nachmanides in any of these excellent qualities that I wish to write here. I shall mostly confine myself to those features and peculiarities in his career and works which will illustrate Nachmanides the tender and compassionate, the Nachmanides who represented Judaism from the side of emotion and feeling, as Maimonides did from the side of reason and logic.

R. Moses ben Nachman, or Bonastruc de Portas, as he was called by his fellow-countrymen, or Nachmanides, as he is commonly called now, was born in Gerona about the year 1195. Gerona is a little town in the province of Catalonia in Spain. But though in Spain, Gerona was not distinguished for its philosophers or poets like Granada, Barcelona, or Toledo. Situated as it was in the North of Spain, Gerona was under the influence of Franco-Jewish sympathies, and thus its boast lay in the great Talmudists that it produced.

Whoever his masters were, they must have been well satisfied with their promising pupil, for he undertook, at the age of fifteen, to write supplements to the Code of R. Isaac Alfasi. Nor was it at a much later date that he began to compose his work, *The Wars of the Lord,* in which he defends this great codifier against the strictures of R. Zerahiah. I shall in the course of this essay have further occasion to speak of this latter work; for the present we will follow the career of its author.

Concerning the private life of Nachmanides very little has come down to us. We only know that he had a family of sons and daughters. He was not spared the greatest grief that can befall a father, for he lost a son; it was on the day of the New Year. On the other hand, it must have been a great source of joy to him when he married his son Solomon to the daughter of R. Jonah, whom he revered as a saint and a man of God. As a token of the admiration in which he held his friend, the following incident may be mentioned. It seems that it was the custom in Spain to name the first child in a family after his paternal grandfather; but Nachmanides ceded his right in behalf of his friend, and thus his daughter-in-law's first son was named Jonah. Another son of Nachmanides whom we know of was Nachman, to whom his father addressed his letters from Palestine, and who also wrote Novellae to the Talmud, still extant in MS. But the later posterity of Nachmanides is better known to fame. R. Levi ben Gershom was one of his descendants; so was also R. Simeon Duran; whilst R. Jacob Sasportas, in the seventeenth century, derived his pedigree from Nachmanides in the eleventh generation.

As to his calling, he was occupied as Rabbi and teacher, first in Gerona and afterwards in Barcelona. But this meant as much as if we should say of a man that he is a philanthropist by profession, with the only difference that the treasures of which Nachmanides disposed were more of a spiritual kind. For his livelihood he probably depended upon his medical practice.

I need hardly say that the life of Nachmanides, "whose words were held in Catalonia in almost as high authority as the Scriptures," was not without its great public events. At least we know of two.

The one was about the year 1232, on the occasion of the great struggle about Maimonides' *Guide of the Perplexed,* and the first book of his great Compendium of the Law. The Maimonists looked upon these works almost as a new revelation, whilst the Anti-Maimonists condemned both as heretical, or at least conducive to heresy. It would be profitless to reproduce the details of this sad affair. The motives may have been pure and good, but the actions were decidedly bad. People denounced each other, excommunicated each other, and did not (from either side) spare even the dead from the most bitter calumnies. Nachmanides stood between two fires. The French Rabbis, from whom most of the Anti-Maimonists were recruited, he held in very high esteem and considered himself as their pupil. Some of the leaders of this party were also his relatives. He, too, had, as we shall see later on, a theory of his own about God and the world little in agreement with that of Maimonides. It is worth noting that Nachmanides objected to calling Maimonides "our teacher Moses" (Rabbenu Mosheh), thinking it improper to confer upon him the title by which the Rabbis honoured the Master of the Prophets. The very fact, however, that he had some theory of the Universe shows that he had a problem to solve, whilst the real French Rabbis were hardly troubled by difficulties of a metaphysical character. Indeed, Nachmanides pays them the rather doubtful compliment that Maimonides' work was not intended for them, who were barricaded by their faith and happy in their belief, wanting no protection against the works of Aristotle and Galen, by whose philosophy others might be led astray. In other words, their strength lay in an ignorance of Greek philosophy, to which the cultivated Jews of Spain would not aspire. Nachmanides was also a great admirer of Maimonides, whose virtues and great merits in the service of Judaism he describes in his letter to the French Rabbis. Thus, the only way left open to him was to play the part of the conciliator. The course of this struggle is fully described in every Jewish history. It is sufficient to say that, in spite of his great authority, Nachmanides was not successful in his effort to moderate the violence of their party, and that controversy was at last settled through the harsh interference of outsiders who well-nigh crushed Maimonists and Anti-Maimonists alike.

The second public event in the life of Nachmanides was his Disputation, held in Barcelona, at the Court and in the presence of King Jayme I., of Aragon, in the year 1263. It was the usual story. A convert to Christianity, named Pablo Christiani, who burned with zealous anxiety to see his former co-religionists saved, after many vain attempts in this direction, applied to the king of Aragon to order Nachmanides to take part in a public disputation. Pablo maintained that he could prove the justice of the Messianic claims of Jesus from the Talmud and other Rabbinic writings. If he could only succeed in convincing the great Rabbi of Spain of the truth of his argument, the bulk of the Jews was sure to follow. By the way, it was the same Talmud which some twenty years previously was, at the instance of another Jewish convert, burned in Paris, for containing passages against Christianity. Nachmanides had to conform with the command of the king, and, on the 21st of July, 1263, was begun the controversy, which lasted for four or five days.

I do not think that there is in the whole domain of literature less profitable reading than that of the controversies between Jews and Christians. These public disputations occasionally forced the Jews themselves to review their position towards their own literature, and led them to draw clearer distinctions between what they regarded as religion and what as folklore. But beyond this, the polemics between Jews and Christians were barren of good results. If you have read one you have read enough for all time. The same casuistry and the same disregard of history turn up again and again. Nervousness and humility are always on the side of the Jews, who know that, whatever the result may be, the end will be persecution; arrogance is always on the side of their antagonists, who are supported by a band of Knights of the Holy Cross, prepared to prove the soundness of their cause at the point of their daggers.

It will thus not be worth our while to dwell much on the matter of this controversy, in which the essence of the real dispute is scarcely touched. There are only two points in it which are worth noticing. The first is that Nachmanides declared the Agadoth in the Talmud to be only a series of sermons (he uses this very word), expressing the individual opinions of the preacher, and thus possessing no authoritative weight. The convert Pablo is quite aghast at this statement, and accuses Nachmanides of heterodoxy.

Secondly,—and here I take leave to complete the rather obscure passage in the controversy by a parallel in his book, *The Date of Redemption,* quoted by Azariah de Rossi—that the question of the Messiah is not of that dogmatic importance to the Jews that Christians imagine. For even if Jews supposed their sins to be so great that they forfeited all the promises made to them in the Scriptures, or that, on some hidden ground, it would please the Almighty never to restore their national independence, this would in no way alter the obligations of Jews towards the Torah. Nor is the coming of the Messiah desired by Jews as an end in itself. For it is not the goal of their hopes that they shall be able again to eat of the fruit of Palestine, or enjoy other pleasures there; not even the chance of the restoration of sacrifices and the worship of the Temple is the greatest of Jewish expectations (connected with the appearance of the Messiah). What makes them long for his coming is the hope that they will then witness, in the company of the prophets and priests, a greater spread of purity and holiness than is now possible. In other words, the possibility for them to live a holy life after the will of God will be greater than now. But, on the other hand, considering that such a godly life under a Christian government requires greater sacrifices than it would under a Jewish king; and, considering again that the merits and rewards of a good act increase with the obstacles that are in the way of executing it—considering this, a Jew might even prefer to live under the King of Aragon than under the Messiah, where he would perforce act in accordance with the precepts of the Torah.

Now there is in this statement much that has only to be looked upon as a compliment to the government of Spain. I am inclined to think that if the alternative laid before Nachmanides had been a really practical one, he would have decided in favour of the clement rule of the Messiah in preference to that of the most cruel king on earth. But the fact that he repeats this statement in another place, where there was no occasion to be over-polite to the government, tends to show, as we have said, that the belief in the Messiah was not the basis on which Nachmanides' religion was built up.

The result of the controversy is contested by the different parties; the Christian writers claim the victory for Pablo, whilst the Jewish documents maintain that the issue was with Nachmanides. In any case, *"der Jude wird verbrannt."* For in the next year (1264) all the books of the Jews in Aragon were confiscated and submitted to the censorship of a commission, of which the well-known author of the *Pugio Fidei,* Raymund Martini, was, perhaps, the most important member. The books were not burned this time, but had to suffer a severe mutilation; the anti-Christian passages, or such as were supposed to be so, were struck out or obliterated. Nachmanides' account of the controversy, which he probably published from a sense of duty towards those whom he represented, was declared to contain blasphemies against the dominant religion. The pamphlet was condemned to be burned publicly, whilst the author was, as it seems, punished with expulsion from his country. It is not reported where Nachmanides found a home during the next three years; probably he had to accept the hospitality of his friends, either in Castile or in the south of France; but we know that in the year 1267 he left Europe and emigrated to Palestine.

Nachmanides was, at this juncture of his life, already a man of about seventy. But it would seem as if the seven decades which he had spent in the Spanish Peninsula were only meant as a preparation for the three years which he was destined to live in the Holy Land, for it was during this stage of his life that the greatest part of his *Com-*

mentary on the Pentateuch was written. In this work, as is agreed on all sides, his finest thoughts and noblest sentiments were put down.

Before proceeding to speak of his works, let us first cast a glance at his letters from Palestine, forming as they do a certain link between his former life and that which was to occupy him exclusively for the rest of his days. We have three letters, the first of which I shall translate here *in extenso*.

The letter was written soon after his arrival at Jerusalem in the year 1267. It was addressed to his son Nachman, and runs as follows:—

"The Lord shall bless thee, my son Nachman, and thou shalt see the good of Jerusalem. Yea, thou shalt see thy children's children (Ps. cxxviii.), and thy table shall be like that of our father Abraham! In Jerusalem, the Holy City, I write this letter. For, thanks and praise unto the rock of my salvation, I was thought worthy by God to arrive here safely on the 9th of the month of Elul, and I remained there till the day after the Day of Atonement. Now I intend going to Hebron, to the sepulchre of our ancestors, to prostrate myself, and there to dig my grave. But what am I to say to you with regard to the country? Great is the solitude and great the wastes, and, to characterise it in short, the more sacred the places, the greater their desolation! Jerusalem is more desolate than the rest of the country: Judaea more than Galilee. But even in this destruction it is a blessed land. It has about 2000 inhabitants, about 300 Christians live there who escaped the sword of the Sultan. There are no Jews. For, since the arrival of the Tartars, some fled, others died by the sword. There are only two brothers, dyers by trade, who have to buy their ingredients from the government. There the Ten Men meet, and on Sabbaths they hold service at their house. But we encouraged them, and we succeeded in finding a vacant house, built on pillars of marble with a beautiful arch. That we took for a synagogue. For the town is without a master, and whoever will take possession of the ruins can do so. We gave our offerings towards the repairs of the house. We have sent already to Shechem to fetch some scrolls of the Law from there which had been brought thither from Jerusalem at the invasion of the Tartars. Thus they will organise a synagogue and worship there. For continually people crowd to Jerusalem, men and women, from Damascus, Zobah (Aleppo), and from all parts of the country to see the Sanctuary and to mourn over it. He who thought us worthy to let us see Jerusalem in her desertion, he shall bless us to behold her again, built and restored, when the glory of the Lord will return unto her. But you, my son, and your brothers and the whole of our family, you all shall live to see the salvation of Jerusalem and the comfort of Zion. These are the words of your father who is yearning and forgetting, who is seeing and enjoying, Moses ben Nachman. Give also my peace to my pupil Moses, the son of Solomon, the nephew of your mother. I wish to tell him . . . that there, facing the holy temple, I have read his verses, weeping bitterly over them. May he who caused his name to rest in the Holy Temple increase your peace together with the peace of the whole community."

This letter may be illustrated by a few parallels taken from the appendix to Nachmanides' *Commentary on the Pentateuch,* which contains some rather incoherent notes which the author seems to have jotted down when he arrived in Jerusalem. After a lengthy account of the material as well as the spiritual glories of the holy city in the past, he proceeds to say:—

> "A mournful sight I have perceived in thee (Jerusalem); only one Jew is here, a dyer, persecuted, oppressed and despised. At his house gather great and small when they can get the Ten Men. They are wretched folk, without occupation and trade, consisting of a few pilgrims and beggars, though the fruit of the land is still magnificent and the harvests rich. Indeed, it is still a blessed country, flowing with milk and honey. . . . Oh! I am the man who saw affliction. I am banished from my table, far removed from friend and kinsman, and too long is the distance to meet again. . . . I left my family, I forsook my house. There with my sons and daughters, and with the sweet and dear children whom I have brought up on my knees, I left also my soul. My heart and my eyes will dwell with them for ever . But the loss of all this and of every other glory my eyes saw is compensated by having now the joy of being a day in thy courts (O Jerusalem), visiting the ruins of the Temple and crying over the ruined Sanctuary; where I am permitted to caress thy stones, to fondle thy dust, and to weep over thy ruins. I wept bitterly, but I found joy in my tears. I tore my garments, but I felt relieved by it."

As to his works, we may divide them into two classes. The one would contain those of a strictly legalistic (Halachic), whilst the other those of a more homiletic-exegetical and devotional character (Agadic). As already indicated in the preliminary lines of this paper, I cannot dwell long on the former class of our author's writings. It consists either of Glosses or Novellæ to the Talmud, in the style and manner of the French Rabbis, or of Compendia of certain parts of the Law after the model set by R. Isaac Alfasi or Maimonides, or in defences of the "Earlier Authorities" against the strictures made on them by a later generation. A few words must be said with regard to these defences; for they reveal that deep respect for authority which forms a special feature of Nachmanides' writings. His *Wars of the Lord,* in which he defends Alfasi against R. Zerahiah of Gerona, was undertaken when he was very young; whilst his defence of the author of the *Halachoth Gedoloth* against the attacks of Maimonides, which he began at a much more mature age, shows the same deference "to the great ones of the past." Indeed, he says in one place, "We bow before them (the earlier authorities), and though their words are not quite evident to us we submit to them"; or, as he expresses himself elsewhere, "Only he who dips (deeply enough) in the wisdom of the 'ancient ones' will drink the pure (old) wine." But it would be unjust to the genius of Nachmanides to represent him as a blind worshipper of authority. Humble and generous in disposition, he certainly would bow before every recognised authority, and he would also think it his duty to take up the cudgels for him as long as there was even the least chance of making an honourable defence. But when this chance had gone, when Nachmanides was fully convinced that his hero was in the wrong, he followed no guide but truth. "Notwithstanding," he says in his introduction to the defences of the *Halachoth Gedoloth,* "my desire and delight to be the disciple of the Earlier Authorities, to maintain their views and to assert them, I do not consider myself a 'donkey carrying books.' I will explain their way and appreciate their value, but when their views are inconceivable to my thoughts, I will plead in all modesty, but shall judge according to the sight of my eyes. And when the meaning is clear I shall flatter none, for the Lord gives wisdom in all times and ages." But, on the other hand, there seems to have been a certain sort of literary agnosticism about Nachmanides which made it very difficult for him to find the "clear meaning." The passage in the *Wars of the Lord* to the effect "that there is in the art (of commenting) no such certain demonstration as in mathematics or astronomy," is well known and has often been quoted; but still more characteristic of this literary agnosticism is the first paragraph of the above-mentioned defences of the *Halachoth Gedoloth.* Whilst all his predecessors accepted, on the authority of R. Simlai, the number (613) of the commandments as an uncontested fact, and based their compositions on it, Nachmanides questions the whole matter, and shows that the passages relating to this enumeration of laws are only of a homiletical nature, and thus of little consequence. Nay, he goes so far as to say, "Indeed the system how to number the commandments is a matter in which I suspect all of us (are mistaken) and the truth must be left to him who will solve all doubts." We should thus be inclined to think that this adherence to the words of the earlier Authorities was at least as much due to this critical scepticism as to his conservative tendencies.

The space left to me I shall devote to the second class of his writings, in which Nachmanides worked less after given types. These reveal to us more of his inner being, and offer us some insight into his theological system.

The great problem which seems to have presented itself to Nachmanides' mind was less how to reconcile religion with reason than how to reconcile man with religion. What is man? The usual answer is not flattering. He is an animal that owes its existence to the same instinct that produces even the lower creatures, and he is condemned, like them, to go to a place of worm and maggot. But, may not one ask, why should a creature so lowly born, and doomed to so hapless a future, be burdened with the awful responsibility of knowing that he is destined "to give reckoning and judgment before the King of kings, the Holy One, blessed be He"? It is true that man is also endowed with a heavenly soul, but this only brings us back again to the antithesis of flesh and spirit which was the stumbling-block of many a theological system. Nor does it help us much towards the solution of the indicated difficulty; for what relation can there be between this *materia impura* of body and the pure intellect of soul? And again, must not the unfavourable condition in which the latter is placed through this uncongenial society heavily clog and suppress all aspiration for perfection? It is "a house divided against itself," doomed to an everlasting contest, without hope for co-operation or even of harmony.

The works *The Sacred Letter* and *The Law of Man* may be considered as an attempt by Nachmanides, if not to remove, at least to relieve the harshness of this antithesis. The former, in which he blames Maimonides for following Aristotle in denouncing certain desires implanted in us by nature as ignominious and unworthy of man, may, perhaps, be characterised as a vindication of the flesh from a religious point of view. The contempt in which "that Greek," as Nachmanides terms Aristotle, held the flesh is inconsistent with the theory of the religious man, who believes that everything (including the body, with all its functions) is created by God, whose work is perfect and good, without impure or inharmonious parts. It is only sin and neglect that disfigure God's creations.

The second of these two works, the *Law of Man,* may be regarded as a sanctification of grief, and particularly of the grief of griefs, death. The bulk of the book is legalistic, treating of mourning rites, burial customs, and similar topics; but there is much in the preface which bears on our subject. For here again Nachmanides takes the opportunity of combating a chilling philosophy, which tries to arm us against suffering by stifling our emotions. "My son," he says, "be not persuaded by certain propositions of the great philosophers who endeavour to harden our hearts and to deaden our sensations by their idle comfort, which consists in denying the past and despairing of the future. One of them has even declared that there is nothing in the world over the loss of which it is worth crying, and the possession of which would justify joy. This is an heretical view. Our perfect Torah bids us to be joyful in the day of prosperity and to shed tears in the day of misfortune. It in no way forbids crying or demands of us to suppress our grief. On the contrary, the Torah suggests to us that to mourn over heavy losses is equivalent to a service of God, leading us, as it does, to reflect on our end and ponder over our destiny."

This destiny, as well as Reward and Punishment in general, is treated in the concluding chapter of the *Law of Man,* which is known under the title of *The Gate of Reward.* Nachmanides does not conceal from himself the difficulties besetting inquiries of this description. He knows well enough that in the last instance we must appeal to that implicit faith in the inscrutable justice of God with which the believer begins. Nevertheless he thinks that only the "despisers of wisdom" would fail to bring to this faith as full a conviction as possible, which latter is only to be gained by speculation. I shall have by and by occasion to refer to the results of this speculation. Here we must only notice the fact of Nachmanides insisting on the *bodily* resurrection which will take place after the coming of the Messiah, and will be followed by the *Olam Habba* (the life in the world to come) of which the Rabbis spoke.

With the rationalist the soul is indeed a superior abstract intelligence created by God, but, like all his creations, has an existence of its own, and is thus separated from God. With the mystic, however, the soul is God, or a direct emanation from God. "For he who breathes into another thing (Gen. ii. 7) gives unto it something of his own breath (or soul)," and as it is said in Job xxxii. 8, "And the soul of the Almighty giveth them understanding." This emanation, or rather immanence—for Nachmanides insists in another place that the Hebrew term employed for it, *Aziluth,* means a permanent dwelling with the thing emanating—which became manifest with the creation of man, must not be confounded with the moving soul (or the *Nephesh Chayah*), which is common to man with all creatures.

It may be remarked here that Nachmanides endows all animals with a soul which is derived from the "Superior Powers," and its presence is proved by certain marks of intelligence which they show. By this fact he tries to account for the law prohibiting cruelty to animals, "all souls belonging to God." Their original disposition was, it would seem, according to Nachmanides, peaceful and harmless.

> About them frisking played
> All beasts of earth, since wild, and of all chace
> In wood or wilderness, forest or den.

It was only after man had sinned that war entered into creation, but with the coming of the Messiah, when sin will disappear, all the living beings will regain their primæval gentleness, and be reinstated in their first rights.

The special soul of man, however, or rather the "over-soul," was pre-existent to the creation of the world, treasured up as a wave in the sea or fountain of souls—dwelling in the eternal light and holiness of God. There, in God, the soul abides in its ideal existence before it enters into its material life through the medium of man; though it must be noted that, according to Nachmanides' belief in the Transmigration of souls, it is not necessary to perceive in the soul of every new-born child "a fresh message from heaven" coming directly from the fountain-head. Nachmanides finds this belief indicated in the commandment of levirate marriage, where the child born of the deceased brother's wife inherits not only the name of the brother of his actual father, but also his soul, and thus perpetuates his existence on earth. The fourth verse of Ecclesiastes ii. Nachmanides seems to interpret to mean that the very generation which passes away comes up again, by which he tries to explain the difficulty of God's visiting the iniquity of the fathers on their children; the latter being the very fathers who committed the sins. However, whatever trials and changes the soul may have to pass through during its bodily existence, its origin is in God and thither it will return in the end, "just as the waters rise always to the same high level from which their source sprang forth."

It is for this man, with a body so superior, and a soul so sublime— more sublime than the angels—that the world was *created*. I emphasise the last word, for the belief in the creation of the world by God from nothing forms, according to Nachmanides, the first of the three fundamental dogmas of Judaism. The other two also refer to God's relation to the world and man. They are the belief in God's Providence and his *Yediah*. Creation from nothing is for Nachmanides the keynote to his whole religion, since it is only by this fact, as he points out in many places, that God gains real dominion over nature. For, as he says, as soon as we admit the eternity of matter, we must (logically) deny God even "the power of enlarging the wing of a fly, or shortening the leg of an ant." But the whole Torah is nothing if not a record of God's mastery in and over the world, and of his miraculous deeds. One of the first proclamations of Abraham to his generation was that God is the Lord (or Master) of the world (Gen. xviii. 33). The injunction given to Abraham, and repeated afterwards to the whole of Israel (Gen. xvii. 2, and Deut. xviii. 13), to be perfect with God, Nachmanides numbers as one of the 613 commandments, and explains it to mean that man must have a whole belief in God without blemish or reservation, and acknowledge Him possessed of power over nature and the world, man and beast, devil and angel, power being attributable to Him alone. Indeed, when the angel said to Jacob, "Why dost thou ask after my name?" (Gen. xxxii. 29), he meant to indicate by his question the impotence of the heavenly host, so that there is no use in knowing their name, the power and might belonging only to God.

We may venture even a step farther, and maintain that in Nachmanides' system there is hardly room left for such a thing as nature or "the order of the world." There are only two categories of miracles by which the world is governed, or in which God's Providence is seen. The one is the category of the manifest miracles, as the ten plagues in Egypt, or the crossing of the Red Sea; the other is that of the hidden miracles, which we do not perceive as such, because of their frequency and continuity. "No man," he declares, "can share in the Torah of our Teacher, Moses (that is, can be considered a follower of the Jewish religion), unless he believes that all our affairs and events, whether they concern the masses or the individual, are all miracles (worked by the direct will of God), attributing nothing to nature or to the order of the world." Under this second order he classes all the promises the Torah makes to the righteous, and the punishments with which evil-doers are threatened. For, as he points out in many places, there is nothing in the nature of the commandments themselves that would make their fulfilment necessarily prolong the life of man, and cause the skies to pour down rain, or, on the other hand, would associate disobedience to them with famine and death. All these results can, therefore, only be accomplished in a supernatural way by the direct workings of God.

Thus miracles are raised to a place in the regular scheme of things, and the difficulty regarding the possibility of God's interferences with nature disappears by their very multiplication. But a still more important point is, that, by this unbroken chain of miracles, which unconditionally implies God's presence to perform them, Nachmanides arrives at a theory establishing a closer contact between the Deity and the world than that set forth by other thinkers. Thus, he insists that the term *Shechinah,* or *Cabod* (Glory of God), must not be understood, with some Jewish philosophers, as something separate from God, or as *glory created by God.* "Were this the case," he proceeds to say, "we could not possibly say, 'Blessed be the glory of the Lord from his place,' since every mark of worship to anything *created* involves the sin of idolatry." Such terms as *Shechinah,* or *Cabod,* can therefore only mean the immediate Divine presence. This proves, as may be noted in passing, how unphilosophical the idea of those writers is who maintain that the rigid monotheism of the Jews makes God so transcendental that He is banished from the world. As we see, it is just this assertion of His absolute Unity which not only suffers no substitute for God, but also removes every separation between Him and the world. Hence also Nachmanides insists that the prophecy even of the successors of Moses was a direct communion of God with the prophet, and not, as others maintained, furnished through the medium of an angel.

The third fundamental dogma, *Yediah,* includes, according to Nachmanides, not only the omniscience of God—as the term is usually translated—but also His recognition of mankind and His special concern in them. Thus, he explains the words in the Bible with regard to Abraham, "For I know him" (Gen. xviii. 19), to indicate the special attachment of God's providence to the patriarch, which, on account of his righteousness, was to be uninterrupted for ever; whilst in other places we have to understand, under God's knowledge of a thing, His determination to deal with it compassionately, as, for instance, when Scripture says that God knew (Exod. ii. 25), it means that His relation to Israel emanated from His attribute of mercy and love. But just as God knows (which means loves) the world, He requires also to be recognised and known by it. "For this was the purpose of the whole creation, that man should recognise and know Him and give praise to His name," as it is said, "Everything that is called by My name (meaning, chosen to promulgate God's name), for My glory have I created it."

It is this fact which gives Israel their high prerogative, for by receiving the Torah they were the first to know God's name, to which they remained true in spite of all adversities; and thus accomplished God's intention in creating the world. It is, again, by this Torah that the whole of Israel not only succeeded in being real prophets (at the moment of the Revelation), but also became *Segulah,* which indicates the inseparable attachment between God and His people, whilst the righteous who never disobey His will become the seat of His throne.

The position of the rest of humanity is also determined by their relation to the Torah. "It is," Nachmanides tells us, "a main principle to know that all that man contrives to possess of knowledge and wisdom is only the fruits of the Torah or the fruits of its fruits. But for this knowledge there would be no difference between man and the lower animated species. The existence of the civilised nations of the world does not disprove this rule, "both Christians and Mahometans being also the heirs of the Torah. For when the Romans gained strength over Israel they made them translate the Torah which they studied, and they even accommodated some of their laws and institutions to those of the Bible." Those nations, however, who live far away from the centre of the world (the Holy Land) and never come into contact with Israel are outside the pale of civilisation, and can hardly be ranked together with the human species. "They are the isles afar off, that have not heard my fame, neither have seen my glory."

What Nachmanides meant by maintaining that all knowledge and wisdom were "the fruits of the Torah, or the fruits of these fruits," will be best seen from his *Commentary on the Pentateuch*. I have already made use of this Commentary in the preceding quotations, but, being as it is the greatest of the works of Nachmanides, it calls for some special attention by itself. Its general purpose is edification, or as he says, "to appease the mind of the students (labouring under persecution and troubles) when they read the portion on Sabbaths and festivals, and to attract their heart by simple explanations and sweet words." The explanations occupy a considerable space. Our author neglected no resource of philology or archæology accessible in his age which could contribute to establish the "simple explanations" on a sound scientific basis. The prominent feature of this Commentary, however, is the "sweet words." Indeed, how sweet and soothing to his contemporaries must have been such words as we read at the end of the "Song of Moses" (Deut. xxxii.): "And behold there is nothing conditional in this Song. It is a charter testifying that we shall have to suffer heavily for our sins, but that, nevertheless, God will not destroy us, being reconciled to us (though we shall have no merits), and forgiving our sins for his name's sake alone. . . . And so our Rabbis said, Great is this song, embracing as it does both the past (of Israel) and the future, this world and the world to come. . . . And if this song were the composition of a mere astrologer we should be constrained to believe in it, considering that all its words were fulfilled. How much more have we to hope with all our hearts and to trust to the word of God, through the mouth of his prophet Moses, the faithful in all his house, like unto whom there was none, whether before him or after him." A part of these sweet words may also be seen in the numerous passages in which he attempts to account for various laws, and to detect their underlying principles.

For though "the Torah is the expression of God's simple and absolute will, which man has to follow without any consideration of reward," still this will is not arbitrary, and even that class of laws which are called *chukkim* (which means, according to some Jewish commentators, motiveless decrees) have their good reasons, notwithstanding that they are unfathomable to us. "They are all meant for the good of man, either to keep aloof from us something hurtful, or to educate us in goodness, or to remove from us an evil belief and to make us know his name. This is what they (the Rabbis) meant by saying that commandments have a purifying purpose, namely, that man being purified and tried by them becomes as one without alloy of bad thoughts and unworthy qualities." Indeed, the soul of man is so sensitive to every impurity that it suffers a sort of infection even by an unintentional sin. Hence the injunction to bring a *Korban* (sacrifice) even in this case; the effect of the *Korban,* as its etymology (*Karab*) indicates, is to bring man back to God, or rather to facilitate this approach. All this again is, as Nachmanides points out, only an affluence from God's mercy and love to mankind. God derives no benefit from it. "If he be righteous what can he give thee?" And even those laws and institutions which are intended to commemorate God's wonders and the creation of the world (for instance, the Passover festival and the Sabbath) are not meant for His glorification.

The lessons which Nachmanides draws from the various Biblical narratives also belong to these "sweet words." They are mostly of a typical character. For, true as all the stories in the Scriptures are, 'the whole Torah is," as he tells us (with allusion to Gen. v. i.), "the book of the generations of Adam," or, as we should say, a history of humanity written in advance. Thus the account of the six days of the creation is turned into a prophecy of the most important events which would occur during the succeeding six thousand years, whilst the Sabbath is a forecast of the millennium in the seventh thousand, which will be the day of the Lord. Jacob and Esau are, as in the old Rabbinic homilies generally, the prototypes of Israel and Rome; and so is the battle of Moses and Joshua with Amalek indicative of the war which Elijah and the Messiah the son of Joseph will wage against Edom (the prototype of Rome), before the Redeemer from the house of David will appear. Sometimes these stories convey both a moral and a pre-justification of what was destined to happen to Israel. So Nachmanides remarks with reference to Sarah's treatment of Hagar (Gen. xvi. 6): "Our mother Sarah sinned greatly by inflicting this pain on Hagar, as did also Abraham, who allowed such a thing to pass; but God saw her affliction and rewarded her by a son (the ancestor of a wild race), who would inflict on the seed of Abraham and Sarah every sort of oppression." In this he alluded to the Islamic empires. Nor does he approve of Abraham's conduct on the occasion of his coming to Egypt, when he asked Sarah to pass as his sister (Gen. xii.). "Unintentionally," Nachmanides says, "Abraham, under the fear of being murdered, committed a great sin when he exposed his virtuous wife to such a temptation. For he ought to have trusted that God would save both him and his wife. . . . It is on account of this deed that his children had to suffer exile under the rule of Pharaoh. There, where the sin was committed, also the judgment took place." It is also worth noticing that, in opposition to Maimonides, he allows no apology for the attack of Simeon and Levi on the population of Shechem (Gen. xxxiv. 25). It is true that they were idolaters, immoral, and steeped in every abomination; but Jacob and his sons were not commissioned with executing justice on them. The people of Shechem trusted their word, therefore they ought to have spared them. Hence Jacob's protest, and his curse against their wrath, which would have been quite unjustified had he looked on the action of his sons as a good work.

Besides these typical meanings, the matters of the Torah have also their symbolical importance, which places them almost above the sphere of human conception; they are neither exactly what they seem to be nor entirely what their name implies, but a reflex from things unseen, which makes any human interference both preposterous and dangerous. Of "the things *called* Tree of Life and Tree of Knowledge," Nachmanides tells us that their mystery is very great, reaching into higher worlds. Otherwise, why should God, who is good and the dispenser of good, have prevented Adam from eating the fruit (of the latter), whilst in another place he says: "And if thou wilt be worthy, and understand the mystery of the word *Bereshit* (with which the Torah begins), thou wilt see that in truth the Scripture, though apparently speaking of matters here below (on earth), is always pointing to things above (heaven)"; or "every glory and every wonder, and every deep mystery, and all beautiful wisdom are hidden in the Torah, sealed up in her treasures."

It is very characteristic of the bent of Nachmanides' mind that he is perhaps the first Jewish writer who mentions the apocryphal book *The Wisdom of Solomon,* which he knew from a Syriac version, and which he believed to be genuine. And when we read there (vii.7-25), "Wherefore I prayed and understanding was given to me. I called upon

God and the spirit of wisdom came upon me. . . . For God has given me unmistakable knowledge to know how the world was made, and the operations of the planets; the beginning, ending, and midst of the times, the alterations and the turnings of the sun, the changes of the seasons, the natures of the living creatures and the furies of the wild beasts, the force of the spirits and the reasonings of men, the diversities of plants and the virtues of the roots. All such things that are either secret or manifest, them I knew"—the wise king was, according to Nachmanides (who quotes the passages which I have just cited), speaking of the Torah, which is identical with this wisdom, a wisdom which existed before the creation, and by which God planned the world. Hence it bears the impression of all the universe, whilst on the other hand when it is said, "The king brought me into his chambers," those secret recesses of the Torah are meant in which all the great mysteries relating to Creation and to the Chariot (Ezekiel i.) are hidden.

We must content ourselves with these few sparks struck from the glowing fires of these inner compartments, which, imperfectly luminous as my treatment has left them, may yet shed some light on the personality of Nachmanides, which is the main object of this essay. But I do not propose to accompany the mystic into the "chambers of the king," lest we may soon get into a labyrinth of obscure terms and strange ways of thinking for which the Ariadne thread is still wanting. We might also be confronted by the Fifty Gates of Understanding, the Thirty-Two Paths of Wisdom, and the Two Hundred and Thirty-One Permutations or Ciphers of the Alphabet, the key to which I do not hold. It is also questionable whether it would always be worth while to seek for it. When one, for instance, sees such a heaping on of nouns (with some Cabbalists) as the Land of Life, the Land of Promise, the Lord of the World, the Foundation Stone, Zion, Mother, Daughter, Sister, the Congregation of Israel, the Twin Rose, the Bride, Blue, End, Oral Law, Sea, Wisdom, etc., meant to represent the same thing or attribute, and to pass one into another, one cannot possibly help feeling some suspicion that one stands before a conglomerate of words run riot, over which the writer had lost all control.

Indeed Nachmanides himself, in the preface to the above-mentioned Commentary, gives us the kind advice not to meditate, or rather brood, over the mystical hints which are scattered over this work, "speculation being (in such matters) folly, and reasoning over them fraught with danger." Indeed, the danger is obvious. I have, to give one or two instances, already alluded to the theory which accepts the Torah or the Wisdom as an agent in the creation of the world. But the mystic pushes farther, and asks for the Primal Being to which this Wisdom owes its origin. The answer given is, from the great Nothing, as it is written, And the Wisdom shall be found from Nothing. What is intended by this, if it means anything, is probably to divest the first cause of every possible quality which by its very qualifying nature must be limiting and exclusive. Hence, God becomes the Unknowable. But suppose a metaphysical Hamlet, who, handling words indelicately, should impetuously exclaim, To be or not to be, that is the question?—into what abyss of utter negations would he drag all those who despair, by his terrible Nothing.

On the other hand, into what gross anthropomorphisms may we be drawn by roughly handling certain metaphors which some Cabbalists have employed in their struggling after an adequate expression of God's manifestations in His attribute of love, if we forget for a single moment that they are only figures of speech, but liable to get defiled by the slightest touch of an unchaste thought.

But the greater the dangers that beset the path of mysticism, the deeper the interest which we feel in the mystic. In connection with the above-mentioned warning, Nachmanides cites the words from the Scriptures, "But let not the priests and the people break through to come up unto the Lord, lest he break forth upon them" (Exod. xix. 24). Nevertheless, when we read in the Talmud the famous story of the four Rabbis who went up into the *Pardes,* or Garden of Mystical Contemplation, we do not withhold our sympathy, either from Ben Azzai, who shot a glance and died, or from Ben Zoma, who shot a glance and was struck (in his mind). Nay, we feel the greatest admiration for these daring spirits, who, in their passionate attempt to "break through" the veil before the Infinite, hazarded their lives, and even that which is dearer than life, their minds, for a single glance. And did R. Meir deny his sympathies even to Other One or Elisha ben Abuyah, who "cut down the plants"? He is said to have heard a voice from heaven, "Return, oh backsliding children, except Other One," which prevented his repentance. Poor fallen Acher, he mistook hell for heaven. But do not the struggle and despair which led to this unfortunate confusion rather plead for our commiseration?

Nachmanides, however, in his gentle way, did not mean to storm heaven. Like R. Akiba, "he entered in peace, and departed in peace." And it was by this peacefulness of his nature that he gained an influence over posterity which is equalled only by that of Maimonides. "If he was not a profound thinker," like the author of the *Guide of the Perplexed,* he had that which is next best—"he felt profoundly." Some

writers of a rather reactionary character even went so far as to assign
to him a higher place than to Maimonides. This is unjust. What a blank
would there have been in Jewish thought but for Maimonides' great
work, on which the noblest thinkers of Israel fed for centuries! As long
as Job and Ecclesiastes hold their proper place in the Bible, and the
Talmud contains hundreds of passages suggesting difficulties relating to
such problems as the creation of the world, God's exact relation to it,
the origin of evil, free will and predestination, none will persuade me
that philosophy does not form an integral part of Jewish tradition,
which, in its historical developments, took the shape which Maimonides
and his successors gave to it. If Maimonides' *Guide,* which he considered as an interpretation of the Bible and of many strange sayings in
the old Rabbinic homilies in the Talmud, is Aristotelian in its tone, so
is tradition too; even the Talmud in many places betrays all sorts of
foreign influences, and none would think of declaring it un-Jewish on
this ground. I may also remark in passing that the certainty with which
some writers deprecate the aids which religion may receive from philosophy is a little too hasty. For the question will always remain, What
religion? The religion of R. Moses of Tachau or R. Joseph Jabez would
certainly have been greatly endangered by the slightest touch of speculation, while that of Bachya, Maimonides, Jedaiah of Bedres, and Del-
medigo undoubtedly received from philosophy its noblest support, and
became intensified by the union.

But apart from that consideration, the sphere of the activity of
these two leaders seems to have been so widely different that it is hardly
just to consider them as antagonists, or at least to emphasise the antagonism too much. Maimonides wrote his chief work, the *Guide,* for
the few elect, who, like Ibn Tibbon for instance, would traverse whole
continents if a single syllogism went wrong. And if he could be of use
to one wise man of this stamp, Maimonides would do so at the risk of
"saying things unsuitable for ten thousand fools." But with Nachmanides, it would seem, it was these ten thousand who formed the main
object of his tender care. They are, as we have seen, cultivated men,
indeed "students," having enjoyed a proper education; but the happy
times of abstract thinking have gone, and being under a perpetual strain
of persecutions and cares, they long for the Sabbath and Festivals, which
would bring them both bodily and spiritual recreation. They find no
fault with religion, a false syllogism does not jar on their ears; what
they are afraid of is that, being engaged as they are, all the six days
of work, in their domestic affairs, religion may be too good a thing for
them. "To appease their minds," to edify them, to make life more sweet

and death less terrible to them, and to show them that even their weaknesses, as far as they are conditioned by nature, are not irreconcilable
with a holy life, was what Nachmanides strove after. Now and then he
permits them a glance into the mystical world in which he himself loved
to move, but he does not care to stifle their senses into an idle contemplation, and passes quickly to some more practical application. To
be sure, the tabernacle is nothing but a complete map of the superlunar
world; but nevertheless its rather minute description is meant to teach us
"that God desires us to work."

This tendency toward being useful to the great majority of mankind may account for the want of consistency of which Nachmanides
was so often accused. It is only the logician who can afford to be
thoroughgoing in his theory, and even he would become most absurd
and even dangerous but for the redeeming fact "that men are better
than their principles." But with Nachmanides these "principles" would
have proved even more fatal. Could he, for instance, have upset authority in the face of the ten thousand? They need to be guided rather
than to guide. But he does not want them to follow either the Gaon or
anybody else slavishly, "the gates of wisdom never having been shut,"
whilst on the other hand he hints to them that there is something divine
in every man, which places him at least on the same high level with
any authority. Take another instance—his wavering attitude between
the Maimonists and the anti-Maimonists, for which he was often censured. Apart from other reasons, to which I have pointed above, might
he not have felt that, in spite of his personal admiration for Maimonides'
genius, he had no right to put himself entirely on the side where there
was little room for the ten thousand who were entrusted to his guidance,
whilst the French Rabbis, with all their prejudices and intolerance, would
never deny their sympathies to simple emotional folk?

This tender and absorbing care for the people in general may also
account for the fact that we do not know of a single treatise by Nachmanides of a purely Cabbalistic character in the style of the *Book of
Weight,* by Moses de Leon, or the *Orchard,* by R. Moses Corduera, or
the *Tree of Life* by R. Isaac Loria. The story that attributes to him the
discovery of the *Zohar* in a cave in Palestine, from whence he sent it to
Catalonia, needs as little refutation as the other story connected with
his conversion to the Cabbalah, which is even more silly and of such a
nature as not to bear repetition. The *Lilac of Mysteries* and other mystical works passed also for a long time under his name, but their claim to
this honour has been entirely disproved by the bibliographers, and they
rank now among the *pseudepigraphica.* It is true that R. Nissim, of

Gerona, said of Nachmanides that he was too much addicted to the belief
in the Cabbalah, and as a fellow-countryman he may have had some
personal knowledge about the matter. But as far as his writings go, this
belief finds expression only in incidental remarks and occasional citations
from the *Bahir,* which he never thrusts upon the reader. It was chiefly
when philosophy called in question his deep sympathies with even lower
humanity, and threatened to withdraw them from those ennobling influences under which he wanted to keep them, that he asserted his mystical theories.

Nachmanides' inconsistency has also proved beneficial in another
respect. For mysticism has, by its over-emphasising of the divine in
man, shown a strong tendency to remove God altogether and replace
Him by the creature of His hands. Witness only the theological bubble
of Shabbethai Tsebi—happily it burst quickly enough—which resulted
in mere idolatry (in more polite language, Hero Worship) on the one
side, and in the grossest antinomianism on the other. Nachmanides,
however, with a happy inconsistency, combined with the belief of man's
origin in God a not less strong conviction of man's liability to sin, of the
fact that he *does* sin—even the patriarchs were not free from it, as we
have seen above—and that this sin *does* alienate man from God. This
healthy control over man's extravagant idea of his own species was with
Nachmanides also a fruit of the Torah, within the limits of which everything must move, the mystic and his aspirations included, whilst its fair
admixture of 365 *Do not's* with 248 *Do's* preserved him from that "holy
doing nothing" which so many mystics indulged in, and made his a most
active life.

Much of this activity was displayed in Palestine, "the land to which
the providence of God is especially attached," and which was, as with
R. Judah Hallevi, always "his ideal home." There he not only completed his *Commentary on the Pentateuch,* but also erected synagogues,
and engaged in organising communities, whose tone he tried to elevate
both by his lectures and by his sermons. His career in Palestine was not
a long one, for he lived there only about three years, and in 1270 he
must already have been dead. A pretty legend narrates that when he
emigrated to Palestine his pupils asked him to give them a sign enabling
them to ascertain the day of his death. He answered them that on that
day a rift in the shape of a lamp would be seen in the tombstone of his
mother. After three years a pupil suddenly noticed this rift, when the
mourning over the Rabbi began. Thus, stone, or anything else earthly,
breaks finally, and the life of the master passes into light.

What life meant to him, how deeply he was convinced that there is no other life but that originating in God, how deeply stirred his soul was by the consciousness of sin, what agonies the thought of the alienation from God caused him, how he felt that there is nothing left to him but to throw himself upon the mercy of God, and how he rejoiced in the hope of a final reunion with Him—of all these sentiments we find the best expression in the following religious poem, with which this paper may conclude. Nachmanides composed it in Hebrew, and it is still preserved in some rituals as a hymn, recited on the Day of Atonement. It is here given in the English translation of Mrs. Henry Lucas.

Ere time began, ere age to age had thrilled,
I waited in his storehouse, as he willed;
He gave me being, but, my years fulfilled,
    I shall be summoned back before the King.

He called the hidden to the light of day,
To right and left, each side the fountain lay,
From out the stream and down the steps, the way
    That led me to the garden of the King.

Thou gavest me a light my path to guide,
To prove my heart's recesses still untried;
And as I went, thy voice in warning cried:
    "Child! fear thou him who is thy God and King!"

True weight and measure learned my heart from thee;
If blessings follow, then what joy for me!
If nought but sin, all mine the shame must be,
    For that was not determined by the King.

I hasten, trembling, to confess the whole
Of my transgressions, ere I reach the goal
Where mine own words must witness 'gainst my soul,
    And who dares doubt the writing of the King?

Erring, I wandered in the wilderness,
In passion's grave nigh sinking powerless;
Now deeply I repent, in sore distress,
    That I kept not the statutes of the King!

With worldly longings was my bosom fraught,
Earth's idle toys and follies all I sought;
Ah! when he judges joys so dearly bought,
    How greatly shall I fear my Lord and King!

Now conscience-stricken, humbled to the dust,
Doubting himself, in thee alone his trust,
He shrinks in terror back, for God is just—
    How can a sinner hope to reach the King?

Oh, be thy mercy in the balance laid,
To hold thy servant's sins more lightly weighed,
When, his confession penitently made,
    He answers for his guilt before the King.

Thine is the love, O God, and thine the grace,
That folds the sinner in its mild embrace;
Thine the forgiveness, bridging o'er the space
    'Twixt man's works and the task set by the King.

Unheeding all my sins, I cling to thee;
I know that mercy shall thy footstool be:
Before I call, Oh, do thou answer me,
    For nothing dare I claim of thee, my King!

O thou, who makest guilt to disappear,
My help, my hope, my rock, I will not fear;
Though thou the body hold in dungeon drear,
    The soul has found the palace of the King!

PART V

RABBINIC JUDAISM IN THE MYSTICAL IDIOM

While the specific theosophical doctrines of Jewish mysticism are interesting, what is more significant for our inquiry is the affect of mysticism upon the society formed by Rabbinic Judaism. The essence of mystical experience—as distinguished from mystical doctrines—is subjective, the direct personal encounter of the private person with God. And, as we now realize, the central, organizing characteristic of Rabbinic Judaism is its stress on the objective requirements of society, on the importance of deeds done by men and women in community. Rabbinic values are intellectual, shared, and amenable to reason; they are sober and stable; they are the foundation of a stable society. We should, therefore, have expected one of two results. Either rabbinism should have produced little mystical experience. Or it should have suppressed or driven out such experience as became public and socially relevant—and dangerous. The first is simply not so. Rabbinic Judaism, so deeply religious and devoted to God and his service, naturally called forth the deep spiritual experience which produces mystic encounter. And only those modes of mystical expression which threatened the integrity of the community and its law were proscribed.

In the main, Rabbinic Judaism welcomed and highly valued the mystical experience induced by prayer, asceticism, and devotion to Godly service. Indeed, so far as rabbinic civilization produced an inner and personal life, as distinct from a public and communal existence, that inner life took form in the direct encounter, through prayer and *mitsvot* at the very least, with God. To people who believed God real and very present, it was natural to seek the unnatural encounter of mysticism, and to attempt to phrase the results of that encounter in publicly accessible language, in specific docrines as to the nature and structure of the Godhead and of transcendant reality.

Among those specific doctrines, one is of greatest social consequence

239

for the vivification of Rabbinic Judaism. That is the conviction that every deed of man on earth has its counterpart in invisible reality. The Talmudic stress on practical action elevated concrete deeds into the highest heavens. What one did affected the most profound reality. "Thus I do such-and-so *mitsvah* for the sake of the unity of the Holy One blessed be he," said by the mystic before performing a commandment, meant that he believed by doing said commandment, he was able to help effect the greater unity of the one God. The doctrinal basis for that conviction need not detain us. Its social effect was to lay stress on the performance of those very deeds which the non-mystic did in a more routine spirit and for more mundane motives, habitually and in a spirit of conformity, because this is what one is supposed to do. But the mystic, knowing that one is supposed to do so for some deeper, or transcendent reason, brought new devotion to the old and established a pattern of deeds, reentered the community ever more concerned to do exactly what everyone else was doing, but for his own reason, and reenforced established social norms.

It is no accident that the great lawyers also were profound mystics. The author of the *Shulhan Arukh,* Joseph Karo, believed he received heavenly visitations. Nachmanides introduced into his commentary on the Pentateuch important mystical considerations. The Gaon of Vilna, that paragon of rabbinic rationality, also devoted his best efforts to the study of mystical literature. It would be difficult to locate a major legal authority who, after the mystic literature became available, also did not give much time to the study of mysticism. The law and the inner life were understood to be one and the same, the latter the spirit, the former the body, the latter the inner meaning, the former the outer capsule. It is no wonder, too, that the asceticism of the mystics of the Middle Ages took the form of ethical behavior, ascetic renunciation meaning the giving up of one's rights in favor of the other. In Rabbinic Judaism, mystical life became normative, even though the doctrines were esoteric. The appeal of mysticism was widespread and profound, and, toward the seventeenth and eighteenth centuries, mystic doctrines became popular, a major social force.

We shall consider four accounts of the role of mysticism in Rabbinic Judaism. The first is Gershom G. Scholem's description of the whole of the structure of mysticism in Judaism. The second is Abraham J. Heschel's portrayal of the spirit and doctrines of Jewish mysticism. The third describes one mode of mysticism, that found in medieval Germany, through the Book of the Pious, a prescription of mystical experience which led toward socially relevant and ethically oriented behavior. The final paper tells us about early nineteenth-century Hasidism, the formulation of Shneyur Zalman of Liady, who bridged the gap between the enthusiasm of early Polish Hasidism, on the one hand, with its stress on piety in preference to learning, and, on the other hand, the devotion of Rabbinic Judaism to mastery of the legal tradition. His synthesis of mystic emotions and rationalist erudition was so successful that it persists, fully vital, into the last third of the twentieth century and probably will go on long into the future.

THE MYSTIC WAY

Certainly the greatest master of the study of Jewish mysticism is Gershom G. Scholem. His *Major Trends* is the authoritative introduction to the subject. Scholem created the modern study of the subject and brought understanding of the Jewish mystical tradition to its present enviable state. Here he defines what we mean by "Jewish mysticism" and shows the important social aspect of any definition. He points out that, "Mysticism is a definite stage in the historical development of religion and makes its appearance under certain well-defined conditions." These are now to be carefully defined.

What is it that the mystic seeks? It is to come into the presence of God. Yet that aspiration, which is so private and personal, in Rabbinic Judaism is given a very public and social meaning. For experience of God's presence reenforces the observance of the law, which makes the mystic quest possible, giving it form and substance.

14.

GENERAL CHARACTERISTICS OF JEWISH MYSTICISM

Gershom G. Scholem

[From *Major Trends in Jewish Mysticism,* by Gershom G. Scholem. N.Y., 1954: Schocken Books, pp. 1-39.]

Since Jewish mysticism is to be the subject of these lectures, the first question bound to come up is this: what is Jewish mysticism? What precisely is meant by this term? Is there such a thing, and if so, what distinguishes it from other kinds of mystical experience? In order to be able to give an answer to this question, if only an incomplete one, it will be necessary to recall what we know about mysticism in general. I do not propose to add anything essentially new to the immense literature which has sprung up around this question during the past half-century. Some of you may have read the brilliant books written on this subject by Evelyn Underhill and Dr. Rufus Jones. I merely propose to rescue what appears to me important for our purpose from the welter of conflicting historical and metaphysical arguments which have been advanced and discussed in the course of the past century.

It is a curious fact that although doubt hardly exists as to what constitutes the phenomena to which history and philosophy have given the name of mysticism, there are almost as many definitions of the term as there are writers on the subject. Some of these definitions, it is true, appear to have served more to obscure the nature of the question than to clarify it. Some idea of the confusion engendered by these definitions can be gauged from the interesting catalogue of "Definitions of Mysticism and Mystical Theology" compiled by Dr. Inge as an appendix to his lectures on "Christian Mysticism."

A good starting-point for our investigation can be obtained by scrutinizing a few of these definitions which have won a certain authority. Dr. Rufus Jones, in his excellent "Studies in Mystical Religion" defines his subject as follows: "I shall use the word to express the type of religion which puts the emphasis on immediate awareness of relation with God, on direct and intimate consciousness of the Divine Presence. It is religion in its most acute, intense and living stage." Thomas Aquinas briefly defines mysticism as *cognitio dei experimentalis,* as the knowledge of God through experience. In using this term he leans heavily, like many mystics before and after him, on the words of the Psalmist (Psalm xxxiv, 9): "Oh taste and see that the Lord is good." It is this tasting and seeing, however spiritualized it may become, that the genuine mystic desires. His attitude is determined by the fundamental experience of the inner self which enters into immediate contact with God or the metaphysical Reality. What forms the essence of this experience, and how it is to be adequately described—that is the great riddle which the mystics themselves, no less than the historians, have tried to solve.

For it must be said that this act of personal experience, the systematic investigation and interpretation of which forms the task of all mystical speculation, is of a highly contradictory and even paradoxical nature. Certainly this is true of all attempts to describe it in words and perhaps, where there are no longer words, of the act itself. What kind of direct relation can there be between the Creator and His creature, between the finite and the infinite; and how can words express an experience for which there is no adequate simile in this finite world of man? Yet it would be wrong and superficial to conclude that the contradiction implied by the nature of mystical experience betokens an inherent absurdity. It will be wiser to assume, as we shall often have occasion to do in the course of these lectures, that the religious world of the mystic can be expressed in terms applicable to rational knowledge only with the help of paradox. Among the psychologists G. Stratton, in his "Psychology of Religious Life" (1911), has laid particular stress on this essential conflict in religious life and thought, even in its non-mystical form. It is well known that the descriptions given by the mystics of their peculiar experiences and of the God whose presence they experience are full of paradoxes of every kind. It is not the least baffling of these paradoxes—to take an instance which is common to Jewish and Christian mystics—that God is frequently described as the mystical Nothing. I shall not try now to give an interpretation of this term, to which we shall have to return; I only want to stress the fact that the particular reality which the mystic sees or tastes is of a very unusual kind.

To the general history of religion this fundamental experience is known under the name of *unio mystica,* or mystical union with God. The term, however, has no particular significance. Numerous mystics, Jews as well as non-Jews, have by no means represented the essence of their ecstatic experience, the tremendous uprush and soaring of the soul to its highest plane, as a union with God. To take an instance, the earliest Jewish mystics who formed an organized fraternity in Talmudic times and later, describe their experience in terms derived from the diction characteristic of their age. They speak of the ascent of the soul to the Celestial Throne where it obtains an ecstatic view of the majesty of God and the secrets of His Realm. A great distance separates these old Jewish Gnostics from the Hasidic mystics one of whom said: "There are those who serve God with their human intellect, and others whose gaze is fixed on Nothing. . . . He who is granted this supreme experience loses the reality of his intellect, but when he returns from such contemplation to the intellect, he finds it full of divine and inflowing splendor." And yet it is the same experience which both are trying to express in different ways.

This leads us to a further consideration: it would be a mistake to assume that the whole of what we call mysticism is identical with that personal experience which is realized in the state of ecstasy or ecstatic meditation. Mysticism, as an historical phenomenon, comprises much more than this experience, which lies at its root. There is a danger in relying too much on purely speculative definitions of the term. The point I should like to make is this—that there is no such thing as mysticism in the abstract, that is to say, a phenomenon or experience which has no particular relation to other religious phenomena. There is no mysticism as such, there is only the mysticism of a particular religious system, Christian, Islamic, Jewish mysticism and so on. That there remains a common characteristic it would be absurd to deny, and it is this element which is brought out in the comparative analysis of particular mystical experiences. But only in our days has the belief gained ground that there is such a thing as an abstract mystical religion. One reason for this widespread belief may be found in the pantheistic trend which, for the past century, has exercised a much greater influence on religious thought than ever before. Its influence can be traced in the manifold attempts to abandon the fixed forms of dogmatic and institutional religion in favour of some sort of universal religion. For the same reason the various aspects of religious mysticism are often treated as corrupted forms of an, as it were, chemically pure mysticism which is thought of as not bound to any particular religion.

As it is our intention to treat of a certain definite kind of mysticism, namely Jewish, we should not dwell too much upon such abstractions. Moreover, as Evelyn Underhill has rightly pointed out, the prevailing conception of the mystic as a religious anarchist who owes no allegiance of his religion finds little support in fact. History rather shows that the great mystics were faithful adherents of the great religions.

Jewish mysticism, no less than its Greek or Christian counterparts, presents itself as a totality of concrete historical phenomena. Let us, therefore, pause to consider for a moment the conditions and circumstances under which mysticism arises in the historical development of religion and particularly in that of the great monotheistic systems. The definitions of the term *mysticism,* of which I have given a few instances, lead only too easily to the conclusion that all religion in the last resort is based on mysticism; a conclusion which, as we have seen, is drawn in so many words by Rufus Jones. For is not religion unthinkable without an "immediate awareness of relation with God"? That way lies an interminable dispute about words. The fact is that nobody seriously thinks of applying the term *mysticism* to the classic manifestations of the great religions. It would be absurd to call Moses, the man of God, a mystic, or to apply this term to the Prophets, on the strength of their immediate religious experience. I, for one, do not intend to employ a terminology which obscures the very real differences that are recognized by all, and thereby makes it even more difficult to get at the root of the problem.

The point which I would like to make first of all is this: Mysticism is a definite stage in the historical development of religion and makes its appearance under certain well-defined conditions. It is connected with, and inseparable from, a certain stage of the religious consciousness. It is also incompatible with certain other stages which leave no room for mysticism in the sense in which the term is commonly understood.

The first stage represents the world as being full of gods whom man encounters at every step and whose presence can be experienced without recourse to ecstatic mediation. In other words, there is no room for mysticism as long as the abyss between Man and God has not become a fact of the inner consciousness. That, however, is the case only while the childhood of mankind, its mythical epoch, lasts. The immediate consciousness of the interrelation and interdependence of things, their essential unity which precedes duality and in fact knows nothing of it, the only monistic universe of man's mythical age, all this is alien to the spirit of mysticism. At the same time it will become clear why certain elements of this monistic consciousness recur on another plane and in different guise in the mystical consciousness. In this first stage, Nature is the scene of man's relation to God.

The second period which knows no real mysticism is the creative epoch in which the emergence, the break-through of religion occurs. Religions' supreme function is to destroy the dream-harmony of Man, Universe and God, to isolate man from the other elements of the dream stage of his mythical and primitive consciousness. For in its classical form, religion signifies the creation of a vast abyss, conceived as absolute, between God, the infiite and transcendental Being, and Man, the finite creature. For this reason alone, the rise of institutional religion, which is also the classical stage in the history of religion, is more widely removed than any other period from mysticism and all it implies. Man becomes aware of a fundamental duality, of a vast gulf which can be crossed by nothing but the *voice;* the voice of God, directing and lawgiving in His revelation, and the voice of man in prayer. The great monotheistic religions live and unfold in the ever-present consciousness of this bipolarity, of the existence of an abyss which can never be bridged. To them the scene of religion is no longer Nature, but the moral and religious action of man and the community of men, whose interplay brings about history as, in a sense, the stage on which the drama of man's relation to God unfolds.

And only now that religion has received, in history, its classical expression in a certain communal way of living and believing, only now do we witness the phenomenon called mysticism; its rise coincides with what may be called the romantic period of religion. Mysticism does not deny or overlook the abyss; on the contrary, it begins by realizing its existence, but from there it proceeds to a quest for the secret that will close it in, the hidden path that will span it. It strives to piece together the fragments broken by the religious cataclysm, to bring back the old unity which religion has destroyed, but on a new plane, where the world of mythology and that of revelation meet in the soul of man. Thus the soul becomes its scene and the soul's path through the abysmal multiplicity of things to the experience of the Divine Reality, now conceived as the primordial unit of all things, becomes its main preoccupation. To a certain extent, therefore, mysticism signifies a revival of mythical thought, although the difference must not be overlooked between the unity which is there before there is duality, and the unity that has to be won back in a new upsurge of the religious consciousness.

Historically, this appearance of mystical tendencies is also connected with another factor. The religious consciousness is not exhausted
with the emergence of the classic systems of institutional religion. Its
creative power endures, although the formative effect of a given religion
may be sufficiently great to encompass all genuine religious feeling
within its orbit for a long period. During this period the values which
such a religious system has set up retain their original meaning and
their appeal to the feelings of the believers. However, even so new
religious impulses may and do arise which threaten to conflict with the
scale of values established by historical religion. Above all, what encourages the emergence of mysticism is a situation in which these new
impulses do not break through the shell of the old religious system and
create a new one, but tend to remain confined within its borders. If
and when such a situation arises, the longing for new religious values
corresponding to the new religious experience finds its expression in
a new interpretation of the old values which frequently acquire a much
more profound and personal significance, although one which often
differs entirely from the old and transforms their meaning. In this way
Creation, Revelation and Redemption, to mention some of our most
important religious conceptions, are given new and different meanings
reflecting the characteristic feature of mystical experience, the direct
contact between the individual and God.

Revelation, for instance, is to the mystic not only a definite historical occurrence which, at a given moment in history, puts an end to
any further direct relation between mankind and God. With no thought
of denying Revelation as a fact of history, the mystic still conceives the
sources of religious knowledge and experience which bursts forth from
his own heart as being of equal importance for the conception of
religious truth. In other words, instead of the one act of Revelation,
there is a constant repetition of this act. This new Revelation, to himself or to his spiritual master, the mystic tries to link up with the sacred
texts of the old; hence the new interpretation given to the canonical
texts and sacred books of the great religions. To the mystic, the original
act of Revelation to the community—the, as it were, public revelation
of Mount Sinai, to take one instance—appears as something whose true
meaning has yet to unfold itself; the secret revelation is to him the real
and decisive one. And thus the substance of the canonical texts, like
that of all other religious values, is melted down and given another form
as it passes through the fiery stream of the mystical consciousness. It is
hardly surprising that, hard as the mystic may try to remain within the

confines of his religion, he often consciously or unconsciously approaches, or even transgresses, its limits.

It is not necessary for me to say anything further at this point about the reasons which have often transformed mystics into heretics. Such heresy does not always have to be fought with fire and sword by the religious community: it may even happen that its heretical nature is not understood and recognized. Particularly is the case where the mystic succeeds in adapting himself to the 'orthodox' vocabulary and uses it as a wing or vehicle for his thoughts As a matter of fact, this is what many Kabbalists have done. While Christianity and Islam, which had at their disposal more extensive means of repression and the apparatus of the State, have frequently and drastically suppressed the more extreme forms of mystical movements, few analogous events are to be found in the history of Judaism. Nevertheless, in the lectures on Sabbatianism and Hasidism, we shall have occasion to note that instances of this kind are not entirely lacking.

We have seen that mystical religion seeks to transform the God whom it encounters in the peculiar religious consciousness of its own social environment from an object of dogmatic knowledge into a novel and living experience and intuition. In addition, it also seeks to interpret this experience in a new way. Its practical side, the realization of God and the doctrine of the Quest for God, are therefore frequently, particularly in the more developed forms of the mystical consciousness, connected with a certain ideology. This ideology, this theory of mysticism, is a theory both of the mystical cognition of God and His revelation, and of the path which leads to Him.

It should now be clear why the outward forms of mystical religion within the orbit of a given religion are to a large extent shaped by the positive content and values recognized and glorified in that religion. We cannot, therefore, expect the physiognomy of Jewish mysticism to be the same as that of Catholic mysticism, Anabaptism or Moslem Sufism. The particular aspects of Christian mysticism, which are connected with the person of the Saviour and mediator between God and man, the mystical interpretation of the Passion of Christ, which is repeated in the personal experience of the individual—all this is foreign to Judaism, and also to its mystics. Their ideas proceed from the concepts and values peculiar to Judaism, that is to say, above all from the belief in the Unity of God and the meaning of His revelation as laid down in the Torah, the sacred law.

Jewish mysticism in its various forms represents an attempt to interpret the religious values of Judaism in terms of mystical values. It concentrates upon the idea of the living God who manifests himself in the acts of Creation, Revelation and Redemption. Pushed to its extreme, the mystical meditation on this idea gives birth to the conception of a sphere, a whole realm of divinity, which underlies the world of our sense-data and which is present and active in all that exists. This is the meaning of what the Kabbalists call the *world of the 'Sefiroth'*. I should like to explain this a little more fully.

The attributes of the living God are conceived differently and undergo a peculiar transformation when compared with the meaning given to them by the philosophers of Judaism. Among the latter, Maimonides, in his "Guide of the Perplexed", felt bound to ask: How is it possible to say of God that He is living? Does that not imply a limitation of the infinite Being? The words "God is living", he argues, can only mean that he is not dead, that is to say, that he is the opposite of all that is negative. He is the negation of negation. A quite different reply is given by the Kabbalist, for whom the distinction, nay the conflict, between the known and the unknown God has a significance denied to it by the philosophers of Judaism.

No creature can take aim at the unknown, the hidden God. In the last resort, every cognition of God is based on a form of relation between Him and His creature, i.e. on a manifestation of God in something else, and not on a relation between Him and Himself. It has been argued that the difference between the *deus absconditus,* God in Himself, and God in His appearance is unknown to Kabbalism. This seems to me a wrong interpretation of the facts. On the contrary, the dualism embedded in these two aspects of the one God, both of which are, theologically speaking, possible ways of aiming at the divinity, has deeply preoccupied the Jewish mystics. It has occasionally led them to use formulas whose implied challenge to the religious consciousness of monotheism was fully revealed only in the subsequent development of Kabbalism. As a rule, the Kabbalists were concerned to find a formula which should give as little offense as possible to the philosophers. For this reason the inherent contradiction between the two aspects of God is not always brought out as clearly as in the famous doctrine of an anonymous writer around 1300, according to whom God in Himself, as an absolute Being, and therefore by His very nature incapable of becoming the subject of a revelation to others, is not and cannot be meant in the documents of Revelation, in the canonical writings of the Bible, and in the rabbinical tradition. He is not the subject of these writings and therefore also has no documented name, since every word of the sacred writings refers after all to some aspect of His manifestation on the side of Creation. It follows that while the living God, the God of religion of whom these writings bear witness, has innumerable names—which, according to the Kabbalists, belong to Him by His very nature and not as a result of human convention—the *deus absconditus,* the God who is hidden in His own self, can only be name in a metaphorical sense and with the help of words which, mystically speaking, are not real names at all. The favorite formulae of the early Spanish Kabbalists are speculative paraphrases like "Root of all Roots," "Great Reality," "Indifferent Unity," and, above all, *En-Sof*. The latter designation reveals the impersonal character as this aspect of the hidden God from the standpoint of man as clearly as, and perhaps even more clearly than, the others. It signifies "the infinite" as such; not, as has been frequently suggested, "He who is infinite" but "that which is infinite." Isaac the Blind (one of the first Kabbalists of distinguishable personality) calls the *deus absconditus* "that which is not conceivable by thinking", *not* "He who is not etc." It is clear that with this postulate of an impersonal basic reality in God, which becomes a person—or appears as a person—only in the process of Creation and Revelation, Kabbalism abandons the personalistic basis of the Biblical conception of God. In this sense it is undeniable that the author of the above-mentioned mystical aphorism is right in holding that *En-Sof* (or what is meant by it) is not even mentioned in the Bible and the Talmud. In the following lectures we shall see how the main schools of Kabbalistic thought have dealt with this problem. It will not surprise us to find that speculation has run the whole gamut—from attempts to re-transform the impersonal *En-Sof* into the personal God of the Bible to the downright heretical doctrine of a genuine dualism between the hidden *En-Sof* and the personal Demiurge of Scripture. For the moment, however, we are more concerned with the second aspect of the Godhead which, being of decisive importance for real religion, formed the main subject of theosophical speculation in Kabbalism.

The mystic strives to assure himself of the living presence of God, the God of the Bible, the God who is good, wise, just and merciful and the embodiment of all other positive attributes. But at the same time he is unwilling to renounce the idea of the hidden God who remains eternally unknowable in the depths of His own Self, or, to use the bold expression of the Kabbalists "in the depths of His nothingness." This hidden God may be without special attributes—the living God of whom the Revelation speaks, with whom all religion is concerned, must have attributes, which on another plane represent also the mystic's own scale of moral values: God is good, God is severe, God is merciful and just, etc. As we shall have occasion to see, the mystic does not even recoil before the inference that in a higher sense there is a root of evil even in God. The benevolence of God is to the mystic not simply the negation of evil, but a whole sphere of divine light, in which God manifests Himself under this particular aspect of benevolence to the contemplation of the Kabbalist.

These spheres, which are often described with the aid of mythical metaphors and provide the key for a kind of mystical topography of the Divine realm, are themselves nothing but stages in the revelation of God's creative power. Every attribute represents a given stage, including the attribute of severity and stern judgment, which mystical speculation has connected with the source of evil in God. The mystic who sets out to grasp the meaning of God's absolute unity is thus faced at the outset with an infinite complexity of heavenly spheres and stages which are described in the Kabbalistic texts. From the contemplation of these 'Sefiroth' he proceeds to the conception of God as the union and the root of all these contradictions. Generally speaking, the mystics do not seem to conceive of God as the absolute Being or absolute Becoming but as the union of both; much as the hidden God of whom nothing is known to us, and the living God of religious experience and revelation, are one and the same. Kabbalism in other words is not dualistic, although historically there exists a close connection between its way of thinking and that of the Gnostics, to whom the hidden God and the Creator are opposing principles. On the contrary, all the energy of 'orthodox' Kabbalistic speculation is bent to the task of escaping from dualistic consequences; otherwise they would not have been able to maintain themselves within the Jewish community.

I think it is possible to say that the mystical interpretation of the attributes and the unity of God, in the so-called doctrine of the 'Sefiroth', constituted a problem common to all Kabbalists, while the solutions given to it by and in the various schools often differ from one another. In the same way, all Jewish mystics, from the Therapeutae, whose doctrine was described by Philo of Alexandria, to the latest Hasid, are at one in giving a mystical interpretation to the Torah; the Torah is to them a living organism animated by a secret life which streams and pulsates below the crust of its literal meaning; every one of the innumerable strata of this hidden region corresponds to a new and profound meaning of the Torah. The Torah, in other words, does not consist merely of chapters, phrases and words; rather is it to be regarded as the living incarnation of the divine wisdom which eternally sends out new rays of light. It is not merely the historical law of the Chosen People, although it is that too; it is rather the cosmic law of the Universe, as God's wisdom conceived it. Each configuration of letters in it, whether it makes sense in human speech or not, symbolizes some aspect of God's creative power which is active in the universe. And just as the thoughts of God, in contrast to those of man, are of infinite profundity, so also no single interpretation of the Torah in human language is capable of taking in the whole of its meaning. It cannot be denied that this method of interpretation has proved almost barren for a plain understanding of the Holy Writ, but it is equally undeniable that viewed in this new light, the Sacred Books made a powerful appeal to the individual who discovered in their written words the secret of his life and of his God. It is the usual fate of sacred writings to become more or less divorced from the intentions of their authors. What may be called their after-life, those aspects which are discovered by later generations, frequently becomes of greater importance than their original meaning; and after all—who knows what their original meaning was?

Like all their spiritual kin among Christians or Moslems, the Jewish mystics cannot, of course, escape from the fact that the relation between mystical contemplation and the basic facts of human life and thought is highly paradoxical. But in the Kabbalah these paradoxes of the mystical mind frequently assume a peculiar form. Let us take as an instance their relation to the phenomenon of speech, one of the fundamental problems of mystical thought throughout the ages. How is it possible to give lingual expression to mystical knowledge, which by its very nature is related to a sphere where speech and expression are excluded? How is it possible to paraphrase adequately in mere words the most intimate act of all, the contact of the individual with the Divine? And yet the urge of the mystics for self-expression is well known.

They continuously and bitterly complain of the utter inadequacy of words to express their true feelings, but, for all that, they glory in them; they indulge in rhetoric and never weary of trying to express the inexpressible in words. All writers on mysticism have laid stress on this point. Jewish mysticism is no exception, yet it is distinguished by two unusual characteristics which may in some way be interrelated. What I have in mind is, first of all, the striking restraint observed by the Kabbalists in referring to the supreme experience; and secondly, their metaphysically positive attitude towards language as God's own instrument.

If you compare the writings of Jewish mystics with the mystical literature of other religions you will notice a considerable difference, a difference which has, to some extent, made difficult and even prevented the understanding of the deeper meaning of Kabbalism. Nothing could be farther from the truth than the assumption that the religious experience of the Kabbalists is barren of that which, as we have seen, forms the essence of mystical experience, everywhere and at all times. The ecstatic experience, the encounter with the absolute Being in the depths of one's own soul, or whatever description one may prefer to give to the goal of the mystical nostalgia, has been shared by the heirs of rabbinical Judaism. How could it be otherwise with one of the original and fundamental impulses of man? At the same time, such differences as there are, are explained by the existence of an overwhelmingly strong disinclination to treat in express terms of these strictly mystical experiences. Not only is the form different in which these experiences are expressed, but the *will* to express them and to impart the knowledge of them is lacking, or is counteracted by other considerations.

It is well known that the autobiographies of great mystics, who have tried to give an account of their inner experiences in a direct and personal manner, are the glory of mystical literature. These mystical confessions, for all their abounding contradictions, not only provide some of the most important material for the understanding of mysticism, but many of them are also veritable pearls of literature. The Kabbalists, however, are no friends of mystical autobiography. They aim at describing the realm of Divinity and the other objects of the contemplation in an impersonal way, by burning, as it were, their ships behind them. They glory in objective description and are deeply averse to, letting their own personalities intrude into the picture. The wealth of expression at their disposal is not inferior to that of their autobiographical confrères. It is as though they were hampered by a sense of shame. Documents of an intimate and personal nature are not entirely lacking, but it is characteristic that they are to be found almost wholly in manuscripts which the Kabbalists themselves would hardly have allowed to be printed. There has even been a kind of voluntary censorship which the Kabbalists themselves exercised by deleting certain passages of a too intimate nature from the manuscripts, or at least by seeing to it that they were not printed. I shall return to this point at a later stage, when I shall give some remarkable instances of this censorship. On the whole, I am inclined to believe that this dislike of a too personal indulgence in self-expression may have been caused by the fact among others that the

Jews retained a particularly vivid sense of the incongruity between mystical experience and that idea of God which stresses the aspects of Creator, King and Law-giver. It is obvious that the absence of the autobiographical element is a serious obstacle to any psychological understanding of Jewish mysticism as the psychology of mysticism has to rely primarily on the study of such autobiographical material.

In general, it may be said that in the long history of Kabbalism, the number of Kabbalists whose teachings and writings bear the imprint of a strong personality is surprisingly small, one notable exception being the Hasidic movement and its leaders since 1750. This is partly due to personal reticence, which as we have seen was characteristic of all Jewish mystics. Equally important, however, is the fact that our sources leave us completely in the dark as regards the personalities of many Kabbalists, including writers whose influence was very great and whose teachings it would be worth while to study in the light of biographical material, were any available. Often enough such contemporary sources as there are do not even mention their names! Frequently, too, all that these writers have left us are their mystical tracts and books from which it is difficult, if not impossible, to form an impression of their personalities. There are very few exceptions to this rule. Among hundreds of Kabbalists whose writings are known to us, hardly ten would provide sufficient material for a biography containing more than a random collection of facts, with little or nothing to give us an insight into their personalities. This is true, for example, of Abraham Abulafia (13th century), of Isaac Luria (16th century) and, at a much later period, of the great mystic and poet Moses Hayim Luzzatto of Padua (died 1747), whose case is typical of the situation I have described. Although his mystical, moralizing and poetical works fill several volumes and many of them have been published, the true personality of the author remained so completely in the shadow as to be little more than a name until the discovery and publication, by Dr. Simon Ginzburg, of his correspondence with his teacher and his friends threw an abundance of light on this remarkable figure. It is to be hoped that the same will gradually be done for other great Jewish mystics of whom today we know very little.

My second point was that Kabbalism is distinguished by an attitude towards language which is quite unusually positive. Kabbalists who differ in almost everything else are at one in regarding language as something more precious than an inadequate instrument for contact between human beings. To them Hebrew, the holy tongue, is not simply a means of expressing certain thoughts, born out of a certain convention and having a purely conventional character, in accordance with the theory of language dominant in the Middle Ages. Language in its purest form, that is, Hebrew, according to the Kabbalists, reflects the fundamental spiritual nature of the world; in other words, it has a mystical value. Speech reaches God because it comes from God. Man's common language, whose prima facie function, indeed, is only of an intellectual nature, reflects the creative language of God. All creation—and this is an important principle of most Kabbalists—is, from the point of view of God, nothing but an expression of His hidden self that begins and ends by giving itself a name, the holy name of God, the perpetual act of creation. All that lives is an expression of God's language,—and what is it that Revelation can reveal in the last resort if not the name of God?

I shall have to return to this point at a latter stage. What I would like to emphasize is this peculiar interpretation, this enthusiastic appreciation of the faculty of speech which sees in it, and in its mystical analysis, a key to the deepest secrets of the Creator and His creation.

In this connection it may be of interest to ask ourselves what was the common attitude of the mystics toward certain other faculties and phenomena, such as intellectual knowledge, and more particularly rational philosophy; or, to take another instance, the problem of individual existence. For after all, mysticism, while beginning with the religion of the individual, proceeds to merge the self into a higher union. Mysticism postulates self-knowledge, to use a Platonic term, as the surest way to God who reveals Himself in the depths of the self. Mystical tendencies, in spite of their strictly personal character, have therefore frequently led to the formation of new social groupings and communities, a fact which is true also of Jewish mysticism; we shall have to return to this fact and to the problem it involves at the end of these lectures. At any rate, Joseph Bernhart, one of the explorers of the world of mysticism, was justified in saying "Have any done more to create historical movement than those who seek and proclaim the immovable?"

It is precisely this question of history which brings us back to the problem from which we started: What is Jewish mysticism? For now the question is: What is to be regarded as the general characteristic of mysticism within the framework of Jewish tradition? Kabbalah, it must be remembered, is not the name of a certain dogma or system, but rather the general term applied to a whole religious movement. This movement, with some of whose stages and tendencies we shall have to acquaint ourselves, has been going on from Talmudic times to the present day; its development has been uninterrupted, though by no means uniform, and often dramatic. It leads from Rabbi Akiba, of whom the Talmud says that he left the 'Paradise' of mystical speculation safe and sane as he had entered it—something which cannot, indeed, be said of every Kabbalist—to the late Rabbi Abraham Isaac Kook, the religious leader of the Jewish community in Palestine and a splendid type of Jewish mystic. I should like to mention here that we are in possession of a vast printed literature of mystical texts which I am inclined to estimate at 3,000. In addition, there exists an even greater array of manuscripts not yet published.

Within this movement there exists a considerable variety of religious experience, to use William James' expression. There have been many different currents of thought, and various systems and forms of speculation. There is little resemblance between the earliest mystical texts in our possession, dating from Talmudic and post-Talmudic days, the writings of the ancient Spanish Kabbalists, those of the school which later flourished in Safed, the holy city of Kabbalism in the sixteenth century, and finally the Hasidic literature of the modern age. Yet the question must be asked whether there is not something more than a purely historical connection uniting these *disjecta membra,* something which also provides us with a hint as to what renders this mystical movement in Judaism different from non-Jewish mysticism. Such a common denominator can, perhaps, be discovered in certain unchanging fundamental ideas concerning God, creation and the part played by man in the universe. Two such ideas I have mentioned above, namely the attributes of God and the symbolic meaning of the Torah. But may it not also be that such a denominator is to be found in the attitude of the Jewish mystic towards those dominant spiritual forces which have conditioned and shaped the intellectual life of Jewry during the past two thousand years: the Halakhah, the Aggadah, the prayers and the philosophy of Judaism, to name the most important? It is this question which I shall now try to answer, though without going into detail.

As I have said before, the relation of mysticism to the world of history can serve as a useful starting-point for our investigation. It is generally believed that the attitude of mysticism toward history is one of aloofness, or even of contempt. The historical aspects of religion have a meaning for the mystic chiefly as symbols of acts which he conceives as being divorced from time, or constantly repeated in the soul of every man. Thus the exodus from Egypt, the fundamental event of our history, cannot, according to the mystic, have come to pass once only and in one place; it must correspond to an event which takes place in ourselves, an exodus from an inner Egypt in which we all are slaves. Only thus conceived does the Exodus cease to be an object of learning and acquire the dignity of immediate religious experience. In the same way, it will be remembered, the doctrine of "Christ in us" acquired so great an importance for the mystics of Christianity that the historical Jesus of Nazareth was quite often relegated to the background. If, however, the Absolute which the mystic seeks is not to be found in the varying occurrences of history, the conclusion suggests itself that it must either precede the course of mundane history or reveal itself at the end of time. In other words, knowledge both of the primary facts of creation and of its end, of eschatological salvation and bliss, can acquire a mystical significance.

"The Mystic," says Charles Bennett in a penetrating essay, "as it were forestalls the processes of history by anticipating in his own life the enjoyment of the last age." This eschatological nature of mystical knowledge becomes of paramount importance in the writings of many Jewish mystics, from the anonymous authors of the early *Hekhaloth* tracts to Rabbi Nahman of Brazlav. And the importance of cosmogony for mystical speculation is equally exemplified by the case of Jewish mysticism. The consensus of Kabbalistic opinion regards the mystical way to God as a reversal of the procession by which we have emanated from God. To know the stages of the creative process is also to know the stages of one's own return to the root of all existence. In this sense, the interpretation of *Maaseh Bereshith,* the esoteric doctrine of creation, has always formed one of the main preoccupations of Kabbalism. It is here that Kabbalism comes nearest to Neoplatonic thought, of which it has been said with truth that "procession and reversion together constitute a single movement, the diastole-systole, which is the life of the universe." Precisely this is also the belief of the Kabbalist.

But the cosmogonic and the eschatological trend of Kabbalistic speculation which we have tried to define, are in the last resort ways of escaping from history rather than instruments of historical understanding; that is to say, they do not help us to gauge the intrinsic meaning of history.

There is, however, a more striking instance of the link between the conceptions of Jewish mysticism and those of the historical world. It is a remarkable fact that the very term *Kabbalah* under which it has become best known, is derived from an historical concept. Kabbalah means literally "tradition", in itself an excellent example of the paradoxical nature of mysticism to which I have referred before. The very doctrine which centres about the immediate personal contact with the Divine, that is to say, a highly personal and intimate form of knowledge, is conceived as traditional wisdom. The fact is, however, that the idea of Jewish mysticism from the start combined the conception of a knowledge which by its very nature is difficult to impart and therefore secret, with that of a knowledge which is the secret tradition of chosen spirits or adepts. Jewish mysticism, therefore, is a secret doctrine in a double sense, a characteristic which cannot be said to apply to all forms of mysticism. It is a secret doctrine because it treats of the most deeply hidden and fundamental matters of human life; but it is secret also because it is confined to a small élite of the chosen who impart the knowledge to their disciples. It is true that this picture never wholly corresponded to life. Against the doctrine of the chosen few who alone may participate in the mystery must be set the fact that, at least during certain periods of history, the Kabbalists themselves have tried to bring under their influence much wider circles, and even the whole nation. There is a certain analogy between this development and that of the mystery religions of the Hellenic period of antiquity, when secret doctrines of an essentially mystical nature were diffused among an ever-growing number of people.

It must be kept in mind that in the sense in which it is understood by the Kabbalist himself, mystical knowledge is not his private affair which has been revealed to him, and to him only, in his personal experience. On the contrary, the purer and more nearly perfect it is, the nearer it is to the original stock of knowledge common to mankind. To use the expression of the Kabbalist, the knowledge of things human and divine that Adam, the father of mankind, possessed is therefore also the property of the mystic. For this reason, the Kabbalah advanced what was at once a claim and an hypothesis, namely, that its function was to hand down to its own disciples the secret of God's revelation to Adam. Little though this claim is grounded in fact—and I am even inclined to believe that many Kabbalists did not regard it seriously—the fact that such a claim was made appears to me highly characteristic of Jewish mysticism. Reverance for the traditional has always been deeply rooted in Judaism, and even the mystics, who in fact broke away from tradition, retained a reverent attitude towards it; it led them directly to their conception of the coincidence of true intuition and true tradition. This theory has made possible such a paradox as the Kabbalah of Isaac Luria, the most influential system of later Kabbalism, though the most difficult. Nearly all the important points and major theses in Luria's system are novel, one might even say excitingly novel—and yet they were accepted throughout as true Kabbalah, i.e. traditional wisdom. There was nobody to see a contradiction in this.

Considerations of a different kind will take us even deeper into the understanding of the problem. I have already said that the mystical sphere is the meeting-place of two worlds or stages in the development of the human consciousness: one primitive and one developed, the world of mythology and that of revelation. This fact cannot be left out of account in dealing with the Kabbalah. Whoever tries to gain a better understanding of its ideas, without attempting anything in the nature of an apology, cannot fail to notice that it contains, side by side with a deep and sensitive understanding of the essence of religious feeling, a certain mode of thought characteristic of primitive mythological thinking. The peculiar affinity of Kabbalist thought to the world of myth cannot well be doubted, and should certainly not be obscured or lightly passed over by those of us to whom the notion of a mythical domain within Judaism seems strange and paradoxical and who are accustomed to think of Jewish Monotheism as the classical example of a religion which has severed all links with the mythical. It is, indeed, surprising that in the very heart of Judaism ideas and notions sprang up which purported to interpret its meaning better than any others, and which yet represent a relapse into, or if you like a revival of, the mythical consciousness. This is particularly true of the Zohar and the Lurianic Kabbalah, that is to say, of those forms of Jewish mysticism which have exerted by far the greatest influence in Jewish history and which for centuries stood out in the popular mind as bearers of the final and deepest truth in Jewish thought.

It is no use getting indignant over these facts, as the great historian Graetz did; they should rather set us thinking. Their importance for the history of the Jewish people, particularly during the past four centuries, has been far too great to permit them to be ridiculed and treated as mere deviations. Perhaps, after all, there is something wrong with the popular conception of Monotheism as being opposed to the mythical; perhaps Monotheism contains room after all, on a deeper plane, for the development of mythical lore. I do not believe that all those devoted and pious spirits, practically the vast majority of Ashkenazic and Sephardic Jewry, ceased, after the exodus from Spain, to be Jews also in the religious sense, only because their forms of belief appear to be in manifest contradiction with certain modern theories of Judaism. I, therefore, ask myself: What is the secret of this tremendous success of the Kabbalah among our people? Why did it succeed in becoming a decisive factor in our history, shaping the life of a large proportion of Jewry over a period of centuries, while its contemporary, rational Jewish philosophy, was incapable of achieving the spiritual hegemony after which it strove? This is a pressing question; I cannot accept the explanation that the facts I have described are solely due to external historical circumstances, that persecution and decline weakened the spirit of the people and made them seek refuge in the darkness of Mysticism because they could not bear the light of Reason. The matter appears to me to be more complicated, and I should like briefly to set out my answer to the question.

The secret of the success of the Kabbalah lies in the nature of its relation to the spiritual heritage of rabbinical Judaism. This relation differs from that of rationalist philosophy, in that it is more deeply and in a more vital sense connected with the main forces active in Judaism.

Undoubtedly both the mystics and the philosophers completely transform the structure of ancient Judaism; both have lost the simple relation to Judaism, that naiveté which speaks to us from the classical documents of Rabbinical literature. Classical Judaism expressed itself: it did not reflect upon itself. By contrast, to the mystics and the philosophers of a later stage of religious development Judaism itself has become problematical. Instead of simply speaking their minds, they tend to produce an ideology of Judaism, an ideology moreover which comes to the rescue of tradition by giving it a new interpretation. It is not as though the rise of Jewish philosophy and of Jewish mysticism took place in widely separated ages, or as though the Kabbalah, as Graetz saw it, was a reaction against a wave of rationalism. Rather the two movements are interrelated and interdependent. Neither were they from the start manifestly opposed to each other, a fact which is often overlooked. On the contrary, the rationalism of some of the philosophical *enlighteners* frequently betrays a mystical tendency; and conversely, the mystic who has not yet learnt to speak in his own language often uses and misuses the vocabulary of philosophy. Only very gradually did the Kabbalists, rather than the philosophers, begin to perceive the implications of their own ideas, the conflict between a purely philosophical interpretation of the world, and an attitude which progresses from rational thought to irrational meditation, and from there to the mystical interpretation of the universe.

What many mystics felt towards philosophy was succinctly expressed by Rabbi Moses of Burgos (end of the 13th century). When he heard the philosophers praised, he used to say angrily: "You ought to know that these philosophers whose wisdom you are praising, end where we begin." Actually this means two things: on the one hand, it means that the Kabbalists are largely concerned with the investigation of a sphere of religious reality which lies quite outside the orbit of mediaeval Jewish philosophy; their purpose is to discover a new stratum of the religious consciousness. On the other hand, though R. Moses may not have intended to say this, they stand on the shoulders of the philosophers and it is easier for them to see a little farther than their rivals.

To repeat, the Kabbalah certainly did not *arise* as a reaction against philosophical 'enlightenment,' but once it was there it is true that its function was that of an opposition to it. At the same time, an intellectual dispute went on between the Kabbalah and the forces of the philosophical movement which left deep marks upon the former's structure. In my opinion, there is a direct connection between Jehudah Halevi, the most Jewish of Jewish philosophers, and the Kabbalists. For the legitimate trustees of his spiritual heritage have been the mystics, and not the succeeding generations of Jewish philosophers.

The Kabbalists employed the ideas and conceptions of orthodox theology, but the magic hand of mysticism opened up hidden sources of new life in the heart of many scholastic ideas and abstractions. Philosophers may shake their heads at what must appear to them a misunderstanding of the meaning of philosophical ideas. But what from the philosopher's point of view represents a flaw in the conception can constitute its greatness and dignity in the religious sense. After all, a misunderstanding is often nothing but the paradoxical abbreviation of an original line of thought. And it is precisely such misunderstanding which has frequently become productive of new ideas in the mystical sphere.

Let us take, as an example of what I have said, the idea of "creation out of nothing." In the dogmatic disputations of Jewish philosophy, the question whether Judaism implies belief in this concept, and if so, in what precise sense, has played an important part. I shall not go into the difficulties with which the orthodox theologians found themselves faced whenever they tried to preserve the full meaning of this idea of creation out of nothing. Viewed in its simplest sense, it affirms the creation of the world by God out of something which is neither God Himself nor any kind of existence, but simply the non-existent. The mystics, too, speak of creation out of nothing; in fact, it is one of their favorite formulae. But in their case the orthodoxy of the term conceals a meaning which differs considerably from the original one. This *Nothing* from which everything has sprung is by no means a mere negation; only to us does it present no attributes because it is beyond the reach of intellectual knowledge. In truth, however, this Nothing—to quote one of the Kabbalists—is infinitely more real than all other reality. Only when the soul has stripped itself of all limitation and, in mystical language, has descended into the depths of Nothing does it encounter the Divine. For this *Nothing* comprises a wealth of mystical reality although it cannot be defined. "Un Dieu défini serait un Dieu fini." In a word, it signifies the Divine itself, in its most impenetrable guise. And, in fact, *creation out of nothing* means to many mystics just *creation out of God*. Creation out of nothing thus becomes the symbol of emanation, that is to say, of an idea which, in the history of philosophy and theology, stands farthest removed from it.

Let us return to our original problem. As we have seen, the renaissance of Judaism on a new plane is the common concern of both the mystics and the philosophers. For all that, there remains a very considerable difference, a good example of which is afforded by the conception of *Sithre Torah,* or "Secrets of the Law". The philosophers no less than the mystics talk of discovering these secrets, using this esoteric phraseology with a profusion hardly distinguishable from the style of the real esoterics and Kabbalists. But what are these secrets according to the philosopher? They are the truths of philosophy, the truths of the metaphysics or ethics of Aristotle, or Alfarabi or Avicenna; truths, in other words, which were capable of being discovered outside the sphere of religion and which were projected into the old books by way of allegorical or typological interpretation. The documents of religion are therefore not conceived as expressing a separate and distinct world of religious truth and reality, but rather as giving a simplified description of the relations which exist between the ideas of philosophy. The story of Abraham and Sarah, of Lot and his wife, of the Twelve Tribes, etc., are simply descriptions of the relation between matter and form, spirit and matter, or the faculties of the mind. Even where allegorization was not pushed to such absurd extremes, the tendency was to regard the Torah as a mere vehicle of philosophic truth, though indeed one particularly exalted and perfect.

In other words, the philosopher can only proceed with his proper task after having successfully converted the concrete realities of Judaism into a bundle of abstractions. The individual phenomenon is to him no object of his philosophical speculation. By contrast, the mystic refrains from destroying the living texture of religious narrative by allegorizing it, although allegory plays an important part in the writings of a great many Kabbalists. His essential mode of thinking is what I should like to call symbolical in the strictest sense.

This point requires a little further explanation. Allegory consists of an infinite network of meanings and correlations in which everything can become a representation of everything else, but all within the limits of language and expression. To that extent it is possible to speak of allegorical immanence. That which is expressed by and in the allegorical sign is in the first instance something which has its own meaningful context, but by becoming allegorical this something loses its own meaning and becomes the vehicle of something else. Indeed the allegory arises, as it were, from the gap which at this point opens between the form and its meaning. The two are no longer indissolubly welded together; the meaning is no longer restricted to that particular form, nor the form any longer to that particular meaningful content. What appears in the allegory, in short, is the infinity of meaning which attaches to every representation. The "Mysteries of the Torah" which I just mentioned were for the philosophers the natural subject of an allegorical interpretation which gave expression to a new form of the mediaeval mind as much as it implied a veiled criticism of the old.

Allegorization was also, as I have said, a constant preoccupation of the Kabbalists, and it was not on this ground that they differed from the philosophers; nor was it the main constituent of their faith and their method. We must look for this in the attention they gave to the symbol —a form of expression which radically transcends the sphere of allegory. In the mystical symbol a reality which in itself has, for us, no form or shape becomes transparent and, as it were, visible, through the medium of another reality which clothes its content with visible and expressible meaning, as for example the cross for the Christian. The thing which becomes a symbol retains its original form and its original content. It does not become, so to speak, an empty shell into which another content is poured; in itself, through its own existence, it makes another reality transparent which cannot appear in any other form. If allegory can be defined as the representation of an expressible something by another expressible something, the mystical symbol is an expressible representation of something which lies beyond the sphere of expression and communication, something which comes from a sphere whose face is, as it were, turned inward and away from us. A hidden and inexpressible reality finds its expression in the symbol. If the symbol is thus also a sign or representation it is nevertheless more than that.

For the Kabbalist, too, every existing thing is endlessly correlated with the whole of creation; for him, too, everything mirrors everything else. But beyond that he discovers something else which is not covered by the allegorical network: a reflection of the true transcendence. The symbol "signifies" nothing and communicates nothing, but makes something transparent which is beyond all expression. Where deeper insight into the structure of the allegory uncovers fresh layers of meaning, the symbol is intuitively understood all at once—or not at all. The symbol in which the life of the Creator and that of creation become one, is—to use Creuzer's words—"a beam of light which, from the dark and abysmal depths of existence and cognition, falls into our eye and penetrates our whole being." It is a "momentary totality" which is perceived intuitively in a mystical *now*—the dimension of time proper to the symbol.

Of such symbols the world of Kabbalism is full, nay the whole world is to the Kabbalist such a *corpus symbolicum*. Out of the reality of creation, without the latter's existence being denied or annihilated, the inexpressible mystery of the Godhead becomes visible. In particular the religious acts commanded by the Torah, the *mitswoth,* are to the Kabbalist symbols in which a deeper and hidden sphere of reality becomes transparent. The infinite shines through the finite and makes it more and not less real. This brief summary gives us some idea of the profound difference between the philosophers' allegorical interpretation of religion and its symbolical understanding by the mystics. It may be of interest to note that in the comprehensive commentary on the Torah written by a great mystic of the thirteenth century, Moses Nahmanides, there are many symbolical interpretations as defined here, but not a single instance of allegory.

The difference becomes clear if we consider the attitude of philosophy and Kabbalah respectively to the two outstanding creative manifestations of Rabbinical Jewry: Halakhah and Aggadah, Law and Legend. It is a remarkable fact that the philosophers failed to establish a satisfactory and intimate relation to either. They showed themselves unable to make the spirit of Halakhah and Aggadah, both elements which expressed a fundamental urge of the Jewish soul, productive by transforming them into something new.

Let us begin with the Halakhah, the world of sacred law and, therefore, the most important factor in the actual life of ancient Jewry. Alexander Altmann, in raising the question: What is Jewish Theology? is quite justified in regarding as one of the decisive weaknesses of classical Jewish philosophy the fact that it ignored the problem presented by the Halakhah. The whole world of religious law remained outside the orbit of philosophical inquiry, which means of course, too, that it was not subjected to philosophical criticism. It is not as if the philosopher denied or defied this world. He, too, lived in it and bowed to it, but it never became part and parcel of his work as a philosopher. It furnished no material for his thoughts. This fact, which is indeed undeniable, is particularly glaring in the case of thinkers like Maimonides and Saadia, in whom the converging streams meet. They fail entirely to establish a true synthesis of the two elements, Halakhah and philosophy, a fact which has already been pointed out by Samuel David Luzzatto. Maimonides, for instance, begins the *Mishneh Torah,* his great codification of the Halakhah, with a philosophical chapter which has no relation whatever to the Halakhah itself. The synthesis of the spheres remains sterile, and the genius of the man whose spirit moulded them into a semblance of union cannot obscure their intrinsic disparity.

For a purely historical understanding of religion, Maimonides' analysis of the origin of the *mitswoth,* the religious commandments, is of great importance, but he would be a bold man who would maintain that his theory of the *mitswoth* was likely to increase the enthusiasm of the faithful for their actual practice, likely to augment their immediate appeal to religious feeling. If the prohibition against seething a kid in its mother's milk and many similar irrational commandments are explicable as polemics against long-forgotten pagen rites, if the offering of sacrifice is a concession to the primitive mind, if other *mitswoth* carry with them antiquated moral and philosophical ideas—how can one expect the community to remain faithful to practices of which the antecedents have long since disappeared or of which the aims can be attained directly through philosophical reasoning? To the philosopher, the Halakhah either had no significance at all, or one that was calculated to diminish rather than to enhance its prestige in his eyes.

Entirely different was the attitude of the Kabbalists. For them the Halakhah never became a province of thought in which they felt themselves strangers. Right from the beginning and with growing determination, they sought to master the world of the Halakhah as a whole and in every detail. From the outset, an ideology of the Halakhah is one of their aims. But in their interpretation of the religious commandments these are not represented as allegories of more or less profound ideas, or as pedagogical measures, but rather as the performance of a secret rite (or *mystery* in the sense in which the term was used by the Ancients).

Whether one is appalled or not by this transformation of the Halakhah into a sacrament, a mystery rite, by this revival of myth in the very heart of Judaism, the fact remains that it was this transformation which raised the Halakhah to a position of incomparable importance for the mystic, and strengthened its hold over the people. Every *mitswah* became an event of cosmic importance, an act which had a bearing upon the dynamics of the universe. The religious Jew became a protagonist in the drama of the world; he manipulated the strings behind the scene. Or, to use a less extravagant simile, if the whole universe is an enormous complicated machine, then man is the machinist who keeps the wheels going by applying a few drops of oil here and there, and at the right time. The moral substance of man's action supplies this "oil," and his existence therefore becomes of extreme significance, since it unfolds on a background of cosmic infinitude.

The danger of theosophical schematism or, as S. R. Hirsch put it, of "magical mechanism" is, of course, inherent in such an interpretation of the Torah, and it has more than once raised its head in the development of Kabbalism. There is danger of imagining a magical mechanism to be operative in every sacramental action, and this imagination is attended by a decline in the essential spontaneity of religious action. But then this conflict is inseparable from any and every fulfilment of a religious command, since every prescribed duty is also conceived as assumed willingly and spontaneously. The antinomy is, in fact, inescapable, and can only be overcome by religious feeling so long as it is strong and unbroken. When it begins to flag, the contradiction between command and free-will increases in proportion and eventually gathers sufficient force to become destructive.

By interpreting every religious act as a mystery, even where its meaning was clear for all to see or was expressly mentioned in the written or oral Law, a strong link was forged between Kabbalah and Halakkah, which appears to me to have been, in large part, responsible for the influence of Kabbalistic thought over the minds and hearts of successive generations.

A good deal of similarity to what I have said about the Halakhah is apparent in the attitude of philosophers and mystics, respectively, to the Aggadah. Here too, their ways part right from the beginning. The Aggadah is a wonderful mirror of spontaneous religious life and feeling during the rabbinical period of Judaism. In particular, it represents a method of giving original and concrete expression to the deepest motive-powers of the religious Jew, a quality which helps to make it an excellent and genuine approach to the essentials of our religion. However, it was just this quality which never ceased to baffle the philosophers of Judaism. Their treatment of the Aggadah, except where it pointed an ethical moral, is embarrassed and fumbling. They almost certainly regarded it as a stumbling-block rather than as a precious heritage, let alone a key to a mystery. And thus it is not surprising that their allegorical interpretation of its meaning reflects an attitude which is not that of the Aggadah. Only too frequently their allegorizations are simply, as I have said, veiled criticism.

Here again the Kabbalists conceive their task differently, although it also involves a transformation of the subject's meaning. It would be too much to say that they leave the meaning of the Aggadah intact. What makes them differ from the philosophers is the fact that for them the Aggadah is not just a dead letter. They live in a world historically continuous with it, and they are able, therefore, to enhance it, though in the spirit of mysticism. Aggadic productivity has been a constant element of Kabbalistic literature, and only when the former disappears will the latter, too, be doomed to extinction. The whole of Aggadah can in a way be regarded as a popular mythology of the Jewish universe. Now, this mythical element which is deeply rooted in the creative forms of Aggadic production, operates on different planes in the old Aggadah and in Kabbalism. The difference between the Aggadic production of the Kabbalah and that of the early Midrash can be easily gauged: in the Aggadah of the Kabbalists the events take place on a considerably wider stage, a stage with a cosmic horizon. Earth and heaven meet already in the ancient Aggadah, but now an even greater stress is laid on the heavenly element which comes more and more to the fore. All events assume gigantic dimensions and a wider significance; the steps of the heroes of the Kabbalistic Aggadah are directed by hidden forces from mysterious regions, while their doings react, at the same time, upon the upper world. Seen that way, there is nothing more instructive than a comparison between the two great and truly comprehensive collections, or *Yalkutim,* each one representing, respectively, one of the two types of Aggadic creation. The compiler of the *Yalkut Shim'oni* collected in the thirteenth century the old Aggadahs which, as preserved by the Midrashic literature, accompanied the biblical text. In the *Yalkut Reubeni,* on the other hand, we have a collection of the Aggadic output of the Kabbalists during five centuries. The latter highly interesting work which was compiled during the second half of the seventeenth century bears full witness to the growing strength and preponderance of the mythical element and to the great difference between Aggadah and Kabbalah in their interpretation of the stories of Biblical heroes. At the same time it is obvious that in comparison with the older Aggadah the realistic element in the later Aggadah has decreased because the realistic foundations, in which Jewish life was rooted, have grown more and more narrow. In fact, this explanation falls in well with the historical experience of the different generations. The old Aggadah is fed by deep and comprehensive experience; the life which it reflects has not yet become colourless, nor did it lose its impetus. The Kabbalistic Aggadah, in contrast, reflects a narrow and circumscribed life which sought, nay, was compelled to seek, inspiration from hidden worlds, as the real world turned for them into the world of the Ghetto. The Aggadic myth of the *Yalkut Reubeni* expresses the historical experience of the Jewish people after the Crusades, and we may say that it is expressed with rather greater force because it is not directly mentioned at all. The depth of the penetration into the hidden worlds which can be encountered here at every step stands in direct proportion to the shrinking perimeter of their historical experience. There is thus a mighty difference of function between the two types of Aggadic creation but no difference of essence.

There is another point worth mentioning. No Kabbalist was ever embarrassed by or ashamed of an old Aggadah; in particular those Aggadahs, which were anathema to 'enlightened' Jews, were enthusiastically hailed by the Kabbalists as symbols of their own interpretation of the Universe. The anthropomorphical and paradoxical Aggadahs belong to this class, as well as certain epigrams, such as R. Abbahu's saying, that before making this world God made many others and destroyed them because he did not like them. The philosophers, who had passed through the school of Aristotle, never felt at home in the world of Midrash. But the more extravagant and paradoxical these Aggadahs appeared to them, the more were the Kabbalists convinced that they were one of the keys to the mystical realm. Their vocabulary and favorite similes show traces of Aggadic influence in proportions equal to those of philosophy and Gnosticism; Scripture being, of course, the strongest element of all.

What has been said of the Halakhah and the Aggadah is also true of the liturgy, the world of prayer; the last of the three domains in which the religious spirit of post-Biblical Judaism has found its classical expression. Here too the conclusion is inescapable that the philosophers had little of value to contribute. Of entire prayers written by philosophers only a few have been preserved, and these are often somewhat anaemic and half-hearted in their approach, especially where the authors were not, like Solomon ibn Gabirol and Jehudah Halevi, motivated in the last resort by mystical leanings. There is in many of them a curious lack of true religious feeling. The case is entirely different when we turn to the Kabbalistic attitude towards prayer; there is perhaps no clearer sign that Kabbalism is essentially a religious and not a speculative phenomenon. The novelty of its attitude to prayer can be viewed under two aspects: the vast number of prayers whose authors were mystics themselves, and the mystical interpretation of the old traditional community prayers—the backbone of Jewish liturgy.

To begin with the former, it is hardly surprising that the new religious revelation, peculiar to the visionaries of the Kabbalah, for which there existed no liturgical equivalent in the older prayers, strove after some form of expression and had already inspired the earliest mystics to write their own prayers. The first prayers of a mystical character, which can be traced back to the Kabbalists of Provence and Catalonia, are carried forward by a long and varied tradition to the prayers in which, about 1820, Nathan of Nemirov, the disciple of Rabbi Nahman of Brazlav, gave valid expression to the world of Hasidic Zaddikism. This mystical prayer, which bears little outward resemblance to the older liturgy, and in particular of course to the classical forms of communal prayer, flows from the new religious experience to which the Kabbalists were entitled to lay claim. Often these prayers bear the mark of directness and simplicity, and give plain expression to the common concern of every form of mysticism. But not infrequently their language is that of the symbol and their style reveals the secret pathos of magical conjuration. This has found a profound expression in the mystical interpretation of the phrase of Psalm cxxx, 1, "Out of the depths I have called unto Thee"; which, according to the Zohar, means not "I have called unto Thee from the depths [where I am]" but "from the depths [in which Thou art] I call Thee up."

But side by side with these original productions of the Kabbalistic spirit we find from the earliest beginnings down to our time another tendency, that of mystical reinterpretation of the traditional community liturgy which transforms it into a symbol of the mystical way and the way of the world itself. This transformation, which has meant a great deal for the true life of the Kabbalist, has become crystallized in the conception of *Kawwanah,* i.e. mystical intention or concentration, which is its instrument. In the words of the liturgy as in the old Aggadahs, the Kabbalists found a way to hidden worlds and the first causes of all existence. They developed a technique of meditation which enabled them to extract, as it were, the mystical prayer from the exoteric prayer of the community the text of which followed a fixed pattern. The fact that this form of prayer was conceived not as a free effusion of the soul but as a mystical act in the strict sense of the term, as an act, that is to say, which is directly linked with the inner cosmic process, invests this conception of *Kawwanah* with a solemnity which not only approaches but also passes the border of the magical. It is significant that of all the various forms of Kabbalistic thought and practice this meditative mysticism of prayer has alone survived and has taken the place of all the others. At the end of a long process of development in which Kabbalism, paradoxical though it may sound, has influenced the course of Jewish history, it has become again what it was in the beginning: the esoteric wisdom of small groups of men out of touch with life and without any influence on it.

As I have already said, mysticism represents, to a certain extent, a revival of mythical lore. This brings us to another and very serious point which I should like at least to mention. The Jewish mystic lives and acts in perpetual rebellion against a world with which he strives with all his zeal to be at peace. Conversely, this fact is responsible for the profound ambiguity of his outlook, and it also explains the apparent self-contradiction inherent in a great many Kabbalist symbols and images. The great symbols of the Kabbalah certainly spring from the depths of a creative and genuinely Jewish religious feeling, but at the same time they are invariably tinged by the world of mythology. In the lectures on the Zohar and on Lurianic Kabbalism I shall give a number of particularly outstanding instances of this fact. Failing this mythical element, the ancient Jewish mystics would have been unable to compress into language the substance of their inner experience. It was Gnosticism, one of the last great manifestations of mythology in religious thought, and definitely conceived in the struggle against Judaism as the conqueror of mythology, which lent figures of speech to the Jewish mystic.

The importance of this paradox can hardly be exaggerated; it must be kept in mind that the whole meaning and purpose of those ancient myths and metaphors whose remainders the editors of the book *Bahir,* and therefore the whole Kabbalah, inherited from the Gnostics, was simply the subversion of a law which had, at one time, disturbed and broken the order of the mythical world. Thus through wide and scattered provinces of Kabbalism, the revenge of myth upon its conqueror is clear for all to see, and together with it we find an abundant display of contradictory symbols. It is characteristic of Kabbalistic theology in its systematical forms that it attempts to construct and to describe a world in which something of the mythical has again come to life, in terms of thought which exclude the mythical element. However, it is this contradiction which more than anything else explains the extra-ordinary success of Kabbalism in Jewish history.

Mystics and philosophers are, as it were, both aristocrats of thought; yet Kabbalism succeeded in establishing a connection between its own world and certain elemental impulses operative in every human mind. It did not turn its back upon the primitive side of life, that all-important region where mortals are afraid of life and in fear of death, and derive scant wisdom from rational philosophy. Philosophy ignored these fears, out of whose substance man wove myths, and in turning its back upon the primitive side of man's existence, it paid a high price in losing touch with him altogether. For it is cold comfort to those who are plagued by genuine fear and sorrow to be told that their troubles are but the workings of their own imagination.

The fact of the existence of evil in the world is the main touch-stone of this difference between the philosophic and the Kabbalistic outlook. On the whole, the philosophers of Judaism treat the existence of evil as something meaningless in itself. Some of them have shown themselves only too proud of this negation of evil as one of the funda-mentals of what they call rational Judaism. Hermann Cohen has said with great clarity and much conviction: "Evil is non-existent. It is nothing but a concept derived from the concept of freedom. *A power of evil exists only in myth.*" One may doubt the philosophical truth of this statement, but assuming its truth it is obvious that something can be said for 'myth' in its struggle with 'philosophy'. To most Kabbalists, as true seal-bearers of the world of myth, the existence of evil is, at any rate, one of the most pressing problems, and one which keeps them con-tinuously occupied with attempts to solve it. They have a strong sense of the reality of evil and the dark horror that is about everything living. They do not, like the philosophers, seek to evade its existence with the aid of a convenient formula; rather do they try to penetrate into its depth. And by doing so, they unwittingly establish a connection between their own strivings and the vital interests of popular belief—you may call it superstition—and all of those concrete manifestations of Jewish life in which these fears found their expression. It is a paradoxical fact that none other than the Kabbalists, through their interpretation of vari-ous religious acts and customs, have made it clear what they signified to the average believer, if not what they really meant from the begin-ning. Jewish folklore stands as a living proof of this contention, as has been shown by modern research in respect of some particularly well-known examples.

It would be idle to deny that Kabbalistic thought lost much of its magnificence where it was forced to descend from the pinnacles of theoretical speculation to the plane of ordinary thinking and acting. The dangers which myth and magic present to the religious consciousness, including that of the mystic, are clearly shown in the development of Kabbalism. If one turns to the writings of great Kabbalists one seldom fails to be torn between alternate admiration and disgust. There is need for being quite clear about this in a time like ours, when the fashion of uncritical and superficial condemnation of even the most valuable elements of mysticism threatens to be replaced by an equally uncritical and obscurantist glorification of the Kabbalah. I have said before that Jewish philosophy had to pay a high price for its escape from the pressing questions of real life. But Kabbalism, too, has had to pay for its success. Philosophy came dangerously near to losing the living God; Kabbalism, which set out to preserve Him, to blaze a new and glorious trail to Him, encountered mythology on its way and was tempted to lose itself in its labyrinth.

THE INNER LIFE OF RABBINIC MYSTICISM

What is important about mysticism within Rabbinic Judaism is the remarkable capacity of the lawyers, disciplined and controlled, to enter into mystic experience, free-ranging and unpredictable. And this was so not of a few remarkable individuals, but of most, though not all, of those who participated in the mystical experience and doctrine. Indeed, the net effect of mystic experience was to deepen the devotee's perception of the profound meanings of the law, therefore to heighten his loyalty to careful observance of the practical commandments of the Torah.

Mysticism, which, by its nature, could have shattered the discipline demanded by the law, in fact reenforced it. That is why we may fairly claim that the mystical quest, like the philosophical one, represents the expression of the fundamental values of rabbinic civilization in a new and fresh, but stable and authentic, idiom. Mystical experience, no less than rational inquiry, found its place within the larger rabbinic structure and made good use of the received images and symbols of rabbinic civilization.

Having outlined the external aspect of mysticism in the larger rabbinic context, let us now turn to its substance. As Heschel explains, the interest of the mystic is to transcend reason, to reconstruct what analysis dissects, to see all things as a unity. The philosophers take matters apart, he stresses, while the mystics put them back together. Mysticism should not, therefore, be seen as the denial of the mind, but rather, the effort to surpass it. What lies beyond what we know and see and touch? This is what the mystic seeks to find out, indeed to experience.

Drawing upon Talmudic and other rabbinic sources, the mystics find doctrines to give substance to these yearnings. Thus Scriptural verses and rabbinic sayings are interpreted in the light of mystic doctrine and experience. All things seem open and clear; the mystic perceives the mystery of these sayings and penetrates into their depths. Imbedded in rabbinic perceptions of the world is the conviction that the earthly realm corresponds to the heavenly one. To the mystic, this belief forms the basis of the view that what man does affects the hidden universe as well. Each action in the here and now carries with it manifold supernatural consequences.

Naturally, the mystic will rely upon intuition, not only on rationality, in the investigation of God's nature. God is perceived as very present in this world, "a most specific reality," in Heschel's words. Just as what man does in this world has its consequences for all reality, so this world contains within itself evidences of the divine presence. Mystic doctrines of God, to be sure, will not be located within the pages of the Talmud or the later rabbinic literature. The doctrine, for example, of the *Sefirot,* the spheres of Divine emanation, or "the garments in which the Hidden God reveals Himself," will hardly be prefigured in the law and theology of the rabbis. But the Jewish mystic transcends that hard fact by assigning to the names of the great legal authorities of the Talmud the very origin and generation of these doctrines. This was possible because it was simply unthinkable to the mystics that the revered authorities of old did not know what they knew, did not attempt to express through the design of patterns of behavior characteristic of Talmudic law what lay at the foundations of all reality.

15.

THE MYSTICAL ELEMENT IN JUDAISM

Abraham J. Heschel

[From *The Jews. Their History, Culture, and Religion.* Edited by Louis Finkelstein. Third Edition, N.Y., 1960: Harper & Brothers. Vol. II, pp. 932-951.]

1. *The Meaning of Jewish Mysticism*

There are people who take great care to keep away from the mists produced by fads and phrases. They refuse to convert realities into opinions, mysteries into dogmas, and ideas into a multitude of words, for they realize that all concepts are but glittering motes in a sunbeam. They want to see the sun itself. Confined to our study rooms, our knowledge seems to us a pillar of light; but when we stand at the door that opens out to the Infinite, we see how insubstantial is our knowledge. Even when we shut the door to the Infinite and retire to the narrow limits of notions our minds cannot remain confined. Again, to some people explanations and opinions are a token of wonder's departure, like a curfew after which they may not come abroad. In the cabbalists, the drive and the fire and the light are never put out.

Like the vital power in ourselves that gives us the ability to fight and to endure, to dare and to conquer, which drives us to experience the bitter and the perilous, there is an urge in wistful souls to starve rather than be fed on sham and distortion. To the cabbalists God is as real as life, and as nobody would be satisfied with mere knowing or reading about life, so they are not content to suppose or to prove logically that there is a God; they want to feel and to enjoy Him; not only to obey, but to approach Him. They want to taste the whole wheat of spirit before it is ground by the millstones of reason. They would rather be overwhelmed by the symbols of the inconceivable than wield the definitions of the superficial.

Stirred by a yearning after the unattainable, they want to make the distant near, the abstract concrete, to transform the soul into a vessel for the transcendent, to grasp with the senses what is hidden from the mind, to express in symbols what the tongue cannot speak, what the reason cannot conceive, to experience as a reality what vaguely dawns in intuitions. "Wise is he who by the power of his own contemplation attains to the perception of the profound mysteries which cannot be expressed in words."

The cabbalist is not content with being confined to what he is. His desire is not only to *know* more than what ordinary reason has to offer, but to *be* more than what he is; not only to comprehend the Beyond but to concur with it. He aims at the elevation and expansion of existence. Such expansion goes hand in hand with the exaltation of all being.

The universe, exposed to the violence of our analytical mind, is being broken apart. It is split into the known and unknown, into the seen and unseen. In mystic contemplation all things are seen as one. The mystic mind tends to hold the world together: to behold the seen in conjunction with the unseen, to keep the fellowship with the unknown through the revolving door of the known, "to learn the higher supernal wisdom from all" that the Lord has created and to regain the knowledge that once was in the possession of men and "that has perished from them." What our senses perceive is but the jutting edge of what is deeply hidden. Extending over into the invisible, the things of this world stand in a secret contact with that which no eye has ever perceived. Everything certifies to the sublime, the unapparent working jointly with the apparent. There is always a reverberation in the Beyond to every action here: "The Lord made this world corresponding to the world above, and everything which is above has its counterpart below . . . and yet they all constitute a unity"; "there being no object, however small, in this world, but what is subordinate to its counterpart above which has charge over it; and so whenever the thing below bestirs itself, there is a simultaneous stimulation of its counterpart above, as the two realms form one interconnected whole."

Opposed to the idea that the world of perception is the bottom of reality, the mystics plunge into what is beneath the perceptible. What they attain in their quest is more than a vague impression or a spotty knowledge of the imperceptible. "Penetrating to the real essence of wisdom . . . they are resplendent with the radiance of supernal wisdom." Their eyes perceive things of this world, while their hearts reverberate to the throbbing of the hidden. To them the secret is the core of the apparent; the known is but an aspect of the unknown. "All things below are symbols of that which is above." They are sustained by the forces that flow from hidden worlds. There is no particular that is detached from universal meaning. What appears to be a center to the eye is but a point on the periphery around another center. Nothing here is final. The worldly is subservient to the otherworldly. You grasp the essence of the here by conceiving its beyond. For this world is the reality of the spirit in a state of trance. The manifestation of the mystery is partly suspended, with ourselves living in lethargy. Our normal consciousness is a state of stupor, in which our sensibility to the wholly real and our responsiveness to the stimuli of the spirit are reduced. The mystics, knowing that we are involved in a hidden history of the cosmos, endeavor to awake from the drowsiness and apathy and to regain the state of wakefulness for our enchanted souls.

It is a bold attitude of the soul, a steadfast quality of consciousness, that lends mystic character to a human being. A man who feels that he is closely enfolded by a power that is both lasting and holy will come to know that the spiritual is not an idea to which one can relate his will, but a realm which can even be affected by our deeds. What distinguishes the cabbalist is the attachment of his entire personality to a hidden spiritual realm. Intensifying this attachment by means of active devotion to it, by meditation upon its secrets, or even by perception of its reality, he becomes allied with the dynamics of hidden worlds. Sensitive to the imperceptible, he is stirred by its secret happenings.

Attachment to hidden worlds holds the cabbalist in the spell of things more basic than the things that dominate the interest of the common mind. The mystery is not beyond and away from us. It is our destiny. "The fate of the world depends upon the mystery." Our task is to adjust the details to the whole, the apparent to the hidden, the near to the distant. The passionate concern of the cabbalist for final goals endows him with the experience of surpassing all human limitations and powers. With all he is doing he is crossing the borders, breaking the surfaces, approaching the lasting sources of all things. Yet his living with the infinite does not make him alien to the finite.

2. *The Exaltation of Man*

In this exalted world man's position is unique. God has instilled in him something of Himself. Likeness to God is the essence of man. The Hebrew word for man, *adam,* usually associated with the word for earth, *adamah,* was homiletically related by some cabbalists to the expression, "I will ascend above the heights of the clouds; I will be like (*eddamme*) the Most High" (Is. 14:14). Man's privilege is, as it were, to augment the Divine in the world, as it is said, "ascribe ye strength unto God" (Ps. 68:35).

Jewish mystics are inspired by a bold and dangerously paradoxical idea that not only is God necessary to man but that man is also necessary to God, to the unfolding of His plans in this world. Thoughts of this kind are indicated and even expressed in various Rabbinic sources. "When Israel performs the will of the Omnipresent, they add strength to the heavenly power; as it is said, 'To God we render strength!' " When, however, Israel does not perform the will of the Omnipresent, they weaken—if it is possible to say so—the great power of Him Who is above; as it is written "Thou didst weaken the Rock that begot thee" (Deut. 32:18). In the *Zohar* this idea is formulated in a more specific way. Commenting on the passage in Ex. 17:8, "Then came Amalek and fought with Israel in Rephidim," R. Simeon said: "There is a deep allusion in the name 'Rephidim.' This war emanated from the attribute of Severe Judgment and it was a war above and a war below . . . The Holy One, as it were, said: 'When Israel is worthy below, My power prevails in the universe; but when Israel is found to be unworthy, she weakens My power above, and the power of severe judgment predominates in the world.' So here, 'Amalek came and fought with Israel in Rephidim,' because the Israelites were 'weak' (in Hebrew: *raphe,* which the *Zohar* finds in the name 'Rephidim') in the study of the Torah, as we have explained on another occasion." Thus man's relationship to God should not be that of passive reliance upon His Omnipotence but that of active assistance. "The impious rely on their gods . . . the righteous are the support of God." The Patriarchs are therefore called "the chariot of the Lord." The belief in the greatness of man, in the metaphysical effectiveness of his physical acts, is an ancient motif of Jewish thinking.

Man himself is a mystery. He is the symbol of all that exists. His life is the image of universal life. Everything was created in the spiritual image of the mystical man. "When the Holy One created man, He set in him all the images of the supernal mysteries of the world above, and all the images of the lower mysteries of the world below, and all are designed in man, who stands in the image of God." Even the human body is full of symbolic significance. The skin, flesh, bones and sinews are but an outward covering, mere garments, even though "the substances composing man's body belong to two worlds, namely, the world below and the world above." The 248 limbs and 365 sinews are symbols of the 613 parts of the universe as well as of the 248 positive and

365 negative precepts of the Torah. Man's soul emanates from an upper region where it has a spiritual father and a spiritual mother, just as the body has a father and mother in this world. The souls that abide in our bodies are a weak reflection of our upper souls, the seat of which is in heaven. Yet, though detached from that soul, we are capable of being in contact with it. When we pray we turn toward the upper soul as though we were to abandon the body and join our source.

Man is not detached from the realm of the unseen. He is wholly involved in it. Whether he is conscious of it or not, his actions are vital to all worlds, and affect the course of transcendent events. In a sense, by means of the Torah, man is the constant architect of the hidden universe. "This world was formed in the pattern of the world above, and whatever takes place in this earthly realm occurs also in the realm above." One of the principles of the *Zohar* is that every move below calls forth a corresponding movement above. Not only things, even periods of time are conceived as concrete entities. "Thus over every day below is appointed a day above, and a man should take heed not to impair that day. Now the act below stimulates a corresponding activity above. Thus if a man does kindness on earth, he awakens loving-kindness above, and it rests upon that day which is crowned therewith through him. Similarly, if he performs a deed of mercy, he crowns that day with mercy and it becomes his protector in the hour of need. So, too, if he performs a cruel action, he has a corresponding effect on that day and impairs it, so that subsequently it becomes cruel to him and tries to destroy him, giving him measure for measure." Even what we consider potential is regarded as real and we may be held accountable for it: ". . . just as a man is punished for uttering an evil word, so is he punished for not uttering a good word when he had the opportunity, because he harms that speaking spirit which was prepared to speak above and below in holiness."

The significance of great works done on earth is valued by their cosmic effects. Thus, *e.g.,* "When the first Temple was completed another Temple was erected at the same time, which was a center for all the worlds, shedding radiance upon all things and giving light to all the spheres. Then the worlds were firmly established, and all the supernal casements were opened to pour forth light, and all the worlds experienced such joys as had never been known to them before, and celestial and terrestrial beings alike broke forth in song. And the song which they sang is the Song of Songs."

Endowed with metaphysical powers man's life is a most serious affair; "if a man's lips and tongue speak evil words, those words mount aloft and all proclaim 'keep away from the evil word of so-and-so, leave the path clear for the mighty serpent.' Then the holy soul leaves him and is not able to speak: it is in shame and distress, and is not given a place as before . . . Then many spirits bestir themselves, and one spirit comes down from that side and finds the man who uttered the evil word, and lights upon him and defiles him, and he becomes leprous."

Man's life is full of peril. It can easily upset the balance and order of the universe. "A voice goes forth and proclaims: 'O ye people of the world, take heed unto yourselves, close the gates of sin, keep away from the perilous net before your feet are caught in it!' A certain wheel is ever whirling continuously round and round. Woe to those whose feet lose their hold on the wheel, for then they fall into the Deep which is predestined for the evildoers of the world! Woe to those who fall, never to rise and enjoy the light that is stored up for the righteous in the world to come!"

3.   *The En Sof and His Manifestations*

Mystic intuition occurs at an outpost of the mind, dangerously detached from the main substance of the intellect. Operating as it were in no-mind's land, its place is hard to name, its communications with critical thinking often difficult and uncertain and the accounts of its discoveries not easy to decode. In its main representatives, the cabbala teaches that man's life can be a rallying point of the forces that tend toward God, that this world is charged with His presence and every object is a cue to His qualities. To the cabbalist, God is not a concept, a generalization, but a most specific reality; his thinking about Him full of forceful directness. But He who is "the Soul of all souls" is "the mystery of all mysteries." While the cabbalists speak of God as if they commanded a view of the Beyond, and were in possession of knowledge about the inner life of God, they also assure us that all notions fail when applied to Him, that He is beyond the grasp of the human mind and inaccessible to meditation. He is the *En Sof,* the Infinite, "the most Hidden of all Hidden." While there is an abysmal distance between Him and the world, He is also called All. "For all things are in Him and He is in all things . . . He is both manifest and concealed. Manifest in order to uphold the all and concealed, for He is found nowhere. When He becomes manifest He projects nine brilliant lights that throw light in all directions. So, too, does a lamp throw brilliance in all directions, but when we approach the brilliance we find there is nothing outside the lamp. So is the Holy ancient One, the Light of all Lights, the most Hidden of all Hidden. We can only find the light which He spreads and which appears and disappears. This light is called the Holy Name, and therefore All is One."

Thus, the "Most Recondite One Who is beyond cognition does reveal of Himself a tenuous and veiled brightness shining only along a narrow path which extends from Him. This is the brightness that irradiates all." The *En Sof* has granted us manifestations of His hidden life: He had descended to become the universe; He has revealed Himself to become the Lord of Israel. The ways in which the Infinite assumes the form of finite existence are called *Sefirot*. These are various aspects or forms of Divine action, spheres of Divine emanation. They are, as it were, the garments in which the Hidden God reveals Himself and acts in the universe, the channels through which His light is issued forth.

The names of the ten *Sefirot* are *Keter, Hokhmah, Binah, Hesed, Geburah, Tiferet, Netsah, Hod, Yesod, Malkut*. The transition from Divine latency to activity takes place in *Keter*, the "supreme crown" of God. This stage is inconceivable, absolute unity and beyond description. In the following *Sefirot*, *Hokhmah* and *Binah*, the building and creation of the cosmos as well as that which divides things begins. They are parallel emanations from *Keter*, representing the active and the receptive principle.

While the first triad represents the transition from the Divine to the spiritual reality, the second triad is the source of the moral order. *Hesed* stands for the love of God; *Geburah* for the power of justice manifested as severity or punishment. From the union of these emanates *Tiferet*, compassion or beauty of God, mediating between *Hesed* and *Geburah*, between the life-giving power and the contrary power, holding in check what would otherwise prove to be the excesses of love.

The next triad is the source of the psychic and physical existences —*Netsah* is the lasting endurance of God, *Hod* His majesty, and *Yesod* the stability of the universe, the seat of life and vitality. *Malkut* is the kingdom, the presence of the Divine in the world. It is not a source of its own but the outflow of the other *Sefirot*; "of itself lightless, it looks up to the others and reflects them as a lamp reflects the sun." It is the point at which the external world comes in contact with the upper spheres, the final manifestations of the Divine, the *Shekinah*, "the Mother of all Living."

The recondite and unapproachable Self of God is usually thought of as transcendent to the *Sefirot*. There is only a diffusion of His light into the *Sefirot*. The *En Sof* and the realm of His manifestations are "linked together like the flame and the coal," the flame being a manifestation of what is latent in the coal. In the process of the emanation, the transition from the Divine to the spiritual, from the spiritual to the moral, from the moral to the physical, reality takes place. The product of this manifestation is not only the visible universe but an endless number of spiritual worlds which exist beyond the physical universe in which we live. These worlds, the hidden cosmos, constitute a most complex structure, divided into various grades and forms which can only be described in symbols. These symbols are found in the Torah, which is the constitution of the cosmos. Every letter, word or phrase in the Bible not only describes an event in the history of our world but also represents a symbol of some stage in the hidden cosmos. These are the so-called *Raze Torah,* the mysteries, that can be discovered by the mystical method of interpretation.

The system of *Sefirot* can be visualized as a tree or a man or a circle, in three triads or in three columns. According to the last image the *Sefirot* are divided into a *right* column, signifying Mercy, or light, a *left* column, signifying Severity, the absence of light, and a *central* column, signifying the synthesis of the right and left. Each *Sefirah* is a world in itself, dynamic and full of complicated mutual relations with other *Sefirot*. There are many symbols by which each *Sefirah* can be expressed, *e.g.,* the second triad is symbolized in the lives of each of the three Patriarchs. The doctrine of *Sefirot* enables the cabbalists to perceive the bearings of God upon this world, to identify the Divine substance of all objects and events. It offers the principles by means of which all things and events can be interpreted as Divine manifestations.

The various parts of the day represent various aspects of Divine manifestation. "From sunrise until the sun declines westward it is called 'day,' and the attribute of Mercy is in the ascendant; after that it is called 'evening,' which is the time for the attribute of Severity . . . It is for this reason that Isaac instituted the afternoon prayer (*Minhah*), namely, to mitigate the severity of the approaching evening; whereas Abraham instituted morning prayer, corresponding to the attribute of mercy."

The plurality into which the one Divine manifestation is split symbolizes the state of imperfection into which God's relation to the world was thrown. Every good deed serves to restore the original unity of the *Sefirot,* while on the other hand, "Sinners impair the supernal world by causing a separation between the 'Right' and the 'Left.' They really cause harm only to themselves, . . . as they prevent the descent of blessings from above . . . and the heaven keeps the blessings to itself." Thus the sinner's separation of the good inclination from the evil one by consciously cleaving to evil separates, as it were, the Divine attribute of Grace from that of Judgment, the Right from the Left.

4.   *The Doctrine of the Shekinah*

Originally there was harmony between God and His final manifestations, between the upper *Sefirot* and the tenth *Sefirah*. All things were attached to God and His power surged unhampered throughout all stages of being. Following the trespass of Adam, however, barriers evolved thwarting the emanation of His power. The creature became detached from the Creator, the fruit from the tree, the tree of knowledge from the tree of life, the male from the female, our universe from the world of unity, even the *Shekinah* or the tenth *Sefirah* from the upper *Sefirot*. Owing to that separation the world was thrown into disorder, the power of strict judgment increased, the power of love diminished and the forces of evil released. Man who was to exist in pure spiritual form as light in constant communication with the Divine was sunk into his present inferior state.

In spite of this separation, however, God has not withdrawn entirely from this world. Metaphorically, when Adam was driven out of Eden, an aspect of the Divine, the *Shekinah,* followed him into captivity. Thus there is a Divine power that dwells in this world. It is the Divine Presence that went before Israel while they were going through the wilderness, that protects the virtuous man, that abides in his house and goes forth with him on his journeys, that dwells between a man and his wife. The *Shekinah* "continually accompanies a man and leaves him not so long as he keeps the precepts of the Torah. Hence a man should be careful not to go on the road alone, that is to say, he should diligently keep the precepts of the Torah in order that he may not be deserted by the *Shekinah,* and so be forced to go alone without the accompaniment of the *Shekinah.*" The *Shekinah* follows Israel into exile and "always hovers over Israel like a mother over her children." Moreover, it is because of Israel and its observance of the Torah that the *Shekinah* dwells on earth. Were they to corrupt their way, they would thrust the *Shekinah* out of this world and the earth would be left in a degenerate state.

The doctrine of the *Shekinah* occupies a central place in the cabbala. While emphasizing that in His essence "the Holy One and the *Shekinah* are One," it speaks of a cleavage, as it were, in the reality of the Divine. The *Shekinah* is called figuratively the *Matrona* (symbolized by the Divine Name *Elohim*) that is separated from the King (symbolized by the ineffable Name *Hashem*) and it signifies that God is, so to speak, involved in the tragic state of this world. In the light of this doctrine the suffering of Israel assumed new meaning. Not only Israel but the whole universe, even the *Shekinah,* "lies in dust" and is in exile. Man's task is to bring about the restitution of the original state of the universe and the reunion of the *Shekinah* and the *En Sof.* This is the meaning of Messianic salvation, the goal of all efforts.

"In time to come God will restore the Shekinah to its place and there will be a complete union. 'In that day shall the Lord be One and His Name One' (Zech. 14:9). It may be said: Is He not now One? no; for now through sinners He is not really One. For the Matrona is removed from the King . . . and the King without the Matrona is not invested with His crown as before. But when He joins the Matrona, who crowns Him with many resplendent crowns, then the supernal Mother will also crown Him in a fitting manner. But now that the King is not with the Matrona, the supernal Mother keeps her crowns and withholds from Him the waters of the stream and He is not joined with her. Therefore, as it were, He is not one. But when the Matrona shall return to the place of the Temple and the King shall be wedded with her, then all will be joined together, without separation and regarding this it is written, 'In that day shall the Lord be One and His Name One.' Then there shall be such perfection in the world as had not been for all generations before, for then shall be completeness above and below, and all worlds shall be united in one bond."

The restoration of unity is a constant process. It takes place through the study of the Torah, through prayer and through the fulfillment of the commandments. "The only aim and object of the Holy One in sending man into this world is that he may know and understand that *Hashem* (God), signifying the *En Sof, is Elohim (Shekinah).* This is the sum of the whole mystery of the faith, of the whole Torah, of all that is above and below, of the written and the oral Torah, all together forming one unity." "When a man sins it is as though he strips the *Shekinah* of her vestments, and that is why he is punished; and when he carries out the precepts of the law, it is as though he clothes the *Shekinah* in her vestments. Hence we say that the fringes worn by the Israelites are, to the *Shekinah* in captivity, like the poor man's garments of which it is said, 'For that is his only covering, it is his garment for his skin, wherein he shall sleep.'"

5. *Mystic Experience*

The ultimate goal of the cabbalist is not his own union with the Absolute but the union of all reality with God; one's own bliss is subordinated to the redemption of all: "we have to put all our being, all the members of our body, our complete devotion, into that thought so as to rise and attach ourselves to the *En Sof,* and thus achieve the oneness of the upper and lower worlds."

What this service means in terms of personal living is described in the following way:

> Happy is the portion of whoever can penetrate into the mysteries of his Master and become absorbed into Him, as it were. Especially does a man achieve this when he offers up his prayer to his Master in intense devotion, his will then becoming as the flame inseparable from the coal, and his mind concentrated on the unity of the lower firmaments, to unify them by means of a lower name, then on the unity of the higher firmaments, and finally on the absorption of them all into that most high firmament. Whilst a man's mouth and lips are moving, his heart and will must soar to the height of heights, so as to acknowledge the unity of the whole in virtue of the mystery of mysteries in which all ideas, all wills and all thoughts find their goal, to wit, the mystery of *En Sof.*

The thirst for God is colored by the awareness of His holiness, of the endless distance that separates man from the Eternal One. Yet, he who craves for God is not only a mortal being, but also a part of the Community of Israel, that is, the bride of God, endowed with a soul that is "a part of God." Shy in using endearing terms in his own name, the Jewish mystic feels and speaks in the plural. The allegory of the Song of Songs would be impertinent as an individual utterance, but as an expression of Israel's love for God it is among the finest of all expressions. "God is the soul and spirit of all, and Israel calls Him so and says: (My soul), I desire Thee in order to cleave to Thee and I seek Thee early to find Thy favor."

Israel lives in mystic union with God and the purpose of all its service is to strengthen this union: "O my dove that art in the clefts of the rock, in the covert of the cliff" (Song of Sol. 2:14). The "dove" here is the Community of Israel, which like a dove never forsakes her mate, the Holy One, blessed be He. "In the clefts of the rock": these are the students of the Torah, who have no ease in this world. "In the covert of the steep place": these are the specially pious among them, the saintly and God-fearing, from whom the Divine Presence never departs. The Holy One, blessed be He, inquires concerning them of the Community of Israel, saying, "Let me see thy countenance, let me hear thy voice, for sweet is thy voice"; "for above only the voice of those who study the Torah is heard. We have learned that the likeness of all such is graven above before the Holy One, blessed be He, Who delights Himself with them every day and watches them and that voice rises and pierces its way through all firmaments until it stands before the Holy One, blessed be He."

The concepts of the cabbala cannot always be clearly defined and consistently interrelated. As the name of Jewish mysticism, "cabbala" (lit.: "received lore"), indicates, it is a tradition of wisdom, supposed to have been revealed to elect Sages in ancient times and preserved throughout the generations by an initiated few. The cabbalists accept at the outset the ideas on authority, not on the basis of analytical understanding.

Yet the lips of the teachers and the pages of the books are not the only sources of knowledge. The great cabbalists claimed to have received wisdom directly from the Beyond. Inspiration and Vision were as much a part of their life as contemplation and study. The prayer of Moses: "Show me, I pray Thee, Thy glory" (Ex. 33:18) has never died in the hearts of the cabbalists. The conception of the goal has changed but the quest for immediate cognition remained. The Merkaba-mystics, following perhaps late prophetic traditions about the mysteries of the Divine Throne, were striving to behold the celestial sphere in which the secrets of creation and man's destiny are contained. In the course of the centuries the scope of such esoteric experiences embraced a variety of objectives. The awareness of the cabbalists that the place whereon they stood was holy ground kept them mostly silent about the wonder that was granted to them. Yet we possess sufficient evidence to justify the assumption that mystic events, particularly in the form of inner experiences, of spiritual communications rather than that of sense perceptions, were elements of their living. According to old Rabbinic teachings, there have always been Sages and saints upon whom the Holy Spirit rested, to whom wisdom was communicated from heaven by a Voice, through the appearance of the spirit of Elijah or in dreams. According to the *Zohar,* God reveals to the saints "profound secrets of the Holy Name which He does not reveal to the angels." The disciples of Rabbi Simeon ben Yohai are called prophets, "before whom both supernal and terrestrial beings tremble in awe." Others pray that the inspiration of the Holy Spirit should come upon them. The perception of the unearthly is recorded as an ordinary feature in the life of certain Rabbis. "When R. Hamnuna the Ancient used to come out from the river on a Friday afternoon, he was wont to rest a little on the bank, and raising his eyes in gladness, he would say that he sat there in order to behold the joyous sight of the heavenly angels ascending and descending. At each arrival of the Sabbath, he said, man is caught up into the world of souls." Not only may the human mind receive spiritual illuminations; the soul also may be bestowed upon higher powers. "Corresponding to the impulses of a man here are the influences which he attracts to himself from above. Should his impulse be toward holiness, he attracts to himself holiness from on high and so he becomes holy; but if this tendency is toward the side of impurity, he draws down toward himself the unclean spirit and so becomes polluted."

Since the time of the prophet Joel the Jews have expected that at the end of days the Lord would "pour out His spirit upon all flesh" and all men would prophesy. In later times, it is believed, the light of that revelation of mysteries could already be perceived.

The mystics absorb even in this world "something of the odor of these secrets and mysteries." Significantly, the Torah itself is conceived as a living source of inspiration, not as a fixed book. The Torah is a voice that "calls aloud" to men; she calls them day by day to herself in love . . . "The Torah lets out a word and emerges for a little from her sheath, and then hides herself again. But she does this only for those who understand and obey her. She is like unto a beautiful and stately damsel, who is hidden in a secluded chamber of a palace and who has a lover of whom no one knows but she. Out of his love for her he constantly passes by her gate, turning his eyes toward all sides to find her. Knowing that he is always haunting the palace, what does she do? She opens a little door in her hidden palace, discloses for a moment her face to her lover, then swiftly hides it again. None but he notices it; but his heart and soul, and all that is in him are drawn to her, knowing as he does that she has revealed herself to him for a moment because she loves him. It is the same with the Torah, which reveals her hidden secrets only to those who love her. She knows that he who is wise of heart daily haunts the gates of her house. What does she do? She shows her face to him from her palace, making a sign of love to him, and straightaway returns to her hiding place again. No one understands her message save he alone, and he is drawn to her with heart and soul and all his being. Thus the Torah reveals herself momentarily in love to her lovers in order to awaken fresh love in them."

6.   The Torah—A Mystic Reality

The Torah is an inexhaustible esoteric reality. To enter into its deep, hidden strata is in itself a mystic goal. The Universe is an image of the Torah and the Torah is an image of God. For the Torah is "the Holy of Holies"; "it consists entirely of the name of the Holy One, blessed be He. Every letter in it is bound up with that Name."

The Torah is the main source from which man can draw the secret wisdom and power of insight into the essence of things. "It is called Torah (lit.: showing) because it shows and reveals that which is hidden and unknown; and all life from above is comprised in it and issues from it." "The Torah contains all the deepest and most recondite mysteries; all sublime doctrines both disclosed and undisclosed; all essences both of the higher and the lower grades, of this world and of the world to come are to be found there." The source of wisdom is accessible to all, yet only few resort to it. "How stupid are men that they take no pains to know the ways of the Almighty by which the world is maintained. What prevents them? Their stupidity, because they do not study the Torah; for if they were to study the Torah they would know the ways of the Holy One, blessed be He."

The Torah has a double significance: literal and symbolic. Besides their plain, literal meaning, which is important, valid and never to be overlooked, the verses of the Torah possess an esoteric significance, "comprehensible only to the wise who are familiar with the ways of the Torah." "Happy is Israel to whom was given the sublime Torah, the Torah of truth. Perdition take anyone who maintains that any narrative in the Torah comes merely to tell us a piece of history and nothing more! If that were so, the Torah would not be what it assuredly is, to wit, the supernal Law, the Law of truth. Now if it is not dignified for a king of flesh and blood to engage in common talk, much less to write it down, is it conceivable that the most high King, the Holy One, blessed be He, was short of sacred subjects with which to fill the Torah, so that He had to collect such commonplace topics as the anecdotes of Esau, and Hagar, Laban's talks to Jacob, the words of Balaam and his ass, those of Balak, and of Zimri, and such-like, and make of them a Torah? If so, why is it called the 'Law of Truth?' Why do we read 'The Law of the Lord is perfect . . . The testimony of the Lord is sure . . . The Ordinances of the Lord are true . . . More to be desired are they than gold, yea, than much fine gold' (Ps. 19:8-11). But assuredly each word of the Torah signifies sublime things, so that this or that narrative, besides its meaning in and for itself, throws light on the all-comprehensive Rule of the Torah."

"Said R. Simeon: 'Alas for the man who regards the Torah as a mere book of tales and everyday matters! If that were so, we, even we, could compose a torah dealing with everyday affairs, and of even greater excellence. Nay, even the princes of the world possess books of greater worth which we could use as a model for composing some such torah. The Torah, however, contains in all its words supernal truths and sublime mysteries. Observe the perfect balancing of the upper and lower worlds. Israel here below is balanced by the angels on high, of whom it says: 'who makest thine angels into winds' (Ps. 104:4). For the angels in descending on earth put on themselves earthly garments, as otherwise they could not stay in this world, nor could the world endure them.

"Now, if thus it is with the angels, how much more so must it be with the Torah—the Torah that created them, that created all the worlds and is the means by which these are sustained. Thus had the Torah not clothed herself in garments of this world the world could not endure it. The stories of the Torah are thus only her outer garments, and whoever looks upon that garment as being Torah itself, woe to that man—such a one will have no portion in the next world. David thus said: 'Open thou mine eyes, that I may behold wondrous things out of Thy law' (Ps. 119:18), to wit, the things that are beneath the garment. Observe this. The garments worn by a man are the most visible part of him, and senseless people looking at the man do not seem to see more in him than the garments. But in truth the pride of the garments is the body of the man, and the pride of the body is the soul. Similarly the Torah has a body made up of the precepts of the Torah, called *gufe torah* (bodies, main principles of the Torah), and that body is enveloped in garments made up of worldly narratives. The senseless people only see the garment, the mere narrations; those who are somewhat wise penetrate as far as the body. But the really wise, the servants of the most high King, those who stood on Mt. Sinai, penetrate right through to the soul, the root principle of all, namely to the real Torah. In the future the same are destined to penetrate even to the super-soul (soul of the soul) of the Torah . . . "

How assiduously should one ponder over each word of the Torah, for there is not a single word in it which does not contain allusions to

the Supernal Holy Name, not a word which does not contain many
mysteries, many aspects, many roots, many branches! Where now is
this "book of the wars of the Lord"? What is meant, of course, is the
Torah, for as the members of the Fellowship have pointed out, he who
is engaged in the battle of the Torah, struggling to penetrate into her
mysteries, will wrest from his struggles an abundance of peace.

7. *The Mystic Way of Life*

A longing for the unearthly, a yearning for purity, the will to
holiness, connected the conscience of the cabbalists with the strange
current of mystic living. Being puzzled or inquisitive will not make a person mystery stricken. The cabbalists were not set upon exploring, or
upon compelling the unseen to become visible. Their intention was to
integrate their thoughts and deeds into the secret order, to assist God
in undoing the evil, in redeeming the light that was concealed. Though
working with fragile tools for a mighty end, they were sure of bringing
about at the end the salvation of the universe and of this tormented
world.

A new form of living was the consequence of the cabbala. Everything was so replete with symbolic significance as to make it the potential heart of the spiritual universe. How carefully must all be approached. A moral rigorism that hardly leaves any room for waste or
respite resulted in making the cabbalist more meticulous in studying
and fulfilling the precepts of the Torah, in refining his moral conduct,
in endowing every-day actions with solemn significance. For man
represents God in this world. Even the parts of his body signify
Divine mysteries.

Everything a man does leaves its imprint on the world. "The
Supernal Holy King does not permit anything to perish, not even the
breath of the mouth. He has a place for everything, and makes it what
He wills. Even a human word, yes, even the voice, is not void, but
has its place and destination in the universe." Every action here below,
if it is done with the intention of serving the Holy King, produces a
"breath" in the world above, and there is no breath which has no
voice; and this voice ascends and crowns itself in the supernal world and
becomes an intercessor before the Holy One, blessed be He. Contrari-
wise, every action which is not done with this purpose becomes a
"breath" which floats about the world, and when the soul of the doer
leaves his body, this "breath" rolls about like a stone in a sling, and
it "breaks the spirit." The act done and the word spoken in the service

of the Holy One, however, ascend high above the sun and become a holy breath, which is the seed sown by man in that world and is called *Zedakah* (righteousness or loving-kindness), as it is written: "Sow to yourselves according to righteousness" (Hos. 10:12). This "breath" guides the departed soul and brings it into the region of the supernal glory, so that it is "bound in the bundle of life with the Lord thy God" (I Sam. 25:29). It is concerning this that it is written: "Thy righteousness shall go before thee; the glory of the Lord shall be thy reward" (Is. 58:8). That which is called "the glory of the Lord" gathers up the souls of that holy breath, and this is indeed ease and comfort for them; but the other is called "breaking of spirit." Blessed are the righteous whose works are "above the sun" and who sow a seed of righteousness which makes them worthy to enter the world to come.

Everything a man does leaves its imprint upon the world: his breath, thought, speech. If it is evil, the air is defiled and he who comes close to that trace may be affected by it and led to do evil. By fulfilling the Divine precepts man purifies the air and turns the "evil spirits" into "holy spirits." He should strive to spiritualize the body and to make it identical with the soul by fulfilling the 248 positive and 365 negative precepts which correspond to the 248 limbs and the 365 sinews of the human body. The precepts of the Torah contain "manifold sublime recondite teachings and radiances and resplendences," and can lift man to the supreme level of existence.

The purpose of man's service is to "give strength to God," not to attain one's own individual perfection. Man is able to stir the supernal spheres. "The terrestrial world is connected with the heavenly world, as the heavenly world is connected with the terrestrial one." In fulfilling the good the corresponding sphere on high is strengthened; in balking it, the sphere is weakened. This connection or correspondence can be made to operate in a creative manner by means of *kawwanah* or contemplation of the mysteries of which the words and precepts of the Torah are the symbols. In order to grasp the meaning of those words or to fulfill the purpose of those precepts one has to resort to the Divine Names and Qualities which are invested in those words and precepts, the mystic issues to which they refer, or, metaphorically, the gates of the celestial mansion which the spiritual content of their fulfillment has to enter. Thus, all deeds—study, prayer and ceremonies— have to be performed not mechanically but while meditating upon their mystic significance.

Prayer is a powerful force in this service and a venture full of peril. He who prays is a priest at the temple that is the cosmos. With good prayer he may "build worlds," with improper prayer he may "destroy worlds." "It is a miracle that a man survives the hour of worship," the Baal Shem said. "The significance of all our prayers and praises is that by means of them the upper fountain may be filled; and when it is so filled and attains completeness, then the universe below, and all that appertains thereto, is filled also and receives completeness from the completion which has been consummated in the upper sphere. The world below cannot, indeed, be in a state of harmony unless it receives that peace and perfection from above, even as the moon has no light in herself but shines with the reflected radiance of the sun. All our prayers and intercessions have this purpose, namely, that the region from whence light issues may be invigorated; for then from its reflection all below is supplied." "Every word of prayer that issues from a man's mouth ascends aloft through all firmaments to a place where it is tested. If it is genuine, it is taken up before the Holy King to be fulfilled, but if not it is rejected, and an alien spirit is evoked by it." For example, "it is obligatory for every Israelite to relate the story of the Exodus on the Passover night. He who does so fervently and joyously, telling the tale with a high heart, shall be found worthy to rejoice in the *Shekinah* in the world to come, for rejoicing brings forth rejoicing; and the joy of Israel causes the Holy One Himself to be glad, so that He calls together all the Family above and says unto them: 'Come ye and hearken unto the praises which My children bring unto Me! Behold how they rejoice in My redemption!' Then all the angels and supernal beings gather round and observe Israel, how she sings and rejoices because of her Lord's own Redemption—and seeing the rejoicings below, the supernal beings also break into jubilation for that the Holy One possesses on earth a people so holy, whose joy in the Redemption of their Lord is so great and powerful. For all that terrestrial rejoicing increases the power of the Lord and His hosts in the regions above, just as an earthly king gains strength from the praises of his subjects, the fame of his glory being thus spread throughout the world."

Worship came to be regarded as a pilgrimage into the supernal spheres, with the prayerbook as an itinerary, containing the course of the gradual ascent of the spirit. The essential goal of man's service is to bring about the lost unity of all that exists. To render praise unto Him is not the final purpose. "Does the God of Abraham need an exaltation? Is He not already exalted high above our comprehension? . . . Yet man can and must exalt Him in the sense of uniting in his mind all the attributes in the Holy Name, for this is the supremest form of worship." By meditating upon the mysteries while performing the Divine precepts, we act toward unifying all the supernal potencies in one will and bringing about the union of the Master and the Matrona.

Concerning the verse in Ps. 145:18, "The Lord is nigh to all them that call upon Him, to all that call upon Him in truth," the *Zohar* remarks that the words "in truth" mean in possession of the full knowledge which enables the worshiper perfectly "to unite the letters of the Holy Name in prayer . . . On the achievement of that unity hangs both celestial and terrestrial worship . . . If a man comes to unify the Holy Name, but without proper concentration of mind and devotion of heart, to the end that the supernal and terrestrial hosts should be blessed thereby, then his prayer is rejected and all beings denounce him, and he is numbered with those of whom the Holy One said, 'When ye come to see my countenance, who hath required this from your hand, to tread my courts?' All the 'countenances' of the King are hidden in the depths of darkness, but for those who know how perfectly to unite the Holy Name, all the walls of darkness are burst asunder, and the diverse 'countenances' of the King are made manifest, and shine upon all, bringing blessing to heavenly and earthly beings."

The lower things are apparent, the higher things remain unrevealed. The higher an essence is, the greater is the degree of its concealment. To pray is "to draw blessings from the depth of the 'Cistern,' from the source of all life . . . Prayer is the drawing of this blessing from above to below; for when the Ancient One, the All-hidden, wishes to bless the universe, He lets His gifts of Grace collect in that supernal depth, from whence they are to be drawn, through human prayer, into the 'Cistern,' so that all the streams and brooks may be filled therefrom." The verse in Psalm 130:1, "Out of the depths have I called Thee," is said to mean not only that he who prays should do so from the depths of his soul; he must also invoke the blessing from the source of all sources.

8.   The Concern for God

The yearning for mystic living, the awareness of the ubiquitous mystery, the noble nostalgia for the nameless nucleus, have rarely subsided in the Jewish soul. This longing for the mystical has found many and varied expressions in ideas and doctrines, in customs and songs, in visions and aspirations. It is a part of the heritage of the psalmists and prophets.

There were Divine commandments to fulfill, rituals to perform, laws to obey—but the psalmist did not feel as if he carried a yoke: "Thy statutes have been my songs" (119:54). The fulfillment of the *mitzvot* was felt to be not a mechanical compliance but a personal service in the palace of the King of Kings. Is mysticism alien to the spirit of Judaism? Listen to the psalmist: "As the hart panteth after the water brooks, so panteth my soul after Thee, O Lord. My soul thirsteth for God, for the Living God; when shall I come and appear before God?" (42:2-3). "My soul yearneth, yea even pineth for the courts of the Lord; my heart and my flesh sing for joy unto the Living God" (84:3). "For a day in Thy courts is better than a thousand" (84:11). "In Thy presence is fulness of joy" (16:11).

It has often been said that Judaism is an earthly religion, yet the psalmist states, "I am a sojourner in the earth" (119:19). "Whom have I in heaven but Thee? And beside thee I desire none upon earth" (73:25). "My flesh and my heart faileth; but God is the rock of my heart and my portion forever" (73:26). "But as for me, the nearness of God is my good" (73:28). "O God, Thou art my God; earnestly will I seek Thee; my soul thirsteth for Thee, my flesh longeth for Thee in a dry and weary land, where no water is . . . for Thy lovingkindness is better than life. My soul is satisfied as with marrow and fatness; . . . I remember Thee upon my couch and meditate on Thee in the nightwatches . . . My soul cleaveth unto Thee, Thy right hand holdeth me fast" (63:2, 4, 6, 7, 9).

In their efforts to say what God is and wills, the prophets sought to imbue Israel with two impulses: to realize that God is holy, different and apart from all that exists, and to bring into man's focus the dynamics that prevail between God and man. The first impulse placed the mind in the restful light of the knowledge of unity, omnipotence, and superiority of God to all other beings, while the second impulse turned the hearts toward the inexhaustible heavens of God's concern for man, at times brightened by His mercy, at times darkened by His anger. He is both transcendent, beyond human understanding, and at the same time full of love, compassion, grief, or anger. The prophets did not intend to afford man a view of heaven, to report about secret things they saw and heard but to disclose what happened in God in reference to Israel. What they preached was more than a concept of Divine might and wisdom. They spoke of an inner life of God, of His love or anger, His mercy or disappointment, His interest or participation in the fate of Israel and other nations. God revealed Himself to the prophets in a specific state, in an emotional or passionate relationship to Israel. He not only demanded obedience but He was personally concerned and even stirred by the conduct of His people. Their actions aroused His joy, grief or disappointment. His attitude was not objective but subjective. He was not only a Judge but also a Father. He is the lover, engaged to His people, who reacts to human life with a specific *pathos,* signified in the language of the prophets, in love, mercy or anger. The Divine pathos which the prophets tried to express in many ways was not a name for His essence but rather for the modes of this reaction to Israel's conduct which could be changed by a change in Israel's conduct. Such a change was often the object of the prophetic ministry.

The prophets discovered the holy dimension of living by which our right to live and to survive is measured. However, the holy dimension was not a mechanical magnitude, measurable by the yardstick of deed and reward, of crime and punishment, by a cold law of justice. They did not proclaim a universal moral mechanism but a spiritual order in which justice was the course but not the source. To them justice was not a static principle but a surge sweeping from the inwardness of God, in which the deeds of man find, as it were, approval or disapproval, joy or sorrow. There was a surge of Divine pathos, which came to the souls of the prophets like a fierce passion, startling, shaking, burning, and led them forth to the perilous defiance of people's self-assurance and contentment. Beneath all songs and sermons they held conference with God's concern for the people, with the well out of which the tides of anger raged.

There is always a correspondence between what man is and what he knows about God. To a man of the *vita activa,* omnipotence is the most striking attribute of God. A man with an inner life, to whom thoughts and intuitions are not less real than things and deeds, will search for a concept of the inner life of God. The concept of inner life in the Divine Being is an idea upon which the mystic doctrines of Judaism hinge. The significance of prophetic revelation lies not in the inner experience of the prophet but in its character as a manifestation of what is in God. Prophetic revelation is primarily an event in the life of God. This is the outstanding difference between prophetic revelation and all other types of inspiration as reported by many mystics and poets. To the prophet it is not a psychic event, but first of all a transcendent act, something that happens to God. The actual reality of revelation takes place outside the consciousness of the prophet. He experiences revelation, so to speak, as an ecstasy of God, who comes out of His imperceivable distance to reveal His will to man. Essentially, the act of revelation takes place in the Beyond; it is merely directed upon the prophet.

The knowledge about the inner state of the Divine in its relationship to Israel determined the inner life of the prophets, engendering a passion for God, a *sympathy* for the Divine pathos in their hearts. They loved Israel because God loved Israel, and they frowned upon Israel when they knew that such was the attitude of God. Thus the marriage of Hosea was an act of sympathy; the prophet had to go through the experience of being betrayed as Israel had betrayed God. He had to experience in his own life what it meant to be betrayed by a person whom he loved in order to gain an understanding of the inner life of God. In a similar way the sympathy for God was in the heart of Jeremiah like a "burning fire, shut up in my bones and I weary myself to hold it in, but cannot" (20:9).

The main doctrine of the prophets can be called *pathetic theology*. Their attitude toward what they knew about God can be described as religion of sympathy. The Divine pathos, or as it was later called, the *Middot,* stood in the center of their consciousness. The life of the prophet revolved around the life of God. The prophets were not indifferent to whether God was in a state of anger or a state of mercy. They were most sensitive to what was going on in God.

This is the pattern of Jewish mysticism: to have an open heart for the inner life of God. It is based on two assumptions: that there is an inner life in God and that the existence of man ought to revolve in a spiritual dynamic course around the life of God.

MYSTICISM AND ETHICS

While most people have heard of the movement called Hasidism, founded by Israel Baal Shem Tov in the eighteenth century, fewer know that an earlier movement, also called Hasidism, developed in twelfth and thirteenth century Germany. The earlier Hasidism produced the "Book of the Pious", a combination of mystical and ethical teaching. The Hasidism of medieval Germany differed from that of eighteenth century Poland in many significant ways and should be considered quite apart from the later movement.

Its primary stress lay not on the esoteric doctrines of which Heschel informs us, but rather upon piety and right behavior. The pious person—the *Hasid*—here is understood as a person who achieves personal serenity, altruism, and asceticism. The ideal is not one of withdrawal from the world, but rather transcendence over the world's hurts and stings. This goal is achieved through concentrating on the earthly law, the *halakhah*, as a means of carrying out the heavenly law, the higher law of true piety.

For the Hasidim of medieval Germany, piety begins beyond the law. Having done what is required, one must then do what is beyond the law's limits and commandments. The Torah permits some things, but the pious man will nonetheless avoid them. The heavenly law is revealed in perfect fairness in human relations, the attainment of a good heart and a good conscience. The ascetic strain is striking: it is through ascetic exercise that mystic experience is attained. But the exercise did not result in removing the ascetic from the community. His ascetic behavior was focused on society and required activity, not passivity.

The selection from *The Book of the Pious* will stress the matter of motivation. The Hasid recognizes that one may do the right thing for the wrong reason, and if so, the meaning of what one does is distorted. One should do the right deed for the right reason, and that is, for the sake of God. If one does so, then the very concrete affairs of everyday life are made into the occasion for the contemplation of, the confrontation with God. It is this sort of practical mysticism, founded upon

301

the common life, which characterizes Rabbinic Judaism, a world which, to begin with, stresses the importance of trivial and concrete behavior in the sight of God. A religious world which believes God wants certain deeds of man is going to produce a mystical movement based upon the higher, or deeper, meanings of those very deeds.

16.

THE BOOK OF THE PIOUS

Sholom Alchanan Singer

[From *Medieval Jewish Mysticism. Book of the Pious,* by
Sholom Alchanan Singer. Northbrook, Ill., Whitehall Co.,
pp. ix-xx, 48-54.]

The rise of Hasidism in the life of German Jewry has long been
regarded as one of the major events in the religious history of that
community. For many scholars it is indeed the only decisive development of major consequence in the spiritual life of German Jewry.

This particular religious growth which bears the name *Ha-Hasiduth
Ha-Ashkenazith,* German Pietism, evolved under the impact of the
crusades and their concomitant persecutions. In essence such newborn
pietism represents a response to the methodical pattern of humiliation
and degradation inflicted upon Jews during the twelfth and thirteenth
centuries; it is a heightened and more intense form of religio-moral
idealism and saintliness. It arose first in the Rhenish Jewish communities. Its representatives were referred to by their contemporaries
as *Haside Ashkenaz,* The Devout of Germany.

The creative period of the movement was relatively short, the century from about 1150 to 1250, but its influence on German Jewry
was lasting. The religious concepts and ideas to which it gave rise and
filled with meaning through their own practice and conduct retained
their vitality for centuries. The protagonists of this heightened pietism
were accepted and regarded as genuine representatives of an ideal
Jewish way of life.

While it is true that the movement itself never achieved the proportions or dimensions of a mass movement, the teachings and leadership did enjoy wide popularity, authority, and prestige. It must, of
course, be recognized that the very nature of the calling with its
demanding and exacting teachings made it a vocation for the few

rather than for the multitude. Nevertheless, it did not preclude the community at large from aspiring to inclusion in its select ranks and being numbered among its devotees. The simple fact that this movement exerted such a powerful influence over a short period of time and a lasting influence over succeeding centuries demonstrates and reveals the deep roots it struck in the heart, life, and mind of German Jewry.

Judah ben Samuel, the Pious of Regensburg (Ratisbon) who is regarded as one of the most prominent and influential of the *Haside Ashkenaz,* the Devout of Germany, was born in Speyer about the year 1140. He died in Regensburg on February 22, 1217. So long as Hasidism remained a living and vital force he held an almost unrivaled position of leadership. There can be no question that his own stature was enhanced by the fact that he was a descendant of one of the most illustrious families in Jewry, the Kalonymides. For many generations his family took a leading part in the development of Jewish learning in Germany. Although originally from Lucca, Italy, the family migrated to many different regions in Europe. A branch of the Kolonymides settled in Speyer, Mayence, and Worms.

Judah the Pious' grandfather, Kalonymus ben Isaac the Elder, already lived in Speyer during the eleventh and twelfth century and established a reputation as rabbi and halakhist. His son Samuel the Pious, the father of Judah, added further to the lustre of the family name through his writings, scholarship, and personal piety. It is, however, unfortunate that most of his writings, which were considerable, have been lost.

Samuel the Pious, his son Judah, and the latter's disciple and relative Eleazar ben Judah of Worms may be regarded as the molders of German Hasidism. The fact that scholarship still remains divided on the question of authorship for the opening sections of *Sefer Hasidim* between Judah, or his father Samuel, reveals the great similarity of ideology and teaching of these two men. Judah the Pious and his brother, Abraham, who was head of an academy in Speyer, were apparently pupils of their father Samuel and received their early instruction from him.

Records indicate that Samuel the Pious was an outstanding Talmudic scholar for his time, in addition to being a pietist of distinction. He maintained an academy in Speyer, wrote commentaries and other works, and is quoted often by contemporary scholars. As far as legend guides us, it seems that Abraham studied with his father Samuel in the conventional and customary setting of student-teacher relationship. Judah's introduction to study was apparently delayed for many years because of his interest in more worldly matters. When he finally began to study, the moment of initiation reverberated with dramatic and prophetic effects, pointing to the fact that Judah would soon overshadow his brother Abraham in mystical knowledge and achievement. After this, Judah applied himself diligently to study.

Later, Judah went to Regensburg, established his dwelling there and was esteemed as one of the foremost scholars and teachers in that town. He wrote many mystical and ethical treatises, the best known being *Sefer Hasidim*. He wrote a commentary on the Pentateuch and books on legalistic matters. Few of these have survived. He was the teacher of Rabbi Eleazar, author of the *Rokeah,* and his mentor in mysticism.

Rabbi Isaac Or Zarua was another of Judah's pupils. A correspondence was carried on between Rabbi Judah and many of the outstanding Franco-German scholars of the day. Rabbi Judah had three sons, Rabbi Samuel, Rabbi Zalman, and Rabbi Moses.

Numerous and illustrious teachers contributed to the personality and development of Rabbi Judah the Pious. Aside from the instruction which Rabbi Judah received from his father in traditional matters, he received his mystical initiation from him as well. The meaning of the "Pyut" he learned from the martyred Rabbi Jom Tob the Holy. He, in turn, influenced very many important rabbis, most especially Rabbi Eleazar b. Judah, called the "Rokeah," Rabbi Baruch of Mayence, Rabbi Isaac Or Zarua. Judah the Pious was referred to by his contemporaries as the "Great Pietist," "Father of Wisdom," and the like.

Legends about Judah abound but their reliability is doubtful. However, through them all there shines the unquestionable impressiveness of his piety and holiness. Tradition states, "If he had lived in the time of the prophets he would surely have been a prophet, if during the time of the Tanaim a Tana, and in the time of the Amoraim an Amora." His contribution to medieval Jewish mysticism is a matter still to be investigated and evaluated fully.

Part of the difficulty of such an investigation stems from the lack of authentic and reliable primary material dealing with the period. Though the life of Francis of Assisi, a contemporary with whom Judah has been compared, is copiously commented upon by medieval writers, Judah's life remains a mystery and virtually unknown. In spite of the fact that we have *Sefer Hasidim* before us, there is still much we should like to know in detail about the man. Even if we presume to attribute authorship to him, which is no small matter, other information about his personal life, and his opinions on important matters are still not available to us.

Concerning the authorship of the book, *Sefer Hasidim,* there is no complete agreement among scholars except on one point, namely, that the book is not the work of one writer but a composite of many writers. This is proved by an internal examination which discloses frequent conflicting statements and sentiments. Some believe that the book in its present form consists of three revisions of a text of which Judah is the original author. . . .

Perhaps the most balanced and measured opinion on the question of authorship has been put forward by Fritz Baer in a view which is shared by most scholars. He says that the teachings of *Sefer Hasidim* form a definite and consistent whole emanating from a specific school and reflecting the spirit of a dominating central figure, Rabbi Judah the Pious. The book itself may be regarded as a collection of ethical and religious precepts for the life of the community and the individual in Germany during the early thirteenth century. It is not an anonymous creation of successive generations; on the contrary, two or three generations of development are seen here, starting with a small group of scholars gathering themselves around a specific leading personality. This one dynamic personality sets the foundation for the *Torath Hasidim,* "Doctrine of the Hasidim," and for most of its conclusions. Baer feels that the tradition ascribing the book to Judah the Pious is quite correct in the sense that Judah stands in the center of the movement. The impact of his personality on his contemporaries may be considered from many points of view. There is hardly a category of thought or action which does not receive his comment. Perhaps it would be incorrect to ascribe all views found in the book to the man directly. But it would be fair to say, in the light of previous remarks, that they come as a consequence of the real and dominating position Judah the Pious enjoyed within the movement. Perhaps in view of the many difficulties that emerge when attempting to ascribe authorship to individuals, it would be more appropriate to refer authorship to a school of thought led by Judah the Pious. This sort of ascription, group or corporate, would of necessity imply in a single work the presence of diverse and often contradictory views. And such is the case here. Nevertheless, contradictions notwithstanding, the book aspires to a higher unity, which is in essence the groundwork and message of the *Haside Ashkenaz.* It represents their interpretation of "Pietism." Naturally, such interpretation embraces a good deal: their view of the reality around them, their interpretation of ritual observance, their conception of Jewishness, of the relationship of man to God, of sin, prayer, and whatever may fall under the rubric of theology and spirituality. Observations on magic, death, and immortality and comments on miscellaneous other subjects are also present in the work. It is this latitude in subject matter, together with the unadorned treatment, that gives the book its intrinsic value as a primary source for the movement which it represents and adorns.

The fact that it represents a departure from certain traditional rabbinic norms and categories of value accounts in part for the ambivalences and contradictions that frequently occur. The departure for new climes of opinion and feeling that characterize it, very often brings a reaction in the form of nostalgia for the older and more familiar traditional touchstones. Moreover, tradition itself, pervasive and all-penetrating as it is, very often makes us heirs of contrary and irreconcilable beliefs and views. The alternation between the old and new may therefore be viewed as being in fact less a matter of contradiction than of tension between two views for greater loyalty. Very often when deeper and more intensive probing occurs, we find that the yield of both views is complete agreement on a more sublime level of aspiration and intent. It is here that a convergence and unity involving religiosity and godliness is ultimately achieved.

In defining the nature of "piety" and the "pious" we can do so from two points of view. One view is that of the masses as reflected in contemporary literature. The other, perhaps more important and to which we will restrict ourselves, is the definition garnered from the book itself. Here, broadly speaking, although a case could be made for additional and, if hard pressed, infinite subtleties and nuances, three main categories of behavior and attitude single out "the pious"; serenity of mind, altruism, and an ascetic renunciation of the things of this world.

A more detailed enumeration of the component elements comprising these major rubrics would be as follows: indifference to offenses of all sorts, doing deeds of kindness, controlling the evil inclination in all its varied manifestations, avoiding all idle and useless occupations and pastimes, purity of intent and the doing of everything almost to extreme for the "sake of heaven." Baer is quite right in saying that all these manifestations of pietism were elicited by a demand embodied in a higher form of law, *Ius Divinum,* heavenly law. The pietist must at times veer from *Ius Positivum,* the demands of conventional law of halakha, in order to fulfill the dictates of "heavenly law."

We find *Sefer Hasidim* describing the substance of pietism as the duty to act beyond the limit of the law. That the law does not represent the ideal optimum of justice has its genesis in Talmudic literature. We have statements in *Sefer Hasidim* to the effect that there may be things which the Torah permits and yet if a man practices them he will be brought to judgment because of them, for man must realize that the Torah permits them only because of the evil inclination. Baer identifies this "heavenly law" which involves human relationships with natural human fairness and equity. Concerning relations between God and man this would provide a stricter interpretation and application of ritual and religious practices. This new line of action governed by good heart and conscience would naturally well up from the soul's assimilation of the divine spirit.

It is quite reasonable to assert that the distinctive element in "pietism" which gives it its most prominent characteristic is the striving to fulfill heavenly law, a demand which is additional, self-imposed by conscience and good heart, a law which is beyond the immediate claims of the traditional law or *halakhah.*

The ascetic strain found within the pietism of the *Haside Ashkenaz* is touched upon by numerous authors. To my mind the subject has not really been given its proper perspective. Baer tries to show differences that exist between the ascetic proclivities of the *Haside Ashkenaz* and that of non-Jewish asceticism. More, perhaps, should have been said about the similarities which are equally interesting but have received sparse comment. Dom Ursmer Berliere's remark concerning Christian mystics can very well apply to our own *Haside Ashkenaz;* that in every mystic there is an ascetic and that asceticism is at the very source of mysticism. This, of course, helps to explain some of the severe forms of penance and self-denial in *Sefer Hasidim.* Moreover, we find in *Sefer Hasidim* overtones and allusions to that triple mystical root which has been sketched for the Christian mystic, purgation, illumination, and union. This is not native to Christianity alone, but was then and is today, shared by many other religions. This can be accounted for by the simple fact that so many faiths drink from a common ideational source.

The period with which we are dealing and which witnesses similar mystical activity in Jewish and non-Jewish camps can be attributed to a religious influence and atmosphere, then prevalent, which affected both equally.

Baer's observation is quite true that the Jewish mystic-ascetic never goes beyond a certain point in self-denial because of legal prohibitions. However, this does not set him apart from the non-Jewish mystic-ascetic in their common striving and spiritual personality. In a manner of speaking, both Christian and Jewish mystics strive and achieve the extreme within their respective faiths that is permissible. It is only in comparison with each other that this "extreme" for the Jewish mystic appears foreshortened. The Jewish mystic goes to the extremity permitted by law as does the Christian; in the latter's case, however, the extent of self-denial permitted is far more generous. The foregoing observation does not indicate at all that the basic concept and mood of Christian and Jewish mystics differ. It is the law which directs and defines the mystical ascetic personality. The Jewish mystic might well be placed beside the Christian and made to appear similar in terms of a common mood, view and aspiration. It is the rule of law and tradition which sets them apart sending them into different areas of mystical preoccupation. In this respect Baer is quite right when he says that *Haside Ashkenaz* did not and could not avoid involvement in the social scene and communal enterprise. The Christian mystical tradition with its greater latitude for escape and isolation could hold out to its contemplative mystics complete insulation from social contact and exposure. The "activists" however might well correspond in terms of their mobility and social exposure to a counterpart in Judaism, namely, the *Haside Ashkenaz*.

46. All your actions should be for the sake of heaven. Let a man not eat nor sleep with the intention of being healthy and fattened in order to engage in matters of this world and to pursue wealth. He should rather say, "I will sleep and I will eat in order that I may be able to stand in fear of my Creator and engage in His Law and commandments." And when he washes his hands and blesses, or if he recites a blessing over fruit, or a blessing involving any other deed, which is fluent in the mouths of all (a common prayer), let him direct his heart to bless in the name of his Creator who does wonderful kindnesses with him and gives him the fruits and bread to enjoy and enjoins upon him the commandments. Let him not act as one who does something because of habit and recites (blessings) without the heart's meditation. For this reason God's anger is kindled in His people and He sent us His servant Isaiah and said, "For as much as this people draw near, and with their mouth and with their eyes do honor Me, but have removed their heart far from Me and their fear of Me is a

commandment of men learned by rote" (Isa. 29:13). The Holy one, blessed be He, said to Isaiah, "Isaiah, see the works of My children, and know that it is all for appearances sake only. They hold fast to Me as a person who holds fast and follows the usage handed down to him from his father. They come into My house and pray in accord with the fixed prayers like the customs of their fathers but without a whole heart. They cleanse their hands and recite the blessing for the washing of the hands, they break bread and recite the blessing over the bread, they drink and bless (only) because the matter is fluent in their mouths, but at the time that they bless, their thoughts are not to bless Me." It is for this reason that His wrath is kindled in Him and He swears by His great name to destroy the wisdom of His wise men who know Him and bless Him (only) out of custom but without devotion, as it is written thereafter, "Therefore, behold, I will again do a marvelous work among this people, even a marvelous work and a wonder and the wisdom of their wise men shall perish, and the prudence of their prudent men shall be hid" (Isa. 29:14). Therefore our sages warned concerning this matter and said "And do things for the sake of their Doer (God). For everything which the Holy One, blessed be He, created, He created for His glory. Do not make of them a wreath with which to adorn yourself, to boast of them when you perform the commandments before people. We will not reach the will of our Creator, because (as in the event mentioned) we labor to find favor in the eyes of men. The reward which we anticipate we lose, there will be none. He who performs secretly, merits greater reward, his deeds are ultimately revealed and he is exalted. (The verse) "The end of the matter, all having been heard" (Eccl. 12:13) the Targum Jonathan translates, "Everything that is done in this world will be made known in the future to all people." It is reported of a certain man that he died prematurely. Long after twelve months he appeared in a dream to one of his relatives. His relative asked him, "How are you faring in the world where you are?" He said to him, "I am punished each day because I was not circumspect in reciting the blessing over the bread, the blessings for fruit and the "Grace" with wholehearted devotion, and they say to me, 'You intended only for your own profit.' " He asked him, "Is it not true that there is judgement for the wicked only for twelve months, and now more than twelve months are past and they are still punishing you?" He said to him, "They do not punish me as severly as during the first twelve months."

47. "Who teacheth us more than the beasts of the earth, And maketh us wiser than the fowls of heaven" (Job 35:11). "Who teacheth us more than the beasts of the earth," (tells) a man to teach his son to be more faithful than a dog that is faithful to its master. "And maketh us wiser than the fowls of the heaven," (this verse) tells a man to learn from the hoopoe, the hen of the prairie. Because, in the time of Solomon, it (hoopoe) did not fulfill its faithfulness to the ruler of the sea involving the "shamir" put in its charge, it choked itself. Therefore let the remainder of Israel apply to itself the syllogism

Another facet of his character is revealed in one of his poems (Shirei ha-Kodesh): "We are children of our father Abraham who stated: 'I am but dust and ashes'; disciples of our teacher Moses who exclaimed: 'What are we but God's servants'; and descendants of King David who said, 'I am a worm.' Whom should we follow: those great teachers, or Jeroboam who, in his pride, knew only to ask: 'Who will be the leader,' and he meant himself."

It was because of this humility that, all urging notwithstanding, he refused to publish even one line during his lifetime. "Almost every author," he would say, "feels proud upon reading his name in print. Such pride ignores the teachings of the Fathers: 'A name made great, is a name destroyed.' Similarly was the writing down of the oral tradition permitted only when it served God's honor but not one's own!" Fortunately he did write down his novellae (Comments on Torah) and responsa to countless inquiries from far and near. After his death, between 1841 and 1861, the latter were published in six volumes. Other books include homiletical and exegetical material.

A Memorial Volume ("Sefer ha-Zikkaron") describes events during the Napoleonic Wars against Austria, when the French Army wrought havoc with the life of the Pressburg Jewish community. It deals with the flight to the countryside and other experiences until the armistice. That volume contains also a number of speeches through which the rabbi endeavored to give courage and strength to his grievously harassed community. The Rabbinical Council of Pressburg had to act in cases between Jews, involving some semi-legal and illegal traffic in arms. R. M. S. was summoned to appear before the French court because he had failed to notify the French authorities of such deals. But his personality and his bearing convinced the authorities of his complete innocence.

Because of the War, the State of Austria declared itself in bankruptcy in 1811, and the official currency was devaluated to one-fifth its original value. This brought forth a flood of inquiries addressed to Rabbi Sofer, concerning the payment of debts, alimony and other obligations.

His answers to every type of question throughout thirty-six years of his rabbinate in Pressburg may offer the key to his spiritual effectiveness.

Even a superficial study of these volumes explains the universal fame of the author throughout the Jewish World. Questions came from the Austro-Hungarian monarchy, from Germany, Italy, Holland, Switzerland, and Palestine. They deal with the whole range of Jewish life and lore, from questions as to the essence of Judaism down to minutiae of law and custom and proper copying of Torah scrolls. We also find questions about civil rights, community and family laws and difficult passages in the Talmud. There is a well-known passage in Berakhoth to the effect that the face of a man who depends on others, will change color. The rabbi offers another interpretation of *"shenitsrakh la-beriyoth,"* to wit: a person whose decision and counsel is wanted by many must have great patience and infinite capacity for adjustment. He will be pale with the exertion, and red with occasional tension.

"Talmudic learning is not enough. A judge must also be familiar with other fields of human knowledge for a proper application of the laws of the Torah to the complexity of everyday problems." Unconsciously, the rabbi described himself.

Many of his answers show his general knowledge, which made him familiar also with problems outside the Jewish realm. As a Torah-scholar he was fully aware of his own limitations. Asked how he was able to give immediate written replies to the most difficult questions, and out of thousands of questions only twice had to admit an error, he explained that since his eighteenth year, with the exception of Tisha be-Av, he never let a day go by without studying the Torah by himself or with his students. Even on the eve of Yom ha-Kippurim he was in the habit of holding a Shiur. The nights, spent with only a minimum of rest, with his feet immersed in cold water, to prevent himself from falling asleep, enabled him in later years to draw out from his phenomenal memory instantaneously the right answer to any question. He interpreted wittily the verse of the Psalms *"Kehitsim beyad ha-Gibbor ken b'ne ha-Neoorim"* to mean: "As arrows in the hand of the hero, so are the children (results) of nights spent awake," *Neoorim* meaning both "youth" and "wakefulness."

Rabbi Moses Sofer not only endorsed the right of the Jews to entrust relevant documents to non-Jewish courts, but declared it incumbent upon the members of the Beth Din to make declarations before a non-Jewish tribunal in order to bring about governmental action— but only in cases where the incorruptibility of the authorities concerned was beyond doubt. With great indignation did he condemn any attempts by Jews to mislead non-Jewish officials through circumlocution or perjury. He declared currency inflation caused by the government binding for all transactions among Jews, including those involving community or charitable institutions. The currency rate established by the State was to serve as basis in the repayment of debts contracted under an earlier rate of exchange. The only exception was the silver payment involved in the Pidyon ha-Ben (the ceremony of the Redemption of the First-born).

Whosoever bribes a judge, whether Jewish or non-Jewish, violates the prohibition: *"Thou shalt not put a stumbling block before the blind."* In the course of this responsum, R. M. S. cited an earlier decision of Rabbi Joel Bacharach (author of *"Havvoth Yair"*, 17th century). Pfalzgraf (Count) Karl Ludwig had bitterly complained about the Jews bribing non-Jewish judges in any litigation between themselves and Christians. Rabbi Bacharach replied: "The Judge's intense Anti-Semitism normally made him decide against the Jew, no matter how much he was in the right. Thus the bribe succeeded in achieving impartiality, and this made a fair trial possible. From the point of view of the Torah a bribe could not be justified, yet the Jews felt they were not doing wrong as they were merely attempting to secure justice". R. M. S. remarks apropos that it is forbidden to make a non-Jew transgress any of the seven Noahide laws, one of them being a fair application of justice.

An interesting responsum concerned a hired maid who had deposited a pair of golden earrings with her employer as a pledge against leaving his employ before the proper time. She disappeared, and could not be found; the earrings therefore could not be returned. R. M. S. decided that since public announcement of a found object is mandatory according to the Talmud, the employer was obliged in this case to search for the maid through newspaper advertisements so that the earrings might be returned to her. If the maid has not called for the earrings within a reasonable period of time, they should be deposited with the community for future surrender to the maid or her representative.

Community Officials

Rabbi Sofer insisted on the autonomous right of the community to choose its spiritual leader: "A rabbi, no matter how great a scholar, if installed by the State without or against the wishes of his community, lacks all authority." Although the laws of the State are generally binding upon its Jewish citizens, the rabbi must inform the authorities that he is not willing to assume his position without the approval of his community, thus preventing non-Jewish authorities from imposing upon the Jews. Rabbi Sofer buttressed his decision by this quotation from Rabbi Meir of Rothenberg:

"In solemn session, we determined to forbid anyone, on penalty
of excommunication, to accept a position of authority over his fellow-
citizens solely with help of a king, judge, or other non-Jewish power.
Such office would breed tyranny in all matters, secular or religious.
Only by a majority vote of the community and on the basis of personal
merit, may such a position be awarded. Anyone who acts against our
decision shall be excommunicated from all Israel, from his own students
as well as from the students of his students. His bread and wine shall
be considered forbidden to fellow-Jews, and as coming from heathens;
his books shall remain unread. Those who follow our decision shall
be blessed."

The other signatories are 150 other rabbis. Rabbi Sofer recommends that the community negotiate with the rabbi foisted upon them
by non-Jewish authorities rather than with the latter, that they read to
him Rabbi Rothenberg's decision and seek a peaceful solution by offering the applicant, if he be worthy, a seat in the local Beth Din, as a
compromise.

Characteristically, Rabbi Sofer would erase all names from copies
of his decisions, or substitute "John Doe" in all cases involving the
wrongdoing of an individual or community.

In a responsum about the rabbi's emolument, R.M.S. considered
himself perchance incapable of an impartial decision, as he himself was
the recipient of a salary. However, on the basis of law and precedent,
he held that every Jew is required to study and teach as far as possible
without compensation. But he is also obliged to take care of his family.
He must not refuse a pupil merely because teaching him might interfere
with his own studies. He could refuse to teach one if thereby his own
income might suffer. For such work he could demand compensation.
On the other hand, every community should employ a person whose
time and energies would be available for teaching and handing down
decisions to any member of the community at any time. Compensation
for such work is to be determined by the financial position of the rabbi.
In case of inflation the community must increase his salary regardless
of the sum stipulated in the original contract.

An extremely difficult and embarrassing question concerned a rabbi
who in theory and practice had violated the Torah and refused to account for his actions to any outside council of rabbis. Very pain-
stakingly R.M.S. examined the credibility of the witnesses and established beyond doubt that the rabbi in question, in spite of repeated
warnings, had committed grave errors in matters of divorce. When
the accused rabbi heard about Rabbi Moses Sofer's decision that the
community should relieve him of his post, he visited R.M.S. in the

hope of affecting a settlement. The discussion only strengthened Rabbi Sofer in his conviction. Nevertheless he made an exact summary of the discussion and transmitted it to the community.

A shohet, in a penitent mood during a dangerous illness, confessed that repeatedly and deliberately he had declared trefah meat kosher. The question arose as to how he should expiate his offenses, whether he should be held responsible for replacing all utensils involved, and whether, after recuperation, he should be permitted to perform Shehitah again. R.M.S. decided that he was unwilling to impose fasting and other self-castigation; that indemnification should not be imposed, but everything should be done to help him do Teshuvah (come back to God). However, for some time to come, he should be permitted to act as Shohet only in the presence of a second, learned and responsible, colleague.

After a rabbi had been elected, a compromising letter revealed that his relatives had influenced the election by buying votes. Rabbi Sofer declared the election void, even though the number of the votes bought had not determined the outcome. If the rabbi himself had been aware of what his relatives were doing, he could no more be a candidate for any other rabbinical position, until he repented and mended his ways. The members of the community who had accepted bribes must be excluded from the new election, even though they had returned them. Electors serve as judges, and a bribe offered to them is as reprehensible as one offered to a judge. Incidentally, Rabbi Sofer condemns the opening of any letter addressed to someone else. Such offense comes under the ban imposed by Rabbi Gershon, The Light of the Diaspora (11th cent.), and re-endorsed in the responsa of Rabbi Meir of Rothenberg.

Differences in Minhagim (Customs)

With the spread of Hassidism, the problem arose in Hungary as to whether the prevailing Ashkenazic ritual should be replaced by the Sephardic one, based on the Siddur of Rabbi Isaac Luria. Disciples of the latter did not hesitate to assert that only prayers of that ritual would be granted. R.M.S. emphatically opposed that opinion and forbade his congregation to change its minhag. He quoted his Frankfort teachers who, although personally using the Luria Siddur, did not encourage their community to do so. Each minhag has its own justification, each one reflects its special tradition. The responsum includes reminiscences of his stay in Mayence, where he visited the house in which Rabbi Ammon, the author of *"Nethaneh Tokef"*, had lived, and the grave of Rabbi Amram, an early editor of the Siddur. He quotes fascinating precedents from the writings of Rabbi Asher and Nahmanides.

As to performing marriage ceremonies under the open sky, he bases the various minhagim in this connection on the differences among Eastern and Western European Jews.

Among other interesting subjects dealt with, are unilateral contracts of rabbis; protection of authors against plagiarism; laws concerning suicide, etc. Noteworthy is a brilliant dissertation on the principles of the Jewish law of acquisition. Rabbi Sofer proves that originally natural law was recognized in Israel, the Torah superseding it only in special cases; in all others the original principle retains its validity. On this basis, a number of otherwise insolvable difficulties involving the acquisition of property find an amazingly simple solution.

Champion of the Faith

In any century or climate R.M.S. would be recognized as a great man. But the significance of his providential role in the 19th century can be comprehended only by one who has studied the life of Central European Jewry in that period. The declaration of human rights enunciated by the French Revolution brought about the emancipation of Jews and, as its corollary, their assimilation. Commonly, the beginning of Jewish assimilation in Western Europe is blamed on Moses Mendelssohn and his followers. The former, indeed, through his Bible translation, unintentionally made the Jewish assimilation movement possible. He was succeeded by Geiger, Jakobsohn and other leaders of Jewish reform who gained tremendous influence among Jews and characterized the classical rabbis as products of medieval ignorance. That schism tore families apart, communities were split, child education was channelled into new spheres, and fashioned after prevailing non-Jewish cults. Jewish family life lost the purity and holiness which had preserved it through two millennia of exile. Reform is one of the greatest spiritual tragedies of Jewish history, from whose consequences we are suffering to this day. Normally, assimilation takes one away from one's traditions. Reform anchored assimilation in Judaism itself. From the beginning of the 19th century, Reform insisted on being recognized as a legitimate school of thought in Judaism and demanded this legitimization from religious Jews.

On Yom Kippur, 1818, for the first time, in the Synagogue of Hamburg the prayers were sung with organ accompaniment, with the text of the Siddur, of course, emasculated, and the choir mixed. The

Dayanim of Hamburg called on all the great rabbis of Germany, Poland, France, Italy, Bohemia, Moravia and Hungary, among them also Rabbi Moshe Sofer, for a statement about the new Temple. As one man, they all condemned this attempt on the life of Judaism. Reform leaders were searching for an authoritative rabbinical body to come to their aid. Germany found only a future convert to Christianity, Rabbi Eliezer Liebermann, to defend their movement. This Liebermann found a fellow-traveller in Rabbi Aaron Chorin of Arad, who became the spokesman for the Reform Movement in Hungary and in a book tried to justify Reform not as a schism but as based on Talmud and Shulhan Arukh. Moses Sofer and others rose to denounce these falsifications. In numerous pamphlets and publications, R.M.S. revealed their weakness and self-contradictions. The Rabbi of Pressburg condemned the three main innovations of Reform: the organ, the substitution of the German for the Hebrew language in worship, and the omission of all prayers relating to the redemption of the Jewish people, as incompatible with our tradition. He declared: "There have always been a few who left the fold and either found their way back or disappeared. The latter are like unto dead leaves dropping from a tree without harming it. But when the apostasies occur in groups, as was the case with Sadducees and Karaites, the breach becomes irreparable. We are facing such group defection in our time. The leaders of this movement have split from us. We must record all the facts of this split so that our ranks may remain unaffected by any contamination."

On another occasion he used this illustration: "A king's child lay deathly ill of a contagious disease. A world-renowned physician, in spite of utmost efforts, saw no hope. At dawn, the amazed king met the doctor in front of the sick-room, his sword drawn. 'What is the meaning of this?' demanded the king. The doctor replied: 'As long as there was any hope, I did my utmost to bring about recovery. Now that all hope is lost, my sword at the threshold is to prevent the spread of contagion.' "

Germany had no Moses Sofer, hence apostasy made great progress and caused tremendous devastation. Only towards the middle of the century did Samson R. Hirsch and Ezriel Hildesheimer arise to defend our heritage, and inspire many followers. They spent themselves in the presentation of true Judaism, in defensive work, and in efforts to win back individual souls. The battle of words had to be waged in German, for only few remained interested in Hebrew or capable of understanding the original language of the Torah. In Austria and Hungary the untiring efforts of Rabbi Sofer met with crisis with much greater success. Like a dam, he prevented every invasion. He trained thousands of his students to preserve traditional Judaism in Hungary and adjacent countries.

Emancipation, Royal Dignitaries, and Other Problems

When the Congress of Vienna brought emancipation to the Jews of Austria and Hungary, all Jewish communities held special thanksgiving services. In his address on that occasion, R.M.S. told this story: "A young prince, for disciplinary reasons, was banished by his father to a village in a far-away land. There he was to share the frugal life of the villagers. After a number of years, the father took pity upon his son and gave instructions to have a palace built for him in the village, and to provide him with servants and comforts befitting his rank. At first, the prince was overjoyed. Yet soon he declared: 'If my father had any intention of calling me home, he would not have bettered my lot in exile. I see now clearly that my days of banishment will last for a long time.' Similarly, the rabbi explained, our hearts at first were overjoyed and thankful that our country had finally granted us equality as citizens. Yet our joy is dampened by the knowledge that our heavenly Father does not deem us worthy at this time to return to our own Palace, in our own country on which the Shekhinah rests."

In the year 1821 the Austrian authorities called on the Rabbinate of Pressburg for a decision regarding the terms of a divorce to be granted by a baptized Jew to his unbaptized wife. In his opinion, written in German, R.M.S. says: 'With regard to the question addressed to me by his Royal Highness and by his Majesty's Chancellery as to whether a form different from the one commonly used for divorce decrees between Jewish marriage partners could be introduced in the case of one who has been converted and who may find its normal provisions disturbing in the exercise of his new religion, the undersigned humbly declares: The document of divorce used in the dissolution of a Jewish marriage is prescribed verbatim in the Talmud as well as in the Jewish Code, together with all formalities attached to its presentation. The laws involved contain not a single passage from which one might deduce that a difference obtains between a divorce in which both partners are conforming Jews and a divorce in which one of them has been converted to Christianity. Therefore the undersigned holds, according to the precepts of his religion and his own conviction, that a marriage between Jews, even if one partner at a later date was converted, cannot be considered dissolved until such time as the husband has presented to the wife, either himself or through a lawfully authorized person, a document of divorce executed according to the precepts of Jewish law. Therefore, no substitute is possible.

In the winter of 1821 the community of Fuerth (Bavaria) approached the rabbi with an urgent request to accept the rabbinate there, not only to lend the glamor of his name to that Kehillah, famous for its learning and practice of Torah, but primarily to become the defender of the faith against the terrific onslaught of the reform movement.

Spokesman for the community was Rabbi Wolf Hamburg, the well-known editor of *"Simlath Binyamin."* Rabbi Sofer, who had spiritually always felt part of German Jewry, was not opposed to heeding the call. Whilst he was wondering as to whether he would be able to maintain the Yeshivah in Fuerth in a manner similar to the one in Pressburg, the latter community, its president, trustees and rank and file, implored him to remain with them.

The decisive moment came when the greatly respected Hirsch Jaffee insisted in moving words that whilst the rabbi might be able to save German Jewry, most of his accomplishments in Hungary would be lost by his departure. Rabbi Sofer accepted that argument and decided to stay in Pressburg.

His Last Will

At the age of seventy-four, R.M.S. wrote his last will for family and community. In this testament, republished many times, he implores his children to pursue their lives as in their father's home, without any deviation, and to beware of pride. Economic problems should not trouble them too much. They are not to be burdened by material needs. God, who had helped them until now, would never fail them. In moving terms, he thanks his community for their aid in expanding the Yeshivah and for having maintained its thousands of students. He begs them not to leave his pulpit vacant too long after his death, but to select as soon as possible a Gaon distinguished by his desire to teach, by financial integrity, by a deep sense of honor, and by popularity. No changes are to be made in either Beth ha-Midrash or Beth ha-Knesseth (synagogue). He blesses the whole community and each one of its members, adjuring them to follow the way of the Lord. His final word to his family: "May the tree not be felled nor the source run dry," closes the document.

His wish was granted. The spirit of their forefathers was maintained by his descendants, who for three generations graced the pulpit of Pressburg. After the defeat of Germany in 1945, the great-grandson of R.M.S., the Rav of Pressburg, moved to the Holy Land, where he re-established the Yeshivah and assumed the leadership of the remnants of his community.

REFORM THROUGH TRADITION

The second response of classical rabbinism to the modern situation is that of Israel Salanter, who took seriously the aspirations of Western Jewry and attempted to show a better way of reform than Reform. Salanter knew that the human dilemmas of the Western Jews could not be ignored, nor could those Jews be offered an impossible choice, the denial of two things which meant much to them, and which came into conflict, the tradition and the new age.

Salanter's stress, on ethical behavior, was remarkably congruent to the emphasis important to Western Jews on acceptable citizenship, but it rested upon much firmer foundations. To Salanter, ethics was not merely socially expedient, but of sacred importance. It was the center of the religious life, the primary mode of service to God. Salanter's response to the modern condition derived directly, and without mediation, from the classical emphasis of rabbinic civilization on practical action, an emphasis important, as we have seen, in the mystical tradition as well as the legal one.

Salanter sought a balance between intellectualism, on the one side, and saintliness on the other. By study of the ethical literature of Rabbinic Judaism he would show a better way. To him this did not mean that one should study only Jewish learning. He understood the importance of mastering secular sciences and skills, though these were of merely contingent importance. He himself lived in Germany and therefore confronted the new age, as other rabbinical authorities of Eastern Europe did not. Like Moses Sofer, he believed that spreading knowledge of the Talmud would cure the ailment of Israel. But he had the vision to recognize that, if the Talmud was good for Israel, it also was good for the gentiles, for its rationality and dialectic logic would improve the mind of all who devoted themselves to its discipline. It was a chimerical notion, but revealing of the man's interest in the changing world and his openness to its opportunities.

What did Salanter seek to establish? Familiar as we now are with some of the high points of earlier Rabbinic Judaism, we may readily propose the answer: to serve, and teach others to serve, God. This means to do the right deed for the right reason and requires that man overcome what is natural in the supernatural discipline of the Torah. The goal of learning is not learning, but moral intelligence.

Like the Hasidim of his day, he meditated deeply on the nature of man, on his dual character. It was through meditation and exercise of self-control that man would overcome the impulse to do evil and discipline himself to do good. Self-search and self-criticism were the way. Salanter aimed at creating a discipline—a habit—to lead to perpetual mindfulness, habitual alertness to what one did and thought. One should have supposed "mindfulness" and "habit" are opposite to one another. But by finding a *routine* of thoughtfulness, Salanter hoped to transform the habitual into the holy. Virtue must be made 'automatic'—yet intentional. Like the German Hasidim six centuries earlier, he held that through asceticism and self-sacrifice one would attain the spiritual goals to which he aspired.

19.

ISRAEL SALANTER

Louis Ginzberg

[From *Students, Scholars, and Saints,* by Louis Ginzberg, pp. 145-194.]

A life wholly consecrated to the third fundamental principle of Judaism, *Gemilut Hasadim,* ethics and morality, was that of Rabbi Israel Lipkin Salanter.

The history of the short-lived but very interesting moralist movement in Lithuania is practically the biography of this man. Rabbi Israel was born on the 3d of November, 1810, in the Russian border province of Samogitia, in Lithuania. His teacher in Talmud and Rabbinics was his father, Rabbi Wolf Lipkin, who was both rabbi and scholar. While still a youth, he married and settled in Salant, the birthplace of his wife. It is from this place that the name by which he is best known is derived. Influences are subtle things, even in one's own case, yet we can clearly discern the influence of two great men of this place who, however diverse they were in capacity and character and mode of life, left their ineradicable marks upon their young and impressionable disciple. The one was the rabbi of the place, Rabbi Hirsch Braude, who was one of the keenest dialecticians among the Talmudists of his generation at a time when dialectics reigned supreme in the domain of the Talmud. Salanter, as a Talmudist, was never able to deny the influence of this master, and he endeavored to transfer this system of dialectics to another sphere of thought, that of ethics.

Quite different was the influence that proceeded from his other master, Rabbi Zundel, whom one would be inclined to describe as a lay saint were it not for the fact that the Jews have no monks, and to them the contrast between the laiety and the clergy does not mean the same as to other peoples.

Rabbi Zundel, though a great scholar, never accepted the position of rabbi but was satisfied to eke out a living from a small shop he kept, or from any odd job that came his way. He even refused to be recognized by any external signs as belonging to the intellectual class and would therefore dress like a common man, disregarding the custom of the country, where even the poor scholar could be distinguished by his garb. This plainness of dress and simplicity of manner were often the causes of great discomfort and unpleasantness to him. Once while travelling among a rather rough lot of people, he was taken to be one of their own class, and as he was unwilling to participate in their vulgar actions and still more vulgar conversation but spent all his time in praying and in studying the Talmud by heart, they decided to punish him for giving himself airs. Surprising him while he was asleep, they attempted to mark him by singeing his beard on one side of his face, and thus disgrace him, as no good Jew would ever dare to shave his beard. Just as they were on the point of carrying out their intention, they heard him exclaiming in great ecstasy, "Only one moment more!" Observing that he was awake, they desisted, though they did not quite understand the meaning of his words by which he expressed his great joy on being able to suffer insults without resisting. His great ideal in life was to make the whole of it a continuous divine service, and the means of realizing this ideal consisted for him in the study of the Torah with its strenuous and solitary discipline of thought and action. From his master, Rabbi Hayyim of Volozhin, he not only learned boundless reverence for the Gaon, Rabbi Elijah Wilna, the master of his master, but he also attempted to live his life in accordance with the ideals set up by this austere and ascetic saint.

The simplicity, humility and saintliness of Rabbi Zundel attracted the young Salanter, who never neglected an opportunity to be near the master that he might be able to see a saintly life with his own eyes instead of studying it from books. It is told that once when Rabbi Zundel noticed the young man following him, he turned suddenly around and said to him: "If you want to lead a pious life, study *Musar*." These simple words were the decisive factor in the life of Salanter.

From now on the driving power in his very active life was the conviction that the study of the Torah and the fulfilment of its commandments, important and absolutely necessary as they are for the salvation of the Jew, do not lead to the desired goal as long as one does not work seriously and steadily at the education of self. This, however, can only be gained by a thorough study of the Musar literature, i.e., the ethico-religious books. How it is to be studied we shall see later; for the present we would remark only that in the importance attached by him to the study of Musar we can see the indirect influence of the Gaon, who declared it to be the religious duty and inviolable obligation of every person to fix a certain time of the day for reflection and meditation. This teaching of the Gaon was made living to the young Salanter by Rabbi Zundel, whose powerful impression on him was so enduring that even in later life the disciple remembered the master with the greatest admiration, and he described him as "a ladder set upon the earth, with its top reaching to heaven."

"To keep aloof from men and to live in retirement from the world" was the highest ideal after which Rabbi Zundel strove, in imitation of that great hermit, the Gaon. Without doubt they also thought of the salvation of their brethren who were in and of the world; but they tried to further it by example only and at most, in cases of pressing necessity, by rare and short apparition. It is therefore not surprising that for a time Salanter was in great perplexity, swaying between the relative merits and advantages of the active and the contemplative life. We thus find in him not merely noble actions, but life in the true meaning of the word, that is, development and struggle. The outcome of this struggle could not be doubtful. Preëminently religious, however, as the motive power of his inner life was, it was essentially of an ethical bent, and hence he could not but come to the conclusion "that true salvation can be gained only by the service rendered by the individual to the community." He became convinced that there is no virtue, strictly speaking, for man as a solitary individual in the world; that virtue begins with sociability. The idea of solidarity is at the root of all our aspirations toward the good. But not only morality, religion also in its higher form, he maintained, can be achieved in social life only, and it is a false show of self-sacrifice when religious duties are performed in partial or complete isolation, as in the cloister of the Bet ha-Midrash. Salanter, therefore, came to the conclusion that it was his duty instead of avoiding the multitude to seek them out in order to enlighten, console and improve them.

While still in the very small town of Salant, Rabbi Israel, at the age of about twenty-five years, became the leader of a small group of students and business men whom he introduced into the study of *Musar*. His fame as a great Talmudist spread very rapidly, and he was scarcely thirty years old when he was appointed head of the Meilishen Academy in Wilna. It is perhaps not without interest to note the fact that his salary amounted to four rubles a week. One is almost inclined to believe that then as now salaries were often in inverse ratio to merits. One takes it for granted that the greater the scholar, the smaller his demands upon life.

In Wilna Salanter found for the first time in his life a large field to display his energies and talents. He had arrived in that "little Jerusalem of Lithuania" at a very critical moment in the history of Lithuanian and Russian Jewry. The Haskalah movement which for about half a century was struggling in vain to gain a foothold in Lithuania, received about 1842 a strong impetus through the activity of Max Lilienthal, the "emissary of Haskalah" and the agent of the Russian government in its endeavor to dejudaize the Jews as a preliminary step toward their conversion to Christianity. It is true that the plain uneducated Lithuanian Jew showed more discernment in judging the "friendly" policy of a most tyrannical government than did the learned German doctor, and Lilienthal had soon to give up the hope of ever realizing his reforms. The agitation, however, caused among the different classes of Lithuanian Jewry by the Lilienthal episode, did not abate even when the educational plans of the government came to a sudden stop, and Lilienthal, their prime mover, finally recognizing whose dupe he was, emigrated to America. Large numbers among the educated classes who hitherto had known only of one form of intellectual activity, the study of Talmud and Rabbinics, began more and more to devote themselves to secular studies, preferably to *belles lettres* in Hebrew and other languages, which they found more attractive and enjoyable, as they satisfied not only the intellect but also the emotions. And, as it is natural for the lower classes to copy the example set by the higher, Jewish studies and consequently Jewish ideals lost their attraction in the eyes of the common people.

To the credit of Salanter it must be said that not only was he the only one among the representatives of strict Talmudism who saw the danger confronting it, but he was also the only one who attempted to protect it against the threatening peril. He cannot be said to have been very successful in his main activities; some will declare that he failed completely, yet surely nobody will deny the religious fervor and sincerity, the high and saintly moral standards of the man who single-handed attempted to fight a world in arms.

Salanter, who lived only two generations after the rise of the great Hasidic movement that threatened to divide the Jewry of eastern Europe

into two hostile camps, had learned from the upheaval caused by a
small band of religious enthusiasts two practical things. The one was
that the preponderance of intellectualism in religion estranges the great
masses, and the other, that those who are to lead them must possess
other qualities besides those of scholarship and saintliness. A favorite
saying of his was that the Hasidim as well as their opponents, the
Mitnagdim, err—the former in believing that they have leaders, the
latter in maintaining that they have no need of them. His activity was
accordingly directed toward the achievement of two objects, the attraction of the masses of the people by emphasizing the emotional element
of religion, and the training of men who would in the true sense of the
word be spiritual leaders of the people.

Shortly after his arrival in Wilna, he established a *Hebrah Musar,*
an institute that had for its object the study of ethical literature—for
example, the works of Bahya, Gabirol, and Rabbi Moses Hayyim Luzzatto. Members of the organization were recruited from all classes of
society—professional scholars, business men, artisans and laborers. At
his instance new editions of a number of ethical works were published
in 1844 and 1845 for the use of the members of the institute as well
as for others who might take up the study of these works if made accessible to them. Salanter was, however, not satisfied with the establishment of a center for those desirous to devote part of their time to
the study of ethics, but he served those seekers after truth as guide
and leader, frequently delivering lectures before them on the subjects
of their studies. In order that his work might spread all over Lithuania,
and likewise continue after his death, he selected a few chosen individuals, distinguished by learning, piety and high moral standards, to
be trained as the spiritual leaders of the people.

In spite of the wide sphere of activity he had created for himself
in the metropolis of Lithuania and although he enjoyed the greatest
respect of the entire community, his stay in Wilna was not of very long
duration. There were many reasons why he left that city. It suffices
here to state that he wanted to avoid an office which it was sought to
impose upon him. In 1848, the Russian Government opened the Rabbinical Seminary in Wilna, and pressure was brought to bear upon
him to accept the professorship of Talmud. That it was his clearsightedness and not fanaticism that forbade the acceptance of this office is
shown by the result or rather lack of result obtained by this class of institutions in Russia. His sound judgment warned him against becoming

the instrument of a government whose politics were directed to the end of extorting money from the Jews to be spent for institutions established for the sole purpose of destroying Judaism. The opposition of Salanter and many of his party to the Haskalah and its schemes was not the result of hostility to secular knowledge, the war-cry of the *Maskilim,* but was mainly rooted in the firm conviction that a government furthering the spread of secular knowledge among the Jews and at the same time curtailing their civil and political rights, can have but one aim in its mind—the destruction of Judaism. There can now be no doubt that this was a just estimate of the policy of the Russian government at that time. With equally fair certainty it may be stated that Salanter was in principle not at all opposed to secular knowledge. Later in life he counted among his very close and intimate friends the leaders of the German orthodoxy, men of the highest type of modern education. It is therefore not at all surprising to find Maskilim cite the authority of Salanter against those who opposed secular knowledge absolutely.

In the year 1848 he left Wilna and settled in Kovno, the second largest Jewish community in Lithuania. The close commercial relations which existed between this city and Germany were not without far-reaching effects upon the life of its Jewish inhabitants. At the time of the arrival of Salanter in Kovno, it was the most modern community in Lithuania, a real hotbed of the Haskalah. When he left it two decades later, it had become the stronghold of orthodoxy and remained such for half a century longer. This change may be said to have been exclusively the work of Salanter who put his stamp upon the spiritual life of this large community.

It was in Kovno that the development of the Musar movement reached its pinnacle. Here arose the first *Musar-Stuebel* (moralist conventicle). The central figure was Salanter and around him gathered a large number of capable young Talmudists as well as many merchants and artisans who were attracted by the high enthusiasm and kindling eloquence of the master. The energy and devotion of Salanter are the more to be admired as his achievements were gained in the face of violent opposition. The opponents were not only the Maskilim but also many among the representatives of the strictest Talmudism. Chief among the latter was the Rabbi of Kovno, Rabbi Loeb Shapiro, a critical mind of the first rank and a man of very independent character. He was frequently in the habit of giving a slight twist to verse 19 of Psalm 135 and applying it maliciously to the Musar-Stuebel:

> O House of Israel, Bless ye the Lord!
> O House of Aaron, Bless ye the Lord!
> O House of Levi, Bless ye the Lord!
> O ye that fear the Lord, Bless ye the Lord!

There is a house for Israel, he said, a house for Aaron, a house for Levi, but there is no mention of a separate house for those who fear the Lord, hence there is no need of establishing conventicles for them. This *bon mot* shows at the same time the course of the opposition which the Musar movement provoked. It is the deep seated opposition of the talmudic Jew to every separatist movement. Against the study of the Musar literature neither Shapiro nor his friends had anything to say; what they condemned was the forming of a society which tended to set its members apart from the rest of the community as "the moralists." The opposition to the Musar movement and its leader was carried on with great bitterness and was not entirely free from personal animosity against Salanter and his disciples. As to the latter it must be stated that their admiration for the master whom they tried to imitate and emulate was sincere and profound, but genius is not to be copied. A good deal of the criticism levelled against the Musar movement had its origin in the extravagancies of those whom the Talmud describes as "disciples who did not wait upon their masters sufficiently," they are those who attempted rather to ape the great than to mirror them.

After living in Kovno for about twelve years, Salanter was forced by a severe illness—a nervous disorder—to change his abode and settle in Germany, where he hoped to regain his health through the famous skill of its physicians. He spent the rest of his life in Memel and Koenigsberg. In these communities new problems awaited him, and, notwithstanding the weakened state of his health, he continued his various activities. These two cities, on account of their proximity to Lithuania, contained large numbers of Jews of that country, some of whom had settled there permanently and others, especially those engaged in importing Russian merchandise into Germany, were forced by their business to spend there many a month of each year. Salanter saw the danger lurking in these large masses of Jews living unorganized in a foreign country, with the Jews of which they neither could nor would form a union. He set himself therefore the task of organizing communities of Lithuanian Jews in these two cities and thanks to his untiring energy and devotion to his people, he succeeded within a short time. He was, however, not interested in organization for its own sake.

What he desired was to transplant the cultural and religious life of the Lithuanian Jews to these communities, and his endeavors were not entirely in vain. The Jewish community in Memel continued up to the great war to be the only one of its kind. Its life resembled that of Kovno and Wilna much more closely than that of Berlin or Frankfort.

A plan that engaged the fertile mind of Salanter for many years was the popularization of the Talmud, that is, first to make the Talmud accessible to the great masses of the Jews and further to introduce its study into the non-Jewish colleges and universities. Being firmly convinced that the knowledge of the Talmud is absolutely necessary for the culture and religious welfare of the Jew, he could not but look with alarm upon the gradual disappearance of talmudic learning from among the great masses of Jewry, even those of Lithuania, the classic land of talmudic study. To stem the tide of ignorance *in re talmudica,* he advised the following means: The publication of a dictionary of the Talmud in Yiddish to help the average business man or artisan among the Lithuanian or Polish Jews in his studies of the Talmud, and the replacement of Rashi's commentary on the Talmud by a more modern one that could be put into the hands of beginners. As usual, Salanter was not satisfied with formulating plans, but immediately set about to carry them out. His plan of a Yiddish dictionary of the Talmud, it is true, did not proceed far, for there were not enough Talmudists who could and would engage in such a work, but the plan of a modern commentary advanced so far that he received a promise of collaboration from a goodly number of prominent Talmudists.

The spread of the knowledge of the Talmud among the educated classes of the Gentiles, Salanter believed would benefit them as well as the Jews. He was of the opinion that the dialectics of the Talmud are the best means for developing the mind of the youth at colleges and universities, who might greatly profit by supplementing their studies in classics and mathematics by courses in Talmud. A better acquaintance with the Talmud by the educated Gentile world would at the same time remove many prejudices against the Jew and his post-biblical literature, which are mostly to be ascribed to the false notion the world has of the Talmud.

Salanter's plan was to petition the authorities of institutions for higher learning in Germany to introduce the Talmud into their regular courses of study. As he did not master the German language, he looked for a man whom he could entrust with the preparation of such a petition that would necessarily have to contain a clear and precise description of the Talmud and its educational potentialities. It seems that Salanter met with some opposition among the Rabbis, who looked with disfavor upon any attempt at secularizing the Talmud.

During his long stay in Germany, he became acquainted not only with the spiritual leaders of the Orthodox but also with the many lay members of this party whom he tried to interest in his educational schemes for the Lithuanian Jews. He finally, in 1878, succeeded in finding a wealthy man in Berlin who set aside a considerable sum of money for the purpose of establishing in Kovno a great Yeshibah for the training of Rabbis, known as the Central Body of the *Perushim*. Perushim were young married men who had left home and family— *Perushim* means those who separated themselves—to devote themselves to study. This idea was quite an original creation of Salanter as all the other Yeshibot up to that time were mainly frequented by young unmarried men.

As the bachelor Rabbi is entirely unknown in Eastern Europe, and maturity is almost a prerequisite of the spiritual leader, it often happened that men who spent their entire youth and a part of their manhood in preparation for the ministry were forced to look for other vocations to enable them to support their wives and children. It could not but result in the increase of an intellectual proletariat—the training of a rabbi does not tend to produce a successful business man—and the gradual elimination of the poorer classes from the Rabbinate, as only the sons or sons-in-law of the wealthy could afford the long preparation. To remedy these evils Salanter established the new educational institute which enabled the poor Talmudist to continue his studies after graduating from the Yeshibah by providing him and his family with the necessary means.

The sum donated by the Berlin Maecenas for the maintenance of the Institute, though very considerable, was not sufficient to assure its permanency, and Salanter, though burdened by old age and many ailments, took upon himself the heavy task of gaining the support of larger classes for his scheme. He addressed a stirring appeal to the Jewish communities of Russia, which was not in vain. The *Kolel* (Central Institute) thus firmly established by him, not only continued to exist for a long time after his death up to the recent war, but even gained in importance very considerably. For a number of years it was the most important center of the higher Jewish learning in Lithuania. The Kolel bore through all the years of its existence the stamp of Salanter by being the only institution of its kind where the study of Musar formed a part of the curriculum.

At the same time while working feverishly at this scheme, Salanter found time and strength to go to Paris to organize there a Russian-Polish community. The conditions in the French metropolis were not dissimilar to those in Koenigsberg and Memel. The lack of organization among the Jews of Eastern Europe who had settled in Paris was greater and in some ways more deplorable than that which Salanter found among his countrymen living in the two cities of Eastern Prussia. The religious life of the French Jews had already at that time reached such a low state that not much good would have been achieved by amalgamating the newcomers with the native Jews even if it had been possible.

After spending almost two years in Paris he succeeded in bringing some order into the chaotic condition of the Eastern Jews. He returned in 1882 to Germany and there took up his residence in Koenigsberg to continue the work that he had interrupted for several years. This however was not granted to him. He died there on the second of February 1883 at the age of seventy-three and a half.

In order properly to estimate the essence of the moralist movement inaugurated by Salanter, it is necessary not only to understand his character and personality but also to become acquainted with the cultural and religious life of the Lithuanian Jews, among whom this movement first arose and developed. The Jewish people, as one of the oldest of the cultural races of the world, place a very high estimate upon intellectualism— indeed sometimes too high an estimate. The older and the more deeply rooted the culture of a nation, the more strongly it is impressed with the truth that "knowledge is power," not only material but also spiritual power. This intellectualism so highly praised by the Jewish people naturally varies with age and country. For Maimonides and his followers in Spain and Provence Judaism consisted essentially of philosophical intellectualism culminating in love of God and love of man. However radically different the Polish-Lithuanian Jew of the eighteenth and nineteenth centuries may be in his entire *Weltanschauung* from the Spanish Jew of the thirteenth century schooled in a scholastic Aristotelianism, both have this belief in common—that it is knowledge that makes a man a man, and a Jew a Jew. The only difference is that the Polish-Lithuanian Jew puts talmudic dialectic, in which he is unsurpassed, in place of Aristotelian philosophy. The rise of the Kabbalah in Provence in the thirteenth century was a reaction against Jewish Aristotelianism of the Middle Ages and similarly the rise of Hasidism in the middle of the eighteenth century was an attempt to aid the emotions in regaining their legitimate place in the spiritual life of the Jew. In Lithuania, the classical land of talmudic learning, the emotional doctrine of Hasidism never secured a firm foothold. The form that Hasidism took in certain parts of Lithuania, the so-called *Habad,* is more intellectual than emotional. To attribute the failure of the Hasidic movement in that country to the violent opposition of the Gaon Rabbi Elijah, the greatest intellectual-religious genius among the Lithuanian Jews, is to take a part for the whole. His opposition did but express the attitude, the natural bent, and the acquired traits of the Lithuanian Jew who seeks first of all to satisfy his intellect. Reaction against the too great preponderance of intellectualism could, however, not fail to make its appearance even in Lithuania. About one hundred years after the rise of Hasidism in the Carpathian Mountains among uncultured and ignorant villagers, we find a parallel phenomenon among the sharp-witted Talmudists of Lithuania. Rabbi Israel Baal Shem Tob, the founder of Hasidism, was a person of "emotion and feeling" and rejected intellectualism instinctively without having intimate knowledge thereof. On the other hand, R. Israel Salanter, the father of the moralist movement, was himself one of the greatest Talmudists of his time and, therefore, although his great heart was not able to be satisfied with a one-sidedness of logic and reason, he nevertheless could not fall into the other extreme of regarding religion as a matter of feeling exclusively.

The keystone of Salanter's teaching is best given in his own words: man is created to labor and to carry on the war of the Lord—the development of the divine in man—and accordingly it is his duty to take great pains in the service of God. It is not sufficient to follow one's good impulses and to do only that which according to one's nature is not very difficult. Such a one does not serve God, he might even be described as one who "casts off the yoke of God," since he permits nature to take its course and does not work in the service of the Lord. The essence of this service consists in man's moral-religious effort to do things which his natural inclinations oppose, and to refrain from others to which he is prompted by them. The development of the moral-religious personality is therefore only possible by the education of self or, to use the favorite phrase of Salanter and other Jewish moralists, by Musar, i.e., self-discipline. One might as well, says Salanter, attempt to see without eyes or hear without ears as to expect moral development without self-education; moral intelligence is the result of education and is not acquired at will.

Man does no wrong wilfully, says Socrates, and similar is the saying of the Rabbis: man does not commit sin unless the spirit of folly has entered into him. The aim of education in general as of self-education in particular is therefore, according to Salanter, to give the reason full power over one's actions, for he who does not act as he thinks, thinks incompletely. To think rightly and completely means of course for Salanter and those to whom he addressed himself to square one's actions with one's belief in God and His revealed will, the Torah. How then, he asked himself, does it happen that people of great intellectual power who are past masters in human wisdom and in the knowledge of Torah do not understand and are, from a moral-religious point of view, idiots or weak-minded? What should the self-education of a man be that would give him the necessary intelligence which makes "the truly wise man," who "sees the consequence of his action?" Salanter's answer to these perplexing questions is that only thought transmuted into emotion has effect on our life or, in his own words: our impulses are swiftly running currents which drown our intelligence if the latter is not carried over them in the boat of emotion and enthusiasm. The purely intellectual idea has no motive power, which can be acquired only by the addition of an emotional and passionate element. Though rational life is moral, life as a whole is non-moral because the emotions are not working. It is therefore not enough for us to form correct opinions; we must pass from mere comprehension to profound conviction; and this requires feeling; we must be carried away. We remain cold even in intense intellectual work. "A passion yields only to a passion," and hence in order that our correct ideas may culminate in correct action, in other words that we may not be carried away by impulses but act in accordance with reason, the mental representation of our action must kindle a desire.

We shall now be able to understand the great importance which the dogma of Reward and Punishment plays in the teaching of Salanter. The precise and detailed definition of this dogma, he remarks, is of no great consequence, what matters is that we firmly believe that there exists after this world a condition of happiness or unhappiness for every individual. The bliss of the righteous surpasses any pleasure conceivable to human imagination. On the other hand, the suffering of the wicked is such that compared with it the greatest earthly pain might be described as pleasure. Faith in the existence of God, Salanter maintains, is of small value in true religion as long as it is not supplemented by the belief in a just God who rewards good deeds and punishes evil ones. It is faith in this sense to which the Rabbis refer in their often-quoted saying: The 613 commandments of the Torah were reduced by the prophet Habakkuk to one, viz.: "The righteous liveth by his faith."

We would do great injustice to Salanter if we maintained that self-interest was for him the only motive power of religion and morality. If there be any need to disprove such a faulty conception, it suffices to quote his words in the last essay published by him; he writes, "The road that leads to eternal bliss is to follow the path of the Torah and fulfil all its commandments for the sake of the Lord. The true service of God is that which is free from the motive of receiving rewards; a person who behaves in this way may be truly described as 'serving God,' while he who does what is pleasing to God with the view of receiving reward, may really be described as 'serving himself.' " As a practical moralist, however, Salanter could not dispense with the dogma of Reward and Punishment. He was firmly convinced that there is but one way to correct a vice, namely to recognize the dangers it entails, and there is but one way of acquiring a virtue, and that is, to see clearly the advantages it brings. Hence he taught that the first step in self-education is the acquisition of the fear of the Lord or, as the Rabbis say, "the fear of sin." By frequent pondering and long meditation upon the consequences of our actions for which we shall be held accountable by a just God, the idea of Reward and Punishment becomes vividly impressed upon our mind. Only when the idea is transmuted into feeling does it become a motive power for our actions. These meditations must therefore be of a nature to stir our hearts and act on our emotions. Salanter accordingly attributed great importance to the mode of studying Musar which, to be effective, must be different from merely intellectual studies. In the Musar Stuebel, by oneself or together with others, preferably at twilight when the falling darkness creates a melancholy atmosphere, one can surrender oneself entirely to one's emotions, one can weep and recite in a loud voice those soul-stirring words of the Prophets, Psalmists and later moralists on the vanity of human life, or give oneself over to reflect in silence upon death, which will bring one before the Heavenly Judge to give an account of one's life.

The sharpening of one's sense of responsibility by the means described is, however, only the first step leading to Musar, self-discipline. When a person is thoroughly permeated with the thought of responsibility in the hereafter for his actions in this world, he has acquired the means necessary for the *Kebishat Yezer ha-Ra,* the suppression of the evil inclination. There are, says Salanter, three stages of the worship of the Holy One, blessed be He. The first is to arouse one's sense of imperfection, the fear that one may not be perfect in the sight of his heavenly Father. By frequent meditation and soulful study of the sayings of our wise men and the dicta of our moralists, this sense is created and then one is in a position to conquer his *Yezer,* which finally leads to "the changing of the Yezer." The Yezer ha-Ra and its opposite, the

Yezer Tob, are defined by him as follows: The evil Yezer is of a two-fold nature—it is (1) the sensual desire in man that often makes him mistake momentary pleasure for the true happiness which he craves, so that he does not act in accordance with the moral-religious principles which he has established in his mind, but succumbs to the pressure of his impulses of passion. The frequent yielding to his sensual desires finally produces in man (2) an impure spirit or, to use modern parlance, the decay of his spiritual energy, with the result that he becomes a slave to his evil habits, committing at the slightest incentive the most depraved actions. Similarly the good Yezer is of a two-fold nature—it is (1) moral-religious clearsightedness unimpaired by passion and evil habits which commands man to struggle against the temptation of passion and sensual desires and to be guided in his actions not by the immediate pleasures which they produce but by their remote consequences. By continually increasing his fund of moral views and strengthening his power of true reason the (2) spirit of purity or, as we might say, automatism of morality is given to him, so that without struggle and combat he always wills the good and the right.

The suppression of the Yezer consists first in the incessant discipline of one's will-power, in order to strengthen and steel it so that it gains perfect control over his passions and no evil temptations have sway over him. Meditation and continuous practice in self-control are the only means of achieving victory. More difficult, and to some extent more important, is introspection and self-analysis. The suppression of the Yezer is not possible without improving "the qualities of our souls" and, as no two men are alike either in temperament or in character, every one must study himself very carefully. Every one, Salanter says, is a world in himself, the knowledge of which is the very first prerequisite for his dealings with the "outer world."

The recognition of one's errors and deficiencies is thus the beginning of salvation, as without it no moral improvement is possible. One must learn to recognize with absolute sincerity the secret springs of his acts. Sincerity is especially important in self-criticism because our judgment of good and evil is not an act of pure reason but is greatly influenced by emotion and sentiment. Accordingly without deep sincerity we should find little to criticise in ourselves; our self-love would blind our judgment. We often, remarked Salanter, meet with people who are extremely conceited and vain, though we fail to detect the slightest reason for their good opinion of themselves. The true reason is that self-love often excites in man so strong a feeling of self-importance that he is unaware of his shortcomings and deficiencies, while those of his neighbor are seen clearly by him. Salanter even goes a step further and maintains that absolute truth can be attained only in the field of material facts directly provable or in the domain of science demonstrable by the methods of logic, while in our moral judgment there is always an element of feeling: In self-criticism our main effort must be directed toward eliminating or at least reducing to a minimum this element of self-love and turning our scrutiny upon ourselves in the same way that we would exercise our criticism upon others.

Our critical abilities should be directed toward our own actions not toward the actions of our fellow-men. We all have an amazingly critical keenness when it is a case of picking to pieces, not our own conduct, but that of our neighbor. We should search again and again the depths of ourselves in the midst of our restless life; we must criticise and correct our actions without pity. We must not allow ourselves to rest on the laurels that we award to ourselves or that others too easily bestow upon us, but should utilize the time rather in self-criticism.

As we devote ourselves to the cultivation of our intellectual powers, so we must pay heed to the development of our moral potentialities. Salanter established the rule among his disciples that each should associate himself intimately with one of his fellows for the purpose of observing and being observed and exchanging friendly cautions and admonitions. In this way all would attain to the self-knowledge that corrects conduct.

The discovery of our faults will not discourage us if we look to the future instead of to the past. Repentance was indeed a doctrine upon which he laid great stress, yet for him as for nearly all Jewish theologians and moralists, repentance is not remorse for the past but a serious attempt to profit in the future by the lessons of the past. When he spoke to the people he was in the habit of making them recite with religious fervor the verse from Lamentations, "Turn Thou us unto Thee, O Lord, and we shall be turned." "Return to God" is the Jewish conception of repentance, and while Salanter was hammering into the minds of the people the great need of self-criticism, that they might be able to change their lives and return to God, he was no less indefatigable in preaching courage. No ailment of the soul, he says, is worse than discouragement; man must again and again renew the idea of courage in his mind. He must not become discouraged if he fails to observe any improvement in his moral qualities after long labor of self-discipline. He should know that his work was not in vain but has left its beneficial effects which, though invisible at the moment, will become visible in time. Drops of water continually falling upon a rock will finally wear it away though the first drops seem to produce no effect at all. It is the same with self-discipline; its effects cannot fail to penetrate our hearts if we practise it continually.

Another form of discouragement against which Salanter warns us is that which has its source in the exaggerated importance attached to the influence of heredity; he writes: "One should not say what the Lord made cannot be changed; He planted in me an evil nature, how can I hope ever to unmake it?" It is not so; man is not only master over the qualities of the soul with which he is born but he is also able to change them.

We all know how great the power of man over animals has been; he has succeeded in imposing his will upon them so that not only originally wild and ferocious animals have lost their ferocity but many species have also been tamed and their natures changed. The same applies to man; he not only can suppress his passions and impulses but he can also change his nature from evil to good by constant study and practice. One must remember further that in the worst of men there is something good and the best are not without a touch of depravity. Hence self-education is the main factor in our development.

Salanter in almost every address was in the habit of quoting the verse from Proverbs: "If thou seekest (wisdom) as silver and searchest for her as for hidden treasures. . . ." The burden of all his exhortations was that the moral life of man is like the flight of a bird in the air; he is sustained only by effort and when he ceases to exert himself he falls.

Moral effort or, to use his own term, the suppression of the evil Yezer, important as it may be, is, however, only the prelude to *Tikkun ha-Middot,* the improvement of character, by which he meant the reduction of virtue to a second nature. Moral effort is the negative part of self-education, which must finally lead to the positive, viz. the entire change of our impulses and inclinations, our passions and desires. We draw nearer to the ideal by always thinking of it, by examining everything in its light. The continuous effort, however, is fatiguing, and therefore when swept by great passions, we are unable to withstand them though we thought we had gained control over our will. Accordingly our only safeguard lies in moral knowledge which must be sufficiently clear to lay hold on us and carry us away; this knowledge must become a passion with us so that we act automatically under its imperious injunction. Impressions upon our emotions such as may be produced by the realization of retribution after death, though they may tend to weaken certain passions and impulses, are not able to change them. Their change can be accomplished only by means by knowledge. We must make ourselves the object of contemplation and, dissecting the stirrings of our hearts, seek to comprehend their complicated machinery. Then and then only will virtue become instinctive in us, so that even our unconscious actions will be directed by it. We must not forget that it is our less conscious thoughts and our less conscious actions which mainly mould our lives.

There are two forms, says Salanter, of intellectual knowledge. The child, for instance, who has just learned his alphabet has great difficulty in combining the letters though he knows well their individual sounds. After exercising for some time he is able to read fluently without being in the least conscious of the single letters and their functions. The same holds good in moral knowledge. For a time we must practise increasing the power of our will over our passions until we become so accustomed to virtue that we perform it unconsciously without being aware of any effort. This will happen when our moral ideals become sentiments by reason of being impressed upon our understanding. The truth of this view Salanter attempted to prove in quite a homely way. He writes: "In our country—Lithuania—the average Jew has trained himself in the observance of the dietary laws to such an extent that without any effort he not only abstains from the use of prohibited food but even abhors it. On the other hand, dishonesty in commercial relations is a frequent occurrence. Many do not trouble themselves to find out whether their dealings with their fellow men are always honest, and not a few will even attempt to cover their dishonest actions when they are found out. Now when we ask, how does it happen that the ceremonial law is automatically observed at great sacrifice of comfort and money, while the ethical is often disregarded— a sin which according to the Rabbis neither the Day of Atonement nor death can atone—we can give only this answer: The long training of the Jew, theoretically and practically, in the observance of the dietary laws has had the result that in following his own nature he feels an abhorrence for everything ritually unclean, while the ethical teachings of the Torah theoretically never formed such an important part of the body of Jewish studies as the dietary laws, and practically did not offer themselves as an exercise in virtue but as something convenient and useful. This, however, is greatly to be regretted; the ethical teachings of the Torah are a most important part thereof, and in practical life we must train ourselves so that we may no longer obey the dicta of morality reluctantly as a severe rule, but that we may follow them with the natural bent of our desires."

Great care, however, must be taken that the automatism of virtue is not turned to that obnoxious form of stoicism which makes man indifferent to the desires and needs of his fellow man. Equanimity and calmness of temper and mind, says Salanter, is a great virtue; we must never allow ourselves to be ruffled even when the greatest misfortunes befall us. "Trust in God," the religious term for this virtue, is, however, an abominable sin if applied to shift from us our obligations towards our fellow men; one must not trust in God at the expense of those who seek our help. Humility is not only a virtue but a demand of common sense, as it is absurd to be proud of a superiority that we owe to the chance of birth or the munificence of Providence; and as to vanity, Salanter could only see in it the most grotesque trait of character. Yet he admonishes us to be very careful of the susceptibilities of others and never fail to pay them our respects in the forms established by society. Withdrawing ourselves from social life is very commendable if it affects only ourselves, but it is the foremost duty of man "to go among the people" and associate closely with them for the benefit and the good of our fellow men. Consequently the positive part of self-education consists not only in acquiring virtue as an instinct, but also in studying to comprehend and understand the desires and impulses of men, so that we may be able to feel their sufferings and wants. The task of combining these two opposites is hard but not impossible.

In spite of Salanter's originality, he has not given us a new system of ethics. He lacked philosophic training and systematic ability. His importance consists mainly in this: that he emphasized and sought to put into their proper light certain aspects of Judaism which previously had been heeded but little or not at all.

The keynote of his teaching is that the aim and task of the Jew is to strive to secure the ethically ideal condition of man and of the world, no matter how far off and perhaps unreachable it may be. Judaism is for him no theoretical system, teaching speculative truths or scientific knowledge concerning a certain province of thought, but it is a doctrine intended to lead man to his moral ennoblement by prescribed ways and means. So far as the moral life is concerned the concrete plays a preponderating and decisive part. On the other hand it cannot dispense with speculative or, let us rather say, religious truths. In fact, it requires some religious truths as a support and a guarantee for the binding force of the moral law. Other religious truths, again, strengthen the will, or are of spiritual value in moral development, because they fuse together practice and theory into a harmonious unity. If morality is to be not merely a theory but a real factor in the life of man, he must so train his thoughts and feelings that his moral consciousness becomes too strong to allow him to act otherwise than morally. The religious truths which are indispensable to the ethical education of man and without which he cannot develop morally, are: Belief in God, Revelation, and Reward and Punishment.

We have seen above what important rôle the doctrine of Reward and Punishment plays in his teachings, and we may add here that Revelation or, to use the rabbinical term, the Torah is of still greater consequence. In his public addresses, Salanter hardly ever touched on any other subject than ethics and the study of the Torah. The latter is to be considered from two different angles. First, as the revealed will of God, it is the only safe guide for our religious and moral life. Hence the duty incumbent upon every one, not only on the professional scholar, to occupy himself with the study of the Torah that his conduct may always be in accordance with the divine Will. The study of the Jewish civil code however, to take one instance, is a religious work not only because it enables the student to know what is right and what is wrong in a given case, but also because it refines and deepens one's conscience. Consequently, strange as it may sound, it is from the point of view of religion more important for the business man than for the Rabbi— the judge—to be thoroughly acquainted with the civil code. The former is often tempted to dishonesty, and by continuous study of the commercial law of the Torah he will be in a better position to withstand his temptations, of which the Rabbi is innocent. Besides the practical parts of the Torah, the study of any portion thereof is a remedy against the Yezer. "The spirit emanating from the Torah makes spiritual him who occupies himself with it."

It would be underrating the importance of Salanter to measure him only by the standard of his theories on ethics. Of him, as in general of all Jewish moralists, it may be said that the practical produced the theoretical, and not vice-versa. The ethical system of the Greeks developed at a time when rapidly growing skepticism threatened to destroy the basis of morality and in part did actually destroy it. The ethical systems framed in those days were the dikes erected by speculative minds to hold in check the devastating flood of immorality. Compare this phenomenon with the long and eventful history of the Jews, and it will become evident that with them there was nothing certain and absolute except God, the source of moral truth. When all things round about tottered and reeled, there always remained one fixed immovable point, that God is good, holy and just, and that it is the duty of man to walk in His ways, the ways of holiness, justice and love. The Jewish moralists, therefore, considered it their chief task not to elaborate new doctrines and speculative truths, but to impress the old lessons with ever greater emphasis upon the consciousness of the people. Their aim was to find means of augmenting the effectiveness of the old truths. And as they always proceeded from the principle that the most successful pedagogic method is teaching by example, they tried to illustrate in their own conduct the truths they wished to inculcate. The Jewish moralists, so far from setting up ideal teachings for the sake of setting them up, demonstrated concretely how the ideal can be made real in the daily walks of life.

It has been well said that a man of rare moral depth, warmth or delicacy may be a more important element in the advance of civilization than the newest and truest idea derived from the fundamental principles of the science of morals. The leading of souls to do what is right and humane is always more urgent than mere instruction of the intelligence as to the exact meaning of right and humanity. If therefore the saint has his place in history, Salanter is one of the outstanding figures in Jewish history of recent times. What most appeals to our imagination and sympathy in history is heroism, and saintliness is only another word for heroism in the domain of ethics and religion. The heroism of the saint is well described by the famous French critic, Sainte Beauve, as an inner state which above all is one of love and humility, of infinite confidence in God, and of strictness toward one's self accompanied with tenderness for others. Saintliness is, however, at the same time preeminently subjective, mainly on account of the great diversity of the means which help to produce the state common to all saints. The glimpses we gain of the life of a saint are therefore of incalculable value to us for the understanding of the religious milieu that produced him. Salanter, for instance, was the product of rigorous Talmudism, and hence to become better acquainted with his heroic life is tantamount to coming nearer to a true understanding of talmudic Judaism. Purity, asceticism and charity are the characteristic practical consequences of the inner conditions of all saintly souls; the forms, however, in which these virtues express themselves vary essentially, and the variation is a safe indication of the culture amidst which the saint arose.

Boundless reverence for the weak and the suffering, the helpless and the needy, best describe the particular form that Salanter's love for his fellow man took. The Lord "dwells with him that is of a contrite and humble spirit," hence Salanter felt himself in the presence of the divine whenever he saw suffering and pain that produce a meek and contrite spirit. His religious enthusiasm, that is his love of God, instead of quenching his love of man, ennobled and transformed it. Too numerous are the stories told about Salanter's kindness and goodness to be given here; a very few characteristics of the saint, may however, be mentioned.

During his sojourn in Kovno it happened on the eve of Yom Kippur, when the Synagogue was filled with devout worshippers awaiting in solemn awe and silence the Kol Nidre service, that suddenly ominous murmurs and whispers arose on all sides. Salanter, wonderful to relate, had not yet arrived. The assembly waited half-an-hour and an hour, and still no trace of the Rabbi. Messengers were sent hither and thither to search for him. All returned from their errand unsuccessful. After long waiting and watching, it was resolved to begin the prayers without Salanter, a course calculated to increase the excitement. All sorts of probable and improbable rumors were circulated about the sudden disappearance of the beloved leader. When the congregation was on the point of dispersing, Salanter appeared in the Synagogue. The joy was great, and equally great was the amazement of the good people when they learned the reason of his absence. On his way to the Synagogue, Salanter told them, he heard a little child cry bitterly. He drew near to investigate why it was whimpering and found that the baby's mother, in order to be at the Synagogue in good time on this holiest of occasions, had put it to bed earlier than was her wont. The child had soon awakened from sleep at an unaccustomed hour and was crying for its mother. As none of the women in the neighborhood signified her willingness to forego attendance at divine services upon the Holy Kol Nidre night, he resolved to stay beside the baby's cradle until its mother returned. To appreciate this act of Salanter, it must be remembered what the service at the Synagogue on the eve of the Day of Atonement meant to a man like him who was in the habit of withdrawing from the world for forty days preceeding Yom Kippur, and spending his time in prayer and devotion.

His great compassion and pity for the poor and helpless often was the cause of clashes between him and the official heads of the communities where he lived as a private man. He had settled in Kovno shortly after the cholera had wrought great havoc among the Jewish population of that city, especially among the poor classes. The hospitals were overfilled with sufferers, so that quite a number were not properly cared for. Salanter insisted that the great Synagogue of the community be temporarily used as a hospital and poor-house. Needless to say that his plan found ill favor in the eyes of many who looked upon it as an attempt at desecrating the house of God. Possibly they were right, as there was hardly any need of such an extreme step to be taken. Salanter, however, in face of suffering and distress could not see their point of view. Courteous and gentle as he otherwise was, he lost his temper on this occasion. Interrupting the address he was delivering in the Synagogue, he pointed his finger in righteous anger at the president of the Congregation, a man distinguished for learning and piety alike, and cried out: "You will have to answer to the Lord for the suffering of the poor. God much rather prefers His House to be used as a sleeping place by "Motel the carpenter"—a very disreputable person but a homeless beggar—than as a place of worship by you." Not long after this incident, Salanter betook himself to the home of the man he had offended, to ask his forgiveness, but he never changed his mind with regard to the justification of his plan to turn the Synagogue into a poor-house.

A year before this he had gotten himself into the bad graces of the spiritual leaders of Wilna. In the year of the frightful cholera epidemic Salanter, after having taken counsel with a number of physicians, became convinced that in the interest of the health of the community it would be necessary to dispense with fasting on the Day of Atonement.

Many a Rabbi in this large community was inclined to agree with his view, but none of them could gather courage enough to announce the dispensation publicly. During the several years of his stay in Wilna he lived strictly the life of a private man, and in his humility would not decide a question of ritual, not even if it occurred in his own house, but would refer it to one of the local Rabbis. When he saw, however, that none of them would act in this case, he thought self-assertion to be his highest duty. He affixed announcements in all Synagogues, advising the people not to fast on the coming Day of Atonement. Knowing, however, how reluctant they would be to follow his written advice he, on the morning of the Day of Atonement at one of the most solemn moments of the service, ascended the reader's desk. After addressing a few sentences to the Congregation in which he commanded them to follow his example, he produced some cake and wine, pronounced the blessing over them, ate and drank. One can hardly imagine what moral courage and religious enthusiasm this action of his required from a man like Salanter to whom obedience to the Torah was the highest duty. He found strength for his heroic action only in the thought that what he did was for the benefit of others. Many years later he used to dwell on this episode and thank with great joy his Creator for having found him worthy to be the instrument of saving many lives. He was convinced that many a person weakened by fasting would have fallen a victim to the frightful disease, and that therefore in making people eat on the great Fast he saved many lives. Others, however, did not share his conviction of the necessity of dispensing with the fast and he was severely censured by them, not only for what he did, but also for having assumed the authority belonging to the official leaders of the community. It is not unlikely that the unpleasantness created by this incident was one of the reasons for Salanter's leaving Wilna for good.

Poor as he was all his life, he had little of worldly goods or, to be accurate, nothing to give others, but he did give them more than this—he gave himself, heart and soul, to those whom he knew to be suffering. The poor and the needy could always count upon his readiness to assist them. No time of the day, no season of the year, no cold winter night, and no scorching summer day could prevent him from walking for hours from house to house to solicit help for those in need. Once a poor scholar confided to him that if he were able to preach he might succeed in maintaining himself and his family by taking up the profession of an itinerant preacher, but as the theory as well as the practice of preaching were quite unknown to him, he must forever give up the hope of gaining a livelihood in this way. Salanter, however, did not despair; he composed a number of sermons, and after spending several weeks in teaching the poor scholar how to deliver them, he dismissed him well prepared for his new calling.

As in the environment of a saint there are often found many who are the very reverse of saints, Salanter's kindness and sympathy were not rarely misused. Sometimes undeserving people would succeed in obtaining from him letters of recommendation, but he would never revoke them, even if informed by reliable persons of the deception practised on him. He used to say that a letter of this sort becomes the rightful property of the person to whom it is given and it would be plain robbery to revoke it.

The fear of being the cause, even in the remotest manner, of injury to the poor, was always present before his eyes. Once when, in obedience to the rabbinical ordinance, he was washing his hands before sitting down to a meal, his disciples noticed that he was exercising great care not to use a drop of water more than the minimum required by the law. In amazement they exclaimed: "Rabbi, does not the Talmud say that he who lets water flow abundantly over his hands will be rewarded with wealth in equal abundance?" "True, but I do not want to enrich myself at the expense of the labor of the water carrier," replied Salanter. He did not for a moment question the binding character of the rabbinical ordinance concerning the washing of hands before meals, but that did not prevent him from remembering and acting in accordance with his great moral principle.

At another time while walking in the outskirts of the city, he noticed the cow of a Jewish farmer straying away and trying to enter a neighboring garden belonging to a Gentile. Knowing the ill-feeling of the Gentile farmers towards their Jewish neighbors in that part of the country, he had no doubt that if the animal should be caught it would be killed or at best kept for a high ransom. He therefore attempted to lead the cow back to the Jewish farmer, but inexperienced as he was in work of this kind, he miserably failed in driving the animal back. Yet he did not give up the fight, and for several hours he held on to the cow, and in this way prevented her from entering the dangerous zone until he was released from his task by people coming along the road. To have permitted the cow to run its own way, he thought, would have been negligence in his duty towards the poor farmer.

No less cautious was he in avoiding offense to the sensibilities of the poor. He was passionately fond of snuff, but he denied himself the pleasure of taking it at sessions of the Charity Board, when the poor appeared to present their cases. He shrank from taking out his silver snuff box in their presence, lest its splendor cause them to feel their poverty more keenly.

The ascetic impulse is a general phenomenon in saintliness, and the Jewish saint does not form an exception to the general rule. Yet there can be no doubt as to the correctness of the view that Judaism is not an ascetic religion. That the highest development of a non-ascetic religion should culminate in ascetic saintliness will appear to many as an inexplicable riddle. If, however, we examine more carefully the form of Jewish asceticism, we shall find the answer to this puzzling question. A religion that sanctifies even the so-called animal appetites and desires of man, elevating them into worship and religious exaltation, and instead of despairing of the flesh, highly recommends the satisfaction and joy of the body,—such a religion could never produce the excesses of asceticism found among other religions to whom the body and the material world are the seat of evil. With very few exceptions, which were of a pathological nature, we hardly ever find among the Jewish saints ascetic mortification, or immolation, and even asceticism as sacrifice to God is very rare among them. Jewish asceticism takes almost always the form which a famous psychologist describes as the fruit of love of purity that is shocked by whatever savors of the sensual.

The life of Salanter offers many instances of this special kind of asceticism. Of fasting and vigils he did not have a high opinion; indeed, he often used to admonish his disciples to eat and sleep as much as they needed. There was little need to preach temperance and sobriety to the Lithuanian Jew, distinguished for extraordinary frugality. Far more stringent was the watch he kept over the things which proceeded from the mouth. He would at times refrain for days and weeks from talking. Idle talk, indulgence in what is ordinarily called conversation, was abhorrent to him, and he employed it only as a means to brighten up people in depressed spirits. The silence he cultivated had its motive neither in the desire for self-mortification nor in that of expiation, but was the direct outcome of his highly developed sense of the purity of life. To his soul whatever was unspiritual was repugnant, and any inconsistency or discord between the ideal and the real was exceedingly painful to him. The average conversation, even of the educated, with its plentitude of insincerity and multitude of pretention, shocked his spiritual sensibility to such an extent that he preferred silence to speech.

There was also always present with him the fear of being admired by others for qualities of heart and soul above what he merited. This fear was so strong with him that he was once found weeping after delivering a brilliant discussion on a talmudic subject; he was afraid that the display of his brilliancy would make people exaggerate his intellect; and what could there be worse than deception? His scrupulousness as to veracity and sincerity knew no bounds. The first essay published by him contains the note that it was put into literary form by somebody other than the author himself, who is rather a poor stylist. He was once asked, how is one to explain the great success of "the liberals" in their fights with "the true believers," since according to a saying of the Sages, "Truth lasts, untruth perishes." The answer he gave was: "Sincerity makes an untruth seem to be a truth, while insincerity makes a truth seem to be an untruth; the liberals succeed because they are sincere; their opponents fail because they are not always sincere."

Salanter lived all his life in dire poverty, as a matter of choice, as there were many who would have considered it a privilege to provide him with comfort. He never accepted the position of Rabbi and only for a short time did he occupy a public office, that of the head of a talmudic school. He was firmly convinced that he could do his work best by being entirely independent of the public, and after a great inner struggle he decided to accept the offer of one of his disciples to support him entirely. This disciple was the only one from whom he accepted assistance, but only as much as was absolutely necessary to keep body and soul together. When Salanter's wife died he found a small sum of money among her effects which she had saved from the weekly allowance granted to her and her family by their benefactor. The money was distributed by Salanter among the poor. He argued, "The money granted to me by my disciple was for my needs, but not to enrich myself; hence I have no right to it nor have my children, the heirs of my wife, and as the original owner refuses to accept it, the poor have the next claim to it."

Though an indefatigable student all his life and in great need of books, he never possessed a single volume. When he died, his room contained, beside a threadbare suit of clothes, nothing else than his *Tallit* and *Tefillin*. It would be a great mistake, however, to believe that Salanter, like the ascetics of other religions, idealized poverty as the loftiest individual state and sang its praises. One of his disciples, trying to persuade him to accept from a rich admirer a new Tallit, said to him, "You are certainly in need of one and the decorum of the services requires that the Tallit be not threadbare. I too hope to buy one as soon as I have the money." And the master's answer was, "I also will buy one as soon as I shall have the money."

Judaism teaches that wealth is a blessing, as it gives time for ideal ends and affords exercise to ideal energies. Jewish saints, therefore, never denounced the possession of earthly goods, provided man does not turn the blessing into a curse by his greed and passion for money. The saint, however, knew also the high moral value of poverty: liberation from material possessions, freedom of soul, and manly indifference. Salanter's craving for moral consistency and purity was developed to such a degree that he could neither occupy a public office in the community nor accept comfort and luxuries from the hand of others. He for a time thought of becoming an artisan that he might be able to support himself by "the labor of his hands," but when he saw the impossibility of such a plan, he gladly submitted to a life of want and hardship.

"Love your enemies" is not a Jewish precept, and one may doubt whether there are any examples of compliance with it. The nearest approach to it is that magnanimity which "repays evil with good," and the life of Salanter is full of acts of this kind. "Imitation of God," he used to say, "is explicitly commanded in the Torah, and accordingly it is our duty not only to confer an act of kindness upon those who have done harm to us, but to do it at the very moment we are wronged. God is kind to the sinner at the time of his sin and rebellion, since without the kindness of God that gives him life and strength he would not be able to sin, and we are to imitate Him so as to be like Him. We must be kind to those who sin against us, at the time of their wrongdoing." He took scrupulous care all his life to act in accordance with this rule. No sooner did he hear of an injury done to him than he hastened to find out whether he could not confer some kindness upon the person who injured him. The continuous practice of this kind of magnanimity, he taught further, develops tolerance and indulgence towards all men.

In one of his letters to his disciples, Salanter expresses the hope that the spark coming from his soul might kindle a holy fire in their hearts. His hope was not in vain. His was one of those conductive natures who, as was well said by a famous author, are effective because the effluence of their power and feeling stirs the hearer or onlooker to a sympathetic thrill. A Jewish saying, "Words that come from the heart enter into the heart," expresses the same thought. Few people who came in personal contact with him could withstand his charm and his power. His influence over the masses as a preacher was unique in the annals of Eastern Jewry. The inner fire of his spirit shot out its lightning flashes, dazzling the inward eye with the clearness of the truth he revealed to the consciences of his hearers. He brought the people no new doctrines to arrest their thought; he was a flame enkindling the smouldering faith of his hearers; for a while he would lift them up into the clear atmosphere of heaven where their souls stood revealed to themselves and their hearts were aglow with unwonted desire of the higher life. He saw truth so clearly that he was able to make others see it.

Salanter's power was, however, in himself not in his words, and we would do injustice to the man if we judged him by his few literary remains. Yet even they reveal not only an intellect of originality but also a soul of rare purity and great nobility, a worthy link in the long chain of Saints in Israel.

BIBLIOGRAPHY ON RABBINIC JUDAISM FROM TALMUDIC TO MODERN TIMES

DAVID GOODBLATT

1. *History and Religion*

This bibliography concentrates on materials available in English. Further resources can be found in Italian, Russian, French, German, and Hebrew in roughly this ascending order of frequency.

The following is an outline of the bibliography:

I. Jewish History
    A. Comprehensive Works
    B. Histories of Jews in Specific Regions
    C. Histories and Studies of the Medieval Period

II. History of Judaism

    A. Halakhah
    B. Philosophy and Theology
        1. Histories
        2. Texts in English Translation
        3. Major Studies in English
    C. Mysticism
        1. Texts in English Translation
        2. Studies
    D. Messianism
    E. Sectarian Movements
    F. Literary and Cultural Matters
        1. Histories of Literature
        2. Anthologies of Texts in English Translation
        3. Poetry
            a. Collections of Hebrew Texts
            b. English Translation
            c. Studies in English
        4. Belletristic and Moralistic Literature
            a. Texts in English Translation
            b. Studies in English

  5. Historiography
     a. Texts in English Translation
     b. Studies in English
  6. Miscellaneous
     Bible commentary, Scientific work, Grammarians,
     Travelogues, Polemics

III. Biographies

The following abbreviations are used:

HUCA   — Hebrew Union College Annual
JAOS   — Journal of the American Oriental Society
JBL   — Journal of Biblical Literature
JJGL   — Jahrbücher für jüdische Geschichte und Literatur
JQR   — Jewish Quarterly Review
MGWJ   — Monatsschrift für die Geschichte und Wissenschaft des
          Judentums
REJ   — Revue des Etudes Juives
pb   = available in paperback

I. JEWISH HISTORY

A. Comprehensive Works

Baron, Salo, *A Social and Religious History of the Jews,* 2nd Ed.,
14 Vols., Philadelphia and New York, 1952-1970.

Dubnow, Simon, *Weltgeschichte des jüdischen Volkes,* 10 Vols.,
Berlin, 1925-1930. Hebrew translation: *Divre Yeme Am
Olam,* Tel Aviv, 1958. English translation: *History of the
Jews,* 3 Vols., So. Brunswick, N. J., 1967-1969.

pb Finkelstein, Louis, ed., *The Jews: Their History, Culture, and
Religion.,* 3rd Ed., 2 Vols., New York, 1960. pb: 3 Vols.,
New York, 1970-1971.

Graetz, H., *Geschichte der Juden,* 3rd and 4th Ed., 11 Vols.,
Leipzig, 1897-1911. The English translation, *History of the
Jews,* 6 Vols., Philadelphia, 1891-1898, omits the notes of the
original and is practically useless. The Hebrew translation,
Divre Yeme Yisrael, 8 Vols., Warsaw, 1905-1908, by con-
trast, adds notes and appendices and is recommended.

pb Grayzel, Solomon, *A History of the Jews,* New York, 1968.

pb Margolis, M. and Marx, A., *A History of the Jewish People,* New
York, 1968.

pb Roth, Cecil, *A History of the Jews,* New York, 1961.

Schwartz, Leo, ed., *Great Ages and Ideas of the Jewish People,*
New York, 1956.

Cahiers d'Histoire Mondiale 11, 1-2, 1968, "Social Life and Social
Values of the Jewish People."

Encyclopedia Judaica, 10 Vols. (Incomplete), Berlin, 1928.

Jewish Encyclopedia, 12 Vols., New York, 1901. Repr. New
    York, 1966
Encyclopedia Judaica, 16 Vols., Jerusalem, 1972.

**B. Histories of Jews in Specific Regions (dealing with the medieval
period)**

BYZANTIUM:
Sharf, Andrew, *Byzantine Jewry from Justinian to the Fourth
    Crusade,* London, 1971.
Starr, Joshua, *The Jews in the Byzantine Empire. 641-1204,*
    Athens, 1939.

EGYPT, SYRIA, PALESTINE:
Mann, Jacob, *The Jews in Egypt and Palestine under the Fatimid
    Caliphs,* 2 Vols., London, 1920-1922.
Strauss, A., *Toldot Hayehudim Bemisrayim Vesurya Tahat Shilton
    Hamamelukim,* Jerusalem, 1944.

ENGLAND:
Adler, Michael, *Jews of Medieval England,* London, 1939.
Hyamson, Albert, *A History of the Jews in England,* 2nd Ed.,
    London, 1928.
Richardson, H. G., *The English Jewry under Angevin Kings,*
    London, 1960.
Roth, Cecil, *History of the Jews in England,* Oxford, 1949.

FRANCE:
Anchel, Robert, *Les Juifs de France,* Paris, 1946.
Berman, Leon, *Histoire des Juifs de France,* Paris, 1937.
Gross, Henri, *Gallia Judaica,* Paris, 1897.

GERMANY:
Agus, I. A., *The Heroic Age of Franco-German Jewry,* New York,
    1969.
Kisch, Guido, *The Jews in Medieval Germany,* Chicago, 1949.
Lowenthal, Marvin, *The Jews in Germany,* Philadelphia, 1936.

ITALY:
Roth, Cecil, *The History of the Jews of Italy,* Philadelphia, 1946.
————, *The Jews in the Renaissance,* Philadelphia, 1959.

NORTH AFRICA:
Hirschberg, H. Z., *Toldot Hayehudim Be'afrigah Hasefonit,* 2 Vols.,
    Jerusalem, 1965. An English translation is in press.

ORIENTAL AREA:
Ashtour, E., "Prolegomena to the Medieval History of Oriental
    Jewry," *JQR* n. s. 50 (1959-60), pp. 55-68, 147-166.
Goitein, S. D., *A Mediterranean Society: The Jewish Communi-*

ties of the Arab World as Portrayed in the Documents of the Cairo Geniza, 3 Vols., Los Angeles, 1970—.

RUSSIA AND POLAND:
Dubnow, Simon, *History of the Jews in Russia and Poland*, 3 Vols., *Philadelphia*, 1916-1920.

pb Dunlop, D. M., *The History of the Jewish Khazars*, Princeton, 1954, New York, 1967.

SPAIN AND PORTUGAL:
Ashtour (Strauss), E., *Qorot Hayehudim Besefarad Hamuslemit*, 2nd Ed., 2 Vols., Jerusalem, 1966.
Baer, Yitzchak, *A History of the Jews in Christian Spain*, 2 Vols., Philadelphia, 1961, 1966.
Katz, Solomon, *The Jews in the Visigothic and Frankish Kingdoms of Spain and Gaul*, Cambridge, Mass., 1937.
Netanyahu, B., *The Marranos of Spain from the Late XIVth to the Early XVIth Century According to the Hebrew Sources*, New York, 1966.
Neumann, Abraham, *The Jews in Spain: their social, political, and cultural life during the Middle Ages*, *Philadelphia*, 1942.
Roth, Cecil, *A History of the Marranos*, Philadelphia, 1932.

TURKEY:
Rosannes, Solomon, *Divre Yeme Yisrael Betogarmah*, 5 Vols, Sofia, 1934-1944, Vol. 6, Jerusalem, 1945.

C. Histories and Studies of the Medieval Period

pb Abrahams, Israel, *Jewish Life in the Middle Ages*, New York and Philadelphia, 1958.
Altmann, Alexander, ed., *Jewish Medieval and Renaissance Studies*, Cambridge, Mass., 1967.
Assaf, Simha, *Beoholei Ya'akov: Essays on the Cultural Life of the Jews in the Middle Ages*, (Hebrew), Jerusalem, 1943.
Baron, Salo, *The Jewish Community*, 3 Vols., Philadelphia, 1942.
Ben-Sasson, H. H., *Peragim Betoldot Hayehudim Bime Habenayim*, Jerusalem, 1962.
Dinur, B. Z., *A Documentary History of the Jewish People*, 2nd Ed., 5 Vols., Jerusalem and Tel Aviv, 1965 (Hebrew).
Finkelstein, Louis, *Jewish Self-Government in the Middle Ages*, New York, 1964.
pb Katz, Jacob, *Exclusiveness and Tolerance*, New York, 1962.
———, *Tradition and Crisis: Jewish Society at the End of the Middle Ages*, New York, 1961.
pb Marcus, Jacob, *The Jew in the Medieval World*, New York, 1969.
Roth, Cecil, ed., *World History of the Jewish People, XI. The Dark Ages: Jews in Christian Europe 711-1096*, Ramat Gan, 1966.

II. History of Judaism

A. Halakhah

Agus, I. A., "Rabbinic Scholarship in Northern Europe" and "Rashi and His School," in C. Roth, ed., *World History of the Jewish People*, XI, pp. 189-209, 210-248.

Aptowitzer, Avigdor, *Mavo Lesefer Rabiah,* Jerusalem, 1932.

Freehof, Solomon, *The Responsa Literature,* Philadelphia, 1955.

pb Ginzberg, Louis, "The Codification of Jewish Law," in his *On Jewish Law and Lore,* Cleveland, New York, and Philadelphia, 1962, pp. 153-184 = "Law, Codification of," *Jewish Encyclopedia*, Vol. 7, pp. 635-647.

———, *Geonica,* 2 Vols., Repr. New York, 1968.

Hones, S., *Toldot Haposqim,* Warsaw, 1922.

Levinger, Y., *Darkhe Hamahshavah Hahilkhatit Shel Harambam,* Jerusalem, 1965.

Mamorstein, A., "The Place of Maimonides' Mishneh Torah in the History and Development of the Halakhah," in I. Epstein, ed., *Moses Maimonides,* London, 1935.

Tchernowitz, H., *Toldot Haposqim,* 3 Vols, New York, 1946.

Twersky, I., "The Beginnings of Mishnah Torah Criticism," in A. Altmann, ed., *Biblical and Other Studies,* Cambridge, Mass., 1963.

pb ———, "The Shulhan 'Aruk: Enduring Code of Jewish Law," *Judaism* 16 (1967), reprinted in Judah Goldin, ed., *The Jewish Expression,* New York, 1970.

Weiss, I. H., *Dor Dor Vedorshav,* 5 Vols., Repr. Jerusalem-Tel Aviv, n. d.

Zimmels, H. J., *Ashkenazim and Sephardim,* London, 1958.

———, "Scholars and Scholarship in Byzantium," in C. Roth, ed., *World History of the Jewish People,* XI, pp. 175-188.

Zucrow, S., *Sifrut Hahalakhah,* New York, 1932.

Liturgy:

Elbogen, I., *Toldot Hatefillah Veha'avodah Beyisrael,* Berlin, 1924

pb Idelsohn, A. Z., *Jewish Liturgy in its Historical Development,* New York, 1967.

Petuchowski, J., ed., *Contributions to the Scientific Study of the Liturgy,* New York, 1970.

Note: The only major code available in scientific English translation is Maimonides' *Mishneh Torah,* published in the Yale Judaica series. Selections from Qaraite law codes appear in Leon Nemoy, *Karaite Anthology*. For translations of responsa see S. Freehof, *A Treasury of Responsa,* Philadelphia, 1962.

See also Section III, Biographies, below. The biographies of the major halakhic authorities contain important material for the history of halakhah.

B.   Philosophy and Theology

    1.   HISTORIES

       Blau, Joseph, *The Story of Jewish Philosophy*, New York, 1962.

pb   Guttmann, Julius, *Philosophies of Judaism*, New York, 1966.

pb   Husik, I., *A History of Medieval Jewish Philosophy*, New York and Philadelphia, 1960.

       Neumark, D., *Geschichte der jüdischen Philosophie des Mittelalters nach Problemen dargestellt*, 3 Vols, Berlin, 1907-1928. Hebrew translation: *Toldot Hapilosofiyah Beyisrael*, 2 Vols., New York, 1921.

       Vajda, G., *Introduction a la pensée juive du moyen age*, Paris, 1947.

    2.   TEXTS IN ENGLISH TRANSLATION (in rough chronological order of philosophers)

       Sa'adyah b. Yosef (Gaon), *The Book of Beliefs and Opinions*, trans., S. Rosenblatt, New Haven, 1948.

pb   ———, "Selections from *The Book of Doctrines and Beliefs*," trans., A. Altmann, in *Three Jewish Philosophers*, New York and Philadelphia, 1960.

       Isaac Israeli, *Works*, trans. and ed., A. Altmann and S. M. Stern, Oxford, 1958.

       Bahya ibn Paquda, *The Duties of the Heart*, trans., M. Hyamson, 2 Vols., Jerusalem, 1965.

       Solomon ibn Gabirol, *The Fountain of Life*, ed. and trans., Harry Wedeck, New York, 1962.

       ———, *The Improvement of Moral Qualities*, trans., S. W. Wise, New York, 1902.

       Abraham bar Hayya (Hiyya), *The Meditation of the Sad Soul*, ed. and trans., G. Wigoder, London, 1970.

pb   Judah Halevi, *Kitab Al Khazari*, trans., H. Hirschfeld, New York, 1964.

pb   ———, "Selections from the *Kuzari*," trans., I. Heinemann, in *Three Jewish Philosophers*, New York and Philadelphia, 1960.

pb   Moses Maimonides, *The Guide for the Perplexed*, trans., M. Friedlander, New York, 1956.

       ———, *The Guide for the Perplexed*, trans., S. Pines, Chicago, 1963.

       ———, *The Eight Chapters of Maimonides on Ethics*, trans., J. I. Gorfinkle, New York, 1912.

       Abraham Maimonides, *The Highways to Perfection*, trans., S. Rosenblatt, Vol. 1, New York, 1927, Vol. 2, Baltimore, 1938.

       Aaron b. Elijah of Nicodemia, *The Tree of Life*, (First Half), trans., Morris Charner, New York, 1949.

Joseph Albo, *Sefer Ha'iqqarim,* ed. and trans., I Husik, 5 Vols., Philadelphia, 1930.

Samuel Usque, *Consolation for the Tribulations of Israel,* ed. and trans., Martin Cohen, Philadelphia, 1965.

Leone Ebreo, *The Philosophy of Love,* trans., F. Friedberg-Seeley and Jean Barnes, London, 1937.

3. MAJOR STUDIES IN ENGLISH

Adlerbaum, N., *A Study of Gersonides in his Proper Perspective,* New York, 1926.

Altmann, Alexander, *Studies in Religious Philosophy and Mysticism,* London, 1969.

Cohen, A., *The Teachings of Maimonides,* Repr. New York, 1968.

Neumark, D., *Essays in Jewish Philosophy,* Vienna, 1929.

Reines, Alvin, *Maimonides and Abrabanel on Prophecy,* Cincinnati, 1970.

Sarachek, J., *Faith and Reason. The Conflict over the Rationalism of Maimonides,* Williamsport, Pa., 1935.

Silver, Daniel J., *Maimonidean Criticism and the Maimonidean Controversy: 1180-1240,* Leiden, 1965.

Stitskin, L. D., *Judaism as a Philosophy: The Philosophy of Abraham bar Hiyya,* New York, 1961.

Strauss, Leo, *Persecution and the Art of Writing,* Glencoe, 1952. *re* Maimonides, Halevi, and Spinoza.

Waxman, M., *The Philosophy of Don Hasdai Crescas,* Repr. New York, 1966.

Wolfson, H. A., *Crescas' Critique of Aristotle,* Cambridge, Mass., 1929.

C. Mysticism

1. TEXTS IN ENGLISH TRANSLATION

The Book of Formation (Sefer Yesirah), trans., Knut Stenring, London, 1923.

The Zohar, trans., Harry Sperling and Maurice Simon, 5 Vols., London, 1931-34.

pb *Zohar: the Book of Splendor,* ed. and trans., G. Scholem, New York, 1949.

Moses Cordovero, *The Palm Tree of Deborah,* trans., Louis Jacobs, London, 1960.

2. STUDIES

Abelson, J., *Jewish Mysticism,* London, 1913.

Altmann, A., *Studies in Religious Philosophy and Mysticism,* London, 1969.

Bokser, Ben Zion, *From the World of the Cabbalah: The Philosophy of Rabbi Judah Loew of Prague,* New York, 1954.

Dan, J., "Beginnings of Jewish Mysticism in Europe," in C. Roth, ed., *World History of the Jewish People*, XI, pp. 282-290.

Heschel, A. J., "The Mystical Element in Judaism," in L. Finkelstein, ed., *The Jews*, etc., Vol. 2, pp. 932-953.

Kramer, Simon, *God and Man in the Sefer Hasidim*, New York, 1966.

Müller, Ernest, *History of Jewish Mysticism*, Oxford, 1946.

pb   Scholem, Gershom, *Major Trends in Jewish Mysticism*, 3rd ed., New York, 1965.

———, *The Messianic Idea in Judaism and Other Essays on Jewish Spirituality*, New York, 1971.

pb   ———, *On the Kabbalah and its Symbolism*, New York, 1965.

———, *Reshit Haqabbalah*, Jerusalem, 1948.

———, *Ursprung und Anfänge der Kabbala*, Berlin, 1962.

———, *Shabbetai Sevi*, 2 Vols., Jerusalem, 1957. An English translation is in press.

Tishby, I., *Niteve Emunah Uminut*, Ramat Gan, 1964.

pb   Trachtenberg, Joshua, *Jewish Magic and Superstition*, New York, 1970.

Vajdo, Georges, *Récherches sur la philosophie et la kabbale dans la pensée juive du moyen age*, Paris, 1962.

See Scholem, *Major Trends*, for further bibliography.
For study of the Zohar, the annotated Hebrew translation by I. Tishby and P. Lahover, *Mishnat Hazohar*, 2 Vols., Jerusalem, 1961, is highly recommended. The text is rearranged on a thematic basis and an extensive introduction is provided.
See also the biographies of Ramban, Rabad, Karo.

D.   Messianism

Aescoly, A. Z., *Hatenu'ot Hameshihiyot Beyisrael*, Jerusalem, 1956.

Cohen, Gerson, *Messianic Postures of Ashkenazim and Sephardim (Before Sabbetai Zevi)*, Leo Baeck Memorial Lecture, IX, New York, 1967 = M. Kreutzberger, ed., *Studies of the Leo Baeck Institute*, New York, 1967, pp. 115-156.

Eppstein, A., "Sefer Eldad Hadani," in *Kitve Avraham Eppstein*, ed., A. M. Haberman, Vol. 1, Jerusalem, 1950.

Even-Shmuel, Y., *Midrashe Ge'ulah*, 2nd Ed., Tel Aviv, 1954.

Mann, Jacob, "Hatenu'ot Hameshihiyot Bime Mas'e Haselav Harishonim," *Hatequfah* 23 (1925) and 24 (1926).

———, "The Struggle between the Omayyid Caliphate and Byzantium for the possession of Constantinople and the Messianic hopes entertained by Oriental Jews," *JAOS* 47 (1927), p. 364.

Moses Maimonides, *Iggeret Teman*, ed., A. Halkin, trans. into English, Boaz Cohen, New York, 1952.

Sarachek, J., *The Doctrine of the Messiah in Medieval Jewish Literature*, New York, 1932.

Scholem, Gershom, *The Messianic Idea in Judaism and other Essays on Jewish Spirituality*, New York, 1971.

——, *Shabbetai Sevi*, 2 Vols., Jerusalem, 1957. An English translation is in press.

Silver, A. H., *A History of Messianic Speculation in Israel from the First through the Seventeenth Centuries*, New York, 1927.

Starr, J., "Le Mouvement Messianique au Début du VIIIe Siecle," *REJ* 101-102 (1937, pp. 81-92).

Werblowsky, R. J. Z., "Messianism in Jewish History," *Cahiers d'Histoire Mondiale* 11 (1968), pp. 30-45.

E. Sectarianism

Ankori, Z., *Karaites in Byzantium*, Jerusalem and New York, 1959.

——, Review of Nemoy's *Karaite Anthology*, *Jewish Social Studies* 15 (1953), pp. 310-312.

Assaf, S., "Letoldot Haqara'im Be'arsot Hamizrah," in his *Beoholei Ya'akov*, Jerusalem, 1943.

Ben-Sasson, H. H., "Rishone Haqara'im—Qavim Bemishnatam Hahevratit," *Zion*, n.s. 15 (1950), pp. 42-55.

Birnbaum, Philip, ed., *Qaraite Studies*, New York, 1971.

Davidson, I., ed. and trans., *The book of the wars of the Lord—Containing the polemics of the Karaite Salmon ben Yeruhim against Saadia Gaon*, New York, 1934.

——, *Saadia's Polemic against Hiwi Al-Balkhi*, New York, 1915.

Friedlaender, I., "Jewish Arabic Studies," *JQR* n. s. 1 (1910-11), pp. 183-215; 2 (1911-12), pp. 481-516; 3 (1912-13), pp. 235-300.

Golb, N., "Literary and Doctrinal Aspects of the Damascus Covenant in the Light of Qaraite Literature," *JQR* 77 (1956-57), pp. 354-374.

——, "The Qumran Covenanters and the Later Jewish Sects," *Journal of Religion* 41 (1961), pp. 38-50.

——, "Who were the Magariya?" *JAOS* 80 (1960), pp. 347-459.

Guttmann, Julius, "The Sources of Hiwi Al-Balkhi," *Alexander Marx Jubilee, Hebrew Volume*, New York, 1950.

Harkavy, Alexander, "Anan der Stifter der Karäischer Secte," *JJGL* 2, pp. 107-122.

——, "Leqorot Hakitot Beyisrael," in H. Graetz, *Divre Yeme Yisrael*, Vol. 3, pp. 493-511.

Mahler, R., *Haqarim: Tenu'at Ge'ulah Yehudit Bime Habenayim*, Merhavyah, 1949. The Yiddish version: *Die Karaimer: A Yiddische Geulahbevegung in Mitalter*, New York, 1949.

Mann, Jacob, "An Early Theological-Polemical Work," *HUCA* 12-13 (1937-38), pp. 411-459.
————, *Texts and Studies in Jewish History and Literature, Vol. II: Karaitica*, Philadelphia, 1935.
Nemoy, L., "Al-Qirqisani's Account of the Jewish Sects and of Christianity," *HUCA* 7 (1930).
————, "Anan b. David: A reappraisal of the historical data," in *Semitic Studies in Memory of Immanuel Löw*, Budapest, 1947, pp. 239-245.
————, "Early Karaism (The Need for a New Approach)." *JQR* 40 (1949-50), pp. 307-315.
————, ed., *Karaite Anthology*, New Haven, 1952.
————, Review of Andre Paul's *Ecrits* etc., JBL 89 (1970), pp. 489-490.
Neubauer, J., "Karäischer Studien," *MGWJ* 82 (1938), pp. 324-352, 404-417.
Paul, Andre, *Ecrits de Qumran et sectes juives aux premiers siècles de l'Islam: Recherches sur l'origine du Qaratisme*, Paris, 1969.
Poznanski, S., "The Anti-Karaite Writings of Sa'adyah Gaon," *JQR* o.s. 10 (1897-98), pp. 238ff.
————, *Karaite Literary Opponents of Saadiah Gaon*, London, 1908.
————, "Meswi Al-Okbari Chef d'Une Secte Juive du IXᵉ Siècle," *REJ* 34-35 (1897), pp. 160-191.
————, "Meyasde Kitot Beyisrael Betequfat Hage'onim," *Reshumot* 1, pp. 207-216.
Revel, Dov (B.), "Hahilufim Ben Bene Bavel Iven Bene Eres Yisrael Umeqorot Hahalakhah Shel Haqara'im," *Horeb* 1 (1934), pp. 1-20.
————, *Karaite Halakhah*, Philadelphia, 1913.
Rosenthal, J., "Hiwi Al-Balkhi: A Comparative Study," *JQR* 38 (1947-48), pp. 317-342, 419-430; 39 (1948-49), pp. 79-94.
————, "On the History of Heterodoxy in the Period of Saadiah," *Horeb* 9 (1942), pp. 21-37. (Hebrew)
————, "She'elot 'Atiqot Batanakh," *HUCA* 21 (1948), pp. 29-91.
Stein, M., "Hiwi Al-Balkhi. The Jewish Marcion," in *Sefer Klausner*, Tel Aviv, 1937, pp. 210-225. (Hebrew)
Wieder, N., *The Judean Scrolls and Karaism*, London, 1962.
Add: Mann, Jacob, "Anan's Liturgy," *Journal of Jewish Lore and Philosophy* 1 (1919), pp. 329-353.
See also S. Baron, *Social and Religious History*, Vol. 5, Chapters 25-26, *plus* notes.

F. Literary and Cultural Matters

　　　1. HISTORIES OF LITERATURE
　　　　　Steinschneider, M., "An Introduction to the Arabic Literature of the Jews," *JQR* o.s. 9 (1897), pp. 224-239, 604-630;

10 (1898), pp. 119-138, 513-540; 11 (1899), pp. 115-149, 305-343, 480-489, 585-625; 12 (1900), pp. 114-132, 195-212, 481-501, 602-617; 13 (1901), pp. 92-110, 296-320, 446-487.

————, *Jewish Literature from the Eighth to the Eighteenth Century*, London, 1857, Repr. New York, 1965.

Waxman, M., *A History of Jewish Literature*, 5 Vols, New York and London, 1960.

Zinberg, I., *Toldot Sifrut Yisrael*, Tel Aviv, 1955.

2. ANTHOLOGIES OF TEXTS IN ENGLISH TRANSLATION
pb Glatzer, N. N., ed., *Faith and Knowledge*, Boston, 1963. Appears as Part Two of *The Judaic Tradition*, ed., N. N. Glatzer, Boston, 1969.

Halper, B., ed., *Postbiblical Hebrew Literature*, 2 Vols, Philadelphia, 1921.

Kobler, F., ed., *A Treasury of Jewish Letters*, 2 Vols., Philadelphia, 1954.

Leviant, Curt, ed., *Masterpieces of Hebrew Literature*, New York, 1969.

Millgram, A., ed., *An Anthology of Medieval Hebrew Literature*, New York, 1961.

3. POETRY
    a. Collections of Hebrew Texts
        Brody, H. and Albrecht, K., eds., *The New-Hebrew School of the Spanish-Arabian Epoch*, Leipzig and London, 1906.

        ———— and Weiner, M., *Mivhar Hashirah Ha'ivrit*, Leipzig, 1922.

        Schirmann, H., *Hashirah Ha'ivrit Besefarad Uveprovans*, 2 Vols., Jerusalem and Tel Aviv, 1956.

    b. English Translations (some with Hebrew text)
        Davidson, I. and Zangwill, I., ed. and trans., *Selected Religious Poems of Solomon ibn Gabirol*, Philadelphia, 1923.

        Goldstein, David, ed. and trans., *Hebrew Poems from Spain*, London, 1965.

        Salaman, Nina and Brody, H., ed. and trans., *Selected Poems of Jehudah Halevi*, Philadelphia, 1928.

        Solis-Cohen, S., ed. and trans., *Selected Poems of Moses ibn Ezra*, Philadelphia, 1934.

    c. Studies in English
        Schirmann, J. (H.), and Haberman, A. M., "The Beginnings of Hebrew Poetry in Italy and Northern Europe," in C. Roth, ed., *World History of the Jewish People*, XI, pp. 249-273.

        ————, "The Function of the Hebrew Poet in Medieval Spain," *Jewish Social Studies*, 16 (1954).

Spiegel, S. "On Medieval Hebrew Poetry," in Goldin, ed.,
Jewish Expression, pp. 174-216 and in Finkelstein,
ed., *The Jews* etc., Vol. 1, pp. 854-892.
See also the extensive bibliography in Schirmann, *Hashirah* etc.,
as well as his introduction and glossary.

4.   BELLETRISTIC AND MORALISTIC LITERATURE
   a.   Texts in Translation
       Abrahams, I., ed. and trans., *Hebrew Ethical Wills*, 2
       Vols., Philadelphia, 1926.
       Cohen, S., ed. and trans., *Orchot Tzaddikim: The Ways
       of the Righteous*, Jerusalem and New York, 1969.
       Epstein, M., ed. and trans., *Tales of Sendebar*, Phila-
       delphia, 1967.
       Gollancz, H., *Dodi Venechdi of Berachya Hanakdan*,
       London, 1920.
       ————, *The Ethical Treatises of Berachya*, London, 1902.
       Hadas, M., ed. and trans., *The Book of Delight by Joseph
       Ben Meir Zabara*, New York, 1932.
       Leviant, Curt, ed. and trans., *King Arturus. A Hebrew
       Arthurian Romance of 1279*, New York, 1970.
       Reichardt, V. E., trans., *The Tahkemoni of Judah Al-
       Harizi*, Vol. 1, Jerusalem, 1964.
       Silverstein, S., trans., *Gates of Repentance of Jonah
       Gerondi*, Jerusalem, 1967.
   b.   Studies in English
       Chotzner, J., *Hebrew Humour and Other Essays*, London,
       1905.
       Davidson, I., *Parody in Jewish Literature, New York*, 1907.
       Marx, Alelander, *Studies in Jewish History and Booklore*,
       New York, 1944
       Morais, Sabato, *Italian Hebrew Literature*, New York,
       1926.

5.   HISTORIOGRAPHY
   a.   TEXTS IN TRANSLATION
       Cohen, Gerson, ed. and trans., *The Book of Tradition
       (Sefer Haqabbalah) of Abraham ibn Daud*, Phila-
       delphia, 1967.
       Salzman, M., ed. and trans., *The Chronicle of Ahimaaz*,
       New York, 1924.
   b.   Studies in English
       Baron, S., *History and Jewish Historians*, Philadelphia,
       1964. *Re* Maimonides and Azariah de'Rossi.
       Neumann, A. A., "The *Shebet Yehudah* and Sixteenth
       Century Historiography," in *Louis Ginzberg Jubilee
       Volume, English Section*, New York, 1945, pp. 253-
       274.

Zimmels, H. J., "Aspects of Jewish Culture: Historiography," in C. Roth, ed., *World History of the Jewish People*, XI, pp. 274-281.

6. MISCELLANEOUS

Adler, Marcus N., ed. and trans., *The Itinerary of Benjamin of Tudela*, London, 1907.

pb Caspar, B. M., *An Introduction to Jewish Bible Commentary*, New York, 1960.

Gandz, Solomon, *Studies in Hebrew Astronomy and Mathematics*, New York, 1970.

Hirschfeld, H., *Literary History of Hebrew Grammarians and Lexicographers*, London, 1926.

Marx, A., "The Scientific Work of Some Outstanding Medieval Jewish Scholars," in *Essays and Studies in Memory of Linda Miller*, New York, 1928, pp. 117-171.

Mierowsky, David, *Hebrew Grammar and Grammarians Throughout the Ages*, Johannesburg, n. d.

Rankin, O. S., *Jewish Religious Polemic*, Edinburgh, 1956.

Segal, M. S., *Parshanut Hamiqra*, Jerusalem, 1952.

pb Spiegel, S., *The Last Trial*, New York, 1967.

Twersky, I., "Aspects of the Social and Cultural History of Provencal Jewry," *Cahiers d'Histoire Mondiale* 11 (1968), pp. 185-207.

III. Biographies

Chavel, C. B., *Ramban. His Life and Teachings*, New York, 1960.

Druck, David, *Yehuda Halevy. His Life and Work*, New York, 1941.

Goldman, Israel M., *The Life and Times of Rabbi David Ibn Abi Zimra*, New York, 1970.

Hailperin, Herman, *Rashi and the Christian Scholars*, Pittsburgh, 1963.

Hershman, A., *Rabbi Isaac Ben Sheshet Perfet and His Times*, New York, 1943.

Liber, Maurice, *Rashi*, Philadelphia, 1926.

Malter, H., *Saadia Gaon. His Life and Works*, Philadelphia, 1921.

Marx, A., *Essays in Jewish Biography*, Philadelphia, 1947. Among others, Saadia, Rabbenu Gershom, Rashi, and Maimonides.

Netanyahu, B., *Don Isaac Abravanel: Statesman and Philosopher*, 2nd Ed., Philadelphia, 1968.

Twersky, I., *Rabad of Posquières. A Twelfth-Century Talmudist*, Cambridge, Mass., 1962.

Werblowsky, R. J. Z., *Joseph Karo: Lawyer and Mystic*, Oxford, 1962.

Yellin, D. and Abrahams, I., *Maimonides*, Philadelphia, 1903.

Yerushalmi, Y. H., *From Spanish Court to Italian Ghetto. Isaac Cardoso: A Study in Seventeenth-Century Marranism and Jewish Apologetics*, New York and London, 1971.

Zeitlin, S., *Maimonides. A Biography*, 2nd Ed., New York, 1955.

2. The Languages of Rabbinic Literature

I. **Rabbinic Hebrew**

Abramson, S., "Mileshon Ḥakhamim," *Leshonenu* 19 (1954), pp. 61-71.

Albeck, H., "Leshon Hamishnah," Chap. 8 of his *Mavo Lamishnah,* Jerusalem and Tel Aviv, 1959, pp. 128-215.

Ben-David, Abba, *Biblical Hebrew and Mishnaic Hebrew,* Tel Aviv, 1967 (Hebrew).

Ben-Hayyim, Z., *Studies in the Traditions of the Hebrew Language,* Madrid and Barcelona, 1954.

Ben-Yehuda, E., *Ad Matai Dibru Ivrit?,* New York, 1919. This originally appeared as part of the Prologomena ("Hamavo Hagadol") to his *Thesaurus totius hebraitatis,* a. v. below under Section IV.

Bergrin, Nisan, "Iyyunim Leksiqaliyim Beleshon Hakhamim," *Leshonenu* 17 (1951), pp. 3-11; 18 (1953), pp. 9-16, 82-88, 161-166. (The latter two omit "Leksiqaliyim" from their titles.)

Birkeland, H., *The Language of Jesus,* Oslo, 1954.

Chomsky, W., "What was the Jewish Vernacular During the Second Commonwealth?" *JQR* 42 (1951-52), pp. 193-212.

Emerton, J. A., "Did Jesus Speak Hebrew?", *JThSt* 12 (1961), pp. 189-202.

Epstein, Y. N., *Mavo Lenusaḥ Hamishnah,* 2nd Ed., 2 Vols., Jerusalem and Tel Aviv, 1964.

————, *Mevo'ot Lesifrut Hatanna'im,* Jerusalem and Tel Aviv, 1957.

Fitzmyer, J. A., "The Languages of Palestine in the First Century A.D.", *CBQ* 32 (1970), pp. 501-531.

Geiger, A., *Lehrbuch und Lesebuch zur Sprache der Mischnah,* Breslau, 1845.

Ginsberg, H. L., "Zu den Dialekten des Talmudisch-Hebräischen", *MGWJ* 77 (1933), pp. 413-429.

Goldberg, A., "Letiv Leshon Hamishnah: Bituyyim Shel Ḥiyyuv Sheyesh Lahem Gam Mashma'ut Shel Niggud", *Leshonenu* 26 (1962), pp. 104-117.

Grintz, J. M., "Hebrew as the Spoken and Written Language in the Last Days of the Second Temple", *JBL* 79 (1960), pp. 32-47.

Har-Zahav, Sevi, "Kelum Leshon Hamishnah Enah Leshon Sifrutit?", *Leshonenu* 7 (1936).

Kutscher, Y., *Halashon Vehareqa Haleshoni Shel Megillat Yishayahu Hashelemah Mimegillot Yam Hemelaḥ,* Jerusalem, 1959. An English translation is in press.

————, "Leshon Hazal," *Sefer Hanokh Yalonfi* Jerusalem, 1963 pp. 246-280. Offprint, Jerusalem, 1967.

————, "Leshonan Shel Ha'igrot Ha'ivriyot Veha'aramiyot Shel Bar Kosebah Ulvene Doro. Ma'amar Sheni: Ha'igrot Ha'ivriyot," *Leshonenu* 26 (1962), pp. 7-23.

————, "Mittelhebräisch und Jüdisch-Aramäisch im neuen Köhler-

Baumgartner," *Supplements to Vetus Testamentum* 16 (1967), (Baumgartner Festscrift).

Lieberman, S., *Hayerushalmi Kifshuto,* Jerusalem, 1935.

———, *Tosefet Rishonim,* 4 Vols., Jerusalem, 1937-39.

———, *Tosefta Kifshutah,* 7 Vols. (so far), New York, 1955-1967.

Margaliyot, E., "Ivrit Ledibbur," *Leshonenu* 24 (1966), pp. 238-241.

———, "Ivrit Ve'aramit Batalmud Uvamidrash," *Leshonenu* 27-28 (1963-64), pp. 20-33.

———, "Leshe'elat Sefat Hadibbur Bezeman Bayit Sheni Uvetequfat Hamishnah Vehatalmud," *Leshonenu* 23 (1959), pp. 49-54.

Melammed, E. Z., "Leleshonah Shel Massekhet Avot," *Leshonenu* 20 (1956), pp. 106-111.

Morag, S., "Binyan Pā'el Uvinyan Nitpā'el (Leveruran Shel Surot Bemesorot Leshon Ḥakhamim)," *Tarbiz* 26 (1956-57), pp. 349-356; 27 (1957-58), p. 556.

Porath, A., *Leshon Hakhamim,* Jerusalem, 1938.

Rabbinowitz, I., " 'Be Opened' = *Ephphatha* (Mark 7:34): Did Jesus Speak Hebrew?" *ZNW* 53 (1962), pp. 229-238.

Schneider, M. B., "Yaḥas Hadiqduq Hamishnati Lediqduq Hamqra'i," *Leshonenu* 3 (1931), pp. 15-28 and cf. 6 (1935), pp. 301-326; 7 (1936), pp. 52-73.

Segal, M. H., *Diqduq Leshon Hamishnah,* Tel Aviv, 1936.

———, *A Grammar of Mishnaic Hebrew,* Oxford, 1927.

———, "Mishnaic Hebrew and its Relation to Biblical Hebrew and to Aramaic," *JQR* o.s. 20 (1908), pp. 647-737.

Sokoloff, M., "The Hebrew of *Beresit Rabba* According to Ms. Vat. Ebr. 30," (Hebrew) *Leshonenu* 33 (1968-69), pp. 25-42, 135-149, 270-279.

Weiss, I. H., *Mishpat Leshon Hamishnah,* Vienna, 1867.

Yalon, H., *Mavo Leniqqud Hamishnah,* Jerusalem, 1964.

———, *Studies in the Dead Sea Scrolls,* Jerusalem, 1967 (Hebrew).

Of great importance are those manuscripts which preserve the original orthography of Rabbinic Hebrew to a greater degree than the standard printed editions. Some are also vocalized. Among the most valuable are the Kaufmann and Parma manuscripts of the Mishnah and the Vatican manuscript of Bereshit Rabbah. The first two have recently been published and the third will appear soon. The Vienna manuscript of the Tosefta, used by Lieberman in his edition, is also important.

II. GALILEAN ARAMAIC

A. Grammars and Studies

Brockelmann, C. and Baumstark, A., "Aramäisch und Syrisch," in *Handbuch der Orientalistik,* III, 2, ed. B. Spuler, Leiden, 1954.

Dalman, G., *Grammatik des jüdisch-palästinischen Aramäisch und Aramäische Dialektproben,* Repr. Darmstadt, 1969.

Kutscher, Y., *Studies in Galilean Aramaic*, Jerusalem, 1966. (Hebrew.) = *Tarbiz* 21 (1951-52), pp. 192-205; 22 (1952-53), pp. 185-192; 23 (1953-54), pp. 36-60.

————, "Mittelhebräisch und Jüdisch-Aramäisch im neuen Köhler-Baumgartner," *Supplements to Vetus Testamentum* 16 (1967), [Baumgartner Festschrift].

Lieberman, S., *Hayerushalmi Kifshuto*, Jerusalem, 1935.

Marshall, J. T., *Manual of the Aramaic Language of the Palestinian Talmud*, Leiden, 1929.

Odeberg, H., *The Aramaic Portions of Bereshit Rabba. II Short Grammar of Galilean Aramaic*, Lund, 1939.

Rosenthal, F., ed., *An Aramaic Handbook*, 4 Vols., Wiesbaden, 1967.

————, *Die Aramäistische Forschung Seit Th. Nöldeke's Veröffent-lichungen*, Leiden, 1939.

Stevenson, W. B., *Grammar of Palestinian Jewish Aramaic*, 2nd Ed., Oxford 1962.

B. Related Dialects

1. OTHER RECOGNIZED WESTERN ARAMAIC DIALECTS
   a. Christian Palestinian Aramaic
       Schultess, F., *Grammatik des christlisch-palästinischen Aramäisch*, Repr. Hildescheim, 1965.
       ————, *Lexicon Syropalaestinum*, Berlin, 1903.
   b. Samaritan Aramaic
       Ben-Hayyim, Z., *Ivrit Ve'aramit Nusah Shomron*, Vol. III, Part 2, Jerusalem, 1967.
       Cowley, A. E., *The Samaritan Liturgy*, Vol. II, Oxford, 1909.
       Nichols, G. F., *A Grammar of the Samaritan Language*, London, n. d. (1858?).
       Petermann, H., *Brevis Lingua Samaritanae*, Carolsruhae et Lipsiae, 1873.

2. JUDAEAN (?) ARAMAIC
    Fitzmyer, J. A., "A Sketch of Qumran Aramaic," Appendix II of his *The Genesis Apocryphon of Qumran Cave I*, Rome, 1966. See also Part V of his Introduction, "The Language of the Scroll," pp. 17-25.
    Kutscher, (E.) Y., "The Language of the 'Genesis Apocryphon.' A Preliminary Study," *Scripta Hierosolymitana* 4 (1958), pp. 1-35. Offprint, Jerusalem, 1964.
    ————, "Leshonan Shel Ha'igrot Ha'ivriyot Veha'aramiyot Shel Bar Kosebah Uvene Doro. Ma'amar Rishon: Ha'igrot Ha'aramiyot," *Leshonenu* 25 (1961), pp. 117-133.
    Mazar, B., "The Inscription on the Floor of the Synagogue in En-Gedi," *Tarbiz* 40 (1970-71), pp. 18-23. (Hebrew with English Summary.)

Rowley, H. H., "Notes on the Aramaic of the *Genesis Aprocryphon," Hebrew and Semitic Studies Presented to G. R. Driver,* ed. D. W. Thomas and W. D. McHardy, Oxford, 1963.
cf. also Dalman, *Grammatik.*

3. THE ARAMAIC OF JESUS

Black, M., *An Aramaic Approach to the Gospels and Acts,* 3rd Ed., Oxford, 1967.
————, "Die Erforschung der Muttersprache Jesu," *ThLZ* 82 (1957), pp. 653-668.
————, "The Recovery of the Language of Jesus," *NTS* 3 (1957), pp. 305-313.
————, "Aramaic Studies and the Language of Jesus," *In Memoriam Paul Kahle, BZAW* 103 (1968), pp. 17-28.
Cantineau, J., "Quelle langue parlait le peuple en Palestine au ler siecle de notre ere?" *Semitica* 5 (1955), pp. 99-101.
Dalman, G., *Jesus-Jeshua,* New York, 1929.
————, *The Words of Jesus,* Edinburgh, 1902.
Diez Macho, A., "La lengua hablada por Jesucristo," *OrAn* 2 (1963), pp. 95-132.
Fitzmyer, J. A., "The Languages of Palestine in the First Century A.D..." *CBQ* 32 (1970), pp. 501-531.
Gundry, R. H., "The Language Milieu of First-Century Palestine: Its Bearing on the Authenticity of the Gospel Tradition," *JBL* 83 (1964), pp. 404-408.
Kahle, Paul, "Das palästinische Pentateuchtargum und das zur Zeit Jesu gesprochene Aramäisch," *ZNW* 49 (1958), pp. 100-116.
————, "Das zur Zeit Jesu gesprochene Aramäisch: Erwiderung," *ZNW* 51 (1960), p. 55.
————, "Das zur Zeit Jesu in Palästina gesprochene Aramäisch," *ThRu* N.F. 17 (1949), pp. 201-216.
Kutscher, E. Y., "Das zur Zeit Jesu gesprochene Aramäisch," *ZNW* 51 (1960), pp. 46-54.
Meyer, A., *Jesu Muttersprache. Das galiläische Aramäisch in seiner Bedeutung für die Erklärung des Reden Jesu und der Evangelien überhaupt.* Freiburg and Leipzig, 1896.
Olmstead, A. T., "Could an Aramaic Gospel Be Written?" *JNES* 1 (1942), pp. 41-75.
Patterson, S. M., "What Language Did Jesus Speak?" *Classical Outlook* 23 (1946), pp. 65-67.
Schultess, F., *Das Problem der Sprache Jesu,* Zurich, 1917.
Segert, S., "Aramäische Studien, II: Zer Verbreitung des Aramäischen in Palästina zur Zeit Jesu," *Archiv Orientální* 25 (1957), pp. 21-37.

Smith, M., "Aramaic Studies and the Study of the New Testament," *JBR* 26 (1958), pp. 304-313.

Torrey, C. C., "Studies on the Aramaic of the First Century A.D. (New Testament Writings)," *ZAW* 65 (1953), pp. 228-247.

————, "The Aramaic Period of the Nascent Christian Church," *ZNW* 44 (1952-53), pp. 205-223.

4. MODERN WESTERN ARAMAIC DIALECTS

Bergsträsser, G., *Glossar des neuaramäischen Dialekts von Ma'lula,* 1921.

Spitaler, A., *Grammatik des neuaramäischen Dialekts von Ma'lula,* Leipzig, 1938.

III. BABYLONIAN TALMUDIC ARAMAIC

A. Grammars and Studies

See the entries in II A above under Brockelmann and Baumstark; and Rosenthal (both entries).

Ben-Asher, M., "Diqduq Hapo'al Ha'arami Be 'Halakhot Pesuqot'," *Leshonenu* 34 (1970), pp. 278-286; 35 (1971), pp. 20-35.

Epstein, Y. N., *Diqduq Aramit Bavlit,* Jerusalem and Tel Aviv, 1960.

Kutscher, Y., "Meḥqar Diqduq Ha'aramit Shel Hatalmud Ha-bavli," *Leshonenu* 26 (1962). Offprint, Jerusalem, 1969.

Levias, C., *Diqduq Aramit Bavlit,* New York, 1930.

————, *A Grammar of the Aramaic Idiom of the Babylonian Talmud,* Cincinnati, 1900. Offprint of articles from *AJSLL* 13-16 (1897-1900).

Luzzatto, S. D., *Elementi grammaticali del Caldeo Biblico e del dialetto Talmudico Babilonese,* Padua, 1865. = *Grammatik der biblisch-chaldäischen Sprache und des Idioms* des *Talmud Babli,* tr. M. S. Krüger, Breslau, 1873. = *Grammar of the Biblical Chaldaic language and of the idiom of the Talmud Babli,* tr. J. Goldammer, New York, 1876.

Margolis, Max L., *Lehrbuch der aramäischen Sprache des babylonischen Talmud,* München, 1910.

————, *A Manual of the Aramaic Language of the Babylonian Talmud,* Munich, 1910.

Schlesinger, Michel, *Satzlehre der aramäischen Sprache des Babylonischen Talmud,* Leipzig, 1928.

B. Related Eastern Aramaic Dialects

1. MANDAIC

Drower, E. S. and Macuch, R., *A Mandaic Dictionary,* Oxford, 1963.

Macuch, R., *Handbook of Classical and Modern Mandaic*, Berlin, 1965.
Nöldeke, Th., *Mandäische Grammatik*, Repr. Darmstadt, 1964.

2. SYRIAC

Brockelmann, C., *Syrische Grammatik*, Repr. Leipzig, 1965.
Nöldeke, Th., *Compendious Syriac Grammar*, Repr. Israel, 1970.
Payne Smith, J., ed., *A Compendious Syriac Dictionary*, Repr. Oxford, 1957.
Robinson, Th. H., *Paradigms and Exercises in Syriac Grammar*, 4th Ed., Oxford, 1962.

3. MODERN EASTERN ARAMAIC DIALECTS

Maclean, A. J., *A Dictionary of the Dialects of Vernacular Syriac*, Oxford, 1901.
————, *Grammar of the Dialects of Vernacular Syriac*, Oxford, 1901.
Nöldeke, Th., *Grammatik der Neusyrischen Sprache*, Leipzig, 1868.
Rivlin, Y. Y., *Shirat Yehude Hatargum*, Jerusalem, 1959.
Socin, A., *Die neu-aramäischen Dialekte von Urmia bis Mosul*, Tübingen, 1882.

IV. LEXICOGRAPHICAL WORKS RELEVANT TO THE LANGUAGES OF RABBINIC LITERATURE

Bacher, W., *Die exegetische Terminologie der jüdischen Traditionsliteratur*, Repr. Darmstadt, 1965.
Barth, J., *Wurzeluntersuchungen zum hebräischen und aramäischen Lexicon*, Leipzig, 1902.
Ben-Yehuda, E., *Thesaurus totius hebraitatis*, 8 Vols., London and New York, 1960.
Dalman, G., *Aramäisch-neuhebräisches Handwörterbuch zur Targum, Talmud, und Midrasch*, Frankfurt a.M., 1901.
Epstein, Y. N. See relevant articles listed in the bibliography of Epstein's works compiled by S. Abramson in the Epstein Festschrift, *Tarbiz* 20 (1949), pp. 7-16.
Ginzberg, L., "Beiträge zur Lexicographie des Jüdische-Aramäisches, I" *Schwarz Festschrift*, Berlin und Wien, 1917, pp. 329-360; "II." *MGWJ* 78 (1934), pp. 9-33; "III," *Essays and Studies in Memory of Linda Miller*, New York, 1938, pp. 57-108.
Jastrow, M., *Dictionary of the Targumim, the Talmud Babli and Yerushalmi and the Midrashic Literature*, New York, 1886-1903.
Kohut, A., ed., *Aruch Completum* (Arukh Hashalem), 8 Vols., Vienna, 1878-1892. A critical edition of the *Arukh* of Natan b. Yehiel of Rome (died 1106) with additional notes. A supplementary

volume, *Additamenta ad Aruch Completum*, ed. S. Krauss, Vienna, 1937, is of great value.

Krauss, S., *Griechische und lateinische Lehnwörter in Talmud, Midrasch, und Targum*, 2 Vols., Repr. Hildesheim, 1964.

Levy, Jacob, *Neuhebräisches und chaldäisches Wörterbuch über die Talmudim und Midraschim*, 4 Vols., Leipzig, 1876-1889, Repr. Darmstadt, 1963.

Lieberman, S., *Greek in Jewish Palestine*, 2nd Ed., New York, 1965.

———, *Hellenism in Jewish Palestine*, New York, 1962.

———, "How Much Greek in Jewish Palestine?" in A. Altmann, ed., *Biblical and Other Studies*. Cambridge, Mass., 1963, pp. 123-141.

Löw, Immanuel, *Aramäische Pflanzennamen*, Leipzig, 1881.

———, *Fauna und Mineralien der Juden*, Hildesheim, 1969.

———, *Die Flora der Juden*, 4 Vols., Vienna and Leipzig, 1924-1934.

Telegdi, S., "Essai sur la Phonétique des Emprunts iraniens en Araméen talmudique," *Journal asiatique* 1935, pp. 177-256.

Yalon, H. See relevant articles listed in the bibliography of Yalon's works compiled by S. Esh in *Sefer Yalon*, Jerusalem, 1963, pp. 37-50.

Journals such as *Leshonenu, Tarbiz, Sinai, JNES, Journal of the American Oriental Society*, etc. and Festschriften contain numerous short lexicographical notes and studies.

ABBREVIATIONS USED

BZAW   Beiheft zur Zeitschrift für die Alttestamentliche Wissenschaft
CBQ   Catholic Biblical Quarterly
JBL   Journal of Biblical Literature
JBR   Journal of Bible and Religion
JNES   Journal of Near Eastern Studies
JQR   Jewish Quarterly Review
JThSt Journal of Theological Studies
MGWJ   Monatsschrift für die Geschichte und Wissenschaft des Judentums
NTS   New Testament Studies
OrAn   Oriens Antiquus
ThLZ   Theologische Literaturzeitung
ThRu   Theologische Rundschau
ZAW   Zeitschrift für die Alttestamentliche Wissenschaft
ZNW   Zeitschrift für die Neutestamentliche Wissenschaft

A TEACHER'S AFTERWORD

Further study of Rabbinic Judaism between Talmudic and modern times will bring the reader into relationship with extraordinary people not represented in this book. It goes without saying, moreover, that much more is to be learned about each figure and idea, movement and spiritual phenomenon, represented here, as Dr. Goodblatt's bibliography makes clear. Two examples of readily available and well-constructed anthologies will suggest the riches awaiting the interested reader.

Isadore Twersky, *A Maimonides Reader* (N.Y., 1972: Behrman House), quoted earlier, is a masterly guide to the greatest of all rabbinic Jews. The introduction printed above gives only a hint of the thoughtful and brilliant account of Maimonides provided by Twersky.

Second, readers who wish to acquaint themselves with a wide range of selected translations of Jewish writings of earlier centuries are advised to consult *The Judaic Tradition, Texts Edited and Introduced* by Nahum N. Glatzer (Boston, 1969: Beacon Press), a massive collection of thoughtfully selected and carefully introduced selections. Glatzer here provides three separate anthologies in one: I. *The Rest Is Commentary,* on the Talmudic Period; II. *Faith and Knowledge,* on medieval Jewish theology and ethics; and III. *The Dynamics of Emancipation,* on modern Judaism, its philosophers, movements, and aspirations, and on the modern Jews and their suffering, on Zionism, and on expressions of piety. Part II, it goes without saying, serves as a valuable counterpart to the present essays.

Four further anthologies pertain to themes introduced in this reader. First is the incomparable *A Rabbinic Anthology, Selected with an introduction* by C. G. Montefiore and H. Loewe (Philadelphia, The Jewish Publication Society of America, and Cleveland and New York, The World Publishing Company, 1963). This work is peculiarly modern. It is a three-way conversation, between a Western Orthodox Jew, Loewe, a Reform one, Montefiore, and the Talmudic tradition. The selections from Talmudic and cognate literature are carefully translated and annotated. But of still greater interest are the responses to those selections on the part of the sage editors. The book is arranged according to themes, for example, God's Love for Israel, Hope and Faith, Prayer, Asceticism, The Life to Come: Resurrection and Judgment, and the like. It includes a considerable apparatus of pertinent information. *A Rabbinic Anthology* certainly is the model for creative and thoughtful anthologization.

The Hasidic Anthology. Tales and Teachings of the Hasidim, edited by Louis I. Newman and Samuel Spitz (N.Y., 1963: Schocken Books), *Judaism,* edited by Arthur Hertzberg, in the series, *Great Religions of Modern Man* (N.Y., 1965: Washington Square Press, Inc.), and *The Jewish Expression, Edited and with an Introduction* by Judah Goldin (N.Y., London, and Toronto, 1970: Bantam Books) bring together important and suggestive writings.

Newman and Spitz provide an extensive selection of Hasidic literature, the richness and piquance of which are scarcely suggested in the single personality dealt with here.

Hertzberg's effort is to "write his own book through the words of others." He contends that there is an essential unity which underlies Jewish faith through all its changing expressions. To demonstrate that unity, he deals with Judaism not historically but conceptually, with "basic values and affirmations" serving as the divisions, a difficult and daring, and, I think, unqualifiedly successful effort. The divisions are fundamental: people, God, Torah: Teaching and Commandment, the cycle of the year, land, doctrine, and prayer. As an introduction both to classical Judaism and to the mind of a considerable, contemporary Jewish thinker, *Judaism* is to be recommended with enthusiasm. Of the several works before us, it probably is the most ambitious effort to construct a coherent account out of discrete materials, a major achievement of synthetic, constructive theology.

Goldin has selected twenty scholarly essays, all written in the present century, of which he approves. The principle of selection is simply the judgment of the editor. As an account of a scholar's opinions about scholarship, it is of intense interest, for Goldin's mode of thought, shaped as it is within the classical literature and disciplines, is as interesting as the things he has thought about. The introduction explains what draws the editor to these particular papers. It is the fact that each paper is the "product of years of research or reflection *cum* study by masters, plus their attempt to reach out to the enduring significance of the phenomenon or event or the literary texts or institutions or period or personality or speculative system which they were discussing at the moment." So Goldin provides both important essays on the history of Judaism and a strikingly original datum for the study of contemporary Judaism through the minds of its most learned men and that of an editor of impeccable taste.

For this writer, however, the present anthology is intended to serve a quite different purpose. It completes a set of text-books and anthologies addressed to a single problem and meant to make possible a cogent course of studies. An autobiographical explanation may not be out of order.

After nearly a decade of university teaching in Judaic studies, I had begun to develop my own theory of how the multiform subjects of Jewish learning might best be introduced into the humanities curriculum. Courses for relatively advanced students in the field of religious studies had taken shape. Then an especially bright undergraduate, who had taken several full-year courses in the history of Judaism, asked, "Why don't you give a course my brother can take?" The brother was not a major in Religious Studies and indeed had taken few courses in humanities. He simply wanted one "survey course," in one semester, to satisfy a modest curiosity about Judaism, into which he had been born. I realized that the courses I had developed left no place for the fulfillment of a perfectly legitimate educational aspiration of a large constituency of students, both gentile and Jewish. What did I have to say to the many who had no time or interest in full-year and multi-year sequences of study? So far as Judaic studies would make a contribution to undergraduate education as a whole, so far as, like Salanter, I had claimed that the study of Judaism is important in the intellectual nurture of any young man or woman, I had accomplished nothing.

But where to start? Merely supplying facts and information seemed to me pointless. A worthwhile, one-semester, undergraduate course should be constructed around two theories, one educational, the other substantive.

My educational theory is simple and unsophisticated. I believe students learn best when they discover, on their own, both information and insight, when they read and reflect in accord with an established, shared agendum of student curiosity and scholarly responsibility. Like American pragmatists in general, I believe in learning by doing and finding things out for oneself. A corollary to this conviction is the view that a course succeeds when it sets up a problem for students' inquiry and concludes with the presentation of students' solutions to, or, still better, analyses of, that primary problem.

The substantive theory for such an introductory course is this: "Judaism" is a massive and meaningless construct, making room for so vast a collection of data as to legitimate a mere rubbish-heap of un-examined, uncriticized facts and notions. While, as is clear, I pro-foundly respect the formulations of "Judaism" accomplished by theo-logians, lawyers, and mystics alike, the respect is for the theological and conceptual achievement of masters within the tradition, not for the descriptive accomplishment of people studying *about* the tradition.

A further substantive theory is that to merit a place in the under-graduate humanities curriculum for the study of religions, the study of Judaism should contribute to the consideration of larger issues within that curriculum. The chief of these is surely, What is meant by "re-ligion"? Since I am neither a philosopher nor a speculative historian of religion, I could obviously not offer an opinion on that pressing ques-tion. But I could supply data, so formulated as to contribute to the thought of those who seek to answer it.

Clearly, the way to develop a cogent, problem-oriented course lay, therefore, in formulating an issue or problem and providing the stu-dents with information and guidance so that *they* could analyze and compose responsible, informed responses. The issue of the course would be to "define Judaism," and the problem would be the analysis of ap-proaches to definition through thoughtful consideration of the rich data, and their formation into a coherent and cogent, descriptive response.

Two bodies of methodology had to be taken into account, first, the internal description, through normative statements of law and theol-ogy, and through apologetics, of theologians, and second, the external description, through attention to the mind and behavior of all who claimed to participate in the tradition, not merely of the elite. The latter task seemed to me best approached through the categories of analysis of historians of religions.

A further factor in planning such a course is my own capacities, such as they are, and my convictions and prejudices. Clearly, I devote my best efforts as a scholar to the study of Talmudic Judaism in late antiquity. The reason is clear from the present anthology: Talmudic Judaism is the primary and formative force in the history of Judaism from the destruction of the Second Temple to our own day. I wanted to analyze its origins and early development. My prejudice is that of an ordained rabbi, and, more important, a believing, and (imperfectly) practicing Jew. To be a rabbi even in the present day means to know at least part of what in classical terms rabbis are expected to know. A rabbi is not an undifferentiated holy man of Jewish origin, but someone devoted to the literature and doctrines of Rabbinic Judaism. So my perception of the history of Judaism and my personal convictions came to a felicitous coincidence.

The course of studies which resulted may be briefly outlined through the description of the textbooks which I wrote, edited, or selected for that purpose.

The first unit is served by *The Way of Torah: An Introduction to Judaism* and *The Life of Torah: A Reader of Jewish Piety and Spirituality* (Encino, 1970, 1974 [second edition], and Encino, 1974, respectively: Dickenson Publishing Co.). This unit is meant to state the problem and at the same time to introduce many important facts and perspectives. The problem is, as stated, that of definition. The task of the student is to confront the meaning of "defining a religion," the general difficulty of doing so, and the specific dilemmas of doing so for "Judaism." The accompanying reader is built along the lines of the outline of the essay in *Way of Torah*, providing both a great many facts, and also an opportunity for direct encounter, through the experience of liturgy, to a less vivid degree through the description of festivals, Sabbaths, religious heroes, and finally, through the consideration of the major movements in modern Judaism, American Orthodoxy, Reform, Conservatism, Reconstructionism, and Israeli traditionalism.

The second unit deals with the origins of rabbinic Judaism in Talmudic times and is served by *From Politics to Piety: The Emergence of Pharisaic Judaism* (Englewood Cliffs, 1973: Prentice-Hall) and *There We Sat Down: Talmudic Judaism in the Making* (Nashville, 1972: Abingdon Press). The formerly asks narrowly historical questions: What do we know about the Pharisees, who formed rabbinic Judaism after the destruction? How do we know it? In what ways shall we analyze the legends and laws to produce a responsible and critical description of Pharisaism? The latter asks questions deriving from the history of religions and is a description of the elements of myth and power in Babylonian Jewry and the ways in which these functioned to generate the form of Judaism known to us, finally, in the pages of the Babylonian Talmud.

These text books are based upon scholarly efforts of some fourteen years: *A Life of Yohanan ben Zakkai* (Leiden, 1962; second edition, 1970: E. J. Brill); *A History of the Jews in Babylonia* (Leiden, 1965-

1970: E. J. Brill, Vols. I-V); *Development of a Legend: Studies on the Traditions Concerning Yohanan ben Zakkai* (Leiden, 1970: E. J. Brill); *Aphrahat and Judaism: The Christian-Jewish Argument in Fourth Century Iran* (Leiden, 1971: E. J. Brill); *The Rabbinic Traditions about the Pharisees before 70* (Leiden, 1971: E. J. Brill, Vols. I-III); *Eliezer ben Hyrcanus: The Tradition and the Man* (Leiden, 1973: E. J. Brill, Vols. I-II); *The Idea of Purity in Ancient Judaism* (Leiden, 1973: E. J. Brill); *The Mishnaic Law of Purities: Kelim. I. Commentary* (Leiden, 1974: E. J. Brill); and two books edited by me, *Formation of the Babylonian Talmud* (Leiden, 1970: E. J. Brill) and *The Modern Study of the Mishnah* (Leiden, 1973: E. J. Brill). It goes without saying that this second unit is the only one based upon the idiosyncratic ideas and methods of this writer.

One further book was written for the second unit of the course, *Invitation to the Talmud. A Teaching Book* (N.Y., 1973: Harper and Row). This book, as its title indicates, introduces Talmudic literature by presenting, after a description of its cultural context, a single unit of Talmudic law, expressed in four closely related documents, Mishnah, Tosefta, Babylonian Talmud, and Palestinian Talmud. The book then ends with a statement of the larger meaning of Talmudic modes of thinking. The final chapter forms a transition to the next unit of the course.

The third stage in the study of the problem of definition introduces the post-Talmudic history of Rabbinic Judaism. Clearly, it is for this unit that the present anthology is intended. At the same time, three other interpretations of the data are offered, Twersky's *Maimonides Reader,* mentioned earlier, and two contemporary efforts at the evocation of the human meaning of mysticism and messianism, respectively: Herbert Weiner, *9½ Mystics, The Kabbala Today* (N.Y., 1969: Holt, Rinehart, and Winston), and Arthur A. Cohen, *In the Days of Simon Stern* (N.Y., 1973: Random House).

Neither is intended as a work of scholarship. The one is a record of encounters with living Kabbalists, people who can tell us what the mystic tradition means today, by a brilliant and learned journalist-rabbi. The other is a novel which takes as its central theme the messianic yearnings of our own times. In bringing the students' attention to creative literature, both through Weiner's essays and through Cohen's novel, I also hope to stress that the expression, therefore, also the study of Judaism takes place through other, entirely legitimate modes of creative expression besides scholarship. The data are to be derived, moreover, not solely or even primarily from books, but from the lives books attempt to record and preserve. And the purpose of study is to *understand* people, not merely to dissect and define them or categorize their ideas.

At this point, the descriptive effort and the first part of the interpretive task are concluded, and the prescriptive, normative statements of theologians are brought into consideration. For that purpose I edited *Understanding Jewish Theology: Classical Themes and Modern Perspectives* (N.Y., 1973: Ktav Publishing House). The first two parts of that book are meant simply to introduce the most fundamental categories of Jewish theological thinking—beliefs in one God, in Torah, and in the chosenness of Israel, the Jewish people, and the centrality of *halakhah* in the expression of those beliefs. Clearly, people who are familiar with the issues of Jewish theological discourse will not need to be told about the meaning of God's unity or about the ways in which "Torah" as a theological category is to be analyzed. But for beginning students, the definition and explanation of these basic categories are valuable.

At later levels of study, particular theological positions of medieval and modern times, specific individuals and movements, may be taken up. Alongside my anthology, I therefore make use of *Between God and Man. An Interpretation of Judaism. From the Writings of Abraham J. Heschel, selected, edited, and introduced* by Fritz A. Rothschild (N.Y., 1959: Free Press). This is intended to accomplish two purposes, first, to extend the discussion, in a learned and classical spirit, of the primary categories introduced in my anthology; and second, to show how a great contemporary theologian does his systematic work. Obviously, my preference for Heschel as archetypal modern theologian may not be shared by others. Students are free to read other fairly systematic theologians, of whom perhaps four or five are worth taking seriously.

With this last unit, the effort to analyze, from the perspectives of theology and history of religions, the classical or pre-modern expressions of Judaism, is concluded. The two approaches to the study of religion are thereupon brought to bear upon the modern period in the history of Judaism.

The history-of-religions agendum is taken up in my *American Judaism: Adventure in Modernity* (Englewood Cliffs, 1972: Prentice-Hall), which is an anthological essay on the foci of holiness, or the structure of the sacred, in American Judaism: holy people, holy faith, holy man, holy land, and holy way of life. To be sure, asking what is understood as sacred or holy about the American Jewish way of life produces ironic and even (intentionally) comical answers. But the serious intent of the book is to underline those very ironies and to ask, Is "the sacred" or "religious" a possibility for such doggedly contemporary, secular, and modern people as American Jews? What do their expressions of their tradition tell us about the potentialities of modernity and the modern meaning of religion? With those questions are supplied the facts in Nathan Glazer's *American Judaism* (Chicago, 1973 [second edition]: University of Chicago Press). A recommended reading is Marshall Sklare's *America's Jews* (N.Y., 1973: Random House).

The approach of modern theology to the classical issues categorized under "God," "Torah," and "Israel" is spelled out in the last third of *Understanding Jewish Theology*. The stress, for thought about the nature and meaning of theology in general and God in particular, is in the writing of Emil L. Fackenheim, on the one side, and Mordecai M. Kaplan, on the other. These theologians also play a role in the other anthologies edited by me, in Kaplan's case, or in other readings in the course, in Fackenheim's. Further, contemporary religious data have already been introduced in *The Life of Torah*. The unit, if somewhat brief, is meant to open the way to the serious consideration of a wide range of theologians and theological thinking, but at the same time to place into proper perspective the nature and meaning of the theological enterprise.

The last unit of the course brings together the concerns of the historian of religion and those of the theologian. This is accomplished through consideration of a specific and imperative issue in contemporary Judaism: the Holocaust, both a historical event of profound impact upon the nature of Jewish religion and a major problem in the minds of theologians and ordinary people alike. No inquiry from the perspective of history of religions has yet developed, though I find much that is suggestive, from that viewpoint, in the writings of Richard Rubenstein, beginning in *After Auschwitz* (Indianapolis, 1966: Bobbs-Merrill).

The students, however, need first of all to experience the profound human crisis of the Holocaust, and for that purpose I turn again to fiction. Student response to Elie Wiesel's writing, in particular, *The Gates of the Forest* (N.Y., 1970: Bard Edition, Avon Library) is keen. Having experienced the Holocaust in their own imagination, they proceed to Emil L. Fackenheim, *God's Presence in History. Jewish Affirmations and Philosophical Reflections* (N.Y., 1973: Harper Torchbooks). After giving a great theologian the last word, the course concludes.

Alongside the readings in history and theology of Judaism, a historical perspective is needed, and for that purpose, nothing is superior to Leo W. Schwarz, ed., *Great Ages and Ideas of the Jewish People* (N.Y., 1956: Random House). Hadassah, the women's Zionist organization, conceived and commissioned this work, the finest achievement of modern American efforts at adult Jewish education. The essays are as follows: *The Biblical Age,* by Yehezkel Kaufmann, translated by Moshe Greenberg; *The Hellenistic Age,* by Ralph Marcus; *The Talmudic Age,* by Gerson D. Cohen; *The Judeo-Islamic Age,* by Abraham S. Halkin; *The European Age,* by Cecil Roth; and *The Modern Age,* by Salo W. Baron.

It goes without saying that other readings are assigned or recommended in the course. I have listed only the primary syllabus and described the theory and logic behind it. In doing so, I hope that the reader may here find a useful course of home study, of these and other books. The place of the present anthology in such a larger course of study and its usefulness for the reader's effort at introducing himself or herself to Judaism should be clear. Perhaps, having surveyed a fairly formidable list of readings, each of which contains its own specialized and excellent bibliography, the reader will find comfort in the counsel of Rabbi Tarfon: "Yours is not to complete the task. But you are not free to desist from it." If even this consolation is insufficient, then let us conclude with Hillel's famous saying: "What is hateful to yourself, do not do to your fellow human being. That is the entire Torah. All the rest is commentary. *Now go forth and learn."*

BIBLICAL PASSAGES CITED

412

INDEX

Aaron ben Amram, 152, 158-60
Aaron ben Joseph ha-Kohen, 149
Aaron ben Meir, 152-53, 159, 166
Abarbanel, 198
Abbahu, R., 271
Abot, 141
Abraham, 140, 287
Abraham, R., 325
Abraham ibn Daud, 203
Abraham ibn Ezra, 163, 170, 203
Abraham ben Maimonides, 191
Abraham ben Samuel, 304-305
Abraham the Angel, 318, 320
Abu Kathir Yahya al-Katib, 150
Abulafia, Abraham, 257
Acre, 188-89
Adar, altering festival, 67
Adler, Cyrus, 153
Adler, R. Nathan, 339-40
Adret, Solomon, 56
Agadoth, 218
Agricultural taboos, 13
Agron, 150, 164
Aha, R., of Shivha, She'iloth, 74
Ahwaz, 161
Akedat Yitzhak, 143
Akiba, R., 69, 140, 232, 259
Akum, business partner, 65-66
Albalag, Isaac, 136
Albo, Joseph, 140, 198
Aleppo, 153, 193, 220
Alexander the First, 324
Alexandria, 92, 137-38, 193, 207
Al-farabi, 203, 205, 265
Alfasi, R. Isaac, 77-79, 81, 113, 221-22; Code of, 216; *Halachoth Gedoloth*, 222
Alfonso X, 91
Al-jamas, 59-60

Al-Kahir, 161
Al-Muktadir, 158, 161
Al-Radi, 161
Altmann, Alexander, 267
Amalek, 229
Amemar, 10
Ammon, R., 347-48
Amoraim, 29-30, 33
Amram, 169
Anabaptists, 252
Anan, 150-51
Animals, sale to gentiles, 66
Annulment of marriage, 79-80
Aptowitzer, V., 104
Aquinas, Thomas, 137, 140, 246
Arad, 349
Arama, R. Yitzhak, 143
Arba'ah Turim, 80-81, 143
Aristotelianism, 78, 265, 271, 364; Israel and faith, 182; Maimonides philosophy, 192, 200, 203, 207; philosophy and mysticism, 213, 217, 223, 233; rationalism, 129, 133, 137-39, 141, 143-44
Arms on Sabbath, 69
Arnold, Matthew, 139
'Aruk, 101, 104
Asher, R., 348
Asher b. Yehiel, R., 79-81
Ashi, Rav, 29, 56; *Geonim, 73*; literature of law, 72-82
Assaf, S., 170
Austria, 343, 350
Averroes, 205
Avicenna, 205, 265

Babel, Tower of, 140
Bacharach, R. Joel, 345
Bachya ben Asher, 56, 233

413

Solomon ben R. Nachman, 216
Solomon b. R. Solomon b. Isaac, 105
Song of Songs, 109
Soul and body, dualism, 43-45
Spain, Islamic and Christian struggle, 173, 175-84; law and its literature, 73-82; rationalism, 135; synagogue and people, 90-92; Talmudic law, 56, 59-60
Speyer, 304
Spinoza, 198
Stalin, Joseph, 5
Statesmanship and rabbinic philosopher, 147-71
Steinschneider, 170
Stratton, G., "Psychology of Religious Life", 246
Succoth, *Ethrog,* 68
Sufism, 252
Suicide, 348
Sura academy, 155-57, 161, 163, 169; literature of law, 73, 75
Surplice, on Day of Atonement, 87
Synagogue, functions, 83-95; height restricted, 91; as institutions, 5
Syria, 137-38

Tagmule ha-Nefesh, 142
Talmud, development and redaction, 39-40; heritage, 23-28; Judaism and Torah, 27-36, law, 53-60, "Sages of the Talmud", 29-30; theology of, 37-50
Tam, R., 65-66, 78, 105, 111, 322
Tannaim, 29-30, 33
Tanya, 315, 319, 322-25, 327-32
Tarfon, R., 56, 69
Targum, 107-109
Tavid, R., 311
Temple at Jerusalem, Second Temple, 11-14, 39
Terwitz, R. Moses, 340
Theology, Medieval Jewish theology, 135-45
Therapeutae, 254
Tiberius, 150-51, 325
Time, computation of, 67
Tithing, 13
Titus, 39
Toledo, 79, 176-77
Torah, and mysticism, 315-32; reading interrupted, 56-57; symbol of, 7-11; Talmudic Judaism and Torah, 27-36

Tov, Israel Baal Shem (Besht), 35, 292, 296, 315, 317-20, 324, 365
Tower of Babel, 140
Treatise on Aggadot, 191
Tree of Life, 234
Treine, 120
Troyes, Champagne, 102-104, 108
Truth, 129
Tsemah ben Shahin, 156
Tsevi, Sabbatai, 320, 322, 340
Turkey, 80
Tusemitz, R. Samuel, 341
Two Hundred Questions on the Bible, 168
Tyre, 102

Ukba, 152, 159
Underhill, Evelyn, 245, 248
Urania of Worms, 91

Vaadim, 59-60
Verona, 142
Vienna, Congress of, 350
Vilna, 104, 317-18, 320-24, 357-59, 362, 376-77
Vital, R. Chayim, 215
Vitebsk, 318
Volhynia, 317-18

Wars of the Lord, 167, 216, 221-22
Washing of hands, 89
Weapons on Sabbath, 69
Will, freedom of, 46-49
Wine, presses, 103; sanctification of, 94
Wisdom of Solomon, 7:7-25
Witnesses, divorce, 66-67
Wolfson, H. A., 207
Women, Sabbath candles, 91; separation in synagogue, 90; witness to divorce, 66-67
World to come: *see* Messianism
Worms academy, 103-105, 110-11, 304

Yad ha-Hazaka, 143
Yaker, R., 104
Yalkut Reubeni, 270-71
Yalkut Shim'oni, 270
Yavneh, 13-14; Origins of rabbinic Judaism, 11-12, 16-19
Yehudai, R., 74
Yehudah Hehasid, R., *Sefer Hasidim,* 76
Yemen, 165, 188, 193, 195
Yitzhak, R. Levi, 331, 325

Indices were prepared by Mr. Arthur
Woodman, Canaan, New Hampshire.